Also by David Rosengarten

The Dean & DeLuca Cookbook
Red Wine with Fish: The New Art of Matching Wine with Food

TASTE

TASTE

ONE PALATE'S JOURNEY THROUGH THE WORLD'S GREATEST DISHES

DAVID ROSENGARTEN

RANDOM HOUSE   NEW YORK

Library of Congress Cataloging-in-Publication Data
Rosengarten, David.
    Taste: one palate's journey through the world's greatest dishes / [David Rosengarten].
        p.   cm.
    Includes index.
    ISBN 0-375-50011-1
    1. Cookery, International.   2. Food—Sensory evaluation.   3. Gastronomy.   I. Title.
    TX725.A1R657   1998
    641.59—dc21   98-16414

Random House website address: www.randomhouse.com
Television Food Network website address: www.foodtv.com
Printed in the United States of America on acid-free paper
9 8 7 6 5 4 3 2
First Edition

Designed by Georgiana Goodwin

To Andrea and Sarah . . .
and the taste of the twenty-first century

A WORD FROM FOOD NETWORK

What is life without food? Every social gathering in every culture around the world centers around a feast. Food is woven into our most intimate stories, our memories, our selves. "Life," as David Rosengarten says, "is a matter of taste."

Taste was the very first in-house production at Food Network and is now our most popular show. A wonderful storyteller and brilliant chef, David enthralls his audience every day with stories about the world's great dishes. His warmth and enthusiasm leap off the screen.

Everyone at Food Network has worked with David at some point in some way. The contributions of Eileen Opatut, Susannah Eaton-Ryan, Wendy Waxman, Heidi Diamond, Julia Harrison, John Jenkins, Georgia Downard, and Susan Stockton have been especially valuable. Along with many others, they have worked tirelessly with David to make his vision become a reality.

For Food Network, it all started with *Taste*. We are proud to have produced David's show from the start and to share with the world his insights, humor, and joie de vivre.

ERICA GRUEN
president and chief executive officer
Food Network

CONTENTS

INTRODUCTION

IS LIFE REALLY A MATTER OF TASTE?

Several times every day, on television sets across the United States, I look into a camera and say, "Life . . . is a matter of taste." I came up with this tag line on the first day of shooting *Taste,* in February 1994, and, almost five hundred shows later, I'm still using it. It has become so widely associated with my cooking show that people regularly write letters to me at Food Network addressed to "David Rosengarten/A Matter of Taste."

Do I believe it? In some senses, life is most certainly not a matter of taste. It would be cruel to insist it is while millions of people around the globe struggle to survive. For them, life is a matter of tasting something before it's too late. And the phrase is potentially troubling in another sense as well. Surely, life is not primarily about aesthetic choices; life is a matter of goodness, of kindness, of ethical conduct long before it's a matter of taste, no?

Well, yes, it is. But taking the time to appreciate the pleasures of the table—if you're lucky enough to be able to do so—brings you about as close to a meaningful life as anything in this world can. Let me explain.

In the early 1980s I began traveling to the small wine villages of Europe. I'd wake up in some bustling town and spend the next few hours working my way from cellar to cellar. When lunchtime arrived, I would emerge from the darkness and return to the village—only to find that it wasn't bustling anymore. It was deserted, as if a neutron bomb had been detonated while I'd been busy tasting Pinot Noir. Where were the people who, just half an hour before, had been walking, talking, laughing, shopping, living?

I later learned that they were, of course, at lunch . . . in their homes, with family and friends. The midday break is the high point of the day in rural Europe—and, in most old villages, it lasts until four or five o'clock. If you've ever tried to buy a hat in a small European village in the hot sun at 3:00 P.M., you know that you'd be better off staying indoors until the sun begins to set and the stores reopen.

When I'm lucky enough to sit at the table at one of these mirthful collations in France's Chambolle-Musigny, or Italy's Castellina in Chianti, or Spain's Haro, I often think about how my family and friends are taking lunch back home: a cold sandwich from a lunch box at school, a nasty bagel on the run with a cup of coffee, a tuna sandwich at a desk while work goes on and on.

And then I realized: these Europeans sitting before me, taking the time to notice the quality of the butter, to discuss the twist of the bread that the baker made that day—these Europeans are really living. Steeped in my own Anglo-American culture, I was positively startled to see this nonpuritanical response to food, this torrent of gastronomic conversation, which really seemed to say, above all else, that the pleasures of the table are worth taking seriously.

That discussion of the cassoulet in southwest France wasn't just idle chatter. By focusing on the proper ingredients (duck? pork? lamb? goose?), or on the texture of the crust, these animated conversationalists were talking in code about their relatives. Everyone knew that Uncle Michel was insane; what else would you expect from a man who substituted goose for duck? And those friends visiting from thirty miles away—when they pointed out how they added bread crumbs to the top of the cassoulet seven times, building up a thicker, crunchier crust—were indicating the superiority of their little village and its traditional ways. And everyone at the table, by taking the time to find God in the details, was mutually affirming the validity of Gallic culture.

Though I didn't have much to add at first, I found that by following the debate I could, simultaneously, get much closer to the food, much closer to the people, much closer to whatever country I was in. Food and wine, if you let them, slow you down, give you the opportunity to withdraw, temporarily, from the battering pace of life, to heal, to show nothing but kindness and charity to those around you. And they provide countless little opportunities for reflection and judgment—which naturally put you in a contemplative state of mind about your own life. Great thoughts, great bonds, and great satisfaction grow out of those hours that we spend with others, sharing food and wine. It can never happen in minutes.

Back in America, I've never seen a reason to stop the process. I probe the world's traditional dishes, under the guise of gastronomic analysis, knowing full well that something greater will grow out of it.

This book is my continuation of that process—and my invitation to you to join it. You'll see how a Spaniard thinks about gazpacho, how an Italian thinks about pasta, how a Frenchman thinks about onion soup. If you join my obsessive quest for gastronomic perfection, we'll all end up as citizens of the world, understanding far more of the lives and cultures around us than we ever thought possible—and we'll also be eating some really great food.

But this book has a larger mission as well. I want to show you how food crept into an American life—mine—and changed that life for the better. How one palate has wandered from the gastronomically unpromising streets of Brooklyn, New York, in the 1950s to the main international culinary avenues of the twenty-first century. Why is that important? I'm anxious to demonstrate what that path was like, in case you want to follow a similar path yourself. Yes, this book will give you great recipes for everything from moussaka to stew. Yes, it will give you the criteria for quality that people who know food employ. But it's an intensely personal book as well—showing you, whenever possible, how I came to appreciate a given dish and suggesting how you might too.

In the end, this intensive food scrutiny will give us all a lot more to talk about at the lunch or dinner table. And more excuses to stay there. For as long as we use that table time properly—nourishing our bodies, our minds, our spirits, and our relationships—life is, most certainly, a matter of taste.

TASTE

1

MY FAVORITE LIGHT APPETIZERS

OYSTERS—CAVIAR—BRUSCHETTA—
COLD CHINESE APPETIZERS—GAZPACHO—
GUACAMOLE—VEGETABLES À LA GRECQUE—
THAI SALADS—CEVICHE

Many of our cookbook authors and TV cooking show hosts are chefs. I am not. *Chef,* in France, means "chief"—as in "the chief of the kitchen." To be a chef, you need a score of galley slaves slicing for you, dicing for you, and squirting brightly colored liquids out of squeeze bottles onto plates containing carefully arranged baby lettuces.

All I do is cook great dinners for family and friends . . . and I can show you how to do the same in your own home.

I am, of course, the undisputed chief of my home kitchen (though my daughters have veto power over what I cook). And when dinner party time rolls around, I love to begin with light and simple appetizers that are easy to make—sometimes at the last moment. If you make the right choice, the ratio of guest excitement to actual cooking work is extremely high—but making the right choice is all-important, so much care must be given to the selection process (that's why this chapter is obsessed with detail). Light appetizers set up palates beautifully for the more substantial thrills that lie just ahead in your stellar dinner party.

Light appetizers . . . good for chefs, great for cooks!

OYSTERS

I'm sometimes asked what my last meal on earth would be. Without a nanosecond of hesitation, I always say that the light appetizer course has to be a gargantuan platter of raw, top-quality oysters—or else I refuse to go!

Why do I love them so? Because the oyster is as much metaphor as meal. Because eating raw oysters is like eating the sea itself, ingesting the origins of life, nibbling on mermaids' toes.

The pleasure I have had eating oysters in restaurants is hard to reproduce at home. For home cooks in America, finding fresh, top-quality oysters is hard. And there is another big problem: it's simply impossible for anyone in America to get what I consider to be the greatest oysters in the world—French oysters—which I've merrily slurped in countless brasseries all over France.

The most widely eaten oyster in France is called the Japonaise. It is cultivated in Brittany and all the way down the west coast of France (some fabulous oysters are cultivated as far south as Bordeaux). The French Japonaise tastes like barely congealed seawater: amazingly thin and light in texture, over-whelmingly briny, salty, with an intense flavor of the ocean. It is the best way on earth to start a French meal.

The problem in America is that we don't have oysters as light in texture or briny in taste as the French ones. Our oysters are usually richer, creamier—as well as less salty, blander. However, though it develops a little differently in American waters, the very same oyster that the French dote on—the Japonaise—is one of the five oyster species commonly available in the United States. If you choose it right, you can come close to the French taste.

So let's look at the five American species, starting with the Japonaise.

1. *Crassostrea gigas.* This is it—an oyster originally from Japan, usually called the Pacific oyster in America. On our West Coast, from Alaska down through Southern

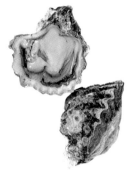

California, it is by far the most widely cultivated species of oyster. Most of those oysters you may have encountered at West Coast restaurants and oyster bars—Quilcenes, Hama Hamas, Totten Inlets, et cetera—are actually Pacific oysters (Japonaises), which are usually specifically named after the bays and inlets in which they were cultivated.

Oyster experts usually call these oysters "fruity" —though the only fruit they really suggest is watermelon, particularly watermelon rind. They also taste like cucumber, the same taste you'll find in these Japonaise oysters in France. Unfortunately, the American versions are usually a little fatter than their French cousins. But if you buy oysters in the coldest months, during the coldest weeks—from the most northerly oyster beds—your odds of getting crisper oysters will increase.

Pacific oysters from Washington, Oregon, Northern California, Alaska, and western Canada are, hands down, my favorite American oysters.

2. *Crassostrea sikamea* (Kumamoto). The Kumamoto oyster's deep-cupped shape sets it apart from the

Pacifics. It does, however, have a fruity taste that is reminiscent of Pacific oysters. It is very trendy just now among American chefs. Kumamotos are raised in Washington State and Northern California.

3. *Ostrea lurida* (Olympia). This tiny

oyster—it's about the size of your thumbnail—is a great favorite of mine. It's also the only oyster species that's indigenous

to the West Coast of America. Once upon a time, it was vastly popular, but you don't see it often today, certainly not in parts of the country other than the Pacific Northwest. I like its user-friendly size and its complex, sweet-earthy-briny-metallic taste.

4. *Crassostrea virginica.* When most Americans think "oyster," it is *Crassostrea virginica* that they visualize. The species is indigenous to the entire Eastern Seaboard of the United States, as well as the Gulf of Mexico. So all those famous East Coast oysters—Blue Points, Wellfleets, Chincoteagues, Gulf oysters—are of this species. The problem is: I'm not crazy about the species. It just doesn't have enough flavor, and rarely does it get briny enough. Sometimes in midwinter, the coldest oysters of this species—ones from eastern Canada, such as Malpeques, or Prince Edward Island—can satisfy me. But I generally look for alternatives, especially to the muddy, flabby Gulf oysters, which I think are best when they're cooked (as in oyster po'boys!).

5. *Ostrea edulis.* This species—which is native to western Europe—has a very particular shape; the oyster shells are round and quite flat, not deep. Additionally, though the texture of the oyster inside is a bit too rich for

most European oyster fanatics, *Ostrea edulis* makes up for it in what can be one of the briniest, most coppery, most penetrating tastes in all of oysterdom. The most famous oysters of this species are Belons, harvested in the Belon River of Brittany in France. I also love Colchesters from southern England, which are the same species. Today, oysters of this species are being farmed in Maine and on the West Coast, where they're sometimes called European flats. Look for them.

A Great American Oyster House

One of my favorite restaurants in California is also one of the best places in the country to eat oysters. It's the Zuni Café, in San Francisco, where Judy Rodgers turns out an amazing range of Mediterranean-California specialties. What makes the oyster eating here so special—other than the freshness and variety—is the way the oysters are listed on the menu. Zuni's oyster list is the only one I've seen that breaks its oysters into the five species and lists specific examples under those five headings. I wish more restaurants would dispel confusion by doing that!

Once you've taken the trouble to learn the five species of oysters, you can order with authority at oyster bars, restaurants, and fish stores. But, aside from mastering the taxonomy, another great problem exists for the American oyster lover: ensuring freshness.

Oysters just hauled out of the water are the best ones to eat, of course. But Nature sometimes assists Commerce—and in this case She did. Oysters that are kept cold, in an air-rich environment (don't seal them in bags), will keep well for at least a week beyond their harvest. This is why it's possible for fresh-tasting New England oysters to wind up on West Coast tables, and vice versa. However, the sad reality is that many of the shelled travelers don't come to the table in optimum condition.

How do you know which ones have? It's exceedingly difficult to tell from the outside of an oyster whether it's going to taste fresh or not. My habitual strategy, whenever it's possible, is to taste one oyster from a batch I'm considering—whether this means ordering a single oyster in a restaurant (sometimes I'll order one each of six different kinds before ordering a dozen more of the one I like best) or convincing the guy in the fish store to open one oyster for me.

What am I looking for? In a word: liquid. The surest signs of an over-the-hill oyster are a lack of liquid (sometimes called oyster liquor) in the shell and a dried-out, shrinking-from-the-shell look in the oyster itself. When I open an oyster, I like to see it swimming in liquid, glistening with moisture. Otherwise, I won't even taste it. Unfortunately, many, many oysters I see in America aren't juicy enough. By comparison, I have virtually never seen a dried-out oyster served in a restaurant in France.

Once you have a batch of wet, juicy, fresh-as-a-daisy oysters on your hands, how do you deal with them? At this point, I turn once again to France as my model—striving to emulate the serving conditions of my favorite Parisian brasseries.

Here's a step-by-step program for serving raw oysters at home to your family and guests.

1. Shucking the oysters. I love opening oysters; I find it much easier than opening clams, which so often offer resistance. The first rule is simple enough: open them *absolutely, positively at the last possible minute.* Oysters are alive, and everything starts changing, taste-wise and texture-wise, once you've opened them.

You need a proper oyster knife to do this job well; the knife has a short, dull, but pointed blade that performs the all-important prying open of the shell. You accomplish this by laying the oyster on a kitchen counter, irregular side down (the flat side of the oyster will be up, facing you). It is a good idea to work with thick gloves, or to hold the oyster in a kitchen towel. At the little peak that can be considered the top of the oyster, there should be a tiny crevice where the shells meet. Poke the pointy tip of your oyster knife into the tiny crevice and start twisting the knife until you've pried open the top shell; just keep digging and twisting until a virtual "pop" occurs. Then simply sweep your oyster knife just under the flat top shell and finish by removing that shell.

Accomplish all of this with the least spillage of oyster liquor you can manage; keep all that juice in the shell. And *never, ever run water over the oyster!* You may be tempted to do so if you have little bits of shell in the oyster, but resist the water routine—just pick out the shell chips with your fingers. Water makes the oyster taste washed out. Now you will have a beautiful oyster on the half shell, which, in France, is ready for the table.

2. To sever or not to sever? Why is your oyster table-ready in France but not in the United States? Because the French, in preparing oysters for the table, never sever the muscle that holds the oyster to the irregularly shaped bottom shell; the theory is that the oyster's freshness is preserved longer by keeping it attached. In America, oyster shuckers tend to take one extra step—cutting the oyster away from the bottom shell—so that the diner can simply lift or slurp the oyster. I prefer the French idea.

3. The oyster fork. If you're doing it the French way, it will help to have a proper French oyster fork. This is not essential, mind you, but it does come in handy. The French oyster fork is designed with a large separation between two of the tines, which enables you to slide the fork through the muscle connection point, severing the muscle mere seconds before consuming the oyster. You could substitute a regular fork at the table, or a small knife.

4. Serving the oysters. The whole idea of oyster service is to keep the critters cold between shucking and eating. The French like to place the shucked oysters on a bed of shaved ice, which usually rests in a round, metal tray (*un plateau*), which is usually placed on a hooplike stand (*un stand*—see how easy French is?). You could just as easily scatter your shaved ice on any kind of dinner plate (for individual portions, like six oysters) or large platter (for table-size portions, like twenty-four oysters) and top the ice with the shucked oysters. Just make sure that the oysters are balanced on the ice, lest their precious juices spill out of their shells. One other consideration: if you're not serving the oysters immediately (and you should!), they may get too cold, may nearly freeze sitting on the ice. In these situations, the French like to strew some seaweed over the ice to act as a thermal buffer—keeping the oysters cold but not frigid.

5. Sauces for oysters. In my oyster universe, sauce wouldn't even be a consideration: nothing improves the taste of a great, fresh, briny oyster swimming in its juice. But, I must confess, when oysters aren't briny enough, I may consider some oyster helper. I do occasionally squeeze a little lemon juice on oysters, to perk them up if they need it. The sauce that the French call mignonette—a combo of vinegar and shallots—is popular with oysters, though I rarely use it. And if I'm eating raw oysters in New Orleans—which I'll only do under duress, and in the coldest months—I'll definitely hit them with a shot of Tabasco (preferably green Tabasco). The one popular oyster sauce that I will never, ever use is cocktail sauce—ketchup and horseradish. It's not that I find the sauce distasteful (I love it with boiled shrimp); it's just that the wonderful, subtle flavor of oyster is completely obliterated by it. I always say that people who eat cocktail sauce with oysters don't really like oysters!

6. Eating the oysters. There are many different oyster-eating styles. Mine is to grab an unsevered oyster on the half shell and detach the meat from the shell with a fork, leaving the oyster and its juice in the shell, ready to be ravished. Then I lift the shell above my mouth and tilt its contents (solid and liquid) past my lips—making sure to ingest every drop of oyster liquor (sometimes called love potion). I like to chew the oyster slowly, savoring its texture. That's all ye know on earth, and all ye need to know.

7. Oyster accompaniments. Something a little dry and starchy between oysters helps set up your palate for the wild, wet shock of the next oyster. The traditional American solution, oyster crackers, accomplishes the job quite well, texturally speaking. But the French method adds a lovely flavor dimension: they serve thin slices of dry, dark bread with a thin schmear of butter that seems to lubricate the whole process.

8. Shell disposal. If you're eating from a communal platter of oysters, always place your empty shells on a plate in front of you. Never return the empty shells to the communal platter; you would be issuing an affront to French civilization. If you're hosting an oyster party, be sure to exchange the shell-laden individual plates for empty ones as soon as they become full.

MIGNONETTE SAUCE FOR OYSTERS

As you may have already gathered, when oysters are perfect I'm not one for oyster sauces. But when oysters are a bit flat and flabby, I perk them up with a little lemon juice. When they're flatter and flabbier still, I reach for the mignonette. This sprightly sauce was traditionally made with red wine vinegar, but many chefs switched to raspberry vinegar in the old nouvelle days. Use about ½ teaspoon of sauce per oyster.

MAKES ENOUGH FOR 2 DOZEN OYSTERS

1/4 cup raspberry vinegar

1 1/2 tablespoons finely minced shallots

1 teaspoon coarse, freshly ground black pepper

1/4 teaspoon salt

Mix all the ingredients together in a bowl. Serve with raw oysters. May be kept for a week in the refrigerator (though the vinegar becomes more shalloty).

RAW OYSTERS WITH SMOKED SALMON AND CAVIAR CREAM

I'm one of those nutty oyster purists who find oyster "dishes" abominable. But about ten years ago, at a restaurant in France's Champagne region, I was served a dish that blew both my oyster prejudices and my mind: raw oysters wrapped in silky smoked salmon, napped with a cold, caviar-studded puddle of cream. Serve each of your guests one of these little packets, as a little preappetizer surprise, or arrange three packets on each of four plates to make a first course for four people.

MAKES 12 OYSTER PACKETS

1/2 cup crème fraîche

1/4 cup heavy cream

2 ounces caviar (beluga, osetra, or sevruga)

1 tablespoon lemon juice

1 tablespoon finely chopped chervil or dill, plus extra
   sprigs for garnish

About 4 ounces top-quality smoked salmon, sliced
   extremely thin

12 cold, freshly opened oysters

1. In a bowl mix together the crème fraîche, heavy cream, 2 tablespoons of the caviar, lemon juice, and chopped chervil or dill. Refrigerate the sauce for 1 to 2 hours before using.

2. Just before serving, cut the salmon into 12 pieces; they should be just large enough to wrap the oysters into roughly square little packets. Wrap the oysters.

3. Divide the cream sauce among the serving plates, creating a pool of sauce at the center of each plate. Divide the wrapped oysters among the plates, arranging them on the sauce pools. Garnish each packet with a generous ¼ teaspoon of caviar and a chervil or dill sprig. Serve immediately.

Finding the Goods

If you live on the West Coast, finding good Pacific oysters (my favorite type harvested in America) is not difficult; fine seafood stores regularly carry them. But elsewhere in the country, you're out of luck. In New York City, I used to beg restaurateurs who had them on their menus (like the people at Union Square Cafe, or at the Grand Central Oyster Bar) to sell me a few. Sometimes they'd do me a favor—but this is not a source that the general public can rely on.

Then came my big discovery. If you telephone oyster producers on the Puget Sound of Washington State and place an order, they will harvest your oysters on, say, Tuesday, ship them off FedEx that day, and have them at your door on Wednesday—twenty-four hours out of the water! They arrive even fresher than they would through the commercial distribution chain. And—a big and—they are cheap! I've purchased oysters this way for a few bucks a dozen. Of course, the FedEx cost bloats the price considerably, but if you're buying hundreds of oysters for a big party, the cost per oyster is still pretty low.

One of the largest and most reliable producers is Taylor United, located in Shelton, Washington; the phone number is 360-426-6178. Another large outfit is Westcott Oysters, at 360-378-2489. A much smaller producer—but one whose products have been magnificent in my experience—is Crescent Beach Oysters, in the San Juan Islands of Puget Sound, at 360-376-4929.

Criteria for Quality

These are the questions for raw oysters:

- *Are they fresh? (swimming in liquid, not dried out, no fishy or "off" odors)*
- *Are they lean and "crisp"? (not fatty, creamy, or soft)*
- *Are they salty/briny? (if they aren't, they've come from lesser waters, or the shucker washed off the oyster liquor)*
- *Were they just opened?*
- *Are there enough of them? (it's only with oysters that I blur quality and quantity)*

When

Raw oysters are the ideal way to start almost any meal imaginable. They're obviously perfect as a kickoff for all kinds of European and American dinners; they're also great as a Japanese starter; and New York City's best Thai restaurant—the Typhoon Brewery—serves them with Thai dipping sauces as a first course. I always eat at least half a dozen raw oysters, usually crave a dozen, and find it hard (despite my Diamond Jim Brady aspirations) to go above a dozen and a half.

In Your Glass

Raw oysters are practically unthinkable without a glass of wine. Recent studies have shown that consuming alcohol with oysters lessens your chances of falling ill if you have the bad luck of eating unhealthy oysters. I take my "medicine" with no complaints.

Which wines are appropriate? With oysters, I love white wines that are light, simple, bone dry, low in alcohol, and, above all, bright with acidity. In France, nothing beats a fresh bottle of bracing Muscadet from the most recent vintage—except, perhaps, Muscadet's even simpler and crisper cousin from the same vineyard area, Gros Plant. Farther east along the Loire River, some good oyster wines are made from the Sauvignon Blanc grape—such as Sancerre and Ménétou-Salon. Be careful, however; modern producers are making these wines richer than ever, and today they can seem clumsy next to oysters. Still farther east, in Alsace, bone-dry Rieslings are produced that can be delicious with oysters—as long as they are simple, light in body, and not from a grand cru vineyard.

One of the most exciting wines of all for oysters—though there are many pitfalls here—is Chablis.

Pitfall 1: Do not attempt to drink anything from California called "Chablis"! We're talking exclusively about the vinous output of a small French village in northern Burgundy called Chablis.

Pitfall 2: The "best" Chablis wines from France are not the best Chablis wines for oysters. Those usually recognized as "best" come from special vineyards designated grand cru by the government; they are big, rich, fat wines, totally inappropriate for oysters. Even most premier cru wines—a step down—are too big. Another, related problem is that many of the top growers age their "big" wines in new oak, which detracts from the true taste of the Chablis soil.

The answer is to seek out wines labeled "Chablis" alone (no "grand cru" or "premier cru"). Buy from a producer who goes easy on the oak (Moreau uses none; Collet uses little). Use only wines from "crisp" vintages (avoid the ones that rate highest on the vintage charts). And try to find Chablis that's at least three to four years old, so that the young Chardonnay fruit will have died down and the special flavor of Chablis emerged.

If you follow all of these suggestions, you may end up with a flinty, steely, minerally bottle of Chablis that is practically the liquid equivalent of oysters—and will make, with those oysters, one of the most memorable wine-and-food matches you'll ever experience.

NAGE OF OYSTERS AND ASPARAGUS IN PERNOD VELOUTÉ

Okay, okay! I confess! Occasionally, I do like oysters that are cooked. If they're Gulf oysters, I like them really cooked—as in fried oysters. But if they're top-quality northern oysters, I do occasionally like them a little cooked, as in this wonderful soup, a fabulous first course for an elegant dinner party. A *nage* is literally a "swim." It's a culinary concept that became quite popular in France during the nouvelle cuisine era—a light soup with prestigious ingredients arranged in it. The "swim" concept implies that the swimming ingredients are not really cooked—they've just gone for a brief dip in the "water." In this delicious *nage*, raw oysters are "cooked" only by pouring hot, creamy soup over them in each serving bowl.

MAKES 6 FIRST-COURSE SERVINGS

4 cups chicken stock

6 tablespoons butter, at room temperature

2 medium leeks, washed and chopped

4 tablespoons flour

3 stalks celery, with leaves, chopped

24 freshly shucked oysters, at room temperature (with up to 1/2 cup oyster liquor)

24 warm asparagus tips, cooked until just tender

2 tablespoons Pernod

Fresh tarragon for garnish, if available

1. Bring the chicken stock to a boil in a small saucepan.

2. In a heavy-bottomed pot, melt 4 tablespoons of the butter over medium-high heat. Add the leeks, and sauté, stirring, for 2 minutes. Turn the heat down to medium, and sprinkle the flour over the leeks. Sauté, stirring, for 2 minutes. Remove from heat, and add the boiling chicken stock all at once. Beat vigorously with a whisk to incorporate the flour into the stock. Return to a boil, and add the celery. Reduce to a bare simmer, and cook for 30 minutes.

3. When you are ready to serve, divide the raw oysters and the cooked asparagus tips among 6 wide, shallow soup bowls. If you find the soup too thick, add some oyster liquor to thin it. Strain the soup, bring it to a boil, add the Pernod, and turn off the heat. Swirl in the remaining 2 tablespoons of butter with a whisk. Season to taste with salt and pepper, and pour immediately over the oysters and asparagus in the soup bowls, keeping the oysters visible just above the surface of the velouté. Garnish with fresh tarragon leaves, if available.

NOTE: A wonderful way to serve this soup is to place the bowls before your guests with the oysters and asparagus already set in them and then ladle out the velouté from a tureen at the table. Serve with dry German Riesling, dry sherry (a Manzanilla would be good), or Marqués de Murrieta Rioja Blanco.

THE GROWTH OF A PALATE: FOODIE FATE? OR FOODIE FREE WILL?

I'm not sure if the force of destiny is operative in this universe, but, if it is, I'm sure I was destined to love food.

This "destiny" wouldn't have been anything as grandiose as two garlic atoms colliding before time in some back forty of the empyrean, logically leading through the aeons to the birth of food-lovin' Dave in 1950. Nor do I think I was "destined" to love food by some divine gastronomic decree, designated the "special of the day" by the Great Menu Maker.

No. It would be, instead, those twin engines of modern destiny that drove me to the table—nature and nurture.

Sometimes, after I'd gone off to live on my own, I'd come home to visit and would barely get through the front door before I'd hear my mom, Lorry, shouting from another part of the house with disdain, "Did you eat garlic again?" And whenever she called me on it, I always had— usually about three days before coming home (I'd never be crazy enough to eat it that day). How could she sense an aroma that was three days old? I don't know. She rarely talked about food, rarely squirmed over its delights—but anything that came within fifty yards of her radar screen was detected with stone-cold precision. I'm sure that I'm not nearly as sensitive to taste and smell as my mom was, but having even a little of her magic goes a long way.

Then there was my dad, Lenny, who had another approach to garlic: he inhaled it on a daily basis. Judging from his lifelong dedication to powerful flavors, I'd say he probably didn't pass on to me an organoleptic gene that yielded the subtlety of analysis my mom's gene did. But here's where nurture kicks in—big time. My dad is the fresser of all fressers, the single most dedicated eater I've ever met. Long before I came along, my dad's eating exploits were legend in the family: his fourteen-lamb-chop dinners in the army, his three-restaurant nights, his long drives to find great steamed clams, great corn, great pizza, great roast beef sandwiches.

It seems that his dad, David Rosengarten—who died shortly before I was born—had set the same agenda for his son Lenny. Old Dave was an MGM executive in the 1920s, who regularly crisscrossed the country on trains and would bring the likes of Louis B. Mayer—as well as the best of what he found to eat across the country—home for dinner in Brooklyn. After dinner, long after dinner, he would wake up young Lenny and take the willing lad to the hottest speakeasy, if it happened to have received a great shipment of oysters that night. I recently took my dad, who's now eighty and still willing, on a gastronomic passage to India; one spicy night in Bombay, he said to me, "I can't believe how lucky I am. When I was young, I had David Rosengarten leading me around New York to find the best things to eat; now I'm old, and I have David Rosengarten leading me around the world for the same reason." Father to son to son: it's the Rosengarten food chain, and it has been going on for most of this century.

C A V I A R

When I was about twenty years old, my theater professor at Colgate University served me real caviar at a dinner party. I'd heard of caviar before then, and had even tasted a few things I thought were caviar . . . like the salty lumpfish eggs, dyed red or jet black, sold in jars in supermarkets. Pretenders all.

When hard-core caviar lovers say "caviar," they mean only one thing: the roe of sturgeon caught in the Caspian Sea. Fish other than sturgeon yield eggs in places other than the Caspian Sea; in some cases, sturgeon themselves yield eggs in other places. But to the true connoisseur they are not caviar.

There are three different types of sturgeon that swim in that sea and, accordingly, three types of true caviar: beluga, osetra, and sevruga.

Beluga. Let's face it—to most consumers, size *does* matter when it comes to caviar. How else would you explain the fact that the largest Caspian Sea sturgeon of all, the beluga, yielding the largest eggs, always gets the highest price by far for those eggs (often around $2,000 retail for a top-grade kilo!). Is beluga caviar worth twice the price of osetra, four times the price of sevruga? It depends whom you ask. It is true that the larger eggs provide a certain textural thrill, and that there is sometimes a fatty-buttery thing going on in beluga caviar. But, to my taste, these grayish eggs (they vary from light gray to dark gray) usually have the least intense marine flavor of the three caviars.

Osetra. I wouldn't lie to you: the lower price of osetra caviar is *not* what makes it my favorite. I have simply found, over time, and over many side-by-side tastings of beluga-osetra-sevruga, that osetra is the one that often stands out for complexity of flavor. I'm told that the diet of the osetra sturgeon differs from the diets of the other two, since it swims at a greater depth than the other two. Did anyone say "bottom feeder"?—a designation that always seems to lead to better taste (it's the bottom-feeding habits of the lobster, I'm convinced, that give it such culinary distinction). You can see the difference immediately in osetra eggs: they're likely to have a yellowish or greenish tinge. And they taste that way too, often hitting the palate with something like an herbal impression. Whether money is or isn't an object, osetra's my choice in caviar.

Sevruga. I also like standing up for poor, underloved, jet-black sevruga. The sevruga sturgeon is the smallest of the three, yielding the smallest eggs, commanding the lowest price. American caviar snobs sneer at the stuff. But it is all the rage among European connoisseurs, who love the very briny taste that it delivers. It is the hardest of the three to match with Champagne, so don't get a kilo for your next bubbles-and-eggs extravaganza. But if the drinks are alternative, so should your caviar be.

JUDGING CAVIAR

First, look at your caviar. Believe it or not, there are unscrupulous producers out there who will sell you sevruga, call it beluga, and charge you beluga prices. Check out color and egg size to make sure the caviar is plausibly in its announced category. Also beware of caviar that does not have a uniform color; a yellow egg here, a black egg there, a gray egg over there means you've got a mix of batches.

In tasting, I pay attention to four main things: texture, fishiness, saltiness, general flavor.

Caviar neophytes are sometimes disappointed that their caviar lacks "crunch," or that they can't feel the separateness of each egg in their mouths. But there's nothing abnormal about this. Caviar eggs do not stand alone; they gather in a thick, creamy, jammy mass. It's very hard to isolate a single egg in your mouth and crunch it as you might a salmon egg. If you can do this with caviar, it's likely your caviar has been pasteurized, i.e., cooked. Pasteurization makes the eggs more separate and crunchy; it is a sign of inferior caviar. At the other extreme, if your caviar is just a homogeneous smoothie devoid of little bumps, something else is wrong; perhaps you've been sold pressed caviar, a spread made of caviar.

Caviar should taste of the sea but not "fishy." If it is fishy, it's likely your caviar is not fresh. Other signs of staleness are sourness and a dry texture.

Good caviar is a little salty, of course, but not unpleasantly so. Unfortunately, caviar sold to the American market is saltier than caviar sold to the European market (see "Producing Caviar," below). Therefore, one of the first things I consider when I'm sampling caviar for purchase in America is the salt level. Sometimes, to my taste, it's too much (and I happen to like salt).

Last, one must consider all the subtleties of flavor. Osetra caviar is the most interesting to me because it has the broadest range of flavors. But all three caviars bring to the table a lot more than fishiness and saltiness. Good caviar has a cleanness, a near-sweetness that is most appealing. Sometimes there's a buttery quality. And occasionally—this is best of all in my book—there's a caviar aftertaste that recalls the taste of, well, eggs, particularly egg yolks.

Producing Caviar: An Essentially Simple Process

The production of caviar—compared with the production of other luxury items, such as smoked salmon, cheese, and wine—is a simple process. The ovaries of the sturgeons, each containing about 400,000 eggs, are removed and pressed into a screen that allows only the eggs to go through. The sieved eggs are rinsed, dried for a few minutes, salted, and packed into tins. Essentially, that's it.

Differences in quality come from differences in the raw material, from the processor's ability to keep the eggs cold, clean, and fresh during the lightning-fast processing, and—most important—from the processor's skill in salting.

Why use salt at all? Primarily because salt is a preservative. But even if you could eat the caviar right after processing, you'd want some salt, since it heightens the flavor of the roe and helps the caviar attain a runny consistency. Too much salt, and the caviar is unpleasant. Too little salt, and the highly perishable product lacks flavor. The master salter gets it just right—juggling factors such as the maturity of the roe (less salt is needed for immature eggs), the size of the roe, the freshness of the roe, and even the exterior weather conditions.

The word malossol, *which you should look for on caviar labels, means "with little salt" in Russian. The best caviars carry this designation.*

However, what most Americans don't realize is that all caviar ticketed for the American market—even top-grade caviar designated malossol—*has about three times as much salt as top-grade caviar ticketed for other places.*

The reason behind this startling fact is the U.S. government's antipathy toward borax, a preservative. All caviar receives a substance, usually amounting to about 3 percent of the caviar weight, to preserve it. For European consumption, the Caspian Sea processors use approximately 2 percent borax (which is not salty in taste) and 1 percent salt. The USDA considers borax a dangerous additive and forbids its use. Therefore, U.S.-targeted caviar gets mixed with 3 percent salt. According to Eve Vega of Petrossian, the ban is absurd. "An American child once died from a borax overdose," she said. "But you'd have to consume forty-eight pounds of caviar at one sitting to be harmed."

If you've noticed that caviar tastes better in Europe, now you know why.

HOW TO EAT AND SERVE CAVIAR

Repeat after me: onions, eggs, and crackers are the enemy.

More precisely, they are the legacy of the Bad Caviar Years—when the authentic, refrigerated roe of Caspian Sea sturgeon was virtually unknown in this country. The onions and eggs covered up the vile, salty, fishy impostor eggs that passed for caviar.

If you have great caviar today—and there's no reason not to, as long as you can afford it—do yourself a favor. Enjoy it only with a spoon—preferably one of horn, ivory, or mother-of-pearl. Make each guest feel special by creating individual servings of caviar; simply place one ounce of it, maybe two, in a small bowl that just contains the eggs. Place that bowl in a large bowl of cracked ice. Give that arrangement of bowls along with a spoon to each guest. You have created the civilized, individualized caviar experience. Life is good.

Individual service of caviar with ivory spoon (left); special instrument for opening jars of caviar (right).

When

Some may have the impression that caviar is a commodity to serve only when you're hosting a posh dinner party. As far as I'm concerned, nothing could be further from the truth. If you're lucky enough to be able to afford copious quantities of the stuff, just watch how much fun caviar ignites when each guest is able to wolf down a few ounces, or more, as the prelude to a barbecue.

In Your Glass

Caviar's classic mate is Champagne, of course. But you'd be surprised how many connoisseurs of each commodity refuse to drink them together.

To my taste, the elegance and harmony of Champagne are usually shattered by its brush with sturgeon roe. Often the finish is harsh, or fishy, or bitter. Why spend so much on Champagne if this is to be its fate? Cheaper, fruitier, less elegant sparkling wines from other places fare even worse.

If you insist on Champagne with caviar, there are a few things you can do to improve your odds. First of all, make sure that your caviar is in tip-top condition; an excess of salt, an edge of fishiness or bitterness, will ruin the match. I have often found peak-condition osetra caviar to be the highest-odds proposition. Next, choose an older Champagne whose fruit has died down. It is important that you avoid aged Champagnes from rich and full vintages. Lighter-style vintage Champagnes from 1975, 1979, 1981, 1983, and 1985 should be just about right.

The last thing you can do to make the "classic" match work is drink your Champagne with caviar in Europe, where the caviar is less salty. Unfortunately, this adds a bit of expense to an already expensive coupling.

Many people turn to vodka as a substitute. Icy cold from the freezer, served in small, frozen glasses, Russian vodka seems a natural partner to Russian caviar. However, be prepared to sacrifice some of the subtlety of your dearly bought caviar; the heady spirit has a tendency to overwhelm the eggs.

For the best-balanced match of all—the one that maintains the integrity of roe and beverage both—drink beer. Beer? Please don't knock it until you've tried it. They do it in Russia all the time. You will find, in addition to extraordinary balance, that beer is supremely refreshing next to caviar. Choose a beer that's on the light side; anything from Beck's and up will start stepping on the eggs. Holsten Dry, from Hamburg, is always a winner. Rolling Rock, a light domestic beer, also works well. It's better to err on the side of insipidity, believe it or not: I'd rather drink Bud with my beluga than Guinness Stout. Just chill it to the absolute max.

Worried that your guests will think you're a low-rent host? Serve your beer, icy cold, in the most elegant small glasses you can find, right out of the freezer, each one topped with a perfect, tiny head of foam. As soon as they follow a spoonful of eggs with the brew you've chosen, I guarantee they'll be toasting your good taste.

STURGEON EGGS: DOOMED TO A LIFE ALONE?

If you blend top-quality caviar with ingredients that are both mild and sensuous (like eggs, smoked salmon, raw fish, mascarpone)—and if you don't allow it to cook!—you can come up with some very sexy combinations that don't make a mockery of what you spent for the caviar in the first place.

One of my favorite combinations is the following—a variation of which is served early in the meal by many chefs in top restaurants in France.

SCRAMBLED EGGS AND CAVIAR IN AN EGGSHELL

The scrambled eggs for this dish may be prepared in any way you wish. But if you use the steam nozzle of a cappuccino machine to scramble the eggs, you will create large, lovely, decadent curds of scrambled egg that go brilliantly with the caviar.

MAKES 6 APPETIZER SERVINGS

6 extra large eggs
2 ounces caviar (I prefer osetra)

6 fresh 4-inch-long spikes of chives
A few spoons of crème fraîche (optional)

1. Put water in a steamer for cappuccino, and heat it until it is steaming.

2. Put 1 egg on a cutting board, and, working with a serrated knife, lightly tap the shell about an inch down from the pointy end—breaking the shell but not cutting through it. Over a bowl, cut through and carefully remove the small end of the shell, and let the white and yolk fall into the bowl. Wash out the large part of the empty shell, and put it in an egg cup. Repeat with 5 more eggs, making 6 egg cups holding 1 empty shell each.

3. Beat the 6 eggs together, and transfer half of the mixture to a small pitcher used for steaming milk for cappuccino. Put the steamer nozzle to the bottom of the pitcher, and steam the eggs on full power until they are mostly coagulated. (Don't worry about leaving some of the egg runny.)

4. Into each of 3 eggshells, spoon 1 heaping teaspoon of cooked egg. Then layer in a generous ½ teaspoon of caviar, another heaping teaspoon of egg, and another generous ½ teaspoon of caviar. Then fill the shells up to the top with egg. Put a ½-teaspoon dollop of caviar on top.

5. Wipe off the steamer nozzle, and repeat the process, filling the rest of the shells with layers of eggs and caviar. You may have a little scrambled egg left over.

6. Garnish each shell with a spike of chive, and, if desired, a small dollop of crème fraîche. Serve immediately.

Bruschetta with warm cannellini bean

Bruschetta with fresh tomato and basil

Plain bruschetta

Bruschetta with Gorgonzola-mascarpone-red pepper

Bruschetta with oven-dried tomato

Bruschetta with olive paste and mascarpone

Bruschetta with anchovy and pimento

BRUSCHETTA

Enough oysters and caviar. These are indisputably great ways to start a dinner party . . . but they are tastes I learned later in life.

I can't wait any longer to tell you about the first great love of my gastronomic life: garlic bread.

We all grew up in America with garlic bread, and most of us loved it. I certainly did at Angelo's, in Brooklyn, my father's favorite restaurant, where I consumed a ton of excellent garlic bread: thick rounds of a good Italian loaf, topped with lots of minced garlic, drizzled with olive oil, and baked briefly in the oven.

But not everybody had garlic bread this good. It was usually cottony loaves of bread slathered with melted margarine and garlic powder, wrapped in aluminum foil and warmed!

In the late 1970s, as the Collective Boomer Palate matured, this type of faux-garlic bread disappeared from our dinner party menus. But, happily, just as we were about to banish garlic bread forever from our adult gastronomic lives—bruschetta came along! Starting in the 1980s, many of the New Wave Italian restaurants in America—that is, those restaurants focusing more on authentic Italian regional food, and those increasingly emphasizing the country food of poorer Italians—featured bruschetta.

What is bruschetta? In its simplest form, it's merely slices of bread that are grilled, rubbed with fresh garlic, and drizzled with olive oil. The word *bruschetta*—which is what they call this dish in Rome—comes from an Italian word for roasting over coals. The same dish has many different names all over Italy, but the other name I like for it is the Tuscan one; the Tuscans love simple foods, so they just call it *fettunta,* or "oiled slice."

Of course, as with so many hot gastronomic commodities in American restaurants, the simple ultimately gave way to the baroque. Rarely, today, do you see bruschetta in restaurants as merely an "oiled slice"; it almost always has something spooned on top of it. Chopped tomatoes with garlic and basil was the first widely popular topping, and probably still is.

I have nothing against bruschetta with toppings; cooks frequently top bruschetta in Italy, and the results can be wildly delicious. I do object to toppings that are defiantly non-Italian.

I especially object to the attention that toppings get, and to the way in which this detracts from the bruschetta itself. I've seen many chefs spend all their mental effort in dreaming up a creative twist on this dish and in acquiring exotic ingredients—without giving much thought to the type of bread they're going to use, or the type of olive oil, or how they're going to cook the bread!

I say: let bruschetta be about bruschetta! The bread itself is one of the most insanely delicious creations to come out of Italy. The rest is a distraction.

Here are some of the key bruschetta "issues," as I see them.

PRONOUNCING BRUSCHETTA

It's probably the *s* before the ch that does it—but almost everyone on these shores wants to say "broo-SHETT-ah." This is *wrong*. The proper pronunciation is "broo-SKETT-ah."

THE TYPE OF BREAD

The Scylla and Charybdis of bruschetta-making are loaves that are too heavy and loaves that are too light. If the bread is too heavy, you'll have a dense, unattractive chew. If the bread is too light, the chew won't be substantial enough.

Most cities today have good bakeries turning out round, crusty breads, which are often called country loaves. Try one. The loaf should have a crunchy brown crust and a serious, moderately chewy bread inside that is lightened by big airholes. This is perfect bruschetta bread.

THE SIZE OF THE BREAD AND THE SLICES

You can make bruschetta with good bread of any size.

Some people like to make it from long, skinny loaves of French or Italian bread, cut into rounds. This works fine—but it is not the way you'll most often see it in Italy, or in restaurants in America.

In those places, and at my house, you'll see bruschetta made from large, round loaves that are 8 to 10 inches in diameter. Slices from those loaves will be in different lengths, depending on how close to the center of the loaf the slice was cut. You can then cut the slices in halves, or thirds, to get pieces of relatively uniform dimensions. I shoot for slices that are 3 to 4 inches long and 3 to 4 inches wide. Remember: they don't all need to be the same size!

One of the most important decisions in bruschetta making concerns the thickness of the slices. If the slices are too thick, the bruschetta will be too bready and may not heat through by the time the outside is grilled. If the slices are too thin, the bruschetta will be too crisp and will lack the substantial chew of good bruschetta. I find that slices of ¾ inch, or a little less, are just about perfect—though you often see them thinner than that in Italy, thicker than that in America.

THE ORDER OF ATTACK

You can oil and garlic-rub your bread in just about any order you like. I prefer to grill the bread first just as it is (no oil, no garlic) and then add the flavorings.

GRILLING THE BREAD

The best way to make bruschetta is to grill the slices of bread over a smoky charcoal fire. It shouldn't be too hot, lest the bread burn on the outside before the inside is heated through. Perfectly cooked bruschetta will look golden brown on the outside (with grill marks, if you wish) and will be soft and warm on the inside.

There are many substitutes for the smoky charcoal fire. You can cook the bread on a gas grill, also on an indoor electric grill, or on a grill pan. I've also placed slices of bread under the broiler with some success (but watch them carefully so they don't burn). If you have a gas range, a surprisingly simple and tasty method is to hold bread slices with tongs over the open fire until they've carbonized evenly on the outside.

ADDING THE GARLIC

Many bruschette go wrong because it's not as easy as it seems to rub garlic onto the bread. If the bread is soft inside (as it should be), you may shred the bread or tear it apart trying to rub garlic over it.

My solution is simple: rub the garlic over only the edges of the bread. Everyone has to bite through the edges to taste the bread, so any biter is sure to get some garlic taste.

I like to smash my garlic cloves with a heavy knife, then rub the fragmented garlic vigorously on the edges of the grilled bread slices.

CHOOSING AND ADDING THE OIL

The olive oil itself is one of the stars of this dish, so make sure you use a fabulous, full-flavored, extra-virgin olive oil. To me, this means Tuscan oil—usually the greenest, fruitiest, and most peppery of olive oils. Make sure to buy one that's not much more than a year beyond the harvest date—certainly no more than two years beyond. Good young Greek or Spanish olive oils are reasonable substitutes.

After the bread slices are grilled and garlicked, break the surface of each slice lightly with a spoon, and drizzle each slice with about 2 teaspoons of olive oil. Turn the slices over, and do it again.

SEASONING THE BRUSCHETTA

I'm not crazy about black pepper on my bruschetta—but I wouldn't consider serving it or eating it without a sprinkling of coarse grains of salt.

Here's my favorite method for making bruschetta.

B R U S C H E T T A

Because I love great olive oil, I usually go oil-overboard when making bruschetta—and apply oil on both sides of the bread. This recipe instructs you to do so, but you might prefer to oil only one side of the bread, in which case you'll need only 1/2 cup of olive oil for these 12 slices.

MAKES 12 SLICES

1 round loaf country bread, not too dense, 8 to 10
    inches in diameter
6 cloves of garlic, smashed

1 cup extra-virgin olive oil (preferably young Tuscan)
Coarse salt

1. Prepare a medium-hot charcoal fire.

2. Cut the middle portion of the round loaf into 6 long slices, each about 3/4 inch thick. Cut these slices in half, making 12 half slices that are roughly 3 by 4 inches.

3. When the fire is ready, place the 12 slices over it in a single layer. Cook, turning once, until the outsides of the bread are golden brown (with grill marks, if possible). This should take about 2 minutes per side; check frequently to make sure the bread isn't burning.

4. When the bread slices are done, rub each one along the edges with smashed garlic cloves (lightly or heavily, depending on your garlic preference). Place the slices on a large platter in a single layer. Sprinkle each slice with 2 teaspoons of olive oil, breaking the surface of the bread lightly with a spoon to let the oil soak in. Season with salt. Turn the slices over, and repeat the oil-and- salt procedure. Let the slices sit for 10 to 15 minutes. Serve as is for simple bruschetta.

As much as I love the Tuscan ideal of the simple "oiled slice," I must confess that the first thing I order at the Union Square Cafe in New York is their Bruschetta rossa—oiled slices with a tomato, basil, and garlic topping. It's delicious. And, over the years, I have developed a number of other bruschetta toppings that I crave.

Here are my favorites.

FRESH TOMATO AND BASIL TOPPING FOR BRUSCHETTA

MAKES ENOUGH TO TOP 12 BRUSCHETTE

2 pounds ripe tomatoes, coarsely chopped
1 cup torn basil leaves, firmly packed
2 teaspoons extra-virgin olive oil

1 teaspoon red wine vinegar
1 clove garlic, pounded into a paste with
    1/2 teaspoon salt

1. In a bowl, mix together the tomatoes, basil, olive oil, and vinegar. Add some of the garlic paste (or all of it, depending on your taste), and blend well. Season to taste with salt and pepper. Let stand at room temperature for 2 hours, if possible.

2. When ready to top the bruschette, drizzle each slice with about 1 tablespoon of juice from the bottom of the bowl containing the tomato mixture. With a slotted spoon, strew the tomato mixture over the bruschette. Serve immediately.

OVEN-DRIED TOMATO TOPPING FOR BRUSCHETTA

The intensified flavor of slow-roasted tomato is fabulous on grilled bread. This method of roasting takes only 4 hours.

MAKES ENOUGH TO TOP 12 BRUSCHETTE

18 plum tomatoes
Coarse salt

Extra-virgin olive oil

1. Preheat the oven to 250 degrees.
2. Cut the tomatoes in half the long way, place them skin side down on a baking sheet, and sprinkle generously with salt. Bake for 4 hours. Cool the tomatoes to room temperature.

3. Place 3 tomato halves on each bruschetta slice, and sprinkle with olive oil and coarse salt. Serve immediately.

GORGONZOLA–MASCARPONE–RED PEPPER
TOPPING FOR BRUSCHETTA

This is a deliciously rich bruschetta—so rich that you may want to use only 2 teaspoons of oil, not 4, per slice of bread.

MAKES ENOUGH TO TOP 12 BRUSCHETTE

1 pound Gorgonzola cheese, at room temperature

1 pound mascarpone cheese

6 red bell peppers, roasted, peeled, and halved
  (see below)

Mix the two cheeses together in a bowl, blending well. Divide them among the 12 bruschette, spreading evenly. Top each slice with a half red pepper. Serve immediately.

Roasting Red Peppers

The simplest way to roast red bell peppers, if you have a gas range, is to cook them over the open fire of your range. Simply rest each pepper on a jet turned up to high flame. Turn the peppers frequently with tongs to ensure even blackening; the peppers should be charred in 5 to 7 minutes.

Place the peppers in a paper or plastic bag, seal, and let them rest for 15 minutes. The steam that's created will separate the charred skin from the flesh. Remove the peppers from the bag, and slide the charred skin off with your fingers. Cut a thin slice from the top of each pepper, then cut each pepper in half longitudinally. Scoop out the seeds, and cut away the thick ribs. The pepper halves are now ready to top the bruschette.

A great substitute: If you can find them, piquillo peppers from Spain's Rioja region are delicious on top of these bruschette—and all you have to do is open a can. They are roasted and packed in brine. Cut them to size, and you've got it made.

OLIVE PASTE AND MASCARPONE TOPPING
FOR BRUSCHETTA

You can use full-flavored, slightly bitter olives for this dish—like the oil-cured black Moroccans—because the creaminess of the mascarpone balances well with the olive's intensity. But feel free to use milder olives, like gaetas or kalamatas.

MAKES ENOUGH TO TOP 12 BRUSCHETTE

1 cup pitted black Moroccan oil-cured olives

1 tablespoon lemon zest

2 teaspoons lemon juice

2 to 3 tablespoons extra-virgin olive oil

12 ounces mascarpone cheese (about 1 1/2 cups)

1. Place the olives, lemon zest, and lemon juice in the work bowl of a food processor. Process, adding just enough oil to make a coarse paste.

2. Spread the marscapone on the bruschette, and spread the olive paste on top. Serve immediately.

WARM CANNELLINI BEAN TOPPING FOR BRUSCHETTA

If you love the simple, elemental taste of beans, serve these bruschette without any of the fancy drizzles suggested in the recipe (white truffle oil or porcini oil). But if you can stand the distraction of these oils on top of your beans, the results are delicious.

MAKES ENOUGH TO TOP 12 BRUSCHETTE

2 cups dried cannellini beans

1/2 pound bacon, sliced

2 teaspoons minced garlic

2 tablespoons minced fresh rosemary

White truffle oil (optional)

Porcini oil (optional)

Finely chopped parsley for garnish

1. Cover the beans with water, and soak overnight.

2. Drain the beans. Put them in a pot, cover them with fresh water, and cook them for 1 hour, or until soft. Drain the beans, and reserve the liquid.

3. Slice the bacon in ½-inch strips. Sauté the bacon in a heavy pot until golden.

4. Add the drained beans, garlic, and rosemary, and stir together. With a fork, mash the beans, adding bean cooking liquid as needed. Leave a few beans whole. You should have a thick, moist bean purée. Season with salt and pepper.

5. Spread the mixture on the bruschette. If desired, drizzle with truffle oil or porcini oil. Top with parsley. Serve immediately.

ANCHOVY AND PIMIENTO TOPPING FOR BRUSCHETTA

Last, there's this unbelievably delicious holdover from my early days. I grew up eating old-fashioned garlic bread with fillets of anchovies and strips of pimiento over the slices. The flavors of youth are preserved in this version, which is better than the original in every way.

MAKES ENOUGH TO TOP 12 BRUSCHETTE

4 small tins flat anchovy fillets

1/4 cup oil from the anchovy tins

1/2 teaspoon very finely chopped garlic

24 ounces coarsely chopped pimientos

12 scallions, minced

4 teaspoons lemon juice

1/4 cup very finely minced fresh parsley

In a bowl mix together all the ingredients. Place the bruschette on a large platter in a single layer. When you are ready to serve, strew the mixture over the bruschette. Serve immediately.

Criteria for Quality

- *Is the bread golden brown—not burned or undercooked?*
- *Has the bread picked up the delicious flavor of the grill?*
- *Does the bread chew correctly—not too dense, or too light?*
- *Is the olive oil full of character?*
- *Is there enough oil to moisten the inside of the bread—but not so much that the bread is inundated?*
- *Can you taste the garlic? (though you shouldn't taste only garlic)*
- *Is the topping appropriate? (it has to make sense with garlic and olive oil)*
- *Is the topping fresh tasting?*

When

Pure-and-simple bruschetta—just grilled bread with garlic and oil—is a fabulous accompaniment to any meal at which bread, garlic, and olive oil seem appropriate. Serve the grilled slices in a covered bread basket, in place of other kinds of bread.

The topped bruschette make fabulous openers for an Italian, Mediterranean, or New American meal. You can pass around trays of bruschetta as your guests eat them with fingers and napkins only.

But topped bruschetta is also a great sit-down first course. I like to serve the lighter ones—such as the tomato-basil-garlic—three to a plate. A serving note: If you serve three to a plate, there's no need to center the topping on each piece of bread. Simply arrange the three toasts on each plate, then casually strew the topping over all three.

In Your Glass

What you drink with bruschetta has everything to do with what you place on bruschetta.

The simplest all-purpose advice, however, is this: choose a young, fruity, simple Italian red to wash everything down. This means young Barbera d'Alba or Barbera d'Asti (don't spend more than $12); young Dolcetto d'Alba; young and simple Chianti; young and simple Valpolicella; or, from November to July, any red wine labeled "Novello" that comes from the most recent vintage.

COLD CHINESE APPETIZERS

Beside Italy, the other great lodestar of my early gastronomic life was China—or, more accurately, China in America. If, on a Saturday night, we weren't heading for a round of shrimp marinara at Angelo's in Brooklyn, we were most likely heading for a big platter of shrimp with lobster sauce at Joy Garden in Manhattan's Chinatown. But the fried rice and egg rolls of the 1950s and 1960s didn't have as much impact as what was to follow.

In the 1970s, New York was invaded by a series of restaurants that, for the first time, featured the spicy cuisines of western China. My palate was warmed up by a few small-scale restaurants serving something called Szechuan food; I immediately fell in love with hot-and-sour soup, cold noodles with a spicy peanut sauce, and stir-fried shrimp with chili-and-garlic sauce. I was amazed to see a dynamic new twist on a cuisine I thought I knew well. It was the first time the thrilling concept of culinary regionality captured my imagination.

But these places merely set the stage for what was to follow. The Szechuan restaurants had a casual feel to them; we were told that Szechuan food was "rural" food. Then the Hunan restaurants took me, and the city, by chili-storm. We were told that Hunanese food was "urban" food, and in the elaborate, uptown decors of these places, the finer service, and the sophisticated cooking techniques, you could understand the claim. Uncle Tai's Hunan Yuan, on the East Side, was the most spectacular place of all, a restaurant that truly changed my gastronomic life. Here, I discovered flaky vegetarian duck (a meatlike dish made from layers of dried bean-curd sheet); Uncle Tai's beef, with an exquisite chew engineered by marinating the beef in baking soda; and Lake Tung Ting shrimp, which—though it didn't feature the spicy thrills of the other dishes—gave me my first taste of shrimp that had been "velvetized" by egg white. Uncle Tai's food was a concerto of textures—the first time in a restaurant I found myself asking not "How'd they get that flavor?" but "How'd they get that feel in the mouth?"

But it also signaled the death of something for me—namely, the pupu platter. I grew up thinking that Chinese people ate egg rolls and other fried tidbits at the start of every meal. One of the biggest differences in this new wave of Chinese restaurants was the array of more sophisticated appetizers—many of them cold—that kicked off the meal. I will never forget the little earthenware pot of slivered cucumbers, glistening with chili oil, punctuated by cilantro, that greeted me on my first visit to Uncle Tai. I was soon copying it and other cold Chinese appetizers at home—and have never stopped.

Here are some of my favorite dishes from twenty-five years of emulation. Each one is delicious, but they're especially spectacular when served together as an elaborate first course for a Chinese dinner party.

Broccoli with Assorted Flavor

This is one of my all-time favorite appetizers from any cuisine. Watch it turn those who are "bored" by vegetables into ravenous eaters of green. It's also a happy time for the cook—since the recipe's a breeze and should be prepared hours in advance. At dinner party time, all you have to do is pick up the platter and put it on the table. I also love the quaint language of the Chinese menu in America: there are so many tastes in here, the flavor is called "assorted."

SERVES 6 AS PART OF A FIRST-COURSE ARRAY

1 large bunch of broccoli

2 tablespoons peanut oil

5 large cloves garlic, finely minced

3 tablespoons peeled and finely minced fresh
    gingerroot

1 tablespoon thin soy sauce

1 tablespoon fish sauce (Thai or Vietnamese)

1 tablespoon Chinese black vinegar (or any other
    vinegar)

1/4 cup chicken stock

1 tablespoon sugar

1/2 teaspoon MSG (optional)

1 teaspoon Chinese sesame oil

1. Separate the broccoli into long, fairly thin pieces; each piece should run from the stalk up to a little "crown" of a broccoli floweret. Some pieces will naturally pull apart this way; but in some cases, you'll have to cut down thicker pieces to arrive at long, thin stalks. The ideal piece is about 4 inches long, with a floweret at the top, and about ½ inch thick.

2. Working with a sharp knife, remove the tough peel on the outside of the stalks; leave the flowerets alone.

3. Parboil the broccoli pieces in a large pot of furiously boiling salted water for 4 minutes. Immediately pour the contents of the pot into a colander, and run very cold water over the broccoli until it cools off.

4. Place the peanut oil in a wok over medium heat. Add the garlic and ginger; stir-fry for 2 minutes. Add the broccoli, soy sauce, fish sauce, vinegar, chicken stock, sugar, and MSG (if using). Stir over heat to blend. Remove the broccoli immediately (you may place it in a bowl or on a plate). Turn off heat under the wok. Swirl in the sesame oil to blend. Adjust the seasoning.

5. For the prettiest results, arrange the broccoli pieces on an oval platter that's just longer than two broccoli pieces laid end to end. Line up half the broccoli pieces on one side of the platter, arranging them carefully with the flowerets toward the left edge of the platter. Place the other half on the other side of the platter, with the flowerets toward the right edge. The broccoli stalks should meet at the center. Pour the sauce over the broccoli, allowing the bits of garlic and ginger to collect at the center, where the broccoli stalks meet.

6. Marinate for 3 hours at room temperature, covered. Serve as is.

COOL NOODLES WITH SPICY SESAME SAUCE

This was one of the very first dishes that told me there was life beyond spareribs.

SERVES 6 AS PART OF A FIRST-COURSE ARRAY

2 tablespoons sesame seeds

2 tablespoons Chinese sesame paste (you may
    substitute smooth peanut butter)

4 tablespoons Chinese sesame oil

2 tablespoons dark soy sauce

1 tablespoon Chinese chili oil (or more, depending on
    your chili lust)

2 tablespoons rice vinegar

2 teaspoons sugar

1/2 teaspoon MSG (optional)

12 ounces fresh or dried Chinese wheat noodles,
    shaped something like spaghetti

Fresh cilantro for garnish

1. Toast the sesame seeds over medium-high heat in a heavy sauté pan, just until they start to darken (about 2 minutes). Remove from the pan and reserve.

2. In a mixing bowl, combine the sesame paste (or peanut butter), 2 tablespoons of the sesame oil, soy sauce, chili oil, vinegar, sugar, and MSG (if using). Stir well to blend, taste for seasoning, and reserve.

3. In a large pot of boiling salted water, cook the noodles (fresh ones will take a minute or two, dried ones

will take longer). When the noodles are just cooked, pour them into a colander, and toss immediately with the remaining 2 tablespoons of sesame oil. Place the noodles in the mixing bowl with the reserved sauce, add the sesame seeds, and toss well to blend. Hold until the noodles cool to room temperature.

4. Place the noodles on a platter, garnish with cilantro leaves, and serve.

AROMATIC SMOKED FISH

Here's another great Chinese appetizer that is cooked in advance and left to cool to room temperature—a perfect party dish! Once again, the Chinese terminology is quaint; the fish is not "smoked" at all but deep-fried in smoking oil. However, there is no crispy coating—and that's why nothing is lost as the fish sits for a few hours, picking up the wonderful flavor of the sauce.

SERVES 6 AS PART OF A FIRST-COURSE ARRAY

1 pound cod steaks, each 3/4 inch thick

2 tablespoons shao hsing (or dry sherry)

2 teaspoons thin soy sauce

1 teaspoon plus 2 tablespoons finely minced fresh
    gingerroot

1 teaspoon plus 3 tablespoons sugar

1/2 teaspoon salt

1/4 teaspoon freshly ground black pepper

4 cups peanut oil for deep frying

2 large cloves garlic, minced

2 scallions, cut into 2-inch lengths

6 pieces star anise

1/4 cup Chinese black vinegar

2 tablespoons Chinese oyster sauce

1/2 teaspoon five-spice powder

Fresh cilantro for garnish

1. With a heavy cleaver, cut the cod steaks into 1-inch pieces that include some skin and bone.

2. In a large bowl, mix together the shao hsing, 1 teaspoon of the soy sauce, 1 teaspoon of the minced ginger, 1 teaspoon of the sugar, the salt, and the black pepper. Add the chunks of cod, and stir well to coat. Marinate for 2 hours at room temperature.

3. Heat the peanut oil in a wok to 375 degrees. Remove the fish from the marinade, dry it off, and, working in batches, fry the chunks in the hot oil until they're brown and crispy (this will take 3 to 5 minutes). Remove the fish to paper towels and reserve.

4. Discard all but 2 tablespoons of the oil from the wok. Place the wok over medium-high heat, and add the garlic, the remaining 2 tablespoons of ginger, and the scallions. Stir-fry for 30 seconds. Add the star anise, vinegar, the remaining 3 tablespoons of sugar, the oyster sauce, the remaining teaspoon of soy sauce, and the five-spice powder. Boil for 2 minutes. Add the reserved fish to the sauce, stir to coat, then remove the wok from heat.

5. Place the fish on a platter, and cool to room temperature. When you are ready to serve, garnish with cilantro leaves.

HACKED CHICKEN WITH HOT OIL AND BROWN SZECHUAN PEPPERCORNS

This dish was another one of the early "classics" in the Szechuan assault on New York in the 1970s—and it has remained a classic on my dinner table. It brought to many of us the intriguing taste of brown Szechuan peppercorns, which are not related to black peppercorns or to chili peppers. They are native to Szechuan and are used today all over China; I love their wild, almost-anise, almost-mint flavor. This dish differs slightly from the preceding ones in that the meat isn't marinated in the sauce; the contrast between the slippery white meat and the dark sauce is one of the joys of the dish. The Chinese like to keep the meat as slippery as possible, so they undercook it; they don't mind chicken that's pink (or even red!) at the bone. My instructions call for "just past pink," but let your thirst for authenticity be your guide.

SERVES 6 AS PART OF A FIRST-COURSE ARRAY

2 whole chicken breasts

6 cloves garlic, peeled

1/4 cup cilantro stems and leaves

4 tablespoons thin soy sauce

6 tablespoons Chinese sesame paste (or smooth peanut butter)

3 tablespoons shao hsing (or dry sherry)

3 tablespoons honey

2 tablespoons Chinese sesame oil

4 teaspoons rice vinegar

1 to 2 teaspoons hot chili oil

3 scallions, green part only, finely minced

1/2 teaspoon brown Szechuan peppercorns

1. Bring a pot of salted boiling water just to the simmer. Plunge the chicken breasts into the water, and cook gently until the chicken is just past pink (this will take 10 to 15 minutes). Place the chicken in a colander, and run it under cold water to stop the cooking. When the chicken is cool enough to handle, remove and discard the skin and bones. Pull the breast fillets apart with your hands into long strips. Reserve.

2. Prepare the sauce: Place the garlic, cilantro, and soy sauce in a small food processor, and purée. Place in a mixing bowl, and blend in the sesame paste (or peanut butter), shao hsing, honey, sesame oil, vinegar, chili oil, and scallions.

3. In a dry cast-iron skillet over low heat, toast the peppercorns for 5 minutes. Remove, grind in a spice grinder, and rub through a sieve. Add the powder to the sauce.

4. When you are ready to serve, arrange the room-temperature chicken shreds on a platter. Pour sauce over all, and serve immediately.

SZECHUAN PICKLED CABBAGE

Extremely simple, and another great room-temperature vegetable dish. The "pickling" process is lightning fast; whereas kimchi takes weeks, this tangy treat is ready in a third of a day.

SERVES 6 AS PART OF A FIRST-COURSE ARRAY

1 pound green cabbage (the round, European type)
1 tablespoon coarse salt
2 teaspoons finely minced fresh gingerroot
1 large clove garlic, finely minced
2 tablespoons plus 1/2 teaspoon Chinese sesame oil

4 dried red chili peppers
3 tablespoons rice vinegar
1 tablespoon sugar
1/4 teaspoon MSG (optional)
1/2 cup seeded and slivered fresh red chilis

1. Cut the cabbage into 1-inch wide strips, and toss the strips in a bowl with the coarse salt. Fit a weight over the cabbage (a plate, perhaps, with some cans stacked on it). Let the cabbage stand at room temperature for 4 hours.

2. After 4 hours, spill the contents of the bowl into a colander. Squeeze the liquid out of the cabbage with your hands. Wipe the bowl dry, and return the squeezed cabbage to the bowl. Add the ginger and garlic, and toss.

3. Place 2 tablespoons of the sesame oil in a wok over medium-high heat. Add the chili peppers, and stir-fry until they turn dark (2 to 3 minutes). Add the vinegar, sugar, and MSG (if using). Bring to a boil over high heat. Immediately pour over the cabbage. Toss the cabbage with the fresh chili slivers. Let sit for 4 hours at room temperature.

4. Just before serving, blend in the remaining ½ teaspoon of sesame oil.

When

One or two cold Chinese appetizers are a great way to start a Chinese meal—followed, perhaps, by a Chinese soup, then an array of main-course dishes, then a grand noodle dish. If it's an especially ambitious meal, you might make all of the appetizers given here. Another idea is to prepare all the appetizers and make a delicious summer meal out of them alone!

In Your Glass

This generally spicy Chinese fare is not that friendly to wine; I could see serving an inexpensive sparkling wine (like a cava from Spain) or a well-chilled white Zinfandel from California with this group of dishes. My first beverage choice, however, would be cold Chinese beer.

SOME REAL SECRETS OF CHINESE FOOD . . . LEARNED IN HONG KONG

Although Chinese food was one of my very early culinary loves, it took me an awfully long time to make an on-site gastronomic inspection: my personal journey from the first taste of Chinese food to the first taste of it in China took over forty years! But what I ate in Hong Kong in 1995 was well worth the wait.

Now, if you don't know Hong Kong, you may ask if the food there is really Chinese. When I visited Hong Kong it was still a British protectorate. Additionally, one doesn't necessarily connect Chinese food with Hong Kong, since this is a city in which you can find anything you want—from a corned beef sandwich to a quesadilla to a wine list with more Château Petruses on it than on any in France—at any time.

Despite all this, however, Hong Kong truly is a Cantonese city—with most of its population, and its restaurants, of Cantonese origin. I also crossed the border into China on that trip, into the nearby province (Guangzhou) and city (Guangdong) of Canton—but I didn't find great food there. Apparently, during the Cultural Revolution, the best chefs fled the mainland for Hong Kong—which may explain the quality of the restaurants there today.

You might call Hong Kong food hyper-Cantonese food. The cuisine of Canton was always influenced by the relative prosperity of that province, and by the fact that Canton had more contact with the West than did other regions of China. Both of those traditional elements have gone berserk in Hong Kong—an international city devoted to wealth. Hong Kong is like an experiment in Cantonese food: let's see what happens to it if we push its fundamentals to the limit.

It was amazing to experience authentic versions of Cantonese dishes that I'd known for so many years, and to discover a greater refinement and subtlety in them. I also tasted foods from other Chinese regions, which gave me standards for other Chinese classics—such as the finest Peking duck I've ever tasted, with pancakes of surpassing delicacy, duck skin of uncanny crispness, and hoisin sauce of uncommon complexity.

But the most important lessons I learned in Hong Kong—whether I was tasting dim sum in a noisy hall or three-star food on the top floor of the Mandarin Oriental—concerned texture. The Chinese are obsessed with it. I consider myself especially sensitive to texture in food. I can wax ecstatic over pasta textures in Italy, fish textures at the sushi bar, cheese textures in France, dhal textures in India . . . you name it. But I have never in my life experienced such a startling range of textures as I did in Hong Kong. Yes, of course, the texture sweepstakes run the gamut from the most shatteringly crisp frying to the sodden gumminess of sea cucumber and other mucilaginous creatures. But the amazement is what goes on in between the end points: chewy, gossamer, rough, slippery, velvety, hairy, airy, dense, spongy, papery, leathery, et cetera. The subtle varia- tions could literally go on forever. Keying in on texture in Hong Kong results in a prime lesson in how Chinese food ought to be, for anyone who wants to make Chinese food at home or enjoy Chi- nese food in restaurants.

The last lesson the food of Hong Kong provided me was of a psychological nature. You can't share a meal with a Chinese person without that person commenting on the medical benefits of the food that hits your table. We in the West increasingly focus on the health aspects of our food—but mostly from the negative perspective ("That'll make you fat"; "That'll make your face break out"; "That'll give you a heart attack"). At the Chinese table, you're more likely to hear— about every ingredient!—such things as "That's good for your skin"; "That will relieve stress"; "That'll improve your digestion"; "That's good for your kidneys." It is a culture that comes to the table with hope, and with the good sense to take food and dining for the miraculous things they are. I came back to the United States more resolved than ever to ignore the "nervous nutritional Nellies" (as Julia Child calls them) who make of the dining table a minefield that will kill you one day. I think that attitude itself is killing us now, as we lose the marvelous opportunity to relax and heal that the dining table provides.

GAZPACHO

In the south of Spain, gazpacho's home, the great velvet purée of peppers, tomatoes, onion, and cucumber is often served without those little salad bar bits that threaten to disturb the velvet.

Of course, the standard way to serve gazpacho around the world today—and, as Spain's most famous dish, it is served around the world—is to give each diner the purée of vegetables in a soup bowl, then present an array of small bowls holding chopped things; each diner chooses chopped bits as garnishes for the soup. Unfortunately, few restaurants in America have gotten the clue that the quality of the chopped bits in bowls has to be high; I've often seen way-over-the-hill veggies, served alongside stale croutons from a box.

In the south of Spain, they also, on occasion, present bowls of gazpacho to be self-garnished with chopped bits—and I've had no problems with quality there. But, more often, they just skip the chopped garnish bit and serve straight gazpacho in tall glasses, poured from a pitcher.

But there's an even bigger difference between southern Spanish gazpacho practice and international gazpacho practice. To wit: Have you noticed how often in our restaurants the texture of this cold soup is disappointing? How the vegetables seem a pulpy mass oozing watery liquid? Real gazpacho in Andalusia, in southern Spain, is smooth and silky, and never separates.

What accounts for the differences? Simple. The answer is bread—which many calorie-counting recipes and chefs leave out of "modern" gazpacho. They might as well call it ga-SPA-cho. Perhaps they don't realize that they are violating the very essence of the dish, which is indisputably bready.

Gazpacho is a very old culinary idea, dating back at least to Roman times. It probably was the Romans who brought it to the south of Spain, and the *pacho* part of *gazpacho* may be derived from the Latin word *pasta,* which means "dough," "bread," or "paste." An alternate theory is that *gazpacho* comes from a Spanish word, *caspa,* which means "a piece of bread in soup." Either way, it's bread. So if you want to save a few calories, eat a little less gazpacho! But don't leave out the bread, which gives gazpacho the smooth consistency it should have. And don't sacrifice the olive oil either.

Gazpacho Reality

There's no question about it: only if you choose top-quality vegetables can you make a top-quality gazpacho. So find tomatoes that are superrich and supersweet (actually, if they're a little squishy that's okay, as long as they taste great). Go for the most expensive red peppers, as long as they're also the sweetest. Use supersweet onions—like Vidalias, Walla Wallas, Texas Sweets, or Maui onions—if you can find them. And make sure your cucumbers are fresh tasting, with rich flesh; I often find that the long English cucumbers have the best texture.

CLASSIC GAZPACHO IN A PITCHER

This is my favorite way to serve gazpacho at home; it will surprise your guests as a dinner party starter. It will surprise them even more when you use bread in the recipe—for they'll probably taste the richest, smoothest, most delicious gazpacho of their lives. Now, when bread is used in gazpacho, most Spanish chefs like to pass the gazpacho through a strainer of some kind; this smoothes out the texture, making it perfect for this gazpacho-in-a-glass. The ultimate texture of your gazpacho has everything to do with the type of strainer you use. The wider the mesh of your strainer, the thicker your gazpacho will be; the thinnest gazpacho will come from the superfine strainer that the French call a *chinois*. Whichever strainer you use, you should get a satiny liquid that has the sheen of a great velouté in a top French restaurant. Just remember to supply lots of elbow grease as you push the soup through the strainer with a wooden spoon. If, when you're ready to serve the gazpacho, it seems a little lumpy, or pulpy, you can pass it through a strainer again, or, better yet, whip it up in a blender.

MAKES SIX 4-OUNCE DRINKS

1 1/2 pounds red bell peppers

1 pound ripe tomatoes

1 pound cucumbers

6 ounces crustless French or Italian bread (weighed after the crust is removed)

2 medium cloves garlic, peeled

1 cup chopped sweet onion

1/4 cup extra-virgin olive oil (preferably Spanish)

1/4 cup sherry vinegar

2 tablespoons good-quality tomato paste

1. Place the red peppers over an open flame (on a grill or on top of a gas range). Cook, turning frequently with tongs, until the peppers are charred on all sides (5 to 7 minutes). Place the charred peppers in a paper bag. After 15 minutes, remove the charred skins from the peppers, making sure no blackened skin remains. Cut the peppers open; discard the stems and seeds. Place the pepper fillets in the work bowl of a food processor.

2. Cut out the stems of each tomato, and place the tomatoes in a pot of simmering water for 1 minute, or until the skins crack. Remove the tomatoes, and, while running them under cold water, peel off the skins. Cut the skinned tomatoes in quarters, and, working with your fingers, remove the seeds from the tomato pieces. Place the skinned and seeded tomatoes in the food processor. Reserve any liquid that's left behind.

3. Peel the cucumbers, and cut them in half the long way. Working with a teaspoon, scoop out the cucumber seeds. Cut the cucumbers into coarse chunks, and add them to the food processor.

4. Place the bread in a bowl of cold water for 30 seconds, then squeeze the water out of the bread. Add the bread to the food processor, along with the garlic, onion, olive oil, vinegar, and tomato paste. Process for at least 2 minutes, or until a smooth purée is achieved.

5. Place the gazpacho in a bowl, cover it, and refrigerate for 2 to 4 hours (the longer it sits, the better the flavors will blend).

6. Working over a bowl, place the gazpacho in a strainer. Mash the gazpacho against the sides of the strainer with a wooden spoon, extracting every possible drop into the bowl, until only a thick, bready mass remains in the strainer; this may take 15 to 20 minutes. Discard the contents of the strainer, unless you're making gazpacho "quenelles" (see below). The gazpacho in the bowl will be medium-thin; if you've used a very fine strainer, you'll have about 3 cups of gazpacho. If the gazpacho seems a little thick, add the reserved liquid from the tomatoes. Season with salt, pepper, and additional vinegar, if desired. Pour the gazpacho into a decorative pitcher. Serve in tall, narrow glasses or wineglasses. The gazpacho tastes best at cool room temperature.

Leftover Pulp = Gazpacho "Quenelles"!

The bready mass that remains in the strainer when you make gazpacho doesn't have to be discarded. If you're feeling resourceful, mix a few olive and green pepper bits into the mass, scoop some of it up in a tablespoon, smooth it out with another tablespoon, scoop it out of the first spoon with the second spoon, and come up with a perfectly rounded oval that we'll call a gazpacho "quenelle"! Place 3 "quenelles" at twelve o'clock, four o'clock, and eight o'clock in a wide soup bowl, pour gazpacho liquid around them . . . and you've got a great presentation.

GARNISHED GAZPACHO IN A BOWL

My favorite way of serving garnished gazpacho is to garnish it myself before it hits the dining room table—especially since the following garnish, though not traditional, is the most alluring version of gazpacho helper I've ever tasted. The trick here is that some of the fillers are creamy (e.g., avocado, egg) and that they're cut in pieces large enough to emphasize that texture. The soft, chunky bits and the light, runny gazpacho positively caress each other.

MAKES 8 FIRST-COURSE SERVINGS

1 recipe Classic Gazpacho in a Pitcher (approximately 3 cups of liquid gazpacho)
1/2 cup peeled, seeded, coarsely chopped cucumber
2 hard-boiled eggs, very coarsely chopped (each egg should yield about 12 chunks)

1/2 cup pitted and very coarsely chopped mild brine-cured black olives
2 Haas avocados
Lemon juice
Minced parsley for garnish

1. Place the gazpacho in a large bowl. Gently stir in the cucumber, eggs, and olives.

2. Peel the avocados, pit them, and cut them into very coarse chunks. Drizzle the chunks with lemon juice to prevent discoloration, and season with salt. Gently stir them into the gazpacho.

3. Serve immediately in small soup bowls, garnished with parsley.

Garnished gazpacho in a bowl with bread "quenelles"

LAYERED GAZPACHO SALAD

Here's another one of my favorite gazpacho ideas, though this one too is untraditional. I first saw it in *Gourmet* magazine almost thirty years ago, and though I've lost the original recipe, I've developed my own variation. The idea is to build layers of the usual gazpacho vegetables in a decorative jar (along with a few anchovies and olives for an extra kick), then to pour a garlic-and-cumin-scented vinaigrette over all. The mixture marinates for twenty-four hours and, when you bring it to the table, resembles one of those dazzling, jewel-like arrangements of vegetables-in-glass that you see at fancy Italian groceries.

MAKES 6 FIRST-COURSE SERVINGS

1/2 pound sweet onions

3/4 pound ripe tomatoes

3/4 pound cucumbers

1/2 pound green bell peppers

6 anchovy fillets

6 large black olives, brine cured (about 2 ounces
    before pitting)

1 large clove garlic, peeled and minced

5 tablespoons olive oil

2 tablespoons sherry vinegar

1 1/2 teaspoons ground cumin

Finely minced parsley for garnish

1. Select a decorative jar that is 7 inches high, 3½ inches in diameter, and holds about 5 cups of liquid. For maximum effect in presentation, come as close as you can to these specifications.

2. Peel the onions, and cut them into small chunks.

3. Stem the tomatoes, and cut them into small chunks.

4. Peel the cucumbers, cut them in half the long way, and scoop out their seeds with a teaspoon. Cut the cucumbers into small chunks.

5. Remove the stems and seeds from the green peppers, and cut the peppers into small chunks.

6. Place ⅓ of the chopped onions in the bottom of the jar. Each time you place a layer of vegetables in the jar, tamp it down to make the layer even, and salt it lightly. Add ⅓ of the tomatoes to the jar (tamp and salt), ⅓ of the cucumbers (tamp and salt), and ⅓ of the green peppers (tamp and salt).

7. Cut the anchovy fillets into 5 pieces each. Strew ⅓ of the pieces over the green pepper layer. Pit the olives, and mince them. Strew ⅓ of the minced olives over the green pepper layer.

8. Repeat the entire layering process, starting with the onions and ending with the anchovies and olives.

9. Repeat the entire layering process a second time. Your jar should now be filled with 12 layers of chopped vegetables, plus anchovies and olives.

10. Place the garlic, olive oil, vinegar, and cumin in the work bowl of a small food processor or a blender. Blend until smooth. Pour the dressing over the vegetables in the jar in 4 or 5 pours, pausing for the dressing to seep down. Cover the jar tightly, and refrigerate for 24 hours before serving.

Serving the Layered Gazpacho Salad . . . and, the Ultimate Gazpacho

You most certainly want your guests to get a look at this layered thing before you divide and conquer it. So I recommend bringing it to the table, collecting your oohs and ahs, then, in full view of your admiring diners, pouring the contents of the jar into a decorative bowl. Give the vegetables a quick toss in the bowl to blend everything well, then divide the gazpacho among 6 individual plates or bowls, which you have at tableside. Garnish with parsley.

This is a great starter for a Spanish dinner. However, there is another cool thing you can do. Along with the Layered Gazpacho Salad, bring to the table a pitcher of the Classic Gazpacho in a Pitcher (about half of the recipe, or 1 1/2 cups, will be sufficient). Serve the Layered Gazpacho Salad in bowls, placing the vegetables at the center of each bowl . . . then pour 1/4 cup of the Classic Gazpacho from the pitcher around the vegetables.

Now, if you really want to go nuts—if you want to present the ne plus ultra gazpacho, the gazpacho after which all other gazpachos are irrelevant—you can bring together all the ideas discussed here. Place 3 gazpacho "quenelles" (see box on page 37) in each soup bowl. Place the chunky garnishes (eggs, avocados, olives, and cucumbers) around them. Place a few tablespoons of the Layered Gazpacho Salad at the center of the bowl, on top of the point where the quenelles meet. Pour gazpacho liquid all around the bowl, and garnish with finely chopped parsley. I will not accept responsibility if your guests start flamenco dancing on your table.

Criteria for Quality

- *Does the gazpacho hold together? (good) Or does it separate? (bad)*
- *Is the gazpacho thin and watery? (bad)*
- *Is the gazpacho too thick and lumpy? (bad)*
- *Are the vegetables fresh tasting?*
- *Is there an ideal balance of vinegar, salt, and pepper—along with sweetness from the vegetables?*

When

- *As a cocktail poured out of pitchers into tall, narrow glasses or wineglasses*
- *As a first course at a Spanish dinner, or any kind of dinner*
- *Particularly in summer (when your guests' desires for light food are strongest), and late summer/early fall (when your vegetables are strongest)*

In Your Glass

If you're serving Classic Gazpacho in a Pitcher . . . obviously you don't need a glass of anything else!

But if you're serving one of the sit-down gazpachos (Garnished Gazpacho in a Bowl or Layered Gazpacho Salad), you'll find a crisp, dry, light Fino or Manzanilla sherry from the south of Spain as delicious with the soup as it is regionally correct.

Soup is sometimes thought to pose problems for wine, because the textures of the two are redundant—so a classic strategy is to serve a wine with higher alcohol, like sherry (about 16 percent), so that it seems richer next to the soup. I also like the nutty flavors of sherry alongside the peppers and olives.

Remember: Do not serve a sweet sherry with this soup! The label should say "Fino" or "Manzanilla." Lustau is a producer to look for, as is Hidalgo. Sherry doesn't have a vintage date, but you do want to drink it not long after it has been bottled—so try to buy it from a store with a big sherry turnover. Once you open it, drink it all; it doesn't keep well.

Chill the sherry until it's extremely cold, then serve it in small, tapered sherry glasses, called copitas *in Spain. If you really want to do it the Spanish way, buy your Fino or Manzanilla in half bottles, and keep several of them chilling in the fridge while you're polishing off the first.*

GUACAMOLE

The first time I tasted guacamole, it really wasn't very good. In the late 1960s, I made a "Mexican" dinner from a magazine. I prepared the guacamole the day before from supermarket avocados, and—since the recipe wasn't specific about avocado-mashing technique—I mashed the daylights out of those suckers. The next night, I served the guacamole to my dad —and he said it tasted like "onion-flavored slime." He was right.

This story would be entirely amusing were it not also sad—for the bad guacamole I made in 1969 is exactly like some of the guacamole I'm tasting across America thirty years later!

There are three keys to great guacamole:

1. Buy the right avocados. Avocados vary wildly in taste and texture; some are oily, rich, and deep flavored, while some are watery and bland. It's obviously the former that you want.

To raise your odds, always buy the pebbly-skinned Haas avocado, sometimes called the California avocado; it's less round than some other avocados, with a shape that suggests a pear. The Haas avocado was hybridized from the ancient, wild Mexican avocado (called the *crillo*), which has a wonderfully nutty creaminess; the Haas is less intense, but it's the best we can do. I usually avoid the large, bright green Florida avocado (hybridized from the ancient Caribbean avocado), because I find it watery and tasteless. You can substitute the Fuerte avocado, which was hybridized from the ancient Guatemalan avocado; it has thick, woody skin, a relatively small seed, and moderate flavor.

When you're buying avocados don't be scared off by a firm texture. The avocado is one of the few fruits that ripens off the tree (the banana is another)—so you can take home rock-hard ones from the store and ripen them yourself. Place the avocados in a paper bag and hold them for two or three days at room temperature. When they yield to gentle thumb pressure, they're ready to eat. You may do so immediately or keep them refrigerated (unpeeled, of course) for another two to three days.

2. Don't mash the avocados to death. There's nothing I hate more than avocado purée masquerading as guacamole. Leave your avocados in chunks—this makes an infinitely more interesting guacamole.

3. Make your guacamole as close to serving time as possible. Avocado, of course, browns with exposure to air—and a guacamole made long before serving is apt to turn brown. Some suggest placing an avocado pit in the center of the guacamole bowl to retard browning—but I think that's a myth. Guac browns no matter what you do.

Second (and of even greater concern to me): all of the flavoring elements in guacamole (like onions, garlic, and cilantro), which are balanced so beautifully with the avocado flavors when the guacamole's first made, grow in intensity as the guac sits around. Eventually (like a day later), all you can taste is the other stuff.

Make your guacamole just before serving it. Two of the best guacamoles in America are at the restaurant Rosa Mexicano, in New York City, and at Gabriel's, just north of Santa Fe, New Mexico, where the dish is made at tableside in the volcanic-rock mortar and pestle called a *molcajete*.

MY FAVORITE GUACAMOLE
(NORTH MEXICAN GUACAMOLE WITH TOMATILLO PURÉE)

In the north of Mexico, they like to blend their avocados with tomatillos (these are not unripe tomatoes but a separate vegetable that happens to be green and look like an unripe tomato). It's a delicious combination, and it forms the basis of the following recipe. I have taken things a step further—by suggesting a tomatillo purée that you can pour around your guacamole, serving them together in a wide, shallow soup bowl as a first course. It's one of the most delicious takes on guacamole I've ever tasted. But if you're just looking for "dip," omit the purée part of this recipe.

MAKES 4 APPETIZER SERVINGS

2 large, ripe Haas avocados

1 clove garlic, smashed

1/4 cup freshly squeezed lime juice

1/2 cup cilantro, firmly packed, including stems, plus
    extra leaves for garnish

1 teaspoon minced fresh jalapeño, or more to taste

1 teaspoon minced white onion

1/2 cup chopped tomatillo

Chopped tomato for garnish

Tomatillo purée (recipe follows)

1. Halve the avocados and remove the pits. Make two long cuts in the flesh of each half and five or six crosswise cuts. Rub the cut surfaces gently with the smashed garlic. Drizzle about half of the lime juice evenly over the cut surfaces.

2. Place the remaining lime juice, cilantro, jalapeño, and onion in the work bowl of a food processor. Purée.

3. Turn the cut chunks of avocado out of their skins and into a large bowl. Toss very gently with the cilantro purée and with the chopped tomatillo.

4. When you are ready to serve, season the guacamole well with salt and pepper. Divide it among 4 wide, shallow soup bowls, placing a scoop of guacamole at the center of each. Spoon the tomatillo purée around the guacamole. Garnish the purée with cilantro leaves and the top of the guacamole with a little finely chopped red tomato. Serve with warmed tortilla chips or warm, fresh tortillas.

TOMATILLO PURÉE

1 pound fresh tomatillos, husked, washed, and
    chopped

1/2 pound red tomatoes, chopped

2 fresh jalapeños, stemmed and seeded

1/2 teaspoon ground cumin

Place all the ingredients in the work bowl of a food processor. Purée. Season well with salt and pepper.

North Mexican guacamole with tomatillo purée

Extracting the Pit

There's a wonderfully simple way to remove an avocado pit. First, you cut a deep, continuous gash all around the avocado, right down to the pit—making sure to cut not at the avocado's equator but from pole to pole. Twist the avocado, and it should separate into two long halves. One of the halves will be holding the pit. Take a large, heavy chef's knife, and sink it forcefully into the pit; it will penetrate the pit by 1/4 to 1/2 inch. Now, simply give the knife a sharp twist in any direction, and pull the pit away from the avocado. It should come right out of the flesh, still attached to the knife.

A Little Avocado and Guacamole History

The avocado is indisputably a native of Mexico. Archaeologists in that ancient land have unearthed small, round seeds of the wild Mexican avocado that date back as far as 8000 B.C. This wild avocado was the ancestor of the current-day Haas avocado. By approximately 6000 B.C. the avocado was being cultivated in Mexico, as we can tell from the changing shape of seeds that have survived. In the millennia after that, the avocado moved southward, through Central America and into South America; it reached the warm valleys near Cuzco, Peru, where it was discovered by Europeans (in this case, the Spaniards) in the fifteenth century A.D.

Before the Spaniards ever got to it, of course, it had a New World name. In the native Nahuatl language of the Aztecs, the avocado was called ahuacatl, a shortened form of their word ahuacacuahatl—which just happens to mean "testicle tree." Was the avocado thought back then to be an aphrodisiac, as this creamy, buttery fruit is sometimes thought to be today? Or were the Aztecs simply great naturalists, merely giving a careful description of a fruit that hangs off its tree in pairs? We'll never know. However, the aphrodisiac theory is given some support by Sir James Frazer's description, in his classical anthropological work The Golden Bough, of a Peruvian avocado harvest as a five-day orgy.

When the Spanish discovered the avocado in Peru, they transliterated the word ahuacatl into something more Iberian: aguacate. From there, it was only a short linguistic step to the current English-language designation.

But where did guacamole come from? Though we don't know very much about the ways avocados were eaten in pre-Columbian America, we do know that the Aztecs made a sauce, or mulli, from avocados—which they called, logically enough, ahuaca-mulli. That works for me as a linguistic progenitor. They apparently added tomatoes, onions, and cilantro leaves to their ahuaca-mulli. Just like we do.

Criteria for Quality

- *Is the guacamole chunky? (it should be)*
- *Does it taste of avocado? (it shouldn't be overwhelmed by the other flavors)*
- *Does it taste fresh?*

When

Guacamole is a great way to start off a Mexican meal—or any kind of southwesternish, Californiaish meal, for that matter. Just serve a bowl with warmed, high-quality tortilla chips, and the party has begun. You might also want to keep it on the table for the remainder of the meal, using it as a kind of salad to accompany the rest of the food.

In Your Glass

You can drink wine, or beer, if you like—but in my glass, next to guacamole, there's always going to be a margarita! I like mine made with one third good tequila (like Herradura reposado), one third freshly squeezed lime juice, and one third Triple Sec. With food, I like it on the rocks—never frozen!—and with no salt around the rim of the glass.

ADIOS, TACO BELL: REAL FOOD IN MEXICO

Mexico grabbed me hard in a number of gastronomic ways when I finally ventured there.

1. Above all, there is corn. The multitudinous variety of corn tortillas and tamales—the subtle degrees of differences in shapes, textures, flavors—hits the virgin American palate as the riot of pasta possibilities in Italy does. Never again, north of the border, could I ever entertain the notion of "tacos" in those stupid, brittle, folded, packaged tortillas. Hit the street food of Mexico, as I did—where talented hawkers manipulate small, soft, divine corn tortillas with the skill of sushi chefs—and you'll know what I mean.

2. I was a veteran of Spanish travel by the time I got to Mexico—and was amazed to find the high degree of "Spanishness" that informs the food scene there. We tend to think primarily of the "native" and "Indian" elements of Mexican food, but those Spanish conquistadores left quite a gastronomic legacy. Above all, I think, is the primacy of meat in Mexico—something else we don't think much about. But just as Spain is a land of great roasters, Mexico is a place where chefs are working overtime to pull carnivorous treasures from their ovens. There is one major difference: in Mexico, the meats usually get chopped by the chefs and folded into tortillas.

3. The real shocker about Mexican food in Mexico is that it's not that hot! Time and again, I've found that the chili burn in Mexico is a have-it-your-way kind of thing: the heat is usually supplied by individual diners, making liberal use of salsas and hot sauces. I was delighted to see this, because it had always been my opinion that Mexican food was not one of the world's great spicy cuisines. A great spicy cuisine has bold flavors that rise above the chilies—like the fragrant spices of India or the great sour-sweet-salty axis of Thai food. Superhot Mexican food, to me, tastes flat. In Mexico, however, they know how to coordinate the level of heat with the level of flavor.

Within three hours of landing in Mexico, of course, I realized that all of the buzz among American foodies is true—what we call Mexican food in America is usually a pitiful shadow of real Mexican food. However, in fairly short order I realized something else as well: there is a new generation of Mexican restaurants in the United States that have nothing to be ashamed of when they're compared with restaurants in Mexico. What I've been tasting at Frontera Grill in Chicago, and at Maya in New York, is as good as anything I've tasted south of the border.

Leeks veritablement à la grecque

VEGETABLES À LA GRECQUE

Maybe it was because I grew up with iced platters of celery hearts, olives, and radishes before dinner . . . but I've always loved the idea of light vegetable starters to a meal. So it was natural indeed, when I started to expand my culinary repertoire in the early seventies, to include the classic cold French vegetable preparation called *à la grecque.* The choice was made even more natural by the fact that my chief cookbook mentor of those years, Julia Child, had a long section in *Mastering the Art of French Cooking,* volume 1, on *"légumes à la grecque."* And probably because of Julia, the dish was something of a rage among the new generation of dinner party hosts in the 1970s.

What are *légumes à la grecque?* They are vegetables (traditionally, you choose one vegetable only each time you make this dish) that are poached in flavored water; the two most popular vegetables to use are mushrooms and leeks. The poaching water is usually flavored with herbs (like parsley and thyme), dried spices (like peppercorns and coriander seeds), a little olive oil, and a little lemon. After the vegetables are cooked, they are removed from the poaching water. Meanwhile, the water is reduced with the flavorings until it's quite concentrated, then poured over the vegetables. The whole is cooled down to room temperature and served; it is a staple of fancy, classic French restaurants that have a chariot of assorted hors d'oeuvres at the front of the house.

Though I made this dish dutifully throughout the seventies, principally with mushrooms or leeks, as I learned more about Greek cooking, I started to wonder why the French ever bothered to call it *à la grecque.* It became clear to me that *à la grecque* is a cooking method devised by a Frenchman who had never been to Greece. The dish is nice enough, but it offers nary a glimpse of the fabulously sunny flavors that are actually used in that eastern outpost of the Mediterranean. Where's the marjoram? The oregano? The cinnamon? The feel of good olive oil?

So, some years later—after I got over my blind allegiance to culinary authenticity—I decided to find a way to make "leeks à la grecque" taste truly grecque, using lively flavors that Greeks have used since, well, . . . the Greeks. The results, if I say so myself, are spectacular; this is now one of my favorite appetizers of all to make for dinner parties. You can serve it all year round, but—because the dish is served cold—it makes an especially wonderful starter for a summer meal.

I'm happy to say that modern French chefs are improving on the old grecque as well. I recently saw a menu from Paris that listed *"Une Grecque Froide de Homard aux Légumes Croquants"* (A Cold "Greek" of Lobster and Crunchy Vegetables). So make the following dish, and be on the cutting edge.

Leeks Veritablement à la Grecque

MAKES 6 APPETIZER SERVINGS

1 pound leeks of uniform size (each not more than
 1 1/4 inches in diameter)

2 cups water

1/4 cup olive oil

3 sprigs fresh marjoram, or 1 teaspoon dried

1 cinnamon stick

3 tablespoons red wine vinegar

3 sprigs fresh oregano, or 1/2 teaspoon dried

Salt to taste

1 cup tomatoes, diced

1/3 cup kalamata olives, pitted and halved

1/4 to 1/2 pound feta cheese, crumbled

Fresh marjoram and fresh oregano, minced, to taste

1. Preheat the oven to 350 degrees.

2. Prepare the leeks: Trim off the root end, and cut each leek so it is approximately 6 inches long. (Discard the dark green part of the leek.) If the leeks are more than 1¼ inches in diameter, cut them lengthwise into halves or quarters. Wash the leeks by making thin, lengthwise slits and placing the leeks under running water. Arrange the leeks in a gratin pan.

3. In a saucepan combine the water, olive oil, marjoram, cinnamon, vinegar, oregano, and salt to taste.

Bring the liquid to a boil, and simmer for 10 minutes. Pour the liquid over the leeks to just cover.

4. Arrange a piece of foil over the gratin pan, and bake 35 minutes, or until leeks are tender. Transfer the leeks to a serving platter.

5. Return the cooking liquid to the saucepan, and reduce to ½ cup. Strain it over the leeks. Chill, covered, for 2 hours or overnight.

6. Just before serving, strew the leeks with the tomatoes, olives, cheese, and fresh herbs.

Cleaning Leeks

Leeks are dirty. As they grow, earth is piled up around them so that the stalks will remain white. Farmers do the same sort of thing with endives and white asparagus—namely, deprive them of sunshine. Some farmers use brown paper collars or black polyethylene tubes to shut out the light, and these plants don't get as dirty, but there's usually some dirt to contend with. So be sure to clean your leeks thoroughly by slicing them lengthwise (not all the way through) and passing the cut leeks under rapidly running water.

When

Classically, any vegetable à la grecque is a cold first course in France; very often you see it as part of a buffet of cold items. And if you make the classic recipe at all, that's where it should stay in the meal.

The updated "grecque" that's presented here is more flexible. You could, of course, easily serve it as a first course, or as a buffet participant. But it's so delicious—and, with its feta cheese and olives, so much richer than the classic version—you could also make it a light luncheon dish. Simply pair it with good bread, good olive oil, and a good glass of appropriate wine.

In Your Glass

I like to emphasize the surprising "Greekness" of these Greek leeks by serving something very Greek with them.

Whenever I tell wine geeks that I like Retsina with Greek food, they all move away from me at the table. Fine. That leaves more Retsina for me. Admittedly, this odd, ancient wine—flavored with pine resin to the point where it tastes a little like turpentine—is not one of the wine world's finest creations. However, it does supply a "spice" to Greek food that makes the whole dining experience seem more authentic.

If you're just getting used to the pine resin taste, buy a bottle of Boutari Retsina, which is Retsina with training wheels—a little lighter on the resinated flavor that is so offensive to wine snobs.

THE COOKING LITERATURE OF THE 1970S

As you probably know by now, I am not a formally trained chef; because my early working years, in the 1970s, were in another field—theater—I did not have the opportunity to lay down a base of culinary knowledge at a cooking school or in a restaurant. However, this doesn't mean that I wasn't actively pursuing my great love of cooking in those years. My work in the theater, and in academia, left me lots of time at night, on weekends, during vacations and summers, to explore in my own kitchen the cuisines of the world. And my trusty vehicle for this exploration was cooking literature; without books, I never could have learned what I did about this subject. To this day, I take tremendous pride in—and make almost constant reference to—my outsize collection of cookbooks.

It all started at Colgate University, in Hamilton, New York—where I was quickly acquiring a reputation for the best table in the class of '71 (though that table was in a somewhat out-of-the-way, ramshackle farmhouse). Away from my dad's cooking for the first time in my life, and from the ethnic restaurants of New York, I was forced to look at recipes if I wanted to eat something other than the slop at the Student Union and the tuna salad special at the Blue Bird.

And that's when, serendipitously, I came across a paperback, first published in 1955, called The World's Best Recipes. *I knew little about it then, and I know little about it now. It was compiled by someone named Marvin Small, whom I'd never heard of before and have never heard of since. However, it was a treasure trove of terrifically authentic ethnic recipes from around the world that always fired my imagination . . . and the recipes always worked extremely well. How can I forget the tortellini, the avgolemono soup, the fondue Neuchâteloise, the lobster Cantonese, the veal paprikash? It was truly a work before its time, and I was lucky to have stumbled upon it—for it shaped my lifelong dedication to ethnic authenticity. I'm sure that if it were available today, it would still be of great use to new home cooks.*

It was at about this time that I became aware of a monthly magazine called Gourmet*—which I cite without shame, since the following accolade has nothing to do with the fact that I'm currently a columnist for the magazine.* Gourmet *always seemed to go a step beyond* The World's Best Recipes *in feeding my appetite for authentic ethnic food; in its pages I would find descriptions of specific dishes at great restaurants around the world (in exotic locations, like Mexico and northern Italy), beautiful photos of those dishes, and, of course, recipes that worked magically in the farmhouse kitchen.*

Then, suddenly, there was James Beard. I'll never forget the fat paperback, with its picture of fat James on the cover, practically drooling over a pile of fat sausages. This was a man after my own heart. His exuberant recipes were somewhere between the known and the unknown; when cooking ideas from other countries appeared, even though I knew nothing about those countries, Beard's techniques and procedures were somehow familiar. I ate up this stuff, roaring through dozens of recipes a month.

But the most important book for me in this era—maybe the most important book for me of any era—was Mastering the Art of French Cooking, *volume 1, by Julia Child, Louisette Bertholle, and Simone Beck. It took me a little while to get started with it, I guess, because I could see that this was a book to work through systematically, not a book to surf. After using it, I discovered, to my joy, that my intuition had been correct: if one does work through this book page by page, recipe by recipe, chapter by chapter, one has taken the equivalent of a cooking course. I am proudly a self-trained chef—but I couldn't have done it without my virtual trainer, Julia Child. If you believe that the most important cuisine in the world, technically speaking, is French—and I do—you owe it to yourself to get a solid grounding in French technique. Cooking school's a great way to do it, but Julia works just fine as well. I did it all from this book—but I was especially grateful for Julia's fabulous chapters on sauces (where I met all the "families"); on luncheon dishes (where the mysteries of quiches, tarts, gratins, soufflés, quenelles, and crepes were revealed); and on cold buffet (which supplied my introduction to vegetables à la grecque, composed salads, aspics, pâtés and terrines, and molded mousses).*

There have been thousands of cookbooks in my life since these first loves, but you never forget your first kiss—or your first soufflé.

THAI SALADS

Thai food hit me like a ton of bricks in the early 1970s. I'll never forget the night I got a call from my dad and my brother, Lewis (who was always the great Asian pioneer of our family); they were so excited they could hardly speak. "Do you know anything about Thai food?" they asked. I admitted I didn't, and they began babbling about this place in Manhattan where the food was spicy, sour, salty, and sweet all at the same time. Salads were unbelievably light and flavorful, appetizers were steamed with coatings of glutinous rice and served with vibrant dipping sauces, rich curries were cooked with coconut milk, noodle dishes went leagues beyond lo mein. We were all there the next night, of course—and, before long, after I'd picked up Jennifer Brennan's groundbreaking *The Original Thai Cookbook,* the extraordinary food of this southeast Asian nation became firmly entrenched in my repertoire.

But I don't think that any aspect of the cuisine had as much impact on me as the remarkable salads. The Thai word for salad is *yum,* which, from one point of view, needs no translation; if you've ever had one, you know exactly what I mean.

I can think of four things that make Thai salads so special. For one, Thai salads seem like exotic versions of the French *salades composées;* in addition to the greens that anchor Thai salads, there are always chunky add-ins such as purple onion, shallots, celery, multiple herbs (like cilantro and mint), and sliced chilies, as well as various forms of protein (like squid, shrimp, chicken, pork, or beef). Thai salads are very complicated dishes that just happen to be called salads.

Second, Thai salads always feature intensely flavored but superlight dressings. Unusually, there is rarely oil in a Thai salad dressing. What there is, however, is lime juice, Thai fish sauce, sugar, chili powder, lemongrass.

Third, Thai salads are also usually garnished to the nines, with vegetables like cucumbers or carrots or chilies or scallions carved into beautiful, intricate geometric shapes.

Last, Thai salads—in Thailand—are always served with the rest of the meal, not as a separate course. That's the tradition, but I like to ignore it—the way they do at Thai restaurants in America—because I think Thai salads make absolutely fabulous first courses for any kind of meal.

When you're ready to make a Thai salad, you'll find—happily!—that it's not really very difficult. Toss together some greens, julienne of celery, sliced onions, slivered fresh chilies, cilantro leaves, fresh mint leaves, and some shredded fresh kaffir lime leaves, if available (you can sometimes find them at Thai groceries). Add to this some grilled squid, shrimp, or any other protein you desire. Then toss the mixture, until just moistened, with some Basic Thai Salad Dressing.

Here's an all-purpose dressing that you can use again and again for Thai salads.

BASIC THAI SALAD DRESSING

MAKES 1³/₄ CUPS

1 cup freshly squeezed lime juice

1/2 cup fish sauce

4 tablespoons sugar

4 tablespoons thin-sliced tender center of
    lemongrass stalk

In a bowl, mix all the ingredients together until the sugar has dissolved. Use on Thai salads.

The following two salads each use the Basic Thai Salad Dressing you've just read about, and each deviates from the standard salad-making formula previously discussed in a few small ways. That's the fun of Thai salad making.

SPICY THAI SHRIMP SALAD

MAKES 4 FIRST-COURSE SERVINGS

2 cups inner stalks of celery, julienned

1/2 cup thin slices purple onion

1/2 cup mint leaves, coarsely torn, plus whole leaves
    for garnish

1/2 cup cilantro leaves, chopped, plus whole leaves for
    garnish

1 pound shrimp, peeled, with tail and last section of
    shell left on, butterflied and deveined

2 teaspoons minced garlic

2 tablespoons vegetable oil

3/4 cup Basic Thai Salad Dressing

1 to 2 teaspoons Thai ground chili powder, to taste*

1 head green leaf lettuce, leaves separated, rinsed, and
    dried

Carved vegetables (optional)

1. Put the julienned celery in a bowl of ice water, and let it sit for about ¾ hour, or until it curls. Drain when ready.

2. In a bowl mix together the drained celery, onion, mint, and cilantro.

3. In another bowl mix the shrimp with the garlic and oil, then grill them over charcoal just until they turn pink. (Alternately, grill them in a cast-iron grill pan or cook them under a broiler.) Mix the shrimp with 4 table-spoons of the dressing, let sit for 10 minutes, then sprinkle with Thai chili powder.

4. Toss the celery mixture with 4 tablespoons of the dressing. Line 4 serving plates with a few leaves of lettuce, drizzle each plate with 1 tablespoon of dressing, and top the lettuce with equal portions of the celery mixture and the shrimp. Garnish with carved vegetables, if desired, and cilantro and mint leaves, and serve immediately.

*You could use crushed red pepper flakes instead.

NOTE: This basic salad also works well with equal quantities of grilled squid or slices of grilled beef. You can serve these salads at room temperature, but the contrast of hot cooked food with the cool of the greens and vegetables is great—so try to serve these salads as soon as you've plated them.

THAI BEEF SALAD

MAKES 4 FIRST-COURSE SERVINGS

1/2 pound filet mignon, in one chunk that's 1 to 1 1/2 inches thick

4 cups firmly packed torn lettuce leaves*

1 cup firmly packed mint leaves, coarsely torn, plus whole leaves for garnish

1 cup cilantro leaves, chopped, plus whole leaves for garnish

1 cup sliced purple onion

1/2 cup firmly packed daikon (white radish) in julienne strips

1 cup finely diced fresh tomato

2 teaspoons finely minced fresh hot chili (preferably Thai bird peppers), or more to taste

4 teaspoons Thai fish sauce

6 tablespoons Basic Thai Salad Dressing

1. Grill the beef to rare over a charcoal fire.

2. While the beef is grilling, combine the lettuces, mint, cilantro, onion, daikon, tomato, and chili in a large mixing bowl.

3. When the beef is rare, remove it from the grill, and let it rest for 5 minutes. Then slice it in ⅛-inch-thick slices, put them in a small mixing bowl, and toss with the fish sauce.

4. Add the beef to the bowl of lettuces, add the salad dressing, and toss.

5. Divide the salad among 4 serving plates, garnish each plate with mint and cilantro leaves, and serve immediately.

A SPECIAL CATEGORY OF THAI SALADS

There is another kind of Thai salad that one frequently sees in Thai restaurants in the United States . . . and I love it. It's called *larb*—which means "to put together, combine"—and it is distinguished by the use of ground meat combined with the greens and a sprinkling of ground, toasted rice.

Larb salads come from the northeastern part of Thailand, which is bordered on the east by the Mekong River. Laos is just across the river, Vietnam is just beyond that, and Cambodia is to the south; because of its geographic proximity, this Thai region, known as Issan, features themes from other southeast Asian cuisines.

Archaeologically, it is a very exciting area; recent discoveries have revealed that a six-thousand-year-old civilization flourished here—making northeast Thailand, like the Tigris and Euphrates River valleys in the Middle East, one of the cradles of civilization. Later on, from the ninth through the fourteenth centuries A.D., this region flourished as a center of the Khmer culture.

But with the decline of the Khmer culture the forests and animal life, which had been bountiful, began to diminish, and the people had to scratch whatever living they could out of an increasingly inhospitable environment. They learned to waste nothing. The fact that they ate fried grub worms and

*For this salad, I like to use a combination of upscale lettuces—like frisée, radicchio, lolla rossa, mâche, et cetera. It's not exactly authentic, but it is delicious.

grasshoppers, ant eggs and semidecayed fish, led the more sophisticated urbanites far away in Bangkok to say disparagingly, "Issan people eat anything."

However, in the latter half of this century, as northeast Thailand has become more and more accessible, it has come to light that Issan cuisine is more than fried grubs and ant eggs. In fact, today Issan cuisine has influenced the rest of Thai cooking, and specific Issan dishes are on the menus of some of the trendiest restaurants in Bangkok.

Issan is a very highly spiced cuisine, more so than any other regional cuisine in Thailand. What better way to disguise the taste of semirotten fish than with a nice hot chili? But the food is filled with wonderful flavors that found their way here from the region's neighboring countries; the cilantro of Thai food probably came to Thailand from Laos through Issan, and the mint of Thai food probably came to Thailand from Vietnam through Issan.

All these flavors—including the explosive heat—get mixed with ground meat and toasted rice powder (a kind of crunchy topping) in larb salads. Of course, we in the United States rarely see the buffalo meat and deep-fried buffalo skin that those foragers use in Issan. Happily, larb salads work just as well with ground chicken, ground pork, or ground beef.

LARB SALAD WITH MINCED PORK

MAKES ENOUGH FOR 4 FIRST-COURSE SERVINGS

1 ounce dried snow fungus*

1 pound ground pork

2/3 cup lime juice

6 tablespoons fish sauce

1 tablespoon sugar

6 tablespoons julienned fresh gingerroot

1 tablespoon Thai chili powder

3/4 cup sliced scallions

2/3 cup coarsely chopped roasted peanuts

4 tablespoons chopped mint

4 tablespoons tender inner stalk of lemongrass, minced

1 to 2 tablespoons finely minced fresh hot chili
    (preferably Thai bird peppers), or more to taste

2 heads green leaf lettuce, leaves separated, rinsed,
    and dried

4 teaspoons toasted rice powder (recipe follows)

1. Soak the fungi in warm water until softened, about 30 minutes, then slice them into 1-inch pieces.

2. Boil the pork in a sieve set in a pot of water for about 1 minute, or until just past pink. Remove and drain.

3. In a mixing bowl mix together the lime juice, fish sauce, and sugar. Add the pork, and mix. Add the gingerroot and chili powder, and mix.

4. Add the fungi, half the scallions, the peanuts, mint, lemongrass, and fresh chilies, and mix.

5. Put 3 lettuce leaves on each serving plate. Divide and mound the pork mixture on top of the lettuce. Sprinkle ½ teaspoon rice powder on each portion, then divide the remaining scallions among the 4 plates. Spoon the liquid left in the bottom of the pork mixture bowl equally over each portion, and serve.

*I love this salad with the big white spongy fungus called snow fungus, which can be found in Chinese or Thai groceries. But you can substitute tree ears, which are easier to find.

TOASTED RICE POWDER

MAKES ¼ CUP

1/4 cup raw sticky rice (you may substitute any kind of rice)

1. Put the rice in a small skillet, and toast it for 3 minutes over medium-high heat, shaking the pan so the grains color evenly. Let the grains cool.

2. Transfer the grains to a spice grinder, and grind to a sandy powder.

Criteria for Quality
- *Does the salad feature the classic Thai collision on your palate of salty, sour, sweet, and hot?*
- *Does it seem freshly tossed?*
- *Are the vegetables crisp?*
- *Is it watery? (it shouldn't be)*

When

In Thailand, Thai salads are served alongside all other dishes as part of the meal; course distinctions aren't made. I say: feel free to serve Thai salads as the first course of a Thai meal, or any Asian meal that features spicy food. To deviate even further from Thai tradition, serve a Thai salad—along with a bowl of rice—as the main course of a light lunch or supper.

In Your Glass

Thai food, when properly prepared, is one of the world's spiciest cuisines. So, unless I'm turning down the BTUs for guests I anticipate can't handle the chilies, I never plan to serve wine with Thai food. Why bother when there's delicious Thai beer at hand? The good news is that the Thai beer Singha, which is so hoppily delicious in Bangkok, is widely available in the United States. The bad news is that most bottles in the United States are not so hoppily delicious; they taste a little sweet and insipid. I suspect the problem is age; try to find a batch of Singha that was recently imported into the country. A new Thai import—Bangkok Beer—seems fresher and hoppier than Singha.

Within a few short hours of my arrival in Bangkok, I went from my lifelong perspective on Thai food as a highly interesting ethnic cuisine that you might want as a change of pace every once in a while to a view of Thai food as one of the world's greatest and most dynamic cuisines.

The differences between here and there are the usual: better technique there, more variety, more exciting ingredients, regional surprises. Additionally, the balance of basic flavors in Thai food—where the primary tastes of hot, salty, sour, and sweet are fused together in a kind of palate explosion—unnaturally tilts toward the sweet in America. It's delightful in Thailand to see the classic balance retained.

But the one element of food in Thailand that took me most by surprise—and that will ever after inform my own cooking in the Thai idiom—is the delirious use of herbs. I knew about coriander leaves, of course, and mint, and—odd as it seemed—basil in Thai cooking. In Thailand, however, you cannot believe how intense these herbs are, or how widely they're used. To draw a parallel to the way I felt upon encountering this herbal paradise, imagine going from Italian cooking in a sterile New York apartment with dried herbs to Italian cooking on a windswept cliff near Naples made with wild thyme and oregano that you've snatched from the ground seconds before plunging it into your food. The Thai basil alone could keep me interested for years—many kinds of it, all backed by conventional wisdom on which is best for which dishes (it's the particularly licorice-scented basil, for example, that they use for seafood curries with coconut milk). And the herbs are not only in the food—most dishes are served with a side dish of herbs, there for you to sprinkle on or chew on as you see fit.

CEVICHE

Ceviche—a white-hot dish of the moment in American restaurants—is raw fish with a Latin accent. And that accent, in most cases, is lime juice. As has so often been the case in culinary history, necessity was the mother of invention. Apparently, it was the Peruvian Indians who first realized that if you toss fresh fish with citrus juice, you are preserving the fish. This was important when they started to migrate inland. The fish travels better because the citrus juice, in a sense, cooks it. Technically, of course, the fish is raw—if you take "cooking" to mean the application of heat to food. But in many ways the citrus-soaked fish does a good impersonation of cooked fish. That's because the citric acid lowers the fish's pH level, which creates an environment that kills off most harmful microorganisms (lime is often used because it's slightly more acidic than lemon). The acid coagulates the protein, just as heat does in the cooking process, turning the raw fish from translucent to opaque. So "cooking," in this case, means that the flesh becomes firm and more stable.

But it's really not cooked. Please keep in mind that the Peruvian Indians were dealing with super-fresh fish, from superclean waters. If you're at all squeamish about eating raw fish, for God's sake don't make ceviche. While the citrus does kill most bacteria, it may not kill them all. I feel confident, when making ceviche, if I purchase superfresh saltwater fish, filleted before my very eyes, preferably by fish experts at a market that caters to a sushi-making Japanese clientele.

Unfortunately, I don't feel so confident when ordering ceviche in most restaurants these days . . . and I don't mean I'm worrying about my health. It's just that, culinarily speaking, lots of crimes are being committed across the country in the name of ceviche.

Problem number 1, to me, is overmarination. Lots of chefs dump the raw fish in a bowl of lime juice and leave it there for twenty-four hours or more. I don't see any need to marinate the fish anywhere near as long as that. When you dunk your fish, you'll see it start to turn white, or opaque, within just a few minutes. I say: remove it from the lime juice right then! You will have ceviche that still has some of the resiliency of raw fish, which I find much more attractive. Otherwise you get falling-apart fish crumbs.

Problem number 2 is that many chefs add other ingredients (e.g., onions, peppers, herbs) to the fish while it's marinating in the lime juice. This may seem logical, if these foods are ultimately going in the ceviche anyway. But it's not—because the lime juice "cooks" these things as well, ultimately yielding a limp, unattractive texture. Add them later.

Problem number 3 is the failure by many chefs to drain off enough liquid after the marination is done; this leads to ceviches that are watery. I like to completely drain the citrus juice off the fish, then toss my fish with vegetables, herbs, oil, and more citrus juice if necessary.

Problem number 4 is the cut of the fish. Many chefs seem to like the texture of fish chunks in ceviche; I find that larger pieces don't create an attractive "chew." I like to use thin, sashimi-like slices (making sure, of course, to keep the marination time short).

Problem number 5 is the predilection our chefs have for raw crustaceans. I guess "lobster ceviche" sounds sexier on a menu than "flounder ceviche"—but the fact of the matter is that crustaceans, though widely used for ceviche in South America, are often blanched there before inclusion in the dish. I'm tired of expensive lobster and shrimp being wasted on ceviche when all crustaceans want is a little heat to be at their best.

SIMPLE CEVICHE WITH HERBS

I hope you'll agree that this great recipe solves all the ceviche problems. It also includes a surprise: I once discovered, serendipitously, that adding a little honey to a ceviche helps smooth out the tang of the citrus juice. I often make this recipe with halibut, but flounder, fluke, sea bass, Spanish mackerel, and other medium-firm white-fleshed fish work equally well. The slightly darker-fleshed red snapper is also good. For this dish (and others), it's well worth acquiring a wonderful brand of Caribbean hot sauce called West Indies Creole Hot Pepper Sauce; it's available from Mo Hotta–Mo Betta (800-462-3220). If you can't find it, use another hot, orange sauce with a fruity taste. Also, a great herbal-tasting Andalusian olive oil—like Nuñez de Prado—will make a big flavor difference. The following recipe is easy to make and easy to serve. If you want a bigger-deal presentation, combine this recipe with the one that follows it.

MAKES 8 SMALL APPETIZER PORTIONS

1 pound very fresh, firm, white-fleshed fish

1/2 cup freshly squeezed lime juice

4 very ripe tomatoes, about 6 ounces each

8 teaspoons West Indies Creole Hot Pepper Sauce

4 teaspoons honey

8 teaspoons very finely minced green chili

8 teaspoons finely minced cilantro leaves, plus extra leaves for garnish

8 teaspoons finely minced mint leaves

2 teaspoons finely minced chives

Extra-virgin olive oil (preferably Andalusian) for drizzling

1. Using a very sharp knife, cut the fish into thin, fairly broad slices. In a bowl, mix it with the lime juice. Let stand for 10 minutes at room temperature.

2. Meanwhile, cut the tomatoes in half horizontally. Rub each tomato half against a coarse grater, catching the juices in a bowl. Discard the tomato skins. Mix the tomato juice with the hot pepper sauce and honey. Blend well.

3. Remove the fish from the lime juice, and discard the juice. Add the tomato mixture to the fish, along with the chili, cilantro, mint, and chives. Taste for seasoning.

4. Divide the ceviche among 8 small plates, drizzle with a little olive oil, garnish with cilantro leaves, and serve immediately.

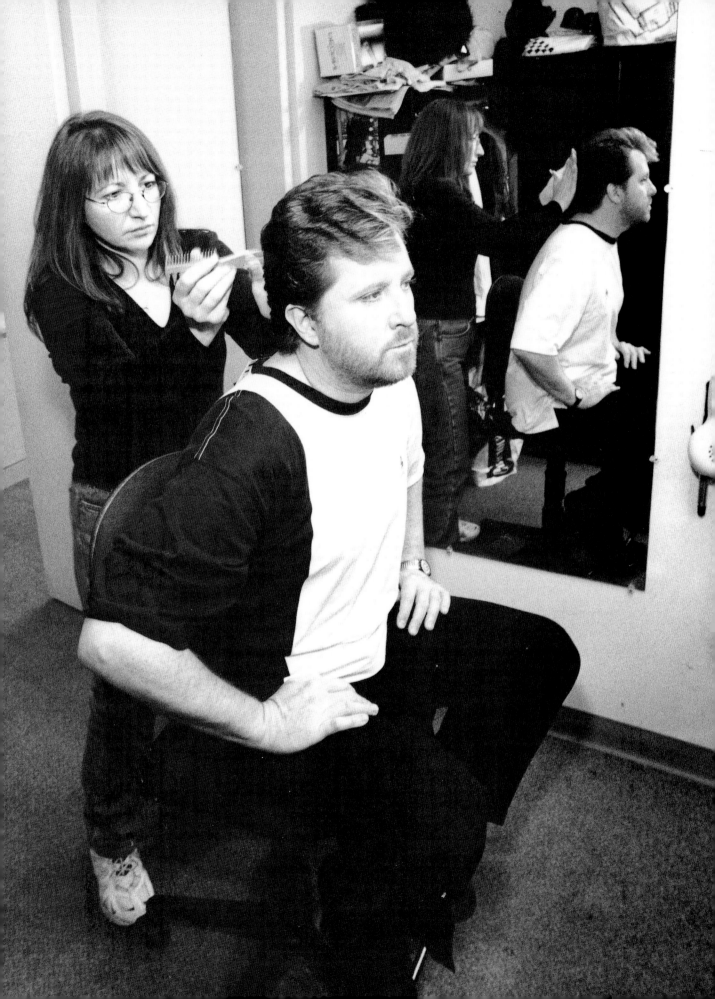

FANCY CEVICHE WITH
FRISÉE AND TOMATO SALSA

If you want to convert the preceding ceviche into a visual masterpiece that will have your guests gasping, all you need are a few extra ingredients (like the red tomato purée, which makes this dish more visually alluring). You'll also need a metal ring of some kind (hardware stores have them, but a cleaned-out, bottomless, topless tuna can will also work). If you really want to do the wizard-chef thing, pick up a squeeze-top bottle from a hair supply store.

MAKES 8 SMALL APPETIZER PORTIONS

1/4 cup red tomato purée, canned

4 teaspoons West Indies Creole Hot Pepper Sauce

2 teaspoons honey

4 ounces frisée, washed and torn into pieces

4 teaspoons extra-virgin olive oil (preferably Andalusian), plus a little more for drizzling

2 teaspoons red wine vinegar

1 recipe Simple Ceviche with Herbs

1. Mix together the tomato purée, pepper sauce, and honey. Reserve.

2. Toss the frisée with the olive oil and vinegar. Season to taste with salt and pepper.

3. Place a metal ring, about 2 inches across and 1 inch high, on a dinner plate. Add ⅛ of the frisée mixture to it. Top the frisée with ⅛ of the Simple Ceviche with Herbs; this should just about reach the top of the ring.

Remove the ring, and decorate the ceviche tower with a little of the tomato purée mixture (out of a squeeze tube, if you desire). Decorate the plate with dabs or squiggles of the tomato purée mixture, and drizzle olive oil over all.

4. Repeat step 3 seven times. Serve immediately.

Fancy ceviche with frisée and tomato salsa

TUNA CEVICHE WITH COCONUT MILK AND GINGER

One of the best ceviches I've ever tasted is at Douglas Rodriguez's wildly creative pan-Latin restaurant in New York City, Patria. Douglas says he got the idea for this spectacular dish in Honduras, a major producer of coconuts—though the inclusion of Asian elements is pure Rodriguez. I've modified his recipe slightly, so you don't need to work with fresh coconuts. And I've changed his chunky cut on the fish, because, in ceviche, I always prefer slices to chunks.

MAKES 8 FIRST-COURSE SERVINGS

1 jalapeño chili, seeded and minced

2 tablespoons grated fresh gingerroot

3 tablespoons Thai or Vietnamese fish sauce

1 tablespoon sugar

1/2 cup freshly squeezed lime juice

14 ounces unsweetened coconut milk (available in cans)

1 1/2 pounds fresh tuna, cut into broad slices about 1/4 inch thick

1/2 purple onion, thinly sliced

2 tablespoons minced scallions

1 tablespoon finely chopped chives

3 tablespoons finely chopped cilantro leaves

1. Place the jalapeño, ginger, fish sauce, sugar, lime juice, and coconut milk in a blender, and purée until smooth.

2. In a large bowl, toss the mixture with the tuna slices. Mix in the remaining ingredients. Divide among 8 plates, and serve immediately.

SERVING NOTE: Douglas Rodriguez likes to serve this ceviche in fresh coconut halves, which sit on red bell pepper– and watercress-strewn shavings of ice.

Naming Ceviche

In Peru, the land of its putative origin, ceviche is called cebiche. The leading theory is that the word was derived from the Spanish verb cebar, which means "to saturate."

However, throughout Latin America you will find a range of spellings. Ceviche, *my preferred spelling, is very common, as is* seviche.

There are also two interesting related words in Peru that you should know about.

- A cebichería *is a little stall (you can find many of them lining the shore in Peru) that serves eight or ten varieties of* cebiche.
- A cebichada *is a feast or dinner where only* cebiche *is served.*

Criteria for Quality

- Is the ceviche watery? (it shouldn't be)
- Is the texture of the fish attractive? (I think large chunks of fish are awkward to chew; I prefer slices)
- If there are herbs and vegetables in the ceviche, are they limp? (they shouldn't be)
- Is there a pronounced flavor in the dish? (there should be—but not so pronounced as to completely drown out the subtle flavor of the fish)

When

Ceviche is one of the all-time great meal starters. I particularly like it, of course, as a first course for any meal that involves the flavors of South America, Central America, Mexico, or the Caribbean. But I've also served it with success as a first course in American Southwest meals, and even in Spanish meals (though I urge you to limit the chili heat if you're taking the European route).

Ceviche also makes a fabulous buffet item, along with other south-of-the-border foods.

In Your Glass

When choosing a wine, a lot depends on the specifics of the ceviche you're making. But my favorite high-odds choice for many types of ceviche is the bubbly Portuguese white wine called Vinho Verde. The bright acidity of this wine buzzes beautifully through raw fish, and its extreme lightness seems perfectly in key with the light weight of ceviche.

There are several small problems, however, in buying Vinho Verde on the American market. In Portugal, they drink it extremely young, when it is very fresh and attractive. In America, it's usually older—and often you can't even determine its age because there's no vintage date on the label. Talk to your wine merchant, and endeavor to get the very youngest Vinho Verde you can find; it should certainly be no more than two years old.

The other problem is sweetness. Vinho Verde consumed in Portugal is bone dry, but some of the bottles destined for the U.S. market are sweetened. Talk to your merchant, experiment—but whatever you do, don't serve the sweetened stuff. My favorite brand is a hard one to find, called Ponte do Lima; a more mass-market brand that's reliably dry is Casal García.

2

MY FAVORITE IN-BETWEEN DISHES

DRIED PASTA DISHES—ORECCHIETTE—
RISOTTO—FRENCH ONION SOUP—
CATALAN LOBSTER AND CHICKEN SOUP—
THAI CHICKEN SOUP WITH COCONUT MILK—
GUMBO—QUESADILLAS—QUICHE—
OEUFS EN MEURETTE—
JAMBON PERSILLÉ—BISTEEYA—
VIETNAMESE SUMMER ROLLS

The great menu model of our times is the three-course meal: appetizer, main course, dessert. But it's not my menu model, not when I can help it.

I think the Italians have it dead right: they favor four courses. At a true Italian meal, things kick off with a light first course, usually cold or at room temperature, featuring vegetables or seafood or sliced meats; this is the *antipasto*. Then, in a stunning defiance of nomenclatural logic, the second course—named *primo*, or "first"—arrives. No matter how you number it, this in-between dish is usually a triumph, perhaps the highlight of any meal in Italy—for this is when the pasta or the risotto or the polenta or the hearty soup hits the table. For me, the main course, the third course—called *secondo*—is often anticlimactic. And then in the fourth position comes dessert.

I love this kind of eating—more variety in a meal, more things to sample and enjoy. I like it so much, in fact, that I construct my dinner party menus with respect to it all the time, whether I'm cooking Italian food or not. A French meal can begin with oysters, then leap to a gooey bowl of onion soup. A Mexican–Latin American meal can lead off with ceviche, then ratchet up to quesadillas or tamales. A Moroccan meal can open with gently spiced Moroccan salads before the flaky pigeon pie appears. And assorted tapas can form a first course for a sit-down Spanish meal, followed by a rich bowl of Catalan Chicken and Lobster Soup.

DRIED PASTA DISHES

Just about the most satisfying in-between dish of all—and the easiest to make—is a steaming bowl of dried pasta. But until I started traveling in Italy, I thought there was something second-rate about it. Silly me.

Many of us in America have felt that way for some time. The problem is that we grew up with dried pasta, the stuff that comes out of a box—and familiarity with all this so-called southern Italian "immigrant" food bred unreasonable contempt. When in the 1970s we started hearing about a different kind of Italian food—the food of the North, the cuisine that includes pasta made fresh every day, usually with eggs in it—everything about the old red-sauce cuisine became suspect to us. If you were gastronomically hip in about 1980, you were literally embarrassed to serve linguine or spaghetti.

When I got to Italy—and not just to the South—shortly thereafter, I discovered that the boxed product is used to make fabulous pasta dishes all over the boot. No one in the North is ashamed to cook dried pasta; it's done every day in homes and restaurants. Some southerners even say that the northerners would like to produce more dried pasta, but, traditionally, they've never had enough sun to dry the pasta out.

The thing to realize is that dried pasta is simply different from fresh pasta—not worse, not better, just different. Some days you want tender, fresh pasta with a buttery-cheesy sauce, some days you want chewier dried pasta with an oily-garlicky sauce. Variety is the spice of life.

Of course, in the United States there is every reason to choose one type of pasta over the other—and I mean you should choose the dried stuff! When *pasta fresca* got hot in the United States in the 1980s, stores started springing up all over that sold freshly made pasta. Fresh pasta started appearing in supermarkets. Restaurants featured it to the near-exclusion of dried pasta, and home cooks started cranking it out of their pasta machines with regularity. But the problem is this: 99 percent of the stuff being made, sold, and served in the United States just isn't any good! *Pasta fresca,* in the hands of a master, can be fabulous stuff—silky, feather light, resilient, as much a cavalcade of textures in Italy as dumplings are in China. Unfortunately, the U.S. versions are usually gummy and sodden.

And this is why I now say: love your boxed pasta! The stuff that's coming into the United States from Italy is just as good here as it is there. Even American brands are often pretty good. It gets better, of course, when you step up to the mass-market Italian brands, like Del Verde and De Cecco. Even better are artisanal Italian dried pastas, such as Martelli and Latini, which are passed through old bronze extruders that give the pasta extra-nubbly texture—a big help in picking up sauce.

COOKING IT RIGHT

One reason dried pasta doesn't get its due here is that most of our restaurants and home cooks prepare it and serve it incorrectly; you often see overcooked, oversauced pasta in the United States that is a million miles from the tight, focused, understated bowls of classic deliciousness you find in Italy.

Here's a step-by-step guide to getting it right. These tips will apply to most dried pasta dishes.

1. Put a tall pot of water to boil; a large quantity of water's important, so that the water will come back to a boil quickly after you've added the dried pasta. Never cook any amount of dried pasta, no matter how little, in less than 4 quarts of water; I like cooking a pound of dried pasta in 8 quarts of water. Cover the pot, and place it over high heat.

2. While the water's coming to the boil, make (or finish or heat up) your pasta sauce. To be really Italian about it, select a sauce that's light and simple. Don't use cream; don't use anything from a jar; and, whatever sauce you've chosen, don't use a lot.

3. When the water is bubbling furiously, add just enough salt to bring the water to the salt level of lightly salted broth. Do not add oil.

4. Add the dried pasta to the water, all at once. If the pasta is longer than the pot is tall, don't break it to fit! Just let it soften a bit, then slide the unsubmerged part of the pasta into the water. You want the water to boil again as quickly as possible; if it's not boiling right away, cover the pot and check it every 20 to 30 seconds to see if the boil has returned. When you check, also scrape a large wooden spoon against the bottom of the pot to make sure no pasta is sticking. When the water's fully back at the boil, remove the cover, and cook the pasta, stirring every few minutes. It is very important to move the pasta vigorously in the pot with a long spoon, so that the strands don't stick together while cooking.

5. The pasta is done when it's just al dente—slightly firm to the bite. The only way to know is to pluck out a strand and taste it. If it seems almost there but not quite, be vigilant; pasta can go from underdone to overdone in a minute or less.

6. When the pasta is done, remove and reserve a cup or so of the cooking water. Set up a large colander in your sink, and spill the contents of the pot into it. *Do not run tap water over the cooked pasta in the colander!* Toss the pasta in the colander to shake off excess water. You can let the colander rest in the sink briefly—but for no more than a minute or so.

7. Meanwhile, working quickly, place the now-empty pasta cooking pot on medium heat and add sauce to it—estimating how much will be just enough to coat the pasta. Add the pasta from the colander to the pasta cooking pot, and blend it with the sauce until it's just coated. If it seems a bit unsaucy, add a little more sauce. If the sauce seems a bit thick or dry, add a little of the reserved pasta cooking water. Stir the pasta with sauce in the pot for 30 seconds. If you are using grated cheese, toss it with the pasta after you take the pot off the heat.

8. Divide the pasta among serving bowls. Top each bowl, right at the center, with a little extra sauce (about ⅓ cup per serving), and serve immediately.

To Cheese, or Not to Cheese?

We in America are passionate about topping our bowls of pasta with grated cheese—and we prove our passion by doing it with even the low-quality sawdust substitutes sold in supermarkets in green containers. But cheese, even good cheese, doesn't get grated on pasta as a reflex in Italy—and I think we can learn something from that. For when you use grated cheese on all pasta dishes, all pasta dishes start tasting alike!

Pick and choose your cheese-intended dishes. Believe it or not, most Italians don't like grated cheese on tomato sauces, or on dishes that are garlicky. And cheese on pasta dishes made with seafood is officially a no-no, though people break that "rule" in Italy all the time. This leaves two big categories that are great for cheese: the buttery sauces of the North and the oil-and-vegetable sauces of the South.

Now, if you really want to do it the Italian way, you'll use different kinds of cheese for these two categories. The buttery sauces are normally sprinkled with Parmigiano-Reggiano—which is made from cow's milk, mostly around Parma. You may substitute a slightly less expensive Italian cheese for this—labeled "grana" in our stores—but don't, by any means, buy something called Parmesan cheese. Make sure you're getting Italian Parmigiano-Reggiano; have the clerk show you that name on the cheese rind. For the oil-based southern sauces, I prefer the bite of pecorino cheese, which is made from sheep's milk in a number of Italian regions; the one you're most likely to see here is pecorino Romano.

Whenever possible, buy these cheeses by the chunk, ungrated. Grate them yourself when you're ready to use them. They'll taste fresher.

Last, there's the question of how to incorporate the cheeses into your pasta dishes. I do not like the custom in American restaurants of the waiter offering to sprinkle grated cheese over everything in sight. When making pasta, I like to take control. If I think the dish needs cheese, I'll stir some into the sauced pasta just before placing it in bowls.

A Few of My Favorite Dried Pasta Shapes

There are hundreds of pasta shapes, of course, but these are the ones I use most frequently.

Pasta Lunga (long strands of pasta)

Linguine. I've been partial to these long, flat strands—"tongues" in Italian—ever since my first linguine with white clam sauce. Great for holding oily sauces.

Capellini. Surprisingly good as well with clam sauce—but also superb for a wide range of light fish and vegetable sauces.

Bucatini. Also known as perciatelli, these long, fat strands are distinguished by the hole that goes right through the middle of each. I love the way they chew, and I love the fact that they take so little time to cook (the hollow center speeds the process up). Great with meat sauces.

Fusilli Lunghi. Corkscrew pasta that is the length of spaghetti—a delightful chew, and also excellent for meat sauces.

Pasta Corta (short pasta shapes)

Gemelli. This means "twins" in Italian; the pasta is made by twisting two "twin" strands of short pasta around each other, creating a very chunky single shape. Great with hearty sauces.

Penne. You'll find penne—straight pasta tubes that are slant-cut—in all sizes and colors today, because they are so popular. I'm especially partial to the smallest, narrowest penne; they're wonderful with light tomato sauces. You can buy either penne lisci, which are smooth, or penne rigate, which have ridges; the latter are better at holding sauces.

Here are four simple recipes for dried pasta dishes. Each one will yield a great bowl of pasta that's authentically Italian in style.

FRANCIS FORD COPPOLA'S SPAGHETTI POMODORO BASILICO

Several years ago I had the pleasure of interviewing the great film director Francis Ford Coppola for a *New York Times* story. The venue was amazing: my apartment, where Francis cooked dinner! He's a deeply thoughtful man, happy to philosophize all night—but also happy to stand at the stove and make his favorite everyday dried pasta dish. I give you the recipe here, for it's as good a basic red-sauce pasta as you're likely to find. Intriguingly, it diverges from what you'd expect the Calabrian Coppolas to be making: it has no garlic, and a knob of butter gets added at the end.

SERVES 8 TO 12

2 tablespoons olive oil

2 medium onions, peeled and coarsely chopped

3 cans imported Italian plum tomatoes (each can 1 pound, 12 ounces)

1 bunch fresh basil

Crushed dried red pepper flakes, to taste

2 pounds spaghetti

1 tablespoon unsalted butter

1. Heat the olive oil over medium-high heat in a heavy saucepan. Sauté the onions in it for 5 to 7 minutes, or until they are transparent and just starting to brown.

2. Using a sharp knife, cut the tomatoes coarsely inside their cans. Drain off and reserve the juice.

3. Add the tomatoes to the saucepan, along with a dozen basil leaves, very coarsely chopped. Season with salt and red pepper flakes to taste. Let the sauce come to a boil, then lower heat, and simmer for 45 minutes. It should have a medium-thick consistency; keep adding back some of the reserved tomato liquid to maintain the correct consistency.

4. When the sauce is nearing completion, boil the spaghetti in a large amount of salted water.

5. When you are ready to serve, add another dozen very coarsely chopped basil leaves to the sauce, and whisk in the butter. Drain the cooked spaghetti in a colander, draining all water from the pasta cooking pot, then return the spaghetti to the pot. Add about ⅔ of the sauce to it, or just enough to lightly coat the spaghetti. Stir well for 1 minute over medium heat.

6. Divide the spaghetti among 8 to 12 bowls, placing a few small basil leaves on each bowl. Top each with a few tablespoons of sauce. Serve immediately. Pass freshly grated Parmigiano-Reggiano if desired.

SPAGHETTI LIMONCELLO

One of the few restaurants in America that consistently serves pasta with real Italian style is Limoncello, in New York City. The chef is from Sicily, and his father is in the lemon business. Perhaps it stands to reason that the chef's best pasta dish at the restaurant is a very southern Italian mixture, fragrant with lemons. If you love the tight focus of spaghetti with garlic and olive oil, you'll probably also love this related dish.

SERVES 4

3/4 pound spaghetti

3 tablespoons olive oil

4 garlic cloves, peeled and very thinly sliced

1 anchovy fillet, finely minced

2 teaspoons freshly grated lemon zest

Pinch dried red pepper flakes

3 tablespoons finely minced fresh parsley

1 tablespoon freshly grated pecorino Romano

1. Cook the pasta in a large pot of salted water.

2. While the pasta is cooking, place the olive oil in a heavy frying pan over moderate heat. Add the garlic, and cook until golden, just before it starts to brown (about 5 minutes). Remove the pan from heat.

3. Add the anchovy, lemon zest, and red pepper flakes to the pan. Remove ½ cup water from the pasta cooking pot, and add it to the pan. Stir well.

4. When the pasta is done, remove it from the large pot and place it in a colander; spill the cooking water out of the large pot, reserving a cup or so. Place the cooking pot back on the stove, over medium-high heat, and put the drained spaghetti back in the pot. Toss for 30 seconds. Add about ⅔ of the contents of the frying pan to the spaghetti and toss. If the spaghetti's not already too saucy, add the rest of the frying-pan sauce. If it's too dry, add a little of the reserved pasta cooking water until the pasta is moist. Cook for 1 minute. Toss with parsley and pecorino Romano, and serve immediately.

Cutting Garlic

You'd be amazed at the difference your cut of garlic makes in the final product. For years, I simply smashed cloves of garlic with a heavy knife to remove the peel, then minced them finely. But after an Italian cook pointed out to me that this leaves a lot of delicious garlic oil on the cutting board, I swung completely in the opposite direction. Now—as in Spaghetti Limoncello—I carefully peel the garlic, then cut it into paper-thin slices. For quick-cooked sauces with garlic, the taste is much more interesting.

FUSILLI PUTTANESCA

This is one of my favorite quick pasta sauces—a hasty toss of tomatoes, anchovies, olives, capers, and pimientos in this version. It works well with all manner of dried pasta, but I like it best with long pasta, particularly with long corkscrew shapes. There's always speculation about the name of the sauce—which means "prostitute." Some say this dish was favored by Neapolitan courtesans, who could throw it together quickly between assignations. A friend of mine recently remarked that if that's the case, it should be very popular among New York psychiatrists.

SERVES 4 TO 6

1 pound long fusilli

1/4 cup fruity olive oil

8 medium cloves of garlic, peeled and cut into thin slices

1 large can tomatoes (1 pound, 12 ounces)

2 tins rolled anchovies, chopped

2/3 cup pitted, coarsely chopped black olives (like kalamata or gaeta)

2/3 cup capers, coarsely chopped*

1 small jar pimientos

*The best capers in the world come from the small islands around Sicily, particularly the island of Pantelleria. These large, flavorful beauties are not packed in vinegar or brine; they're dry packed in salt. Before using them, be sure to wash off the salt. If you're salt sensitive, you might want to soak them for a few minutes to reduce the saltiness.

1. Cook the pasta in a large pot of salted water.

2. Place the olive oil in a saucepan over medium heat. Add the garlic slices, and sauté until they start to turn golden (2 to 3 minutes).

3. Meanwhile, drain the tomatoes, and place them on a cutting board. Cut them into small dice. Add them to the saucepan, leaving behind as much of the tomato liquid as possible. Add the anchovies, olives, and capers.

Blend, and cook for 1 minute. Dice the pimientos, and add them to the sauce. Cook for another 30 seconds.

4. When the pasta is ready to serve, drain it in a colander. Place the pasta cooking pot over medium heat. Add the drained pasta and ⅔ of the sauce. Toss for 30 seconds. Taste, and, if necessary, season with coarse salt and black pepper. Divide among pasta bowls, and top each with a bit of remaining sauce. Serve immediately.

SPAGHETTI WITH RED CLAM SAUCE

As a great lover of clams, I'm partial to dried pasta with *white* clam sauce—a dish that concentrates on the briny little mollusks. I'm certainly no fan of the unclammy, drenched-in-tomato-sauce dish that usually arrives when you order red clam sauce in this country. However, recent trips to southern Italy have shown me that there is a wonderful compromise at hand. Around Naples, the sauce is basically what we would call white—except for the addition of a few chunks of tomato (often their wonderful cherry tomatoes, or *pomodorini*). And guess what: the bits of red create a lovely counterpoint to the salty clams. The following recipe is an *Italian*-style red clam sauce. Try it, you'll love it!

SERVES 4 TO 6 AS A PASTA COURSE

1 large head of garlic
10 tablespoons medium-quality extra-virgin olive oil, plus a little extra for drizzling
One 28-ounce can whole tomatoes (preferably Muir Glen from California)

1 1/4 cups shredded fresh basil, plus a few sprigs for garnish
12 very large chowder clams, each 8 to 10 ounces
1 pound spaghetti
2 pounds Manila clams or New Zealand cockles, washed

1. Separate the cloves of garlic, and peel each one. (To facilitate this, you can soak the separated cloves in warm water for ½ hour.) Cut the peeled cloves into broad, thin slices.

2. Place 6 tablespoons of the olive oil in a very wide sauté pan or a very wide Dutch oven over medium-high heat. Add the garlic, reserving about 4 cloves' worth of slices. Cook, stirring occasionally, until the garlic is almost brown (about 5 minutes).

3. While the garlic is cooking, place the contents of the 2 tomato cans in a colander. Working over the sink, squeeze the tomatoes in your hands until they are a coarse pulp.

4. When the garlic is almost brown, add the tomatoes and ¼ cup basil. Cook over medium heat for 10 minutes, uncovered, then remove from heat and reserve.

5. Open the clams with a clam knife, reserving the juice. Chop the clams coarsely and reserve.

6. Add the spaghetti to a large pot of salted boiling water. Cook until al dente (about 10 minutes). When the pasta is done, spill the contents of the pot into a colander. Toss the hot pasta in the colander with a little olive oil, and reserve.

7. Meanwhile, place the remaining olive oil in the now-empty pasta pot over high heat. Add the reserved garlic. Sauté until almost brown. Add the Manila clams or New

Zealand cockles. Add ½ cup of basil. Add the reserved tomato sauce. Add a few tablespoons of the reserved clam juice. Cover the pot, and cook until the Manila clams open (3 to 4 minutes). Add the chopped clams, stirring.

8. Stir the reserved spaghetti into the pot. Blend well with the sauce. Add the remaining ½ cup of basil. Season to taste with salt and pepper.

9. Turn out onto a large pasta platter. Garnish with extra sprigs of basil. Serve immediately.

Beyond Clams

If you want to turn your spaghetti with clam sauce into a shellfish bonanza, it's easy to do. Simply sauté some additional sliced garlic (5 or 6 cloves) in a few tablespoons of olive oil in a large sauté pan. When the garlic is golden, add shellfish: cut pieces of raw lobster, shrimp, squid, scallops—whatever's at hand. Sauté until the shellfish is just cooked. If using mussels, cover the pan so that they can open quickly. When the fish is cooked, season with salt and pepper, toss with finely minced parsley, and add the contents of the pan to the sauced spaghetti in the pot (step 8 of the red clam sauce recipe). Stir well. As you can see from the cover of this book, it's one happy eating event.

Dried Pasta for Clam Sauce

It is axiomatic in America that linguine goes with clam sauce. But surprise, surprise: linguine is not nearly as popular in Italy as it is here. Around Naples, it is most likely spaghetti that's served with clam sauce. After careful deliberation, I'm ready to agree that spaghetti—which doesn't lie as flat in the sauce as linguine does—is a better choice for clam sauce.

Clams for Clam Sauce

The one type of clam that I absolutely, positively will not choose for clam sauce is canned clams. Beyond that, I'm open to all hard-shell possibilities. However, experience has taught me that the very best combination of quality and value is provided by superlarge hard-shell clams, the ones called quahogs in New England, or chowder clams. And, to really gild the lily, I like to add tiny whole clams—such as Manila clams, or New Zealand cockles—to the dish. Both of these are readily available these days in better seafood stores. If you can't find them, you can substitute littlenecks—though the result will be a much tougher, more rubbery clam.

Criteria for Quality

Different dried pasta dishes have different criteria. But a few basic questions must be asked about every dried pasta dish:

- *Is the pasta of good quality (a firm chew, a slightly nutty taste)?*
- *Is it cooked al dente?*
- *Is there just enough sauce to cover the pasta, not so much that the pasta is smothered? (a proper bowl of pasta should have no sauce collecting in the bottom)*
- *Is the dish relatively free from lots of chunky stuff? (it should be; in Italy, the pasta itself is the star)*
- *Is the dish watery? (it shouldn't be)*
- *Is the dish properly seasoned?*

When

In their most authentic, natural setting—Italy—dried pasta dishes are served as the second course of a meal. Italians like to serve a little something before the "first" course, which they, and we, call antipasto. *Whatever it's called, I like this meal order very much—an array of vegetables, or salads, or cold meats first; a steaming bowl of dried pasta second; a simple grilled meat dish third.*

It has become very popular in America to serve pasta as the one-and-only course of a meal (maybe with bread and a salad). I've even seen this done in Italy. I even do it myself sometimes. But the pasta always seems lonely to me, somehow, without neighboring courses. Perhaps this is why Americans load up the pasta bowl with too much sauce and too many chunks of other things: they're trying to make up for the neighboring courses that they've eliminated from their menus.

In Your Glass

It's hard to generalize about wine for dried pasta dishes, because there are so many variations. I'll make this generalization, though: drink some kind of wine with your pasta, please!

Many dried pasta dishes feature tomato sauces. Lots of wines may go with these, but a great all-purpose solution is a simple red wine from the Piemonte region: Barbera. It's very low in tannin, which makes it food friendly, and very high in acid, which makes it particularly friendly to tomatoes. Beware, however: lots of producers today are trying to make a grander style of Barbera and are charging $30 and up per bottle. This is not the pasta wine I have in mind. Just find a simple Barbera, priced at $12 or under, with the denominazione *Barbera d'Alba, Barbera d'Asti, or Barbera del Monferrato.*

Looking for white wine? With dishes of the oily-garlicky school, with perhaps a few vegetables thrown in, I like crisp whites. The Tuscan wine Galestro is always a good bet for these dishes, as is the Sardinian wine Vermentino. Neither is very expensive—but expect only a refreshing, food-friendly drink, not a wealth of flavor.

Orecchiette with beans and mussels

ORECCHIETTE

Orecchiette—or "little ears"—occupy a special place in the pasta pantheon. There's fresh pasta in the North of Italy and dried pasta in the South—but orecchiette are somewhere in between. Oh, geographically they're southern all right—a specialty of Puglia, a terrific gastronomic region that features chunky little pasta shapes. But orecchiette, as I learned on a trip to Puglia a few years back, can be made with or without egg, can be made to be eaten fresh or to be eaten dried. It's pasta at the crossroads, and I love it.

I find orecchiette special in another way, as well. I can think of no pasta shape that more efficiently picks up the proper sauce. This is because the little "ears"—rounded shapes, actually, with a depression at the center—trap small bits of food in the concave center. This doesn't work, of course, if your sauce includes long strips of food; but if you've wisely chosen little bits of things, you'll have an ideal textural marriage of pasta and sauce. Because of this, orecchiette are among my very favorite of all pasta shapes.

These days you can buy good dried orecchiette from artisanal producers in Puglia. And if you don't have time to fuss, just prepare this packaged pasta with one of the following sauces. But if you do have a little extra time, I strongly urge you to give the following recipe for homemade orecchiette a try; I guarantee they are the best little ears you'll ever nibble.

HOMEMADE ORECCHIETTE

I developed this basic recipe for Dean & DeLuca soon after I returned from a trip to Puglia. It doesn't take that much actual work; however, because of the various stages of drying, you'll have to keep coming back to it. So make it on an afternoon when you need to be in the house for a few hours doing something else.

MAKES ABOUT 6 OUNCES, ENOUGH PASTA FOR 2 PEOPLE

1 cup unbleached flour
1/4 teaspoon salt
4 to 5 ounces water

1. In a large bowl, mix together the flour and salt. Add water until a fairly dry dough is formed. Turn out onto a floured board, and knead for 10 minutes, until smooth and firm.

2. Cut the dough in 2 pieces, and roll each piece into a long cylinder, about ½ inch in diameter. Cut the cylinders crosswise into small pieces, making a cut every ¼ inch or so. With your fingers, round out each little piece of dough until it's a small circle, about ⅛ inch thick and ⅔ inch in diameter. Let them stand on kitchen counter, in a single layer, for 15 minutes.

3. After 15 minutes, flip each piece of dough over. Now, working on the counter, press your thumb into the center of each one, creating a depression. When you've finished all the orecchiette, let them rest on the counter for 1 hour.

4. After 1 hour, pick up 1 piece, place it in your palm, and depress it again (in the same spot) with your thumb. You should now have a fairly deep depression. Try to make the rim of the piece approximately the same thickness as the center. Return the piece to the counter, depression side down, and continue with the rest until all of the orecchiette are done.

5. You can cook the orecchiette immediately, but I like the texture better if the pasta dries for a few hours.

Orecchiette usually take 7 to 8 minutes to cook. They can be a little trickier than most pastas to cook, since the rim of the "ear" can be a little thicker than the depression; this means that each little ear cooks unevenly. Obviously, you have to cook them until the rims are finished—meaning the centers might be slightly past al dente.

Here are two traditional Pugliese dishes made with orecchiette.

ORECCHIETTE WITH BROCCOLI RABE AND SAUSAGE

This is the classic Pugliese treatment for orecchiette; the bitterness of the broccoli rabe is a particularly characteristic element of Pugliese cooking. I adapted this recipe from the best version of the dish I ever tasted in America—which is served at Limoncello, in New York City, where you'll find some of this country's best southern Italian pasta dishes.

MAKES 4 TO 6 SERVINGS

1 pound orecchiette (either buy a pound of dried orecchiette, or triple the preceding recipe for Homemade Orecchiette)

2 bunches broccoli rabe, about 2 pounds altogether

1 cup olive oil

10 medium cloves garlic, peeled and sliced thin

1 pound sweet Italian sausage, skin removed and crumbled in large chunks

8 medium plum tomatoes, diced

Red pepper flakes, to taste

1/2 cup grated pecorino

1. Cook the orecchiette in boiling salted water.

2. While the orecchiette are cooking, cut off about 1½ inches from the bottom of the broccoli rabe stems and discard them. Chop the remaining broccoli rabe into pieces approximately 1 inch long. You should have about 14 cups.

3. When the orecchiette is almost al dente, add the broccoli rabe, and cook an additional 3 minutes.

4. Place the olive oil in a heavy pot over medium-high heat, and add the garlic. Sauté until golden. Add the sausage meat, and sauté, stirring, for 3 minutes. Stir in the tomatoes and red pepper flakes.

5. When the orecchiette and broccoli rabe are done, drain them, and add them to the sausage mixture. Heat and stir all the ingredients until they are well combined. Toss the ingredients with the cheese. Season with salt and pepper. Serve immediately.

ORECCHIETTE WITH BEANS AND MUSSELS

This is a dish that took me completely by surprise. I'd never heard of it before my trip to Puglia—but after I tasted it there, I knew I'd want it many times again. The beans and shelled mussels fit especially niftily into the crevices of the orecchiette.

MAKES 2 SERVINGS

1/2 cup fresh cranberry beans, shelled (or canned cannellini beans)

Extra-virgin olive oil, to taste

2 tablespoons fruity olive oil

2 large cloves garlic, finely minced

1 carrot, very finely minced

1 celery stalk, very finely minced

1 cup water

1 1/3 pounds mussels

12 cherry tomatoes

2 tablespoons fresh oregano, minced

1/3 pound orecchiette (buy dried orecchiette, or use a scant recipe of Homemade Orecchiette)

1. Boil the cranberry beans until they are just tender, drain them, and season with salt, pepper, and extra-virgin olive oil. (If you are using canned beans, simply season with salt, pepper, and oil.) Reserve.

2. Place the fruity olive oil in a heavy pot over medium-low heat, and slowly sauté the garlic in it for 10 minutes. Add the carrot and celery, and sauté slowly for another 15 minutes.

3. Add the water, raise the heat, and reduce rapidly for 5 minutes. Over high heat, add the mussels, cover, and steam until they open. Remove them, shell them, and reserve. Simmer the liquid in the pot for another 15 minutes, until it's well reduced.

4. Mince the tomatoes. Toss them with the fresh oregano.

5. Boil the orecchiette until just al dente.

6. When you are ready to serve, warm the tomatoes with oregano in the mussel-cooking liquid for 1 minute. Add the beans, mussels, and orecchiette. Toss them together over medium heat for 30 seconds. Season with salt and pepper and extra-virgin olive oil. Serve immediately, garnished with mussels in the shell if desired.

Criteria for Quality (for Orecchiette in General)

- *Is each "little ear" evenly cooked? (this is tricky, since the outer part of the orecchiette can be thicker than the central part)*
- *Does the sauce make sense for orecchiette? (large chunks of things that don't fit inside the "ears" wouldn't be appropriate)*

THE LURE OF REAL ITALIAN FOOD

Food writers who spend a great deal of time in Italy and France—the two prime destinations of those in our field—are fiercely divided. Some think Italy is heaven on earth (and dream of buying a home there); others have the same feelings for France. I make no bones about my preference: I'm a France guy.

What I love about France so much is the balance it strikes between the cool logic of northern Europe and the sunny exuberance of southern Europe. I find this balance in many aspects of French culture but tend to focus on its gastronomic implications. Because France is beautifully poised between North and South, many comestibles—from wine grapes and apples to tomatoes—grow beautifully there, yielding foods (and wines) that are intensely focused in flavor but not overripe. The cooking as well, it seems to me, strikes the right balance between North and South, high and low, classic and creative, high art and folk art. France is the land of Cartesian equanimity, of the Golden Mean.

Italy is the land of Chaos. I say that lovingly, though not everyone does; some Francophiles are positively turned off by the more freewheeling spirit of Italy, the greater confusion, the higher randomness. Those who thrive on the crisp orderliness of public crowds in France, or the precision work of waitstaff in French restaurants, are sometimes driven to distraction by the tendency of public crowds in Italy to push in closer, or by the failure of Italian servers to reach the polished heights of French ones.

One of the implications of "chaos" that has always marked life in Italy to me is what seems to be the unshakable destiny of all plans to go awry. I exaggerate for effect—but it has happened to me on many an occasion that the best-laid plans have done a severe Robert Burns.

For example, I was once driving to an inn in the Chianti Classico region, where I would be headquartered for several days while researching a wine story. It was a miserable November afternoon, with a bone-chilling rain pouring down; I'd made an arrangement to arrive at 2:00 P.M., and, when I drove onto the grounds at 2:00 P.M., all I wanted was a room, a hot bath, maybe a fireplace, maybe a bowl of pasta.

I never got even close. There were a number of possible entrances to the inn, none of which was clearly the main entrance; I left my car, ran through the downpour, and knocked on the likeliest door. No answer. More knocks. More silence. I went to another door . . . and another. No matter where I knocked, and no matter how loudly—I was banging and screaming by the sixth door—silence was the only response. Soaked, I walked dejectedly to the car, cursing those who fail to keep appointments. I waited in the car for fifteen or twenty minutes, hoping someone would show up. I wasn't sure what to do next but had half a mind to drive on to Pisa and catch a plane to Paris.

A few miles down the road, however, my eye was caught by a small, tasteful sign on the road for an albergo, *with an arrow pointing towards a driveway. I'd researched the local lodging possibilities well and had never heard of this one; impulsively, however, I took the turn. What was waiting for me, of course, was one of the most beautiful and comfortable old inns I've ever stayed in, amazingly gracious people, an antique-laden room with a four-poster, plenty of hot water, blazing fireplaces galore . . . and a delicious, soul-satisfying Tuscan meal that the owners whipped up for the unexpected drop-in at about 3:00 P.M.*

There's something of this spirit in Italian food, as well. It's hard to predict what's going to be excellent to eat in Italy. I go into the highest-rated restaurants—like those that get three stars from the Michelin guide—and I'm continually disappointed. After such an experience, I might stop off at a little trattoria I've never heard of, where the chef looks like he's making it up as he goes along—and the food is brilliant.

What does traveling in Italy teach you about Italian food? Don't be formal, don't be French, don't be tied to recipes. Be freewheeling, loose, and improvisational. If you've developed a feel for the tastes of Italy, and some basic technique, benevolent Chaos will reign in your kitchen as well. It is important, however, to put in your time in Italy. Many of the Italian dishes we think we know in America taste completely different in Italy—and, if you want to dazzle your friends and family with your Italian cooking, you must use the food of Italy—in Italy!—as your model.

Here are a few important Italian items that differ so in Italy.

Pasta. *This is one of America's favorite foods, of course—but pasta in America is very different from pasta over there! The most important difference is in the amount of sauce used in the dish; whereas Italians like to use only enough sauce to just coat the pasta, Americans like to smother their noodles in sauce.*

Another difference is the type *of sauce used on pasta. Once, in America, tomato sauce was ubiquitous; then we learned about so-called northern Italian food, and "fancy" Italian restaurants here started serving alternatives to tomato sauce—like cream sauce. But Italy herself holds two surprises: (1) tomato sauce is much more popular in the North than we've been led to believe; and (2) sauces using cream are very rare. Even fettuccine Alfredo, in the classic recipe, has no cream.*

Last, there's the issue of pasta quality. Today, the best Italian brands of dried pasta are available to us in the United States, so—as long as you're cooking it properly—you don't have to travel to see what that tastes like. (Those who say the water it's cooked in makes the dried pasta taste different in Italy are a little loony, I think.) But when it comes to fresh pasta, or pasta fresca, *or* pasta all'uovo, *I contend that travel is a necessity. Maybe the water does make a difference in this case; whatever it is, you just never find in America the amazing resiliency, stretch, tenderness that you find in* pasta fresca *in Italy—and certainly nothing near the variety.*

Mozzarella. It is possible to find good-quality mozzarella in the United States—but the good stuff is just a tiny, tiny percentage of the supermarket soap that most Americans have to buy. Once you've had it in southern Italy, however, you'll never stop being haunted by mozzarella: the thin layers of cheese that seem practically like puff pastry; the dripping wetness; the chewy but soft texture in the mouth; a taste that seems to suggest sweet, concentrated milk. In the region of Puglia, I once sat at dinner with about thirty American journalists and was served burrata—a local specialty of runny cheese wrapped inside fresh mozzarella. Conversation was animated as the course was served—but five minutes later, you could hear a pin drop. Most agreed, with a kind of awe, that it was the greatest mozzarella they'd ever tasted.

Olive Oil. We do get the same olive oil in the United States that they have in Italy . . . but we get it almost a year later! The dirty little secret of olive oil is that—unlike wine—it never tastes better than the moment it's made. That's when the full intensity of olive flavor is present. A few months later, the thrill is gone. A year or two later, the oil's health is gone—it's well on the way to rancidity. This is why it's very important to get to Tuscany, some year, in November. That's when the greatest olive oil in the world—deep green, blazing with fruit and wheatgrass flavors, dazzlingly peppery and pungent—has just emerged from the presses. Padrones at restaurants all over Tuscany are parading to tables with flasks of the brand-new elixir—pouring it on bread, on beans, on grilled meats.

RISOTTO

Risotto is one of the most immediately appealing dishes in the whole Italian repertoire: a warm and creamy bowl of plump, just-tender rice grains suspended in a kind of porridge, the whole made even richer by immoderate amounts of butter and Parmigiano-Reggiano. It is comfort food of the very highest order—and, on a cold winter's night, perhaps the one dish more than any other I feel comfortable ordering.

It was only about fifteen years ago that I first went to Italy and experienced real risotto for myself. Before that, I had had only bad versions to contend with, and descriptions in books that weren't precise enough. Before learning about risotto, I was programmed to believe that, in rice dishes, fluffy equals good. But no cookbook was spelling out the risotto reality for me, loud and clear:

This is one rice dish that's not fluffy. This stuff is creamy and wet. When you think of risotto, think of the texture of hot breakfast cereal!

Once you know that, once you have that goal to shoot for, you should have no problem making risotto at home. It's a very hands-on process: no measuring out of liquid and rice, no covering the pot and going away to watch Food Network for twenty minutes. In risotto making, you are constantly on the scene—adding liquid bit by bit, stirring, judging doneness.

These are the basic steps.

1. Sauté something flavorful (like chopped onions) in butter or oil.

2. Add the rice, and stir well, making sure each grain is coated.

3. Add a fairly large quantity of broth, and stir until the rice absorbs the broth.

4. Keep adding broth in small quantities, stirring almost continually (as soon as the broth is absorbed, add more).

5. Add other stuff, if you wish (mushrooms for mushroom risotto, shellfish for shellfish risotto, et cetera).

6. Stop cooking when the rice is tender almost all the way through (a little firmness at the center of each grain is good).

7. "Mount" the risotto with butter and/or Parmigiano-Reggiano just before serving (this fat-adding but absolutely indispensable fillip is called the *montecato* by Italians).

All the specifics follow in my favorite risotto recipe.

It really couldn't be simpler, but there is one cloud of confusion: You will find some controversy concerning the final texture of the dish.

1. Some people like it thicker, pastier, with the grains of rice holding together.

2. Some people like it loose and runny, with what amounts to a medium-bodied sauce holding the rice grains in suspension.

I am in the latter camp, all the way. In fact, when I finish cooking a risotto—after the grains of rice have absorbed enough liquid and are just al dente—I usually give my risotto an extra ladleful of broth, just to make sure it comes to the table in a runny-creamy state. I even do this off the heat, to limit the chances of the rice thirstily stealing the liquid from the sauce.

Without any further ado, then, the basic risotto from the Rosengarten house.

Thick and pasty risotto

Medium-thick risotto

Loose and runny risotto (my choice)

CAULIFLOWER RISOTTO WITH SAFFRON

There are thousands of risotto possibilities in the world: hundreds of classic variations, and ever more variations cooked up daily by creative chefs. I like my risotto simple. I find that all kinds of stuff in it, and—as is the fashion today—other kinds of stuff on top of it, tends to obscure the dish's wonderful, rudimentary simplicity. Risotto Milanese—just chicken broth and saffron in addition to the basics—has always been my favorite. Once, however, I added some cauliflower to a risotto Milanese, in the hope of supplying a hint of the flavor that expensive white truffles can bring to the dish. It was superb—and has become my risotto staple.

SERVES 6 TO 8 AS A RISOTTO COURSE

4 ounces unsalted butter

1 1/4 cups finely chopped onion

2 1/4 cups superfino or fino rice (see "The Choice of Rice" on page 89)

1 teaspoon saffron threads

9 to 12 cups light, boiling chicken broth

4 cups small cauliflower florets, each the width of a thumbnail

3/4 cup freshly grated Parmigiano-Reggiano

1. Melt 2 ounces of butter over medium heat in a large, heavy stockpot. Add the chopped onion, and sauté until the onion is soft and golden, stirring occasionally (about 7 minutes).

2. Add the rice. Stir well to coat the rice with the butter. Sprinkle with the saffron threads. Cook for 1 minute, stirring.

3. Turn heat to medium-high. Add 2 cups of the chicken broth (or enough to just cover the rice). Stir continually, and keep the broth at a gentle simmer. When most of the broth has been absorbed, add the cauliflower, and stir well. When all the boiling broth has been absorbed, add approximately 1/2 cup more, stirring until it is absorbed. Keep adding broth, 1/2 cup at a time, until the rice is al dente.

4. Stir the remaining butter into the rice, along with the freshly grated cheese. Adjust the texture with additional broth, if desired. Taste for seasoning, and serve immediately.

Nothing but Truffles

As much as I love the purity of a simple risotto, I am driven nuts by the flavor combo of risotto and white truffles. The truffles taste something like a combination of cheese, garlic, cauliflower, and sex—and if you can get a hold of a few ounces of these obscenely expensive fungi, I highly recommend that you shave them with impunity over the cauliflower risotto once you've served it in individual bowls at the table.

Of course, fresh white truffles—most of which are sniffed out by dogs in the environs of Alba, in northwestern Italy—come but once a year. The season begins in September and is over by December. Despair not. For the rest of the year, you do have other white truffle options. There is, of course, a bevy of black truffle options as well. But for me this is a black-and-white case: the latter's better in risotto.

White Truffle Oil. This product has become so popular in recent years that up-to-the-minute foodies are now complaining about its ubiquity in trendy restaurants. Their complaints are justified when the oil is used inappropriately, and when it is of inferior quality. But if you can find a good one—I'm happy with the product Urbani makes—and if you can find one made not more than a year ago, I say go for it at risotto time. After you take the risotto off the heat, stir in a few teaspoons (or more) of oil just before serving. You can gild the lily by drizzling a little oil over each portion.

White Truffle Paste. This is a bit harder to find, but it is more consistent in quality. Use it the same way: blend the white truffle paste into the risotto just before serving.

White Truffle Butter. This is the most difficult to find, but white truffle butter is my favorite alternative to fresh white truffles (because it tastes the freshest). You buy white truffle butter refrigerated, and you melt a few tablespoons into your finished risotto—once again, just before serving.

What's in a Name?

A lot of confusion—since there is a good deal of controversy about the original meaning of risotto. Some people assume that it means "rice"—but that's one thing it definitely does not mean. In Italian, rice is riso. Obviously, however, the words are related. Some linguistic detectives believe the word originally meant something like "rice under a sauce" or "rice under vegetables." Others believe it originally meant something like "riced."

Risotto in Italy

Once upon a time, risotto was truly a dish of Italy's northernmost regions—Piemonte, Lombardy, the Veneto. It was almost never seen in the South, and it was even less than acceptable in the center. The great cookbook writer Pellegrino Artusi—whose classic nineteenth-century work documented the food of the central regions of Tuscany and Emilia-Romagna—wrote that "rice . . . is a fattening food that the Turks have administered to their women to make them like corpulent cushions."

Today, much has changed. The North still loves its risotto—but, truth be told, I have seen and tasted many fabulous risotto dishes all over Italy.

The Broth

Most Italian chefs are very insistent about the difference between the meat "stocks" that French chefs use and the meat "broths" that Italian chefs use. They view Italian broth as much lighter than French stock, less full flavored, less seasoned—in general, a better liquid to use when you don't want the subtle flavor of something like rice to be masked.

I must confess that I love risotto so much, and sometimes need it so impetuously, that I do use good canned chicken stock to do the job. The results are still delicious. But, of course, if you have the time, nothing is better for risotto than a lovely, gentle, subtle, homemade Italian-style broth (less intense than French stock).

Whichever liquid you use, just make sure that it's not salty, because this may overseason your risotto. You can always add salt at the last minute—preferably after you've added the also-salty Parmigiano-Reggiano.

Panning Out

Never forget that risotto is a touchy-feely thing; getting its texture perfectly right depends on some magical mixture of just the right pan, just the right quantity of risotto, just the right amount of heat, just the right rhythm in adding liquid, and just the right total cooking time.

There is a theory behind "just the right pan." First of all, you need even heat to cook the rice evenly—so your pan should be of good, heavy material so the heat is distributed evenly. But it's also important to make risotto in a fairly wide pan, so that the rice doesn't "stack up" on itself in the pan and cook unevenly. I like to expose as much of the rice to the surface of the pan as possible. For the amount of rice in the Cauliflower Risotto recipe, a Dutch oven that's 8 or 9 inches in diameter is just about right. I use an anodyzed aluminum pan like Calphalon at home for risotto.

By the way, as you make risotto at home, always remember exactly what you did (quantities, heat, time, stirring methods, et cetera). If your risotto comes out perfectly, you'll want to remember just how you did it so that you can reproduce it next time!

The Choice of Rice

The textural miracle that is risotto occurs only when short-grained rice is used. Why? Because short-grained rice is high in amylopectin, a type of starch that dissolves in the pot—which is what builds the creamy sauce that surrounds the grains of rice in a good risotto.

In Italy, four types of short-grained rice are grown: superfino, fino, semifino, and ordinario. When risotto started to catch on in America, we heard much about one type of superfino: Arborio, grown in Piemonte. For a while, everyone assumed you had to use Arborio rice to make risotto—and, since Arborio is particularly high in amylopectin, it does make the creamiest risotto. But there are other types of superfino available. One of them, Carnaroli, makes what I consider to be an even better risotto than Arborio does—because grains of Carnaroli rice remain a little chewier on the inside.

And now the shocker: for my money, it's not superfino rice that makes the best risotto of all! I prefer a type of fino called Vialone Nano, which is available in the United States. I first tasted it at a great albergo on the west shore of Lake Garda, in northern Italy. When I was served risotto there, I noticed how loose and runny it was, how much less sticky it seemed. The chef explained to me that fino, particularly Vialone Nano, is lower in amylopectin than superfino is—which means there's less starch in the rice to thicken the "sauce." In Venice, they call this looser risotto all'onda ("in a wave"). This is my favorite kind of risotto. And you get the added bonus from Vialone Nano of a good al dente chew in the center of each grain.

Serving Tips

My favorite way to serve risotto is just as they do it in the countryside in Italy. Pour it out of the pot as quickly as possible onto a long, oval platter (for the recipe given here, you'll need a very large platter). Make sure each of your guests has a wide, shallow soup bowl; it's especially nice if the bowls are heated. Bring the platter into the dining room and, using a large serving spoon, spoon a portion into each of the soup bowls. Encourage your guests to eat the dish with large spoons.

Creativity Alert!

As you probably know, I hate stupid culinary creativity. And, as you know by now, I love risotto so much I'd especially hate some kiwifruit-crazed chef to do something stupid with my beloved dish. So you must understand that I present the following risotto *only because, despite all presentiments you may have, it is unbelievably delicious!*

We stumbled upon it one day while playing around with ideas for a strawberry show. Georgia Downard, Food Network's culinary director, suggested that the pleasing texture of rice pudding could probably be achieved by using the risotto method—and the resulting dish would be soothingly hot in temperature to boot!

Oh come on . . . try it! It's extraordinary!

STRAWBERRY RISOTTO

Sometimes, when I'm cooking an Italian dinner party, a terrible choice confronts me: pasta or risotto for the *primo*—the course before the main course? Sometimes pasta wins, and I feel as if my poor guests missed a great risotto opportunity. Well, here's the solution to that dilemma—if the meal isn't too heavy, serve pasta before the main course and serve this amazing strawberry risotto as a dessert.

MAKES 4 DESSERT SERVINGS

2 cups milk

2 cups unsweetened coconut milk (a good brand of canned Thai milk is fine)

1/2 cup sugar

1 vanilla bean, halved lengthwise

2 strips lemon peel

2 tablespoons butter

2/3 cup Arborio rice

Up to 1/2 cup heavy cream, heated (optional)

2 tablespoons eau-de-vie de fraise

1 cup sliced strawberries

Lightly toasted sweetened, flaked coconut, for garnish (optional)

Lightly toasted sliced almonds, for garnish (optional)

1. In a saucepan combine the milks, sugar, vanilla bean, and lemon peel. Heat until the liquid is very hot and bubbles appear around the edges of the pan. Reduce heat and keep warm.

2. Meanwhile, in another saucepan melt the butter over medium heat. When the foaming subsides, add the rice, and stir to coat with butter.

3. Add the simmering milk, ½ cup at a time, stirring vigorously. Let each addition be absorbed by the rice before adding more. Regulate heat under the rice so the milk is absorbed at a brisk simmer. It should take from 30 to 35 minutes to add the liquid. Begin tasting toward the end of the cooking time—the rice should be tender but still firm to the bite. It will form its own sauce.

4. If you like your risotto runnier, stir in some or all of the heated cream. Remove from heat, and stir in the eau-de-vie and strawberries, saving a few perfect strawberry slices for garnishing. Serve in shallow bowls, and, if desired, sprinkle with coconut and almonds.

Criteria for Quality

- Is the risotto loose and creamy, not gluey and/or gloppy?
- Is the rice itself cooked just al dente, not too firm, but not too mushy?
- If other ingredients are used, does the supporting cast of characters (e.g., mushrooms, vegetable, seafood) seem appropriate?
- If other ingredients are used, does the risotto taste of those ingredients? (it should)
- If other ingredients are used, are they used in small enough proportions that the rice itself is still the star?
- Is the risotto served hot?

When

In the classic Italian meal order, antipasti get things started. Then come primi—which are usually pasta dishes, polenta dishes, or risotti. After the risotto comes the third course, or main course.

Today in top American restaurants—Italian restaurants, New American restaurants, even French restaurants—risotto is often served as a first course. At home—particularly on a cold night—I think it's a great starter for a dinner party.

Lots of risotto-struck Americans, however, are finding it satisfying enough to stand all by itself as a main course. If you serve risotto this way, it's fun to gather your family or friends in the kitchen to watch you and shout words of encouragement as you stir.

In Your Glass

In Italy, wine is sometimes used along with broth in cooking risotto; if it is, the wine served with the risotto is determined by the wine used in the risotto. Most wine-producing regions have local risotto specialties, like risotto al soave (made with white wine in the Veneto) and risotto al barbera (made with red wine in Piemonte).

As you can see, risotto wine can be either white or red. But I think there's one thing it absolutely must be: simple. Don't pour big, oaky Chardonnays or tannic, alcoholic Cabernets with risotto. Light, fruity, young, well-balanced wines work best.

My favorite all-purpose choice is young Soave Classico from a good producer, like Anselmi. But all kinds of simple Italian whites—Galestro, Lacryma Christi, Bianco di Custoza—seem right with most risotti.

FRENCH ONION SOUP

In 1970, I was a theater student on my first trip to Paris. My paucity of francs didn't allow me to sample too many of the French capital's gastronomic glories. But every day, at lunch, I'd make my way to a café on the Boulevard Raspail, where I ordered the same thing over and over again: an incredibly deep, nearly sweet bowlful of cooked onions and broth, which was crowned by a gooey mass of bubbling gold, a thick, perfectly melted patch of Gruyère cheese, a virtual security blanket. There was great French bread on the side, and a *pichet* (small pitcher) of the most wickedly delicious red wine I'd ever tasted. Later on, I discovered it was Beaujolais Nouveau. The cost of lunch? About $3.50, including wine!

Happily, that soup is still part of my life—because it's extremely simple to make and serve at home. There are only a few principles by which you must abide:

1. Use great beef stock. The lifeblood of an onion soup is its stock. If you use water, it's not gonna happen. If you use chicken stock, your soup will be too light (in color and flavor). If you use canned beef stock, you'll end up with a commercial taste.

2. Cook the onions slowly. It may surprise you to learn that I'm not going to force you to use Vidalia onions, or Walla Wallas, in making your onion soup; the French have never heard of a supersweet American onion, and they've been doing just fine for centuries, *merci*. But sweetness is an issue here—because, by cooking your onions extremely slowly in butter in a sauté pan, you caramelize them, bringing out a rich natural sweetness that suffuses the soup. You can use supersweets if you want, or even add a touch of sugar—but make sure you also get the sweetness of slow caramelization.

3. Use last-minute add-ins before finishing the soup. An onion soup is greatly improved in flavor if, just before sealing it with cheese and running it under the broiler, you drop a few last-minute flavorings into the individual crocks. Season with salt and pepper, of course. Along with that, I like to add a little minced onion (this provides another layer of onion flavor) and a little cognac.

4. Use firm, full-flavored croûtes. Individual crocks of onion soup should be layered, just under the cheesy mantle, with slices of toast. It's important, however, that the toasts be very dried out, lest they instantly turn to soggy mush. Additionally, I like to flavor the toasts with garlic so that they add a little something beyond texture.

5. Select great cheese, and layer it properly. One of the world's great melting cheeses is Swiss Gruyère—both for its chewy texture when melted and for its strong, deep, nutty flavor. I love to emphasize its cheesiness by sprinkling it with a little Parmigiano-Reggiano. Finally, the way you apply it to the crock is of supreme importance; I've seen many a chef merely grate the Gruyère and sprinkle it on top. No! It must be sliced and laid over the bowl—otherwise you won't get that tight cap of cheese, that meltdown that occurs not just over the soup but all around the rim of the crock.

FRENCH ONION SOUP GRATINÉE

MAKES 2 SERVINGS

3 tablespoons unsalted butter, plus melted unsalted
 butter to taste
1 tablespoon olive oil
1 1/2 pounds yellow onions, peeled and sliced thin
Large pinch of sugar
2 tablespoons flour
4 cups Homemade Beef Stock (recipe follows)
1/2 cup dry white wine
Cheesecloth bag containing 1 teaspoon dried thyme,
 12 parsley sprigs, 8 peppercorns, and a bay leaf

About 6 slices day-old crusty French baguette (enough
 to cover the surface of each soup bowl), cut 1 inch
 thick
1 large clove garlic, halved
1/2 cup finely minced onion
2 to 3 tablespoons cognac
6 ounces Gruyère, shaved into thin slices
1/3 cup freshly grated Parmigiano-Reggiano

1. Place the butter and olive oil in a large saucepan over moderately low heat. Add the onions, and toss them with the sugar. Cook, covered, stirring occasionally, until soft. Uncover and cook over moderate heat, stirring occasionally, until golden brown, about 30 minutes.

2. Add the flour, and cook, stirring, for 30 to 60 seconds. Add the stock, wine, cheesecloth bag, and salt and pepper to taste, and cook, partially covered, skimming off fat occasionally, for 40 minutes.

3. Preheat the oven to 350 degrees. Arrange the slices of bread on a baking sheet, brush both sides with melted butter, season with salt and pepper, and bake, turning once, for 15 minutes, or until golden and firm. Rub with garlic.

4. Transfer the soup to individual ovenproof crocks, each 4 to 5 inches across the top. Stir the minced onion and cognac into each crock, dividing evenly. Cover the soup with bread slices, fitting 3 slices into each crock so they cover as much of the surface as possible. Lay the slices of Gruyère over each crock, letting the cheese hang 1 inch over the sides of the crocks. Sprinkle with Parmigiano-Reggiano, and drizzle with melted butter. Bake for 15 minutes, until the cheese has melted.

5. Run the crocks under a preheated broiler until the cheese is bubbling and lightly browned. Serve immediately.

HOMEMADE BEEF STOCK

A rich homemade beef stock is crucial to the success of this dish. Here's how to make one.

MAKES JUST UNDER 2 QUARTS

3 pounds meaty beef bones, including bones with
 marrow
2 carrots (3/4 cup), peeled and coarsely chopped
1 large onion (1 cup), peeled and coarsely chopped
1 1/2 tablespoons olive oil
1 leek, coarsely chopped
2 celery stalks, coarsely chopped

4 tomatoes, quartered
6 cloves garlic, peeled and crushed
1/4 cup tomato paste
1/2 cup fresh parsley, chopped
5 sprigs fresh thyme
4 bay leaves
1/2 cup red wine

1. Preheat the oven to 450 degrees.

2. Put the bones in a large, heavy roasting pan with the carrots and onion. Drizzle the oil over the bones. Put in the oven, and roast for 15 minutes.

3. Remove the pan, and add the leeks, celery, tomatoes, and garlic. Spread the tomato paste with a pastry brush over the bones. Roast for 30 more minutes, until the bones are brown and the vegetables are soft.

4. Remove the bones and vegetables, and place them in a large stockpot. Add the fresh herbs and bay leaves.

Cover with 2 inches of water, and season to taste with salt and pepper.

5. Deglaze the roasting pan over high heat with the red wine, scraping up all the browned bits on the bottom. Add the wine to the pot.

6. Simmer the liquid, partially covered, for 4 hours. Do not let it boil.

7. Strain the stock, and cool it in a bowl in an ice bath. Refrigerate or freeze the stock.

Criteria for Quality

- *Is the broth rich and multidimensional in flavor?*
- *Does it have the telltale sweetness of caramelization?*
- *Does it have good compensating acidity (from the wine)?*
- *Are there plenty of burnished onions floating around?*
- *Is there toast on top? Is it firmer than soggy mush? (it should be)*
- *Does the cheese have lots of flavor? Is it chewy? Does it drape over the sides of the crock? (the answers to all of these questions should be yes)*
- *Does the soup seem like more than a bowl of soup—something like a whole meal, perhaps?*

When

Following the circumstances of my original encounter with French onion soup, I like to serve this dish for lunch—when all that's needed to round out the meal is a good baguette and a glass of red wine. You can add a green salad as well, if you wish.

I would, however, also consider a slightly smaller bowl of soup as a good early-course choice in a French-bistro type of meal. Give your guests some oysters, or a frisée salad, hit them with the onion soup as an in-betweener, then go on to a main course that's not too saucy (roast chicken or a chunk of grilled steak would be ideal).

Last, of course, there's the late-night thing. I've always been a sucker for after-midnight goodies—and, if you happen to have the stock lying around, it won't take you too long to rustle up the most satisfying post-theater supper you've ever supped.

In Your Glass

Cheese goes especially well with white wine, and one of those magical French whites that seem to be rich and light at the same moment is a lovely onion soup mate. Alsatian Pinot Blanc is perfect, perhaps the fine one made by Ostertag; don't chill it too much.

Of course, I'll never be able to think of French onion soup without simultaneously thinking of Beaujolais; this is still my number-one choice. But don't get fancy for this match with any of those single-village Beaujolais. Stick to a simple Beaujolais, or Beaujolais Nouveau, from the most recent vintage, chilled in the refrigerator for about 15 minutes.

THE FIRST TIME I SAW PARIS

I woke up one January morning, in the first week of the 1970s, at a dingy bed-and-breakfast in London. I'd been there for a week, studying theater with a group from my college, and with my Anglo-Francophile theater professor, Atlee Sproul. The theater in London had been great; the food dreary. I knew we were going to France that day, but—since French food to me for most of my life had meant ersatz crepes at bad restaurants in New York—I wasn't on gastronomic alert.

I woke up that foggy getaway day in London, a Saturday, thinking that it would not be too different from all the other days of my life. Oh, it was a little more than usually exciting, I guess, hurtling on a bus through the misty English countryside towards Dover, and boarding a hovercraft, which whisked us over the English Channel. Soon, however, I was deep asleep on another bus, this one French.

I woke up in Paris at about 4:00 P.M., when the bus stopped in front of our quarters on the Left Bank, not far from the Sorbonne. This was no palace. The great neo-Gothic architecture of rural Normandy had yielded to the neo-Dormitory style of our lodgings. I was groggy. I was home-sick. I was mildly depressed. Furthermore, the concierge made no effort to understand me.

Then it started to happen. The first tremor occurred at about 5:00 P.M., when a friend stopped by my room and asked if I wanted to take a walk; he'd heard about some shops near our hotel, though he wasn't sure what they were. I was willing, and we strolled into the night, darkening, towards the Rue Mouffetard.

I can't begin to describe adequately what happened to me as we turned the corner onto that street. Suddenly, without any warning, sprawling before me, in the unnatural, intoxicating mildness of a fifty-five-degree January night, was an open-air market in full swing—the first time I had ever laid eyes on such a thing.

The first thing that hit me, aside from the sheer mass of humanity, was the quality of light. It was fully evening now, but the dazzlingly bright street was awash in a theatrical glow, something you might see in the frenetic crowd scenes in Act 2 of La Bohème. *There was a glamour to it, a festiveness; the light seemed to celebrate as well as illuminate. It was a revelatory light also, showing with almost unnatural clarity the colors worn by the Saturday night shoppers who filled the old street. Encouraged by this light, I fantasized that I'd stepped into another world, in another time; since the Rue Mouffetard street market has always had a strong Greek dimension, I felt as if the whole of the sunny Mediterranean was opening up for me, as well as the heart of historic Paris. I was giddy, light-headed, and dizzily time-traveling through Homer's Trojan War as well as Victor Hugo's Notre-Dame.*

Then the sounds reached my ears. Dogs, vendors, shoppers, and vociferous hagglers all blended in laughter, animated discussion, and the occasional cry of delight.

But all of this was merely prologue to the food. My friend and I barely spoke as we moved, wide-eyed, from one gorgeous display to the next. The produce stalls held the most beautiful specimens of fruits and vegetables that I'd ever seen. Everywhere I saw fruits and vegetables that I didn't know. Fish stalls were full of huge crates of shellfish, with hues and shapes that were completely new to me. Butcher stands, right on the spot, showed me a whole new way of thinking about meat: what you buy comes from animals, they seemed to be saying, so you should see it in its full zoological context. The reality of skinned, hanging rabbits, and perfectly intact sheep's heads, and piles of untrimmed pigs' feet, and gooey collections of innards, was as far from Waldbaum's sanitized, plastic-wrapped cuts of what was once living as a guy could get. Though initially a little alarmed by these sights, I soon found that my stronger emotion was fascination with the culinary frankness of the French.

But it didn't stop there—for our noses were then assaulted by something unfamiliar, something rich, and ripe, and earthy, and just a little naughty. We were approaching a cheese shop, which held an assortment that, as powerfully as it worked on the nose, worked even more powerfully on the eyes. Here were flat disks, fat rounds, huge wheels, towering pyramids, plump squares, little buttons, thick cylinders of cheese. Here were whites, yellows, ivories, greens, blacks, browns, and grays—the outer colors of cheeses. Here were the collected milks of goats, sheep, and cows, turned into a staggering array of shapes, sizes, colors, smells. Or maybe it was the charcuterie that did it—the dizzying cornucopia of hams, dried sausages, and pâtés that I saw in the next shop. There were scores of each, and each one looked better than the one before it.

Finally, we couldn't take it anymore. We were starving. We bought an immoderate amount of charcuterie and cheese (who could choose just a few things?), then stumbled into a boulangerie. Oh God, no! There was more! The whole French world of bread to explore and understand! We started off with a simple baguette, baked a few hours before and costing the equivalent of a few pennies. Were we done? No—a wine shop was just around the corner! We reached, by instinct, I'm sure, for the Beaujolais—a perfect beginner's red wine, a silly, simple party in a bottle, with straightforward strawberry fruit and nary a lick of astringency to slow you down. And, as if all that weren't enough, one last shop attracted us with its lights on the way home. . . . It was a patisserie. It was happening all over again! Another set of new and dazzling culinary stimuli, another discipline to conquer! The rows of little tarts, and babas, and puff pastries, and Dieu knows what else, were glistening like jewels; we were mentally exhausted at this point, but couldn't leave without scooping up a goodie . . . well, maybe just a small boxful of goodies.

You know my appetite. Can you imagine how the magic of that early Paris evening washed over me? I felt that I'd reached some time-space-food warp in the deep stretches of the universe, had been sucked into it with tremendous force—and was, of course, praying that I'd never get out. Over our incredible feast in the hotel room—purities of taste, subtleties of texture, levels of freshness that I'd never experienced before—I more or less intuited that something was born on this evening, and something died. As we opened the second bottle of Beaujolais, I solemnly vowed to dwell among the living.

The excitement never stopped on that trip. Every day, after a meeting in the morning to discuss the play we'd seen the night before, Atlee would announce which great French restaurant he was attending that evening and would issue an open invitation to anyone willing to share the check. It was very kind of him to request our company—but I guess I felt a little guilty about going through my dad's allowance more quickly than I had to, especially when I was enjoying such great food for mere centimes.

One morning, however, Atlee told us that before that evening's performance of Molière's L'Avare (The Miser) *at the Comédie-Française, he would be going to a relatively inexpensive bistro right near the theater. I was jumping out of my skin with culinary curiosity, and the invitation proved irresistible.*

It was a simple, lovely restaurant, with an utterly bewitching rusticity: the French equivalent of checkered-tablecloth, wax-encrusted Chianti-bottle dining. The patron *seemed to know Atlee and treated our group of six with obvious warmth, a palpable delight in sharing his food. The gaiety was not impeded by the sudden appearance on the table of—guess what—a bottle of Beaujolais. It was years later that I realized my first trip to Paris had taken place less than two months after the release of the 1969 Beaujolais Nouveau, one of the greatest vintages ever in all of Burgundy. Certainly what was on the table that night seemed finer than any Beaujolais I'd ever tasted before.*

Atlee suggested that we start with snails—something I'd heard about but never tried. I'd seen them at neighboring tables, though, and the garlic-butter-drenched nuggets being extracted from the snail shells seemed rather small. So, when everyone ordered a half-dozen snails, I spoke up in my best high school French and said, "Pour moi, douze." The owner smiled at my order of a dozen. "Vous aimez les escargots?" he asked. Did I like snails? I didn't quite know how to say, "I've never really tasted any, I'm just a knee-jerk glutton"—so I simply replied, "Oui." And ooh la la, they were marvelous little critters—plump, earthy, chewy, drenched in buttery herbs and garlic, which got soaked up by our baguettes working overtime.

On to the coq au vin—a scented platter of chicken that really tasted like chicken (a new one on me), sweet little onions, earthy mushrooms, and a purply wine sauce that was undoubtedly made with . . . well, you know what. Speaking of which, it was the third bottle of Beaujolais the owner was opening when he ran into a little cork-extraction problem. Slightly embarrassed, he said, "C'est difficile à ouvrir," while he was struggling—"It's difficult to open." Riding the wave of the first two bottles, feeling the bonhomie of the moment, and willing to fall resoundingly on my linguistic face, I essayed my first joke in French: "Oui, mais il n'est pas difficile à boire." Did I get the syntax right? Did I say something like "I'm difficult when I drink a lot," rather than what I intended to say—"Yes, but it's not difficult to drink"? The French are reputedly prickly about tiny errors; was he going to snub me, shoo me out of the restaurant, take away my passport? None of the above, thank God. Instead, he broke into a profound laugh from his belly, just as he popped the cork and, to the accompaniment of winy laughter from Atlee and the others, poured the purple juice into my glass so rapidly it almost spilled. I'd always heard about the great good fellowship of the French table, but here I was, right in the heart of Paris, my head swimming, in the middle of an honest-to-God Gallic food fest.

But we had a play to catch. So plates were cleared, cheese was skipped, and the apple tart was presented—a warm, buttery, tender thing that hit the table like a force of nature; somehow, it put the whole meal in perspective. I don't know if I'd ever before sat through a tripartite progression like this one: a meal that just felt right, felt practically ordained, felt impossible to change.

I guess it was about ten minutes into the play when I realized that, on this night, Molière at the Comédie-Française might as well have been Leave It to Beaver *in my living room. Couplets? Plot development? Actors? All I could think about were escargots, chickens, and apple tarts. Have you ever replayed something in your head, over and over again, and gotten so excited about it that you just couldn't sit still? This was my fate, on my first visit to the Comédie-Française—and I hope I didn't offend the people in my row too deeply when I stood up and walked past them towards the aisle for some breathing room.*

For the next few hours, I paced the corridors and lobbies, thinking through every moment of that culinary masterpiece. Oh, I peeked in every once in a while, to see how Harpagon was doing. But I wasn't truly interested. I was bursting with the joy of that meal, and didn't want to have it squelched just then by the straitjacket of a seat in the theater. But I loved the theater! This was why I was in Europe! This was going to be my life! I was sober enough now to see the conflict in symbolic terms; I knew I was standing at a crossroads and, though my life would be able to accommodate both loves in one fashion or other, right there, at that temple of European theater, I could see that someday, somehow, my true love would gain the upper hand.

I realized in France, on this, my first trip abroad, that even in the best of culinary situations, you simply cannot get a feel for the cuisine of a country unless you go there. Some cuisines transplant relatively well; some don't. French cuisine doesn't—because it's so vitally dependent on the quality of its raw material. Someone in New York could have made that pre-Molière meal for me—but without the fresh Burgundian snails, the fresh Normandy butter, the light-touch baguettes, the essence-of-poultry chicken, the French apples, it just wouldn't have been the same. Even Beaujolais Nouveau tastes fresher in France (I love watching cases of wine being carried off of trucks and into restaurants every morning in Paris; it's just another fresh agricultural product, like cheese, or lettuce, or flour, being hauled down from the hills into the big city).

But there's another principle at play. Dining on someone else's national cuisine in New York is essentially dining out of context. When you're in the country itself, you're right in the stew pot. Every sensation you experience—the look of the room, the conversation of the people around you, the attitudes of your servers—is an integral part of the true dining experience. This is especially so in countries that make a special place for food in their cultures. To eat French food without observing the centrality of the food in everyday life is really not to eat it at all.

I have a little theory about France. People who work in the French food industry could be a lot richer if they produced food of lower quality and charged more for it—just as people do in other countries, all over the world. But I think the French mind doesn't work this way. Jacques the cheese maker says to himself, "I could make an extra 20,000 francs a year by buying lower-quality milk. But if I did that—and if everyone did the same—what would I spend my extra 20,000 francs on?" It's a version of Kant's moral principle; let's call it the Gastronomic Categorical Imperative. It's a social contract, or a national conspiracy, to ensure that France will always be France. The conspiracy gets rocked now and again, but, thirty years after I first stumbled upon food in France, I can happily report that France is still France. The conspiracy goes on.

CATALAN LOBSTER AND CHICKEN SOUP

One trip to Spain, and you'll learn a culinary lesson that'll last a lifetime: despite popular belief in America, the food of Spain is very different from the food of Mexico. So when you think Spanish food, don't think "former Spanish holdings in the New World"; instead, think "classic European wine country." For the truth is that the food of Spain is much more like the food of France than it's like the food of Mexico.

One of the best places in Spain to learn this lesson, of course, is in the northeast corner of the country, the part closest to France. There you'll find a number of intriguing cuisines that challenge French food for complexity and refinement.

One of the best is Catalan cuisine, from the province of Catalonia, which surrounds and includes the great city of Barcelona. It's an archaic cuisine, probably tracing its roots to the Romans who occupied the area, but showing much influence from the hordes of variegated invaders who, over many centuries, passed through this corridor that lies between the Iberian Peninsula and the rest of Europe.

One of the Catalan dishes that seems most archaic, in many ways, is a main course that features pieces of lobster and chicken held together by a ground-nut sauce. In Catalan, it's called *mar i muntanya* (logically enough, "sea and mountain"). I love the flavors of this dish—but I'm not so crazy about the surf-and-turf aspect, which seems as much tacky 1950s as it does historic 1550s.

Oh, there is no dearth of shellfish-and-poultry pairings in very old European cuisine; the French did it to ennoble humble chicken dishes, just as the Catalans ennobled their commonplace bounty of seafood by adding pieces of relatively scarce chicken. Today, however—with a lobster tail resting on one side of the plate and a chicken breast reposing on the other—I find the juxtaposition ennobling for neither player. And after tasting this dish in Catalonia, and in many Spanish restaurants in the United States, I decided to modify it. In my version, I retain all of the wonderful flavors—but integrate the dish by turning it into a soup.

Catalan Lobster and Chicken Soup

CATALAN LOBSTER AND CHICKEN SOUP

MAKES 4 SERVINGS

1 lobster, about 1 1/4 pounds

6 tablespoons olive oil

1 cup chopped onions

3 chicken breast halves, bone in and skin on, patted dry

1/2 cup dry (Fino) sherry

2 tablespoons Spanish brandy

3 cups fish stock

1 1/2 cups dry white wine

1 cup peeled, seeded, and chopped fresh or canned
    tomatoes

1 bay leaf

1/2 teaspoon dried thyme

1 tablespoon chopped parsley, plus additional for garnish

16 blanched almonds

10 hazelnuts

1 large clove garlic

1 1/2 teaspoons grated unsweetened chocolate

1/8 teaspoon sugar

Pinch of saffron dissolved in 2 to 3 tablespoons
    hot fish stock

2 tablespoons arrowroot, dissolved in 3 to 4
    tablespoons cold water

1. Prepare the lobster: Place the live lobster on its stomach, and drive a sharp knife into the point where the tail meets the head to kill the lobster. Halve crosswise where the tail meets the chest cavity. (Or have the fishmonger do this.) Drain the liquids from both halves into a small bowl. Spoon the tomalley (and coral, if the lobster is female) into another small bowl (tomalley is a dark gray-green mass in the head section or upper tail; coral will appear as a very dark red or black mass). Twist off the claws close to the lobster body, split again at the elbow, and crack each piece with a heavy knife. Discard the head. Split the tail in half lengthwise, and remove the brown intestinal vein. Halve each piece crosswise, keeping the lobster meat in the shell. You will have 8 pieces in all. (If you're squeamish about cutting up a live lobster, lightly steam it before cutting it in pieces.)

2. In a large, heavy saucepan, heat the oil over medium heat. Add the onions, and cook until they are wilted. Turn heat to high, and add the lobster pieces to the saucepan. Sauté, shaking the pan and turning the lobster, until the shells turn bright red (4 to 5 minutes). Remove and reserve the lobster. Add the chicken breasts, skin side down. Cover and cook about 10 minutes, or until just cooked through. Remove and reserve the chicken.

3. When it is cool enough to handle, remove the meat from the lobster and chicken pieces, and return the shells and bones to the saucepan over high heat. Sauté for 3 minutes. Then deglaze the pan with the sherry and brandy, scraping the bottom of the pan to incorporate all the browned bits. Add the fish stock, white wine, reserved lobster liquids, tomatoes, and herbs; bring to a boil, partially cover, and reduce heat to a simmer. Cook for another 30 minutes.

4. Meanwhile, in a food processor, process the nuts to a fine powder. Add the reserved lobster tomalley (and coral), garlic, chocolate, sugar, and saffron. Process until smooth.

5. When the lobster stock is done, strain it into a bowl, discarding the shells and bones. If desired, chill the stock and remove any fat that accumulates on top; reheat before continuing. Transfer the nut mixture to a saucepan, and beat in the hot stock, whisking well to combine. Simmer for 15 minutes, stirring occasionally. For the smoothest texture, strain the soup again into the cleaned saucepan, and return to a simmer. Stir in the arrowroot-and-water mixture in a thin stream, whisking until the soup thickens slightly. Slice the reserved lobster and chicken meat, add it to the soup, and warm for 5 minutes. Serve sprinkled with parsley.

When

After a few light tapas, this would be a great in-between course at a Spanish dinner party. But by upping the quantities of lobster and chicken, you could easily turn it into a main course; serve a salad on the side that features roasted red peppers and green olives, a big hunk of bread, and a glass of Spanish wine.

In Your Glass

One of the things I like to drink with soup—any kind of soup, not necessarily Spanish soup—is dry sherry; its higher alcohol content, which makes it a lot richer, seems to work better with thin liquids like soup. With this dish, it's even better than usual, since the Spanish flavors of this soup meld with the sherry like nobody's business. Just make sure that you select a dry sherry from Spain—labeled either Fino or Manzanilla—and that you serve it very cold, in wineglasses.

Another common soup solution on my table is sparkling wine—the bubbles of which also make a nice contrast with thin soup. Once again, a local answer is at hand—for Spain's top region of sparkling wine production happens to be in Catalonia. If you can find a sparkling wine by Raimat, that's your best choice; failing that, the familiar brands of Codorníu, Freixenet, or Paul Cheneau will do just fine.

Last, one of my favorite flavorful whites in the world also comes from Spain—the white Rioja made by Murrieta. With this soup, don't substitute another white Rioja; only the Murrieta has the flavor to stand up to and the acidity to cut through the rich lobster.

THAI CHICKEN SOUP WITH COCONUT MILK

This fabulous, world-class soup was one of the first Thai dishes I tasted when I stumbled upon Thai cuisine in the early 1970s. I loved the soup immediately . . . perhaps because in one bowl it sums up Thai food, that incredible collision of basic flavors. *Tom kha kai* has the tartness of lime, the sweetness of palm sugar, the saltiness of Thai fish sauce, and the heat of chilies, along with the lemon-oil fragrance of lemongrass, the citrus essence of kaffir limes, the mustardy kick of galanga root, and the soothing creaminess of coconut milk. Plus, it's a damned good chicken soup!

If you use enough of all these ingredients, it's hard to mess up this dish. However, I must report that, after having eaten *tom kha kai* for twenty years in Thai restaurants in America, when I tasted it on my first trip to Thailand, it was a revelation all over again. There, the flavors were unbelievably intense, and the proportions of the varying flavors in the bowls that I tasted were magically right.

The hardest part of making this soup is getting the ingredients—but if you can locate a store in a Chinatown near you that sells Thai groceries, your soup is made. Or, you can find a great mail-order source for these provisions (see page 105).

THAI CHICKEN SOUP WITH COCONUT MILK
(TOM KHA KAI)

And here's the final revelation: after returning from Thailand, I tasted one of the best *tom kha kai*s ever at a restaurant in New York! It was made at the Typhoon Brewery by the great American chef James Chew, who studied cooking in Thailand and has an uncanny feel for the cuisine. Unfortunately, he's no longer at the restaurant—but the following adaptation of his recipe can put his great soup on your table any time you want it.

MAKES 4 SERVINGS

For the broth:

4 cups unsweetened coconut milk

4 cups chicken stock

A 4-inch piece of fresh lemongrass, outer dry leaves removed, sliced very thin on the bias

6 thin slices fresh or frozen galanga root

5 fresh kaffir lime leaves (or 1 tablespoon grated lime rind)

3 Thai bird chilies (or 1 jalapeño), seeded and finely chopped

3 tablespoons Thai fish sauce (nam pla)

1 teaspoon fresh lime juice

2 pinches palm sugar (or light brown sugar)

2 medium chicken legs (2 drumsticks and 2 thighs), boned, skinned, and cut in 1/2-inch dice

3 ounces assorted fresh mushrooms (like oyster, cremini, or shiitake), sliced

For the garnish:

1 tablespoon scallions, chopped

1 tablespoon fresh kaffir lime leaves, in very thin julienne

1/2 teaspoon Thai bird chili (or other hot chili), very finely minced (use at your discretion)

12 cilantro sprigs

1. In a large pot, combine the coconut milk, chicken stock, lemongrass, galanga root, lime leaves, chilies, fish sauce, lime juice, and palm sugar. Bring to a boil, then lower heat. Simmer for 20 minutes.

2. Add the chicken, and simmer for 5 minutes, or until cooked.

3. Add the mushrooms, and simmer for an additional 3 minutes. (The balance of this dish is a subtle thing. You might want to taste it at this point and, if necessary, correct the seasoning with salt, fish sauce, lime juice, and palm sugar.)

4. Ladle the soup into 4 hot bowls, divide the garnish among the bowls, and serve.

Coconut Milk for Thai Food

You have several choices when it comes to procuring coconut milk for Thai dishes. The most authentic method, but the most trouble, is making your own; to do this, you must crack open fresh coconuts, grate the flesh, and steep it in hot water. An easier method is to buy dried, grated coconut—make sure it's not sweetened!—and steep it in hot water or hot milk. However—though I usually go for the most authentic methods, no matter how laborious they are—these days I almost always use coconut milk from a can. There are a number of terrific brands on the market today, and I see no reason not to take advantage of them. Make sure to buy canned coconut milk that hasn't been sweetened—like my favorite canned coconut milk, JFC, imported from Thailand by a company in San Francisco.

Thai Sources

Here are a few sources across the United States that will mail-order Thai ingredients to you:

The Oriental Pantry
423 Great Road
Acton, MA 01720
978-264-4576
800-828-0368

Spice Merchant
P.O. Box 524
Jackson Hole, WY 83001
307-733-7811

Mo Hotta–Mo Betta
P.O. Box 4136
San Luis Obispo, CA 93403
805-544-4051
800-462-3220

Criteria for Quality

- Is the soup intense in flavor? (it should be)
- Is it vibrant with chili heat? (it should be)
- Is there a good proportion of solids floating in it? (there should be)

When

Tom kha kai, like all soups in Thailand, is not served as a separate course—because there are no separate courses in Thailand. Everything is served at once at a Thai dinner. To keep the soup hot throughout the meal, it is traditionally placed over a small fire. This is a lovely way to dine and, if you're so inclined, a lovely way to present Thai food to family and friends.

Of course, you can very easily Westernize it. You might include tom kha kai as the soup course in a multicourse dinner that includes other Thai dishes—or Asian dishes, or fusion dishes. Another possibility is to make the soup a main course—which you can easily do by doubling the amount of chicken in it. Simply serve it with steamed rice and a salad dressed with Thai flavors (see the Basic Thai Salad Dressing on page 54).

In Your Glass

I like bubbles with soup; still, wine can seem texturally redundant next to the liquid in soup. A good but not great sparkling wine, perhaps something from Spain or California, is very good with tom kha kai; the chili heat in the soup would wipe out the finesse of French Champagne.

Of course, in Thailand you would drink Singha, their great beer, with the soup. It's available in the United States, though it doesn't taste nearly as good here as it does there; the slightly bitter, deliciously hoppy backbone of the beer is gone. A new Thai beer in the U.S. market—Bangkok Beer—does come closer to the real Thai taste. The best news, however, is that almost any European-style lager will do. Possibly the most delicious match of all would be with German or Belgian weiss beer, or Weizenbier, or wit beer, or wheat beer.

GUMBO

Sometimes a dish is a perfect expression of its place and culture; such a dish is gumbo, the emblematic soup of New Orleans. The complicated history of Louisiana cooking can be read in a bowl of gumbo, like reading the rings of a tree; in that deep-tasting bowl, you can readily discern the six influences that, in the eighteenth century, merged to form the extraordinary cooking of this part of the world.

The story starts with the native Choctaw Indians, who noticed that a local tree—the *Sassafras albidum*—has a deliciously flavored bark, which the Choctaws used in making "sass tea" (and which was later used in making root beer). They also noticed that the leaves of the tree, when pounded into a powder, function as a thickening agent for soups and sauces.

In the early eighteenth century, the French arrived in Louisiana, bringing with them their penchant for elegant, fastidiously prepared food—a quality that has survived today in the "fancy" restaurants of New Orleans, such as Arnaud's and Galatoire's. Thickening soups and sauces was very important to them, of course; that rich "feel" of French food wouldn't exist without great thickening techniques. Their chief method for thickening was making a roux—a combination of butter and flour that's briefly cooked before liquid is added. But they were intrigued by this Choctaw Indian sassafras leaf and called the powder *filé;* they noticed that *filé* (if cooked too long) makes threads in the soup as it thickens it, so the French verb they named it for means "to make threads" (like *fila*ments).

A little later in the eighteenth century, slaves were brought from Africa to work on the local plantations—but they brought something as well: okra seeds. Believe it not, the plot thickens still further here, for it was discovered that the mucilaginous nature of gumbo pods will also turn a thin broth into a thick one. Okra not only went into this evolving soup called gumbo but gave it its name; the Bantu word for okra is *gombo,* and the Umbundu word for okra is *ochinggombo.* An international sensation was born and christened.

In 1762 France gave up New Orleans and the French Caribbean Islands to Spain—whereupon the Spaniards arrived in Louisiana, bringing a fourth culinary influence to the melting pot. This Spanish influence was manifest in the widespread use of rice and in the growing popularity of combining meat and fish in the same dish (as in the Spanish paella). Many of the Spaniards married people from Louisiana French families, and their children were known as Creoles (from a Spanish verb meaning "to create, to be born"). So that's the original definition of Creole: a light-skinned person born in the New World, whose recent ancestors came from Spain and France. And the Creoles of Louisiana were very strict about this definition.

This became an issue, because some years later French people living in Canada began migrating to Louisiana; they were from Acadia, which today is called Nova Scotia. With their French heritage and New World birth, they assumed they were Creoles. But the Creoles of Louisiana said, "No! You're from Canada! And you don't have Spanish blood! You're Acadians!" . . . which, of course, became Cajuns. And these transplanted Canadians, denied access to Creole society, exerted the fifth culinary influence on local cuisine, a very powerful one. They took up residence in the bayous of southern Louisiana, developing, ultimately, a rustic cuisine that became the "country" equivalent of the more citified "Creole" cuisine. Most important, they brought their Nova Scotian love of lobster and shellfish to the bayous of Louisiana—transferring their crush on northern crustaceans to the local crawfish and shrimp.

One more culinary element rounds out the picture. In the latter part of the eighteenth century, a group of Creoles splintered off to live in the Caribbean. But their stay was not a happy one—for, some years after their arrival, violent slave revolts on the islands of Haiti and Martinique forced them to return to New Orleans. Happily, however, they brought something back with them—a newfound love for the spice of the islands, particularly for hot red pepper. Where would Louisiana food be without Tabasco? Now you know where its chief ingredient came from.

Once you know *all* of this fascinating history, eating a bowl of gumbo is elevated from taking sustenance to taking a history lesson. The spice of the refugee Creoles is there. The Spanish penchant for meat and fish together is there. The Cajun predilection for shellfish is there. And the Choctaw, French, and African ideas about thickening are most certainly there.

Thickening, in fact, is at the heart of what you'd have to call the Gumbo Controversy. Gumbo is one of those classic dishes that are interpreted liberally every day; everyone accepts that anything goes: crawfish gumbo, sausage gumbo, chicken gumbo, vegetarian gumbo (Gumbo Z'Herbes), ad infinitum. But gumbo connoisseurs do argue about the proper thickening. Here are the leading schools of thickening thought.

Thickening by Roux. Traditionally, all gumbos start with a roux base. Now, Louisiana roux has evolved beyond French roux: butter is rarely used in Louisiana (they use oil instead), and, whereas the French cook roux for about two minutes, the Louisianans may cook it for half an hour! The longer you cook it, the browner it gets, the more of a flavor it adds to the dish it will thicken—but the more diminished it is in thickening power! So the first big gumbo question is: How long do you cook your roux? It is traditional in gumbos that contain seafood (like the following one) to cook the roux for a long time, until it becomes very dark and loses much of its power to thicken the gumbo; Louisianans like seafood gumbos that are a little thinner than most gumbos.

There's more controversy today, however—because some Louisiana chefs don't even use roux anymore, claiming that the addition of flour is unnecessary! They depend on the other thickeners instead.

Thickening by Okra. Though gumbo is named for okra, a modern gumbo does not necessarily have okra in it. Many do, however. And when okra gets put in the pot—especially if the okra has been cut—it spills its mucilaginous contents into the soup, making it delightfully gummy. I love everything about okra—its taste *and* its texture.

Thickening by *Filé* Powder. It is not necessary to use *filé,* so, if you can't find it, by all means make a delicious gumbo anyway. But *filé* does add a nice textural touch to a gumbo. Remember: if you use it, add it at the very last minute—otherwise, it turns into threads and makes the soup unpleasantly gummy.

Now here are the permutations of thickening you usually see these days:

- *filé* alone
- okra alone
- *filé* and roux
- okra and roux

Cajun chefs tell you never to use *filé* and okra together; they say doing so thickens the soup too much. Well, I've ignored their advice on occasion—and have always been happy with the results.

Shrimp and Andouille Gumbo with Oysters

In this version of gumbo—one of my favorite ones—I've chosen to use long-cooked roux and okra as thickeners. I also use the spicy Cajun sausage called andouille along with two kinds of shellfish. Though I'm not partial to cooked oysters, I often think of them when I think about Cajun food—the best "cooked-oyster cuisine" in the world. If you want to serve your gumbo in the authentic manner, fill a small teacup with hot white rice, then invert the cup in the center of a wide soup bowl. You'll have a small dome of rice—around which you ladle the gumbo.

MAKES 6 TO 8 FIRST-COURSE SERVINGS

3/4 cup vegetable oil

3/4 cup flour

2 cups chopped onions

2 cups chopped green bell peppers

2 cups chopped celery

4 cups sliced okra (about 1 1/2 pounds cut into 1/3-inch chunks)

1 tablespoon minced garlic

2 bay leaves

1/2 teaspoon cayenne, or more to taste

1 teaspoon black pepper

1/2 teaspoon dried thyme

1/4 teaspoon dried oregano

6 cups shrimp stock (recipe follows)

1 cup peeled, chopped tomatoes

1 pound andouille sausage, cut into 1/2-inch chunks

2 pounds medium shrimp, peeled and deveined, shells reserved for stock

24 raw oysters, shucked

1. In a deep, heavy skillet, heat the oil over high heat until it is just smoking. Add the flour, whisking constantly until it is incorporated. Turn heat down to medium-low, and continue to cook, whisking, until the roux darkens to a rich, deep, nutty color, about 20 minutes.

2. Immediately add the onions, green peppers, and celery, and cook, stirring, for 3 minutes. Add 3 cups of the okra, the garlic, bay leaves, cayenne, black pepper, thyme, and oregano.

3. Meanwhile, in a large Dutch oven or heavy soup pot, bring the stock to a vigorous boil. Spoon the stock a little at a time into the hot roux mixture, stirring well after each addition until it is dissolved and the liquid has thickened. Reduce heat to a simmer, and add the tomatoes and andouille. Simmer for 15 minutes, stirring frequently.

4. Add the remaining 1 cup okra, and simmer for 10 minutes more.

5. Add the shrimp, and simmer for 3 minutes, or until just cooked through.

6. Add more stock or water for a thinner gumbo, if desired. Just before serving, add the oysters; cook them for 1 minute or less, just until their edges start to curl. Season to taste with salt and pepper, and serve immediately.

NOTE: If you want, you can dust the oysters with some kind of Cajun spice blend just before adding them to the gumbo. This'll kick it up a notch.

SHRIMP STOCK

MAKES 8 CUPS STOCK

2 tablespoons vegetable oil

Shells from 2 pounds medium shrimp

1 onion, chopped

2 celery stalks, chopped

4 bay leaves

1/2 teaspoon dried basil

1/2 teaspoon dried thyme

1 teaspoon dried oregano

1. Place the oil in a large, heavy pot over high heat. Add the shrimp shells, and cook, stirring, until the shells have gotten crispy-brown (about 5 minutes).

2. Add the rest of the ingredients, and cover with 2 quarts of water. Bring to a boil over high heat. Reduce heat to low, and simmer for 40 minutes.

3. Allow the stock to cool, then strain.

Criteria for Quality

- *Is the gumbo properly thickened? (I like it not too thin, not gummy-thick)*
- *Is it brimming with chunks of various things? (I like a gumbo that's practically a stew)*
- *Have main ingredients been chosen that blend well in flavor?*
- *Is there an underlying taste of roux? (the antiroux forces be damned; I like gumbo that tastes of roux!)*

When

Gumbo makes a great soup course in a New Orleans–style meal, of course. But a hearty gumbo can also be a meal in itself—needing only some bread and salad to round things out.

In Your Glass

You could find wines that will go well with gumbo—but it's hard to generalize about wine and gumbo since the main ingredients you've chosen for your gumbo, and the level of spice, will all make a difference in the wine requirements.

Let's simplify matters. When I'm in New Orleans, I drink beer with gumbo. A light, crisp, clean one—like Rolling Rock or Corona—will always go just fine. If you want to step up in body, flavor, and authenticity, try to find a terrific Louisiana-brewed beer called Abita Amber.

I found New Orleans embarrassingly late in life. I must confess another sin as well: it's a place I thought I had gastronomically figured out before I arrived. One reason I thought I knew something about Cajun food was that I'd had a lot of it around the country in the late 1980s; Cajun was hot then, and the bombardment was coming from all sides. At one point, the only things not being "blackened" in trendy restaurants were soup and the reputations of top Cajun chefs.

But I didn't quite get it. The cynic in me arose, and I believed that the Cajun craze was manufactured by marketers. Oh, the food was fine—but not fine enough, in my opinion, to fuel this furor. Any cuisine that depends on garlic powder and onion powder as major seasonings, I reasoned, can't be considered world class.

And then I hit New Orleans. And then I knew I was wrong. I wasn't wrong about the versions of Cajun cuisine being made around the country. But this is a cuisine that has to be tasted on its home turf to be understood. Why? Because this part of Louisiana is the only section of America I've ever been to that feels like those sections of France, or Italy, or Spain, where there are fabulous, thriving, gastronomic traditions, where local specialties hit you at every turn, where the whole thing is kept alive by the absolute fever of the local people for their local food.

But when you go to New Orleans, you have to do it right in order to get this impression. There are many restaurants there, and I quickly learned which are the best to patronize: the funky little places that serve the cheapest, simplest, most authentic Cajun cuisine. Raw oysters at the Acme Oyster House, with a squirt of green Tabasco. Fried oysters anywhere, alone or in po'boys. Fried soft-shell crabs, the best I've ever tasted, particularly at the mind-bendingly transcendent dive called Uglesich's (where I sat in a state of blissed-out gastronomic shock with Emeril Lagasse and Curtis Aikens, who seemed to be enjoying themselves as well). Crawfish, coated with spices, at a hundred dirty bars (eat 'em warm, not hot, for more flavor). Gumbo everywhere but the fancy places. Sandwiches with roast beef "debris" (the tasty bits of meat in the pan) at Mother's. Red beans and rice with ham hocks on Mondays, using up the leftovers from Sunday ham dinner. Mufulettas, those great meat-and-olive sandwiches, at the Central Grocery, where they were born. And, of course, the commercialized but still wonderful beignets, unholy little doughnuts, at the Café du Monde, with a blast of chicory-flavored coffee on the side.

What can you learn from New Orleans, home to such an untransportable cuisine—other than which places you'll have to go back to on your next visit? Plenty. Because after I visited Louisiana, my Cajun cooking at home improved dramatically. There's a spirit that rolls through this food—and you can't begin to capture it unless you've been at the fount.

QUESADILLAS

The simple quesadilla—the grilled cheese sandwich of Mexico—is actually a very complicated subject. On its home turf, you're likely to see it made with either corn tortillas or flour tortillas, with a bewildering range of indigenous melting cheeses, and with a wide variety of fillings. Furthermore, it may be cooked in deep oil, on a griddle, or in the oven—and it may be constructed in one layer or multiple layers.

Here in the States, it has gotten both more and less complicated. On the simple side, we gringos usually use flour tortillas only, usually melt only Monterey Jack, almost always make only one layer, and almost never put these things (or anything, anymore) in deep oil. But then we go and do to quesadillas what Wolfgang Puck did to pizzas: we complicate the subject endlessly by adding all kinds of "upscale," "New Wave," "multi-culti" ingredients, from smoked salmon to kiwis.

I'm happy to say that I have reached quesadilla peace, in my own mind. I've never had a quesadilla that I enjoy more than the very simple ones I make at home, using the best possible ingredients. They are quick and easy, and have truly become for me the grilled cheese sandwiches of the nineties.

Here are my basic choices:

I use flour tortillas. Though I love the taste of fresh corn tortillas—made from masa and widely used in Mexico for quesadillas—good ones are almost impossible to find across America. Moreover, the corn tortillas you do find in markets, made weeks or months ago from masa harina, are almost always leathery and dry. This texture used to be standard for supermarket flour tortillas as well . . . but no more. Pretty good ones are now available in many stores, and they have become my tortilla of choice for this quick-to-make, everyday snack.

I'm not fanatic about the "right" cheese. In Mexico, you're likely to find chihuahua, asadero, or quesillo cheese used in quesadillas; in our own West and Southwest, Monterey Jack and brick cheese are often used. I say: virtually any melting cheese will be fine as a quesadilla filler. I've often used mozzarella and mild cheddar, and am especially partial to the texture of Danish fontina. I've even used, with good results, the supermarket packages (in the refrigerated case) of preshredded cheese, sometimes made from a blend of melting cheeses. Some people like to blend in more strongly flavored melting cheeses, such as Swiss Gruyère; I've even seen full-flavored Parmigiano-Reggiano blended with other cheeses for quesadillas. These stronger cheeses will yield less Mexican-tasting results, but the quesadillas will be yummy nevertheless, and I use them all the time.

I always use a frying pan or a griddle. Sure, you can skip a little fat by steaming your quesadillas or baking them in the oven . . . but would you do that to your grilled cheese sandwiches? I love the flavor that quesadillas pick up from a hot pan with butter or lard—and the method is easy as pie (cooking takes about 4 minutes from turning the gas on to turning the quesadilla out).

My principle for filling quesadillas is: the simpler, the better. With good tortillas, good cheese, and good technique, why would you want anything more? But if you want something more—and, I must confess, sometimes I do vary a bit from the basic formula—don't get too baroque. Stick to Mexican themes (e.g., avoid the smoked salmon), and your quesadillas will be magnificent.

BASIC CHEESE QUESADILLA

So simple . . . and so damned good.

MAKES 2 QUESADILLAS OR 12 WEDGES (A GOOD SNACK FOR 6 PEOPLE)

4 wide flour tortillas (about 7 to 9 inches in diameter)
1/2 pound melting cheese, grated

2 tablespoons fat (see page 114)

1. Lay 2 of the tortillas out on a counter, browner side down. Divide the cheese between the tortillas, spreading it as evenly as possible, right up to the outer edges of the tortillas. Top each with a second tortilla, and press the top tortillas down lightly. Sprinkle one side of each quesadilla lightly with a few drops of water, flip the quesadillas over with a wide spatula, and sprinkle the other sides with water.

2. Choose a heavy, no-stick skillet that's larger than the diameter of the tortillas. Over medium-high heat, add 1 tablespoon of fat. When it is hot, carefully add 1 quesadilla to the pan. Cook for about 1 minute, pressing down on the quesadilla with your spatula to melt the cheese as quickly as possible. Check to make sure the bottom is lightly browned, then flip the quesadilla over in the pan. Cook, pressing, for another minute or so, or until the second side is also lightly browned and the cheese has melted completely.

3. Remove the quesadilla from the pan, and, when it has cooled slightly, cut it into 6 wedges and serve. Meanwhile, spill the remaining fat out of the pan, add another tablespoon of fat, and cook the second quesadilla in exactly the same fashion.

NOTE: A little steamed spinach on top of the cheese inside the quesadilla—something I tasted in San Antonio—is a surprisingly delicious variation.

POBLANO-ONION QUESADILLAS WITH CHORIZOS AND CILANTRO

These are about as baroque as I like to get with quesadillas. Note, however, that all of the ingredients are very Mexican—and the taste of the finished product is as well. These quesadillas are so rich and hearty that you might want to consider serving them as a main course, along with a bevy of other Mexican specialties (salsa, rice, beans, et cetera).

MAKES 2 QUESADILLAS, OR 12 WEDGES (A GOOD SNACK FOR 6 PEOPLE OR A MAIN COURSE FOR 2 PEOPLE)

4 tablespoons fat (see page 114)
1 pound onions, peeled and thinly sliced
1/4 pound ground Mexican-style chorizo
1 teaspoon dried oregano, preferably Mexican

1/2 pound poblano chilies
1/2 pound melting cheese, grated
1/2 cup minced cilantro leaves
4 wide flour tortillas (about 7 to 9 inches in diameter)

1. Place 2 tablespoons of the fat in a heavy sauté pan over medium heat. Add the onions, and cook until they are almost tender and lightly browned, about 15 minutes. Push the onions to one side of the pan, and sauté the chorizo. Remove the chorizo when it has warmed through (about 5 minutes), and mix the onions with the orange fat that the chorizo has left behind. Mix in the dried oregano. Cook the onions for another 5 minutes, then remove them from the pan.

2. While the onions are cooking, place the poblanos over an open fire (either on a grill or on top of your range). Cook, turning frequently with tongs, until the poblanos are charred on all sides (about 10 minutes). Place the charred poblanos in a paper bag. After 15 minutes, remove the charred skins from the poblanos. Cut the poblanos open, discard the stems and seeds, and cut the poblanos into strips about ⅓ inch wide.

3. Mix together the onions, poblanos, cheese, and cilantro leaves. Work the mixture with your hands until the ingredients are evenly distributed throughout.

4. Lay 2 of the tortillas out on a counter, browner side down. Place ¼ of the cheese-onion-poblano-cilantro mixture on each tortilla, spreading it as evenly as possible, right up to the outer edges of the tortillas. Top each with half of the ground chorizo. Then top the chorizo with the remaining cheese-onion-poblano-cilantro mixture—once again spreading it as evenly as possible, right up to the outer edges of the tortillas. Top each with a second tortilla, and press the top tortillas down lightly. Sprinkle one side of each quesadilla lightly with a few drops of water, flip the quesadillas over with a wide spatula, and sprinkle the other sides with water.

5. Choose a heavy, no-stick skillet that's larger than the diameter of the tortillas. Over medium-high heat, add 1 tablespoon of fat. When it is hot, carefully add 1 quesadilla to the pan. Cook for about 1 minute, pressing down on the quesadilla with your spatula to melt the cheese as quickly as possible. Check to make sure the bottom is lightly browned, then flip the quesadilla over in the pan. Cook, pressing, for another minute or so, or until the second side is also lightly browned and the cheese has melted completely.

6. Remove the quesadilla from the pan, and, when it has cooled slightly, cut it into 6 wedges and serve. Meanwhile, spill the remaining fat out of the pan, add another tablespoon of fat, and cook the second quesadilla in exactly the same fashion.

Special Quesadilla Techniques

There are two special challenges in cooking quesadillas in a skillet or on a griddle.

First of all, you want the finished texture of the outside to be slightly crisp from the heat, but the tortillas should retain some of their softness. My solution is to sprinkle a little water on each side of the quesadilla before you put it in the pan; this prevents extreme crisping and leads to a lovely crisp-tender texture.

Second, you must have a good feel for heat when cooking quesadillas. If the pan is too hot, the outsides of the quesadillas will burn. If it's too cool, the cheese won't melt quickly enough, and the outsides of the quesadillas will turn crunchy by the time the cheese melts. I use medium-high heat and always press on the quesadilla with the spatula to speed up the melting of the cheese. I check after a minute or two and, if I see the cheese melting nicely, I flip the quesadilla over for another minute or two.

As soon as the cheese is fully melted, the quesadilla is ready.

By the way, I once discovered by accident a little trick that makes quesadillas taste even better. If, after your quesadilla is in the pan, you sprinkle just a little bit of cheese on the edge of it, all around the circle, the finished quesadilla ends up with a lovely, brown, cheesy, slightly crunchy rim.

Which Fat?

To my taste, butter and lard both have strong points in making quesadillas.

The flavor of butter interacts with the flavor of cheese to create a palate-caressing, wonderfully heartwarming taste. The downside is that using butter leads to a quesadilla that's crisper and browner on the outside.

The flavor of lard in quesadillas is earthier and seems more "Mexican." Additionally, it's easier to achieve a crisp-tender texture on the outside of the quesadillas if you use lard.

I see no advantages whatsoever in using vegetable oil.

TOMATILLO SALSA

Quesadilla wedges are delicious by themselves—but if you're passing them around on platters at a dinner party, they can be dressed up by placing a tablespoon or so of salsa on each wedge. This is my favorite salsa for quesadillas.

MAKES ENOUGH FOR 2 QUESADILLAS, OR 12 WEDGES (A GOOD SNACK FOR 6 PEOPLE)

8 medium tomatillos

2 tablespoons red onion, finely chopped

2 tablespoons cilantro, minced

2 tablespoons lime juice

1 teaspoon finely minced jalapeño pepper,
   or more to taste

1 1/2 teaspoons finely minced fresh red chili,
   or more to taste

2 teaspoons rice wine vinegar

1 teaspoon sugar

1 teaspoon lime zest, grated

1. Husk and rinse the tomatillos, then chop them finely.

2. Mix the tomatillos in a bowl with the rest of the ingredients. Serve the salsa immediately, before it starts to get watery.

Criteria for Quality

- *Is the quesadilla crisp-tender on the outside?*
- *Is it lightly flavored with fat—but not overly saturated with it?*
- *Has the cheese fully melted and stayed within the quesadilla?*
- *If there are additional fillings, do they seem appropriate (i.e., do they complement the cheese and seem reasonably Mexican)?*
- *Is the quesadilla served hot?*
- *If you are using flour tortillas, do the tortillas seem light and flaky?*

When

I love quesadillas cut into 6 wedges each and served as pass-around starters for a Mexican meal.

They also make a terrific side dish at lunch, served with a steaming bowl of Mexican soup (made with beans, perhaps).

Or wedges of quesadillas—particularly hearty ones, such as the Poblano-Onion Quesadillas with Chorizos and Cilantro—can be served alongside other Mexican dishes (salsas, beans, rice, et cetera) as the main component of a buffetlike meal.

In Your Glass

There's little hesitation for me here: the flavor of tequila is almost mystical with Mexican food, and my drink of choice with quesadillas is a margarita. I like mine made with good tequila (see page 312) and served on the rocks (no salt on the rim, please, when serving margaritas with food).

QUICHE

Whoever said real men don't eat quiche either knew very little about men or knew very little about quiche. Or both. I have witnessed, with my very own eyes, real men eating quiche. How real? Suffice it to say they were truck drivers. Okay, they were French truck drivers in France. *Routiers,* in French—driving semis just like real men do, spewing exhaust just like real men do, pulling off the road to chow down at a truck stop just like real men do. And what were they chowing down, along with their bottles of wine? You guessed it. Q-U-I-C-H-E. Not only eating quiche but devouring it.

Only one thing was different from what we have here in the United States—these real men were eating real quiche! Quiche is not something that was invented in a fern bar in Santa Monica in 1972. Quiche is one of the great regional dishes of France. Forget the scrambled egg texture of some American quiches. Forget the rubbery, hardened eggs of other American quiches. Real quiche is a miraculous custard, set inside a pastry shell, that quivers to the touch; it is simultaneously creamy and firm, a textural triumph. Every time I have it in Alsace, right near its ancestral home, it blows me away. It's fabulous food that, skillfully interpreted or not, fully deserved its fifteen minutes of fame in the United States

When Julia Child made quiche on the eighty-seventh show of her series *The French Chef* in the mid-1960s, things went completely nuts. Shortly thereafter, quiche became the beef Wellington of the seventies. Quiche at every party. Quiche at every restaurant. Frozen quiche in the supermarket.

Then, of, course, the quiche backlash set in. Reaction-to-quiche books. People parodying the dish by calling it *quish* (pronounced "kwish"). Jokes on Johnny Carson. But these jokes weren't nearly as funny as the quiche being passed off as the real thing.

- A magazine in the seventies published a recipe for cottage cheese quiche with canned French-fried onion rings.
- Another had one for cranberry-carrot dessert quiche with whipped cream.
- Another had one for chocolate chip quiche.

Chocolate chip quiche! Of course real men don't eat that! Real anythings don't eat that!

Let's roll this back a few centuries. We can trace the origins of quiche to the 1500s in the city of Nancy, in the Lorraine region of northeast France. Quiche was also widely served next door, in Alsace—the region that's most famous for it today. The name actually means something like "cake"; it comes from *kuche,* a word in the Lorraine dialect taken from the German word for cake, *Kuchen.* Chefs in Alsace-Lorraine never could figure out which country they belonged to.

Quiche does have many variations in France (sorry, no chocolate chips)—but the classic quiche, the most famous version, is quiche lorraine, in which the custard is flavored with bacon. In the truly classic version, no cheese is added, but lots of chefs in France today add Gruyère cheese, and—since it's so yummy—so do I.

Remember: forget all those "creative" quiche ideas. This is one dish that gets worse the further it gets from the original. Real quiche, for real tasteful people, comes down to only two things:

1. The quality of the crust

2. The quality of the custard inside

The following recipe, I guarantee, will provide you with the highest quality of both.

QUICHE LORRAINE

The trick to the crust is using ice water; mixed with the egg yolks, it helps to keep the pastry dough cool so that the butter and shortening don't melt. The small pieces of these fats form pockets in the dough, and, when the dough is cooked, these pockets form the layers that make the pastry flaky. This is the same principle that makes the more complicated puff pastry puffy. You should start with cold butter and cold shortening, form the dough quickly, and avoid overworking it to keep from melting the fats. The trick to the custard also involves temperature, in a way: by boiling the cream before incorporating eggs into it, you get a richer, sexier custard texture. Finally, my innovation with quiche lorraine makes it a bit deeper in flavor and more exciting to chew: I like to sprinkle freshly cooked bacon bits over the quiche when it's done.

MAKES 8 TO 10 SERVINGS

1 1/2 cups all-purpose flour

1/2 teaspoon salt

7 tablespoons cold unsalted butter, cut into small pieces

2 tablespoons cold vegetable shortening, cut into small pieces

1 egg yolk mixed with 3 tablespoons ice water

2 tablespoons freshly grated Parmigiano-Reggiano

1/2 pound slab bacon, cut into 1-inch-by-1/4-inch pieces, or lardons

2 cups heavy cream

3 eggs

1 egg yolk

Freshly grated nutmeg

1 1/4 cups freshly grated Gruyère cheese

Finely minced parsley, for topping

Finely crumbled crisp bacon, for topping

1. In a bowl combine the flour and salt.

2. Blend in the butter and vegetable shortening until the mixture resembles coarse meal.

3. Add the egg yolk mixture, working the dough until it is just moistened and comes together. Shape the dough into a disk, and wrap it in plastic wrap. Chill for 30 minutes.

4. Preheat the oven to 375 degrees.

5. Lightly butter a 10- to 12-inch quiche pan, preferably black steel with a false bottom.

6. Roll out the dough on a lightly floured surface to a circle 2 inches larger than the pan. Fit the dough into the pan, centering it; there will be an overhang. Sprinkle the overhang with Parmigiano-Reggiano, and fold it into the pan to form a loose, rustic edge. Prick the bottom of the dough all over with a fork, and line it with wax paper. Weight with beans.

7. Bake the shell for 10 minutes. Remove the beans and paper, and bake for 5 minutes more. Remove the shell from the oven.

8. Place a skillet over medium-high heat. Add the bacon, and cook until it is golden brown (not too crisp). Remove, and drain on paper towels.

9. Boil the cream in a saucepan until lightly thickened, about 2 minutes. Cool completely.

10. In a bowl whisk together the cooled cream, the 3 eggs, the egg yolk, and nutmeg. Season with salt and pepper.

11. Scatter the cooked bacon and 1 cup Gruyère in the bottom of the quiche shell. Place it on a baking sheet, and pour the custard over the filling. Bake for 20 minutes. Sprinkle the top with the remaining ¼ cup of Gruyère, and cook the quiche until the center is puffed and golden, an additional 10 to 15 minutes.

12. Sprinkle the quiche with minced parsley and finely minced bacon. Let it cool for a few minutes, then cut it into wedges and serve.

Criteria for Quality

- Is the crust flaky, buttery, light—not heavy, dense, dry, stiff, chewy, or crumbly?
- Is the custard soft, quivering, creamy—not curdled, rubbery, or unattractively wet?
- Do the flavorings seem appropriate? (kiwi quiche just doesn't work for me)

When

In France, quiche would normally be served as a first course, or as an in-between course after a light first course like oysters. As a follow-up main course, a big platter of choucroute (see page 183) would be both regionally correct and delicious.

It just so happens, however, that a big slice of well-made quiche is also a delicious entrée for lunch or a light supper. Forget all those horrors of the 1970s, and serve your guests an authentic slice of this stuff—with a very French green salad (with mustardy vinaigrette), a baguette, and some white wine.

In Your Glass

Quiche lorraine is very wine-friendly food; there aren't too many white wines in the world that won't find at least a modicum of happiness beside it. The only potential pitfalls are too much alcohol (harsh against the salty bacon) and too much wood (ditto). Look for light, graceful whites.

If you want to be regionally authentic, serve a white wine from Alsace. Paradoxically, the northern region of Alsace produces some big, ripe, almost southern-tasting wines that would be too much for quiche. Avoid Pinot Gris and Gewurztraminer with this dish. But the lighter Alsatian whites—like Pinot Blanc and Sylvaner—are lovely with quiche lorraine. And Alsace's best wine, Riesling, will go well with quiche as long as it's not a big, expensive one from a grand cru vineyard.

OEUFS EN MEURETTE
(Poached Eggs in Red Wine Sauce)

In America, we like to put ketchup on everything . . . even eggs. In France, they like to put wine on everything . . . even eggs. I don't mean to be unpatriotic, but I'm gonna have to give this round to the French.

I guess I've felt this way ever since that delicious night in January 1970, in a cozy Parisian bistro, when I was exposed to my first Burgundian wine sauce—in a glorious coq au vin. I learned later that the suave purple pool that surrounded that chicken is not confined, in classic Burgundian cooking, to chicken. The sauce is a combination of red Burgundy wine, stock that is flavored with bacon or some kind of cured pork, and vegetables; if it sounds familiar, that's because you may know the dish called boeuf bourguignon, which uses the same sauce. Furthermore, the sauce is the same medium Burgundians use to poach fish in a dish called *matelote,* the same medium they use for rabbits and, quite commonly, for brains.

This sauce is called a *meurette* in Burgundy—possibly derived from *muire,* a word in Old French for brine. One of the most interesting uses for the sauce is in *oeufs en meurette*—eggs poached in red wine.

Unfortunately, I almost never see *oeufs en meurette* in America. Here, red wine is considered a natural enough cooking medium for meat, and is beginning to become an acceptable sauce base for some fish dishes; but to most Americans this whole idea of poaching an egg in red wine and then serving it with a red wine sauce just doesn't sit right. We are great egg consumers, we Americans, but for some reason we find it hard to make a leap from our beloved, plain old fried-scrambled-boiled to more sophisticated egg dishes that include sauces.

But think about it for a minute. The egg is a natural for sauce. The egg, in fact, is one of the few naturally occurring foods that come with their own sauce. Prepare a soft-boiled egg, break it open . . . and the yolk oozes over the egg white, just like any self-respecting sauce would.

Consider the glories of *oeufs en meurette.* For starters, the colors are extraordinary; in this dish, when you break into the soft eggs, the bright yellow yolk squirts into a wine-dark sea, creating the prettiest sight this side of a sunset on the ocean. Then there are the flavor affinities: the richness of the egg perfectly cut by the acidity of the wine sauce; the bacon bits cuddling up to the chunks of egg in a marriage of flavors that needs no explanation; the supporting cast of shallots, garlic, and bay leaf pushing the eggs way beyond mere breakfast duty. It is a brilliant peasant dish, much loved in France and a must in my kitchen every November and December.

Why in those months? Well, Burgundians are likely to make this dish with all manner of Burgundian red wines. But the first time I ever tasted *oeufs en meurette* was in November, at a celebration of the release of Beaujolais Nouveau. The eggs tasted great *with* the wine, and the eggs tasted great *in* the wine. Some years later I kitchen-tested the dish with a wide range of red wines to see which one made the most delicious poaching medium and sauce; the winner, hands down, was Beaujolais Nouveau.

What is Beaujolais Nouveau? It's a special category of Beaujolais: *new* Beaujolais. All Beaujolais (most of it is not *nouveau*) comes from the Beaujolais region of France, just north of Lyons, on the southern rim of Burgundy. Beaujolais is very simple red wine, meant to be drunk young for its pure taste of exuberant, cherry-banana-strawberrylike fruit. What's special about Beaujolais Nouveau is that it's even simpler than regular Beaujolais and meant to be drunk even younger.

Every fall Beaujolais producers rush some of their wine into bottles so that this Beaujolais *nouveau* comes to market on the third Thursday of November. This is usually only about two months after the grapes were picked! Most of the Beaujolais won't see a bottle until at least April of the next year, five to six months down the road. But in November the world is treated to its first taste of the new vintage in France—in the form of simple, cheery, unpretentious Beaujolais Nouveau. It is shipped to Paris with great haste and flown to countries all around the globe . . . where thousands of Beaujolais Nouveau parties are waiting to receive it.

The downside of Beaujolais Nouveau is that it doesn't last; once it loses its youthful fruit and baby fat, it goes downhill fast. Regular Beaujolais might hold up for a few years; a few rare, very serious versions of Beaujolais, in great vintages, might still have something to say after ten years. But Beaujolais Nouveau is best consumed by spring, certainly by summer. I like it best when it first hits the streets . . . and *oeufs en meurette* is my best excuse for using lots of it.

Oeufs en meurette

OEUFS EN MEURETTE

This delicious, slightly gussied-up version includes roasted shallots and mushrooms, elements that give the Beaujolais even more to play with. And I'm suggesting a technique that removes the last-minute anxiety of poaching eggs—which is great if you're making a party. The eggs are half-poached in advance, saved in cold water, then finished in the Beaujolais liquid at serving time. In fact, this recipe offers you the opportunity to do almost everything in advance, and to pull the dish together within minutes of serving.

MAKES 2 SERVINGS

For the vegetable garnish:

6 small shallots

2 medium white mushrooms, quartered

8 pieces of bacon, each 1 by 3/4 by 1/8 inch

About 1/2 cup very young Beaujolais (Nouveau, if possible)

For the croûtes:

4 slices of French bread, crusts removed, cut 1/3 inch thick, about 2 inches in diameter

1 garlic clove, smashed

1 tablespoon butter

For the poaching liquid:

1 tablespoon butter

2 tablespoons chopped bacon

6 tablespoons chopped shallots

1 teaspoon chopped garlic

2 cups very young Beaujolais (Nouveau, if possible)

1 bay leaf

1/2 cup chicken stock

For the beurre manié:

1 tablespoon softened butter

1 1/4 tablespoons flour

For setting the eggs:

4 large, very fresh eggs

1 tablespoon red wine vinegar

Final assembly:

1 tablespoon very young Beaujolais (Nouveau, if possible)

1 tablespoon very finely chopped parsley

1. Preheat the oven to 400 degrees.

2. Prepare the vegetable garnish: Peel the shallots, but be careful to keep them intact at the root end so they won't fall apart while roasting. Place the shallots in a buttered roasting pan, and place in the preheated oven. Roast until they are well browned on the outside, soft on the inside (about 45 minutes). While they're roasting, baste occasionally with Beaujolais to prevent them from burning. Remove and reserve. Place the mushroom quarters in the roasting pan, and place the pan under a hot broiler until the mushrooms are nicely browned (about 5 minutes). Add the bacon pieces to the mushrooms for 2 minutes, then remove from heat. Reserve the shallots, mushrooms, and bacon pieces together.

3. Prepare the croûtes: Place the slices of bread on a roasting pan. Rub well with the smashed garlic clove. Place the butter in a small, heavy saucepan along with the garlic clove. Melt the butter over low heat, stirring.

After it melts, stir it over a low flame for 1 minute. Then drizzle the butter through a sieve onto the bread slices, distributing evenly. Place the slices under a broiler until they become golden brown on one side, 3 to 4 minutes. Turn them over, and broil them until the other side becomes golden brown. Divide among 2 dinner plates, and reserve.

4. Prepare the poaching liquid: Place the butter in a heavy sauté pan over medium-high heat. Add the chopped bacon, shallots, and garlic, and sauté until the shallots just start to turn brown (about 5 minutes). Turn the heat to high, and add the Beaujolais and bay leaf. Boil until the wine is reduced to 1 cup (about 10 minutes). Add the chicken stock, bring the mixture back to the boil for 2 minutes, then remove from heat and reserve.

5. Prepare the beurre manié: Mix the butter and flour until they are well blended. Reserve.

6. Set the eggs: Bring 1 quart of salted water to a simmer in a 10-inch pan or Dutch oven. Add the vinegar. Slip the eggs into 4 teacups, and, with the water at a gentle simmer, slip the eggs into the water, holding the teacups close to the water. The idea is to keep the whites as close to the yolks as possible. As soon as the eggs hit the water, push the whites toward the center of each egg with a wooden spoon (this takes just a few seconds). Simmer for about 2 minutes (the eggs will be just set). Remove the eggs to a wide, shallow pan, then fill the pan with cold water. The eggs will keep nicely in the water for at least an hour.

7. When you are ready to serve, bring the Beaujolais poaching liquid to a rapid simmer. Add the eggs to the simmering liquid, and poach them for 2 minutes, or until the whites are firm and the yolks still runny. While the eggs are poaching, baste the tops with some of the poaching liquid. Remove the cooked eggs with a slotted spoon, letting all the liquid run off, place them on the croûtes, which are on dinner plates, and keep them warm for a moment under aluminum foil. Meanwhile, bring the poaching liquid to a rapid boil, and begin beating in the beurre manié with a whisk. The sauce should be medium thick within a moment or two. (Use your judgment as to how much beurre manié to add.) Season to taste with salt and pepper. Add the whole shallots, mushroom quarters, and bacon pieces. Add the tablespoon of Beaujolais, and stir. Pour the thickened sauce over and around the eggs, dividing the vegetable garnish evenly between the 2 plates. Top with parsley.

Why Vinegar in Poached Eggs?

One of the goals in poaching an egg is to coagulate the proteins in the white, a process that keeps the egg together. But when you put the whole egg in the poaching liquid, the white begins to float away from the yolk, making for a messy, irregularly shaped result, with strings of egg white streaming off in all directions. The solution? Adding vinegar to the poaching liquid helps to prevent this disaster by speeding the coagulation of the white's albumen, thereby preserving the egg's shape.

Criteria for Quality

- *Are the eggs properly cooked: solidified whites, runny yolks?*
- *Is the sauce neither too thick nor too thin?*
- *Does the dish taste of raw wine? (it shouldn't)*
- *Does it have layers of flavor? (you should taste more than just wine)*

When

I have, with great results, served oeufs en meurette *as an in-between course at a hearty bistro-style dinner: a bistrolike salad first, then the eggs, then something grilled as a main course.*

Alternatively, oeufs en meurette *is a great luncheon dish; serve it with a salad on the side—and a bottle of Beaujolais—and you're all set.*

Last, of course, if you are planning to celebrate the arrival of Beaujolais Nouveau some year—the wine becomes legal at the stroke of midnight on the third Thursday of November—there's no better soul mate for the new wine than this dish. Happily, it makes a great midnight snack.

In Your Glass

I think that subject has been pretty well covered.

Jambon persillé

JAMBON PERSILLÉ

We live in an age of endangered species—but in this case I'm not talking about flora or fauna. I'm talking about great traditional dishes, many of which are being ignored by the top chefs in the regions that created these dishes. Why? Because chefs want to "express" themselves these days, because they perceive it as boring to turn out one more perfect version of a local classic. And we, of course, are the losers—we who are anything but bored by authentic versions of the classics but must now travel through a gastronomic world that persecutes these dishes.

The region of Burgundy in France—which, thank God, is preserving its traditional wines, perhaps my favorite wines on earth—is a prime offender in this culinary regard. Oh, you can find the Burgundian classics in take-out shops and, sometimes, in simple bistros; but try to find a great Burgundian classic like jambon persillé—ham in parsleyed aspic—prepared by a great regional chef (of which there are many), and you're out of luck.

For the life of me, I can't understand how anyone could ignore this great creation. However—and this is what really hurts—jambon persillé is the victim of a second kind of persecution: Americans who know about the dish also ignore it. Why? *Alas, because we don't like aspic.*

Let's start at the beginning. In Burgundy—or at least in Burgundy in the old days—no Easter Day luncheon would have been complete without a terrine filled with jambon persillé. To make it, chefs took a lightly salt-cured ham (known in France as *jambon demi-sel*)—which once upon a time chefs cured themselves—and poached it for hours in white wine with an array of vegetables and herbs, and some gelatinous hunks of the calf. Then—after the rich stock was clarified and blended with a shower of chopped parsley—pieces of the now-cooked, now-flavorful ham would be layered in a terrine with the stock to gel together. At serving time, slices of *jambon persillé* (parsleyed ham) would be extracted from the terrine—each slice a jeweled mosaic. Ham alone could never be as delicious as the combination of ham with that flavorful, parsleyed stock—which, as a shimmering aspic, makes a bite of ham seem lighter, more elegant, than it ever could be by itself.

But that's where I probably lose you. Americans get positively cranky when the subject of aspic comes up. Salmon in aspic? Chicken in aspic? Pâté with aspic? "No, no!" comes the usual reply. "Not aspic!" But aspic and America's beloved Jell-O are the same thing: liquids (usually stock in aspic, usually water in Jell-O) that have been firmed up, and left clear, by the addition of gelatin. And what is gelatin? It's a collagen derived from the connective tissue of animals. Now if you ask me, the only weird thing about eating gelatin-based foods is combining cherry-flavored sugar water with calf's-foot derivative. Folks, it's *Jell-O* that's weird! But lovely, flavorful gelatin around a meat product is much more logical! So please, give up this crazy prejudice against something quite natural, and try in your own kitchen one of the great regional dishes of France. You'll be ahead of most of the great chefs in Burgundy.

JAMBON PERSILLÉ

You can make a good jambon persillé with packaged, powdered gelatin. But I say, if you're gonna martyr yourself as the upholder of Burgundian tradition, why not go all the way and make it with veal bones and calves' feet instead of powdered gelatin? The result will be an aspic that's firm enough to cut but will feel soft and meltingly luscious in your mouth. Just ask your butcher for the bones and feet in question.

MAKES 8 HEFTY APPETIZER SERVINGS

one 8-pound mild-cured smoked ham

2 pounds veal bones, cracked (preferably knuckles)

2 calves' feet, split (about 2 pounds each)

4 stalks celery, chopped

1 large onion, chopped

3 large carrots, coarsely chopped

8 large garlic cloves, peeled

1/2 cup minced fresh tarragon

2 tablespoons minced fresh thyme

12 whole black peppercorns

6 whole allspice

4 cloves

18 parsley stems

2 bay leaves

8 cups chicken stock

4 cups dry white wine, plus 2 tablespoons

3 tablespoons minced shallot

2 tablespoons white wine vinegar

6 egg whites, shells reserved

2 fat leeks, washed and chopped

1 cup very finely minced fresh parsley, leaves only

1. In a large, heavy pot combine the ham, veal bones, and calves' feet, and cover them with cold water. Bring it to a boil, and simmer for 5 minutes. Spill the contents of the pot into a large colander, and refresh under cold running water. Rinse out the pot, and return the ham, bones, and feet to it.

2. Add 2 celery stalks to the pot, along with the onion, 1 carrot, 4 garlic cloves, a cheesecloth bag with 6 tablespoons minced tarragon, the thyme, peppercorns, allspice, cloves, 12 of the parsley stems, and the bay leaves. Add the chicken stock, wine, and enough water to cover by 2 inches. Bring to a boil, and simmer, partially covered, skimming the froth, for 2 to 2½ hours. Let the mixture cool for 1 hour.

3. Remove the ham to a cutting board. Remove the skin and fat, if desired, and cut the meat into large sections. Pull the ham apart with a fork or cut it into 1-inch-square pieces, trimming off all gristle.

4. Finely mince the remaining 4 cloves of garlic, and mix them with the ham chunks in a large bowl. Add the remaining 2 tablespoons of minced tarragon, the remaining 2 tablespoons of white wine, shallots, and vinegar. Toss well, and chill, covered, for 1 hour.

5. Meanwhile, strain the stock through a fine sieve, discarding all the solids. Skim the fat from the stock with a spoon; or, if you have time, refrigerate the stock until the white fat solidifies on the surface, then remove the fat. When you're done defatting, you should have about 6 cups stock. If you have more, reduce it over high heat to 6 cups. When the stock is ready, let it cool.

6. Clarify the stock: Lightly beat the egg whites until they just start to mount; coarsely crush the eggshells. In a large saucepan, combine the whites and the shells with the remaining celery, carrots, and parsley stems, all chopped. Whisk in the ham stock over high heat, and bring it to a boil, whisking constantly. Lower heat, and simmer, uncovered and undisturbed, for 30 minutes. The egg whites and vegetables will form a crust over the top; remove this, using a wide skimmer, and discard. Ladle the remaining stock through a colander lined with a double thickness of rinsed cheesecloth into a large bowl. Season to taste with salt. (Since it will be served cold—which dulls saltiness—the stock should be well salted.)

7. Set the bowl of aspic in a larger bowl of cracked ice, and stir until the aspic thickens to the consistency of raw egg white. Stir in the minced parsley.

8. To build the jambon persillé, you may use either a white porcelain terrine or a round glass bowl; whichever you choose, make sure it just holds the full amount of ham and stock that you've prepared. Working quickly (to keep the texture of the gelled stock), put ⅓ of the ham mixture in the container you've chosen. Pour ⅓ of the parsleyed aspic mixture over the ham, and gently combine the two. Chill in the refrigerator, covered, until it is firmly gelled. Repeat the process 2 times with the remaining ham and aspic. When the last layer is firmly gelled, the jambon persillé is ready to serve—but the flavors will intensify if the terrine is chilled for 1 to 2 days.

9. To serve, you may cut slices directly out of the terrine or bowl. Or you can unmold the jambon: set the terrine or bowl briefly in a pan of hot water, run a knife between the jambon persillé and the inner wall of the terrine or bowl, and invert the aspic onto a serving plate. Cut it into wedges, and serve with crusty bread.

The Right Jambon

Let's face it, there are an awful lot of cheap, mediocre hams out there, fobbed off on the American public as high-quality hams. If you're used to these spongy, waterlogged, overprocessed monstrosities, you've got a real treat in store—hams that actually taste like meat that came from an animal.

Let me steer you directly to my favorite widely available ham: Tobin's First Prize, made near Albany, New York. For starters, it is a bone-in ham—which, for any gastronomic purpose, is my favorite kind. However, a bone-in ham is especially important for jambon persillé; while the ham is poaching, the bone will help add flavor to the stock.

Another general reason I like the Tobin's ham is that it's still smoked the old-fashioned way, over hardwood; the added flavor is always to my liking, but in jambon persillé it has the happy quality of standing up to all the other flavors (parsley, garlic, wine) that come into the dish.

If you're sold, call John Morrell & Co. at 800-666-MEAT; they'll be happy to ship you a Tobin's ham. If you're planning to make your ham at Easter time—or anytime between Thanksgiving and New Year's—give them a call a few weeks in advance.

Clarifying Stock Clarification

The most elaborate process in this recipe is the clarification of the stock (step 6); you must simmer the stock with the egg whites and eggshells for 30 minutes so that the egg parts can trap any impurities that may dirty and/or cloud the stock. Then you must pour the stock through a double thickness of cheesecloth to remove any minute particles the eggs missed.

Why go to the trouble of it all? Because, classically, an aspic is supposed to have a perfectly clear transparency. This makes it look jewel-like. Cloudy aspics, or aspics with particles trapped in them, are considered unappetizing.

Do you have to clarify? I'll leave that up to you. It's something like the deveining of shrimp: if you don't do it, no one will get sick from it. Some diners may find the result unappealing. But the food itself won't taste any different.

A Big Success: Jambon Persillé Manqué

Once I was making a jambon persillé that didn't gel, so to speak: the aspic never firmed up properly. I thank my lucky stars that this happened . . . . because I was able to improvise a twist on jambon persillé that I now go out of my way to reproduce.

I simply took my pieces of cooked and chunked ham and arranged them on a dinner plate attractively, in a small mound. Then I took the parsleyed, partly gelled stock—which was like a green sauce—and poured it over the ham. A few parsley leaves for garnish . . . and I had something with all the magic of jambon persillé but less formally constructed, at once more casual and more trendy looking on the plate.

I urge you to improvise with this time-saving variation. Prepare the recipe through step 6. When you get to step 7, stir the stock over ice only until it achieves the thickness of a medium sauce. Add the parsley. Then, make decorative arrangements of the ham on plates and top them with the "sauce." Work quickly so the "sauce" doesn't change texture, garnish with parsley, and serve immediately.

Jambon persillé manqué

Criteria for Quality

- Is the aspic perfectly clear? (this is a classical criterion to which I adhere, but you may wish to skip the fuss)
- Is the aspic firm but not rubbery? Does it melt softly in your mouth?
- Is the aspic well seasoned?
- Is the ham tender, moist, well flavored?
- Is there enough parsley to justify the inclusion of parsley in the dish's name?

When

Jambon persillé is a classic Burgundian appetizer; a cold wedge of it, with some mustard on the side, and a hunk of crusty bread, is a great way to kick off a country meal (some kind of stew—fish, fowl, or red meat—seems a perfect main-course follow-up to me).

However, I see no reason not to convert this great dish into a main course at a lunch or a light supper, particularly in warmer weather. I like to serve it accompanied by an array of French vegetable salads—some of them vinaigrette based (like French potato salad), some of them mayonnaise based (like celeriac rémoulade). Cornichons, mustard, bread, and white wine round out a great meal.

In Your Glass

Most charcuterie in France is eaten with white wine, and this dish is no exception. Classic Burgundian practice, of course, calls for a white wine from Burgundy. But I think you'd be making a mistake to serve one of the region's famous, expensive, rich white wines (made from Chardonnay) with this dish; the combination, for me, goes over the top; the wine seems too fat. If you must pour a Chardonnay-based wine from Burgundy, use a much crisper, lighter one from the Chablis region, in the northwest corner of Burgundy. Once again, don't select a heavy grand cru; look for village wines (they say only "Chablis" on the label) from vintages that aren't highly rated by American wine writers.

Good acidity is the ticket here (to cut through the rich jambon), along with earthy, minerally, not particularly fruity flavors (which seem odd to me against the meatiness of this dish). Another Burgundian possibility is the local white wine that Burgundians actually drink while they're shipping their expensive Chardonnays off to America: Bourgogne Aligoté, made from the crisp Aligoté grape. I love the one made by Jayer-Gilles in cool vintages, particularly three or four years after the vintage.

Other possibilities—if you're willing to break out of Burgundy—are the crisp Sauvignon Blanc–based whites of the Loire Valley (their herbaceousness is great with the parsley). Again, avoid the big-ticket wines from big vintages. But there are modest Sancerres, Pouilly-Fumés, Ménétou-Salons, Reuillys, and Quincys out there that are wonderful mates for jambon persillé.

BISTEEYA

If you travel to Morocco with high culinary expectations, you may find the food disappointing—with one glaring exception. Bisteeya, a flaky pie stuffed with pigeon, simultaneously sweet and savory, is the one Moroccan specialty that unquestionably belongs in the exclusive circle of World's Greatest Dishes. And though bisteeya can never be exactly the same when made in the United States, if you follow the recipe just ahead, you can come pretty darned close.

Why is bisteeya so good? It starts with the amazing pastry, probably the flakiest in the world, called *warka*. I got to watch the laborious *warka*-making process when I was in Morocco. Women (always women!) prepare a very wet dough, then dab the bottom of a large, hot pan with it until every spot on the pan is dabbed. The dabbing leaves a ghostlike film of dough on the pan—but after a few seconds of heat, an unbelievably thin sheet of pastry starts to form. Moments later, the women carefully lift this off the pan bottom, and one sheet of *warka* is ready. It takes hours to make enough *warka* for a few party-size bisteeyas. The dough is made precisely the same way spring roll skins are made in China; it was probably the Persians who learned to make it there, and other migrating Arabs who took it from the Persians and brought it to Morocco.

Inside the pie, there are three exciting layers. Usually the meat is pigeon—a filling undoubtedly devised by the native Berbers, inhabitants of Morocco's Atlas Mountains, who cooked the birds with saffron and butter. Next comes a contribution of the inhabitants of Tétouan, in the North, not far from Spain (geographically and gastronomically): an onion purée containing eggs that have been deliberately curdled by lemon juice. The Tétouan gourmands prefer the taste of tart to sweet. Last, the southern taste for sweetness is satisfied by the addition of toasted and sweetened almonds—not to mention the sugar-and-cinnamon dusting the exterior of the pie receives.

Crunching together the contrarieties of taste experience in your mouth—the tart and the sweet, made even more interesting by the gamy pigeon and the subtle Moroccan spices—is one of the world's great treats. Even if your tooth is not especially sweet, there's something absolutely irresistible about the way the sugar in this dish combines with the other ingredients—you feel as if you're eating something you're not supposed to be eating, and getting away with it. This dish should be extremely popular in America because it has two qualities that Americans are wild about—sweetness and crunchiness. So how come, in this golden age of esoteric ethnic food, almost no one in America has ever heard of it?

Well, to begin with, there are not very many Moroccan restaurants in this country, and our opportunities to sample this dish are limited. Another problem is that you can't get that flaky pastry, *warka*, here. But, you can still make a good bisteeya by using phyllo dough. The frozen stuff in the supermarket will do a fine job—but if you live near a good Greek bakery, like Poseidon in New York City, the fresh phyllo you can buy there will make the dish very close to the *warka*-wrapped item in Morocco. So now you have no excuse not to try bisteeya.

When you do try it—and I know you will, right?—you may want to take a note from Moroccan restaurants. When bisteeya is made in homes in Morocco, it's usually more than 20 inches in diameter, because it feeds a large crowd. Moroccan restaurants can't do this, because once the bisteeya is cooked, it must be served immediately; you can't hold bisteeya, then warm up a slice in the microwave, because the crunch won't be right. So Moroccan restaurants always make individual-size bisteeyas, which can be cooked when they're ordered. I like the idea of these smaller bisteeyas for use in American homes—because they're more appropriate for the size of American families, and because the smaller pie is easier to manipulate as you're filling it.

BISTEEYA

Pigeon is used in the classic bisteeya—and pigeon with bones, at that. I love pigeon, but I've found that cheaper, more widely accessible chicken is a fine substitute, particularly if you stick to the dark meat. And, though I like my bisteeya crunchy, I don't like it *that* crunchy; I prefer to remove the bones from the chicken before it goes into the pie. The following recipe—adapted from a terrific bisteeya served at the Andalousia restaurant, across the street in Greenwich Village from Mario Batali's restaurant, Pó— will yield six individual pies. I caution you, however—they are intended for six large individuals; you could easily serve a half pie each to twelve, or a quarter pie each to 24.

MAKES 6 INDIVIDUAL PIES

3 pounds skinless chicken legs and thighs

3/4 pound butter

1 1/2 pounds finely chopped onion

1 teaspoon ground ginger

1 pinch saffron

2 cinnamon sticks

1 teaspoon ground cinnamon, plus more for garnish

1 1/2 cups blanched almonds

1/4 cup granulated sugar

13 eggs

24 phyllo leaves

Confectioners' sugar for garnish

1. Preheat the oven to 350 degrees.

2. Place the chicken in 1 quart of water in a large pot. Add ½ pound of butter, the onion, ginger, saffron, cinnamon sticks, and ground cinnamon. Simmer the chicken until it is tender, about 1 hour. Let it cool in the pot. When it's cool enough to handle, remove the chicken from the pot, and shred the meat. Discard the bones. Reserve the broth.

3. Toast the almonds on a roasting pan in a 350-degree oven until they are lightly brown, about 10 minutes. Shake the pan occasionally. When the almonds are done, chop them coarsely. Mix the chopped almonds with the granulated sugar.

4. Bring the chicken broth back to a slow boil. Beat 12 eggs well. Add the eggs to the slowly boiling broth, stirring. Simmer the eggs, stirring, for 10 minutes (they will curdle), then remove them with a skimmer. Place them in a sieve, and let them cool.

5. Mix together the shredded chicken meat and the cooked eggs. Moisten with broth if the mixture is too dry.

6. Melt the remaining ¼ pound of butter. Place a leaf of phyllo on a counter, lightly brush it with melted butter, top it with another leaf, and brush the second leaf with melted butter. Spoon 1½ tablespoons of the almond mixture onto the center of the leaves, and spread it into a circle about 3 inches in diameter. Then put ⅙ of the chicken-egg mixture on the almonds, spread it out into a circle that's about 5 inches in diameter, and top it with another 3-inch circle of almond mixture (about 1½ tablespoons). Fold the outsides of the two leaves inward, forming a closed circle. Lightly brush a third leaf of phyllo with melted butter, top it with another leaf, and brush the fourth leaf with melted butter. Working with a wide spatula, place the chicken-and-almond-stuffed round onto the third and fourth sheets of phyllo, top side down; as you move the chicken-and-almond-stuffed round, you will turn it over. Beat together 1 egg and 2 tablespoons water to make an egg wash, and dab it on the edges of the third and fourth sheets of phyllo. Fold them in so that they completely cover the stuffed circle. Turn the bisteeya over, and, working with your hands, make sure that the whole structure is fairly evenly round. With a large spatula, carefully place the bisteeya on a cookie sheet lined with parchment paper, and brush the top lightly with melted butter. Repeat this process 5 times to make a total of 6 bisteeyas.

7. Bake the bisteeyas in a 350-degree oven until brown, about 35 minutes.

8. Sift confectioners' sugar on top of the bisteeyas, and run crisscrossing lines of ground cinnamon over the top.

How Do You Spell It?

Considering the number of sources that have influenced this dish, it is not surprising that the name has a number of spellings and pronunciations. The original Berber name is bestila—*but it's also called* bistayla *or* pastilla. *I use* bisteeya *because it seems to be the most commonly accepted name.*

Finger Food

If you want to eat bisteeya like a Moroccan—if you want to eat anything like a Moroccan—pick up portions of the food between the thumb and the first two fingers of your right hand. It's a little messy, but it's your socially sanctioned chance to revert to childhood.

Regional Bisteeya Variations

The bisteeya recipe here is in the style of Fez—a style that you'll see in restaurants in Morocco's major cities, like Marrakech and Casablanca. In Tétouan, in the North, they prefer to leave out the sweetened almonds and sugar. In Rabat, north of Casablanca, they make it with rice cooked in almond milk perfumed with orange water. And in Marrakech—in addition to the classic bisteeya—they make a dessert version with a custard of milk and orange water poured between layers of crispy fried warka *leaves.*

Criteria for Quality

- *Is the bisteeya crisp-crunchy-flaky on the outside?*
- *Is it buttery—but not greasy?*
- *Does the filling seem moist enough? (many a bisteeya is brought down by a dry filling)*
- *Are the sweet and savory flavors in good balance, each contributing an exciting dimension?*

When

If you want to eat bisteeya as the Moroccans do, you'll have to follow the fairly wacky order of a Moroccan meal. First comes an array of salads, some of which are lightly sweet (think of these as Moroccan antipasti). Then comes the bisteeya course—which is very odd, because the dish is very sweet. What's even odder is that, in Morocco, it seems just right. After bisteeya, if it's a feast, the Moroccans will go on to a stew (called a tagine), a very unsweet spit-roasted lamb (called méchoui*), and, last, a big platter of couscous, which will be topped by a stew that may or may not be sweet.*

You could, of course, skip the Moroccan meal order and simply serve your bisteeya as a main course. It makes a great luncheon dish.

In Your Glass

Despite the Muslim proscription against alcohol, a good deal of wine is produced in Morocco. After all, the French were there! There's some good rosé being produced around Meknes, and some awfully good—believe it or not—Cabernet. Unfortunately, I was not crazy about any of these wines with bisteeya.

If you want wine with bisteeya—and I say, Why not?—you should find a good wine with moderate sweetness to balance the sweetness of the dish. But it should have good acidity as well, to cut through the richness of the dish. What better candidate for this job than my old friend German Riesling? Look for a label that says QbA Halbtrocken, Kabinett, Kabinett Halbtrocken, Spätlese Halbtrocken, or Auslese Halbtrocken.

THE LESSONS OF MOROCCO

Paul Bocuse, the great French chef, once opined that there were two other great cuisines in the world: Chinese and Moroccan. I think what he really meant by this was that there are two other kinds of restaurants in Paris: Chinese and Moroccan. I don't think anyone who has traveled the world and tasted sensitively could conclude that this is one of the world's greatest cuisines.

I traveled to Morocco in part because I'd heard all of this French hype about the food. I soon discovered the source of the hype: Morocco was colonized by the French, and the French feel very comfortable around a restaurant culture that is so French influenced (native restaurants in Morocco use French on the menus, and many of the restaurant personnel speak French). However, though I wasn't bowled over by the cuisine, I'd recommend a trip to Morocco for anyone interested in broadening his or her palate.

Problems first. Morocco was important in my travel history for a negative reason. I saw there something I would see again and again as I set out for destinations beyond western Europe: the lack of a restaurant culture. There may be great food within people's homes in any given country, but when a country lacks great restaurants, it's awfully hard for gastronomic travelers without personal connections to find its culinary soul. The standard of quality at Morocco's restaurants—and I had lots of help in researching the best—was surprisingly low. With the exception of Yacout in Marrakech—one of the most mesmerizing settings for dining anywhere in the world, with very good food—I couldn't find anything that rose above mediocre. This alerted me to problems that lie on the road ahead, and got me thinking about solutions for dedicated travelers.

Second, I ran into another perennial problem: gracious hosts who will do anything they think it takes to please you. Unfortunately, they usually think it takes bowdlerizing their food, transforming it into something more recognizable to Americans. This problem set me off on a life-long search for solutions on the road that get you closer to the place's real food.

Last on the debit side, I saw how easy it was to make second-rate Moroccan food. People often talk of Moroccan spices as if something special is going on here. I say no; the spice blends of Indian cuisine are far more intoxicating than those of Moroccan cuisine. Only ras-el-hanout—an amazingly exotic blend of Moroccan spices that can include Spanish fly, even marijuana—stood out as something unique. The rest of the spices, and the ways in which they're used, are like second-string Indian. Nevertheless, I was able to see in Morocco the importance of fresh *spices—for when I really enjoyed something in Morocco and asked the chef the secret, I was always told that his or her spices were freshly ground. Indian food still tastes intense with less than fresh spices; the more subtle Moroccan food needs a jolt of freshness.*

The most important gastronomic lessons I took back from my Moroccan sojourn involved specific dishes. I'd never been a great couscous fancier before—but my standards were set in Morocco forever by fabulous mounds of freshly rolled semolina pellets, far more fragrant and chewable than any I'd had before. Tagines—stews, which in the United States usually take the form of too-sweet fruit-and-meat stews—were usually steam table–like in Morocco; however, the lamb-and-quince stew I tasted at Restaurant Yacout also set standards forevermore (and the conical pot I bought in the souk at Fez, also called a tagine, forevermore gives me the chance to live up to those standards).

Pride of gastronomic place, however, goes to Morocco's one true entry in the worldwide sweepstakes for great dishes: bisteeya.

VIETNAMESE SUMMER ROLLS

Owing to a distinct dearth of Vietnamese restaurants in New York City—and because, happily, I didn't get to travel to Vietnam in my formative years (1967–1974)—I came to Vietnamese cuisine pretty late in life. Now, I'm happy to say, Vietnamese food is hot across the United States, even in New York—and, finally, I'm reveling in it.

It represents an extraordinary blend of influences. Vietnam—unlike Thailand, which has enjoyed a relatively insular existence—has been perennially overrun by foreigners. In the first millennium (until about 1000 A.D.), Vietnam was subjugated by China—which means that chopsticks, woks, noodles, bean curd, and soy sauce became staples of the Vietnamese kitchen. In the thirteenth century, invaders from Mongolia left their imprint—mostly in the north of Vietnam, and mostly in the form of beef. (Today, one of the best-known Vietnamese dishes in America is pho, a noodle soup that usually includes beef.) Furthermore, there has always been a good deal of exchange between Vietnam and its southeast Asian neighbors, which brought spicy pastes into the Vietnamese kitchen (as well as the Indian curries that came to the region with Indian émigrés). And in the sixteenth century, European merchants who had traded with the New World started introducing foods from the Americas (like tomatoes, potatoes, and corn) to Vietnam.

Most important, of course, was the French occupation of Vietnam from the midnineteenth to the midtwentieth century. No other Asian country has a cuisine that is as Westernized as Vietnam's. Today, many Vietnamese—thanks to the French—enjoy baguettes, milk, butter, yogurt, ice cream, French pastries, coffee (delicious coffee!) with condensed milk, tea with milk, and a great crème caramel made with coconut milk. You may not see all of these things at Vietnamese restaurants in the United States, but you will see a delicacy and refinement in Vietnamese cooking that is unmistakably French.

You will certainly see it in the one dish (aside from pho) that has become the calling card of Vietnamese restaurants: summer rolls. Perhaps reflecting the French love of gastronomic intricacy, there are many kinds of rolls in Vietnam. But it is the summer roll that stands out as a unique, purely Vietnamese creation—and it is the summer roll that I love the most.

In case you're not among the initiated, the summer roll is a room-temperature wrap of translucent rice paper around a filling that usually includes salad, herbs, and noodles. Its beauty is that it doesn't get cooked once the soft, pliable dough wrapper goes into place—making it light, delicate, fat free, and *the* roll of choice for Americans who have sworn off all those deep-fried egg rolls and spring rolls.

The secret behind this dish is a remarkable ingredient called *bánh tráng,* or Vietnamese rice paper. To make it, producers soak rice in water overnight. The next day they mash the rice in a mortar, adding water, until they have a paste. Then they spread the paste in a very thin layer on a muslin cloth stretched over a pot of simmering water. They cover the pot with a lid and cook the dough—which is essentially a form of crepe—until it firms up just enough. Then they quickly transfer it to a woven bamboo mat to rest and dry in the sun; the weave of the mat makes an impression on the rice paper, and this gives it its characteristic crisscross pattern.

You can buy packages of *bánh tráng* in many Asian groceries, and certainly in any grocery that has Vietnamese products. It is one of the handiest Asian wraps because the dough is dried; unlike egg roll skins or wonton wrappers, you don't have to refrigerate it. You can keep packages of *bánh tráng* in your pantry indefinitely—and you can have them ready for the table in three seconds! Because the other miracle of *bánh tráng* is its quick preparation. To bring it back to life, you merely dip a sheet in a basin of warm water for two or three seconds. When you remove it and place it on a cloth, it won't yet feel entirely softened up. However, within a moment or so of hitting the cloth, it becomes completely soft and pliable. You could, at this point, use the softened *bánh tráng* as a wrapper for foods that you wish to steam, sauté, or deep-fry. But my favorite way to use it is to wrap it around greens, herbs, a little protein, and a few Vietnamese flavorings—and create a summer roll, instantly ready to serve.

Of course—as you might anticipate—there really is much to be said about what goes inside the summer roll. If truth be told, lots of Vietnamese restaurants in America serve summer rolls that are delicate to the point of blandness, with ingredients inside that barely register on the palate. But recently, at a restaurant called Vietnam in New York's Chinatown, I tasted a summer roll that was simultaneously delicate *and* brimming with flavor. It was made with shrimp and grilled pork meatballs, along with the usual array of greens and flavorings. I loved it, asked a few questions, got to work in my kitchen . . . and came up with the tastiest version of this Vietnamese classic that you're likely to find anywhere in the United States.

VIETNAMESE SUMMER ROLLS WITH SHRIMP AND GROUND PORK

The chef at Vietnam—the New York restaurant that inspired my version of the summer roll—likes to form the ground pork into meatballs, steam them lightly, then grill them. The texture and taste of these morsels make all the trouble worth it. Depending on the rest of your menu, you can serve one, two, or three summer rolls to each diner as a great appetizer.

MAKES 8 SUMMER ROLLS

1/2 pound fatty ground pork

2 medium cloves garlic, finely minced

1 thin scallion, finely minced

3 1/2 tablespoons nuoc mam, Vietnamese fish sauce, plus extra for sprinkling

1 tablespoon plus 1/2 teaspoon sugar

1 egg, beaten

1 tablespoon cornstarch

8 medium-size shrimp, about 1/4 pound

8 square sheets of *bánh tráng*, 8 1/2 inches per side (see note, page 138)

1 cup shredded lettuce

1/2 cup mung bean sprouts

1/2 large carrot, shredded

4 teaspoons chopped dry-roasted peanuts

1 large bunch fresh mint

1 large bunch fresh cilantro

1. In a bowl, mix the pork with the garlic, scallion, 1½ tablespoons of the nuoc mam, ½ teaspoon of the sugar, the egg, and the cornstarch. Leave the mixture in the refrigerator for ½ hour. Meanwhile, prepare a charcoal fire (or heat up an indoor grill).

2. When you are ready to cook the pork, shape the mixture roughly into 6 Ping-Pong-size balls. Lightly oil a steamer tray, and steam the pork balls for 5 minutes. Transfer the partially cooked pork balls to a hot grill fire. Cook for 10 minutes, turning occasionally, so all sides of the balls get golden brown. Remove the pork balls from the fire, cut them in half, and return them to the fire, cut side down. Grill them for 5 more minutes. Remove the pork, and, when it is cool enough to handle, cut it in shreds roughly 1½ inches long and ¼ inch thick. Reserve.

3. Bring a few quarts of salted water to the boil. Plunge the shrimp into the boiling water, and turn the heat off. Remove the shrimp from the water when just cooked (2 to 3 minutes). In a bowl, mix together the remaining 2 tablespoons of fish sauce and the remaining tablespoon of sugar. When the shrimp are cool enough to handle, peel them, and slice them in half the long way (cutting each shrimp into 2 thin, C-shaped pieces). Reserve the shrimp and fish sauce–sugar mixture.

4. Submerge 1 sheet of *bánh tráng* in a basin of warm water for 2 to 3 seconds, then remove it immediately. Try to dip all of it into the water simultaneously, and handle it carefully so it doesn't tear. Place the sheet on a dry towel.

5. Roll the sheet right on the towel: About 1 inch above the lower edge of the sheet, spread out ⅛ cup of shredded lettuce. Leave a 1½-inch gap between the left edge of the sheet and the lettuce, and the same between the right edge of the sheet and the lettuce. Define a rectangle with the lettuce that's about 5 inches wide and 3 inches long (towards the center of the sheet). Now evenly top the lettuce rectangle with ⅛ of the bean sprouts, ⅛ of the shredded carrot, and ⅛ of the peanuts. Evenly distribute ⅛ of the grilled pork shreds over the rectangle. Tear 5 to 6 mint leaves, and an equal amount of cilantro, and distribute those over the rectangle. Top everything with a few sprinkles of nuoc mam.

6. Carefully pick up the right edge of the sheet, and fold it towards the center of the filling. Make sure the folded sheet is even and uncreased. Do the same with the left edge of the sheet. The rectangle of filling should now be covered by the folded sheet, with the left and right edges meeting each other at the center of the rectangle. Pick up the bottom edge of the sheet, and start rolling away from you, making sure to tuck the filling in tightly as you roll. When you have rolled about halfway to the top of the sheet, dip the shrimp halves in the reserved fish sauce–sugar mixture. Place 2 shrimp halves along the cylinder that you have half-rolled, and keep on rolling until a fully rolled cylinder has been formed. Place it under a damp towel.

7. Repeat the process 7 times to make 7 more rolls. Serve immediately, or cover the rolls with damp towels and save at room temperature for several hours. Serve with Vietnamese peanut dipping sauce (recipe follows).

NOTE: *Bánh tráng,* or Vietnamese summer roll wrappers, come both round and square. The square shape is easier to work with when making summer rolls. The product I use is manufactured in Singapore and called K&M; each sheet measures 8½ inches per side.

PEANUT DIPPING SAUCE FOR SUMMER ROLLS

My only break with Vietnamese tradition in the preparation and serving of summer rolls concerns the sauce. Vietnamese chefs like to serve a thick, sweet peanut sauce for dipping—which I find totally out of whack with the delicacy of the dish. I must confess, however, that the peanut flavor is delicious with these rolls. So I've created a new peanut sauce that is much lighter than the traditional one, and I think the very best dipper of all. To make it, you must purchase a jar of chili-garlic sauce in an Asian grocery; if you can, find the one made in Hong Kong by Lee Kum Kee (it's widely available in the United States).

4 tablespoons chili-garlic sauce
   (preferably Lee Kum Kee)
4 tablespoons water

4 tablespoons finely chopped peanuts
4 teaspoons hoisin sauce

Mix all the ingredients together. Let them stand for 1 hour. Serve with Vietnamese Summer Rolls.

Vietnamese Fish Sauce

Asian fish sauce is an acquired taste for some—and I urge you to acquire it immediately! It is made by salting little fish that are similar to anchovies and placing them in barrels, in the hot sun, for as long as six months! The strong-flavored liquid that develops—salty and cheesy more than it is fishy—is poured off, clarified, and bottled as fish sauce. It is an essential ingredient in the cuisine of many southeast Asian countries.

If you're new to it, you might want to purchase a bottle of nam pla, or Thai fish sauce. When I was in Thailand, a cooking teacher told me that Thai fish sauce is far superior to Vietnamese fish sauce, because the Vietnamese sauce is too strong; this makes the Thai sauce perfect for beginners. But the Vietnamese, of course, think that their sauce, called nuoc mam, is superior; they call the Thai product wimpy.

Where do I stand? Clearly on the side of the Vietnamese. In fact, my favorite fish sauce of all time is a Vietnamese brand called Three Crabs; it is distributed by the Viet Huong Fish Sauce Company in San Francisco (415-822-0612).

Criteria for Quality

- *Is the rice paper soft and pliable?*
- *Is it smooth (free from cracks)?*
- *Is the summer roll tightly and neatly rolled?*
- *Do the ingredients inside taste fresh?*
- *Is there a bright flavor inside the roll?*

When

Summer rolls are great appetizer food—in any season! If you're making a Vietnamese meal that features successive courses of one dish each, you could go two ways. Either (1) start with a light vegetable or noodle salad, then serve the summer rolls as a second course; or (2) start with the summer rolls, then serve a hot noodle soup (like pho) as a second course.

Another option is to serve the summer rolls alongside a range of other Vietnamese dishes as part of a Vietnamese buffet.

In Your Glass

Unless you're using inappropriate amounts of inappropriately thick and sweet dipping sauce with your summer rolls, French Champagne is an excellent accompaniment for summer rolls. Don't splurge on the older, more complex Champagnes for this dish; their subtleties might get wiped out by the fish sauce and other elements. This is one situation in which the fruit and straightforwardness of a young, nonvintage Brut is preferable. Good California sparkling wine would do the trick as well.

3

MY FAVORITE MAIN COURSES

SOFT-SHELL CRABS—
SZECHUAN SHRIMP WITH CHILI AND
GARLIC SAUCE—CRAB CAKES—
DOVER SOLE—SINGAPORE CHILI CRAB—
PAELLA—MOUSSAKA—
CHOUCROUTE GARNIE—
BOEUF BOURGUIGNON—
JERKED CHICKEN—
ALLA-FRANCESE DISHES—
BARBECUED RIBS

One consistent element in the maze that is "modern restaurant food" is the Main-Course Letdown. Have you noticed that the contemporary chef's arsenal—originality, whimsy, pretty-as-a-picture plating—works best in the smaller, opening courses of a meal? When this current brand of kitchen witchcraft (which dates back to the indulgent days of "nouvelle cuisine") is applied at main-course time, the results are often less successful. Why? Perhaps it has to do with our main-course expectations: at main-course time we're used to a crescendo in the meal that normally takes the form of a mound of "real" food. Three tiny bay scallops tucked into a few miniature lasagna leaves with a drizzle of oregano oil and a sun-dried tomato swan ain't gonna do the trick.

And that is why, when the main course rolls around, I urge a return to simple, straightforward food, not dazzle food. Oh, I don't mind a little creativity—a de rigueur lightening here, a technical improvement there. But I'd be a whole lot happier in my dining life if restaurant chefs paid more attention to the main-course dishes that have fed us well for hundreds of years.

It has been a long time since I've gone "artistic" over a main course at a dinner party. So in this chapter you will find the yummiest classics that have been making my dinner guests the very happiest for the last decade or so.

SOFT-SHELL CRABS

Peepers. Busters. Peelers. Southern terms of endearment for one of the great treats of American gastronomy . . . and one of the great oddities of the gastronomic world.

Why are soft-shell crabs odd? Because they're almost uniquely American. Theoretically, any crab-producing area anywhere in the world could specialize in soft-shell crabs—for soft-shells are, after all, just regular old hard-shell crabs that have shed their shells. They do this because their shells cannot grow, but their insides can—so the only way for a crab to get bigger is to shed its shell, grow its body, then accrue a larger shell.

But a whole industry has to be set up to capture these critters at just the right time and then care for them en route to the consumer. And the region from the Chesapeake Bay in Maryland down to the Gulf of Mexico in Louisiana—going back less than a hundred years—is the only crab-producing region in the world that has taken the trouble to set up a large-scale soft-shell crab industry. That's what's odd.

Indeed, most Europeans traveling to America for the first time find soft-shell crabs surprising (initially; then they find them delicious). Impervious to surprise may be travelers from the northeast coast of Italy, because the area around Venice is the only other coastal region I know of that's set up to produce soft-shell crabs (*moleche*)—but their industry is minuscule compared with ours.

So remember: soft-shell crabs are not freaks of nature. We have them in America because of a marketing decision. They are freaks of commerce.

Now, as to nature: the great blue crab of Maryland (which is actually found up and down the Eastern Seaboard and all the way over to Texas) spends most of its life—which would be about three years, if the crabbers left it alone—in a hard-shell condition. If it lived a full life, it would shed its shell as many as twenty-three times. Soft-shell crabbers, however, rarely allow that to happen. When crabs are large enough to go to market, the crabbers watch for telltale signs that the crabs are about to shed their shells; then they spring into action and catch them. The crabbers do have to spring, by the way, because if the crabs remain in the water for even a few hours after shedding, the new hard shells begin to form. Happily for the crabbers, hard shells will not form once the soft-shell crabs have been taken out of the water.

So what are the shedding clues? Ten to fourteen days before the blessed event, little white lines begin to appear on the shell. Crabbers pluck crabs with these lines from their natural waters and move them to holding floats. Two days before the shedding (or molting), the crab's hind legs turn from pink to red—and the vigil really begins. Skilled professionals in places like Crisfield, Maryland—the center of the industry—stay with the crabs round the clock so that the peelers may be plucked from the tank as soon as the shells come off. At the decisive hour, the body of the crab starts to expand, and, like a small, oddly shaped balloon, a bulbous dark mass begins to emerge slowly from the rear opening of the crab; after a lot of seemingly painful pushing and puffing and panting, the soft-shell crab emerges from its prison 25 to 40 percent larger than its former self.

For the first few hours after molting—when she's exposed and squeezable—the female crab, ironically, has her only opportunity to mate. Male crabs are furiously trying to grab her—but the bay crabber is trying to do the same, with an altogether different purpose in mind.

THE SOFT-SHELL CRAB PROBLEMS

On the gastronomic front, there are two groups of obstacles blocking your path to the blissful delectation of soft-shell crabs: buying difficulties and cooking difficulties.

Buying Difficulties. When soft-shell crabs are taken out of the water, they will live for only a few days. So they are shipped immediately, usually by air, to markets around the country. Unfortunately, the longer they're out of the water, the less sweet and intense they'll taste; that's why it's a good idea to make sure you're getting very fresh crabs, i.e., live crabs that are particularly lively looking, flailing around when provoked.

There is a season, of course, for live soft-shell crabs: they're a spring thing. But lately, live soft-shell crabs from warmer waters have been arriving in northern markets earlier in the year. I've seen Gulf of Mexico soft-shell crabs in New York as early as February. Now, I've got no prejudice against Gulf crabs—in fact, the best soft-shell crab I ever tasted was a Louisiana crab, at Uglesich's in New Orleans. But it has been my experience in the North that the best-tasting soft-shell crabs arrive from Maryland in June.

And one more tip: don't buy the larger crabs. Soft-shells usually range from 2 to 5 inches across, and many markets seem to think that Americans will pay more if the crabs are at the upper end of the continuum. I encourage my fish market, however, to get me the smaller ones; they seem more succulent, and I find them easier to cook well.

Now, if you love soft-shell crabs, you may be tempted to buy them frozen at other times of the year. In a word: don't. Not only are frozen soft-shell crabs more insipid in flavor, but they can be wet and watery—a problem that plagues even live soft-shell crabs and leads to all kinds of cooking difficulties.

Cooking Difficulties. So there you are, in a fine restaurant, with rising anticipation over the imminent arrival on your table of the season's first soft-shell crabs. The chef is sautéing them in butter, as many chefs do, and you can't wait. As soon as you cut into them, however, you realize that something is wrong: namely, they're squishy, watery, leaky, insipid. The plump meat you visualized just isn't there. It has probably happened to you so many times you've come to accept that this is the way soft-shell crabs are supposed to be.

And there's another problem as well. Though I fully appreciate the softness of soft-shell crabs—after all, the point of the thing is that you can eat the whole crab—sometimes I find them too soft, find myself yearning for a little crunch, a little textural resistance. And this is why I believe one of the secrets of cooking soft-shell crabs to be *the restoration of the shell*. Yes, some supreme power took the shell off—but supreme chefs restore a little firmness to the crab that makes it perfect.

One of the best ways to do this is by deep-frying the crab. Japanese chefs in America get this dead right. They quarter the crabs (creating even more surface area to crunch up), toss them in some flour, dip them in beaten egg, then roll them in a particularly crunchy type of bread crumb called *panko*. After the crabs fry for a few minutes at 365 to 375 degrees, they're crisp and altogether wonderful on the outside.

They may, however, still be watery on the inside. Why? Because they are supposed to be like this. In order to crawl out of its shell, a crab has to convert some of its flesh into water. Of course, soft-shell crabs are watery. But now—read on—they don't have to be.

A few years ago I was on a mission to solve the watery-within problem, and I tested scores of methods. The one I finally came up with is something of a miracle: while you're sautéing the crabs in a pan, you lay a heavy weight—like a brick—over the crabs. The weight forces the crabs to spit out all their excess liquid while helping to develop a crunchy sear on the sides of the crabs that're next to the pan. The result tastes intensely of crab, but the meat within has practically the texture of lobster.

WEIGHTED AND PANFRIED SOFT-SHELL CRABS

This is it. The ultimate soft-shell crab cooking method, the one that removes all the watery liquid from inside the crab. Try it!

MAKES 4 SERVINGS

1 cup flour

1 tablespoon salt

1 teaspoon fresh ground black pepper

1/2 teaspoon cayenne

12 small soft-shell crabs, cleaned (see note, opposite)

Unsalted butter for pan frying

1. In a bowl, mix together the flour, salt, black pepper, and cayenne.

2. Dredge the crabs in the flour, shaking off the excess.

3. Choose several heavy frying pans that will hold the crabs in one layer without crowding. Place the pans over moderately high heat, and add enough butter to create a thin layer (about ¼ inch) in each pan. After the foam subsides, add the floured crabs and weight them (with bricks, other heavy pans, or anything you can improvise). Cook for 2 to 3 minutes, or until the crabs are golden brown on the underside. Turn the crabs over, and weight them again. Cook for 2 to 3 more minutes, or until the other side is golden brown. Transfer them to paper towels to drain briefly, and serve, 3 to a portion.

NOTE: You should always buy live soft-shell crabs, and that means they have to be cleaned. Most fishmongers will gladly do this for you—but it should be done very shortly before you plan to cook them. That's why I usually prefer to do the cleaning myself at home, just before cooking time. It's actually quite simple. First you take a pair of scissors and snip off the front of the head, about ¼ inch behind the eyes and mouth. This kills the crab immediately, even though it may continue to twitch. Fear not, he (or she) cannot feel a thing now. The next thing to do is squeeze out the amber-colored sac that lies just behind the mouth. Then lift the pointed side on the left and pull out the spongy gills. Repeat on the right side. Place the crab on its back, and you'll see that its chest looks like a catcher's chest protector. At the bottom of the chest protector is a flap called an apron; twist this apron off, and you're done.

Saucing Your Crabs

I find these brick-weighted crabs absolutely delicious just as they are. But there are endless good ideas if you want to jazz them up a bit. Here are a few possibilities:

- A tart grapefruit-tomatillo–red pepper salsa
- A Thai dipping sauce consisting of lime juice, fish sauce, green chilies, sugar, and cilantro
- Browned butter with capers
- Extra-virgin olive oil in which lemon slices, herbs, and garlic have soaked for a few hours
- A mayonnaise made with sherry vinegar and walnut oil

Sourcing Your Weight

Where can you find a weight to place on your soft-shell crabs? Specialty food shops sometimes sell glazed culinary bricks that are designed to top terrines, so that the pâté inside can be consolidated, squeezed down, by the weight; these bricks are also excellent for topping your soft-shell crabs. Another method is to put a sauté pan on top of the crabs (obviously, one that's a little smaller than the one they're cooking in) and to load it with heavy items (such as large cans of tomatoes).

Criteria for Quality

- *Are the crabs sweet tasting? crabby tasting? free from off-flavors? (if they're old, they can taste ammoniac, for example)*
- *Are the crabs golden brown and crunchy in some way on the outside?*
- *Are the crabs watery on the inside? (they shouldn't be)*
- *If the crabs are sauced, is the sauce appropriate? does it distract from the crab flavor? (it shouldn't)*

When

Three or four small soft-shell crabs make a great main-course portion. If you're serving them plain, go American all the way—and partner them with French fries and coleslaw. If, however, you're making a fancy, creative dinner party, you might want to consider appetizer portions of soft-shell crabs—like one per person—drizzled with some fancy-schmancy condiment.

Don't forget: a deep-fried soft-shell crab also makes a mighty fine sandwich at lunchtime—on either a good bun or good white bread, with lemon and homemade tartar sauce.

In Your Glass

The precise wine you choose for your soft-shell crabs will have much to do with the way you've chosen to sauce them. But for the crabs themselves, unadorned, my favorite wine is the same wine I prefer for lobster itself: dry Riesling from Germany.

Of course, if you're deep-frying the crabs, then one of my favorite wines for deep-fried food comes into play: Champagne. If you're serving the deep-fried crabs plain, choose a refined, elegant, lightish Champagne from the Champagne region of France—such as a Blanc de Blancs from Pol Roger.

THE CREATIVITY I APPLAUD: INNOVATIONS IN TECHNIQUE

The preceding recipe may seem simple to you, and it is—but it may also be, in fact, the most creative culinary contribution I've ever made. Ever since I showed on Taste *the technique of brick-weighting soft-shell crabs, chefs from across the country have been contacting me to let me know that they're loving it too.*

You may wonder why chefs get so excited by small advances such as this one—particularly in a culinary world brimming every day with more spectacular "innovations." The answer, I'm happy to say, is that chefs are finally starting to get fed up with a brand of culinary nonsense that has passed for "creativity" for too many years now. For over a decade, whenever we've heard about culinary innovation, we've heard chiefly about flavor combining—the juxtaposition, the yoking together of surprisingly diverse ingredients. Some hotshot chef in a midsize city combines Thai curry paste and kalamata olives, and everybody gets excited—never mind that the fish lying underneath this mess is badly cooked. Menus don't get noticed anymore unless they contain entries like "Marjoram-Rubbed Orange Roughy with Cherimoya Essence, an Infusion of Hojo Santa Leaves, and a Port Wine Reduction, Served with Sesame Seed Risotto and Yuca Fries."

I wouldn't be so upset about this culinary development if chefs were more responsible in their flavor combining; perhaps we should require chefs to be trained and licensed before they start messing around. But the sad fact of the matter is that anybody can throw disparate ingredients together . . . and almost everybody does. This is not what I call creativity. This is gustatory anarchy. Necessity is still the mother of invention, and the only necessity driving the flavor combiners is the necessity to be more outrageous today than they were yesterday.

Sometimes, however, there is a necessity for culinary invention—particularly when perspicacious chefs have noticed that the old, traditional ways of cooking something are yielding less than ideal results. Then, they start making innovations in technique *that are designed to yield a better product. This technical creativity, to me, is true creativity: not just anyone can do it; real understanding and intuition are needed; and the results can be revolutionary. Very often I say of these innovations what scientists say when they see a new proof or theorem: "That's an elegant solution." There's nothing elegant, believe me, about whizzing bean curd, olive oil, epazote, and herring in a food processor.*

Here are a few wonderful examples of creativity that arise from the need to improve something technically.

- ***The Watery Soft-Shell Crab Problem*** *(see page 146)*
- ***The Eggplant-on-the-Grill Problem.*** *Have you ever noticed that when you grill slices of eggplant over a fire, the slices can turn hard as cardboard on the outside by the time the inside is cooked? A chef once told me that the definitive way to prevent this problem is to blanch the eggplant slices for 30 seconds in simmering water, then throw them on the grill.*
- ***The Smoky Pizza Quest.*** *The owners of Al Forno in Providence, Rhode Island—two of the most creative chefs anywhere, by my measure of culinary creativity—loved the smoky flavor of pizza cooked in a wood-burning oven and wondered how they could make that flavor even more pronounced. The answer was simple, logical, and wonderful—cook the pizza on a grill, directly over a smoky hardwood fire. Works like a charm.*
- ***The Dry Lean Meat Problem.*** *Now that pork has been bred to have little fat, it joins turkey breast as a "problem" meat: How do you get this lean flesh to be juicy? I'm not sure who invented this solution, but a number of chefs across the country are now placing turkeys and pork chops in brine for a few hours before cooking. I don't know why this works, but I know that it is a brilliant innovation, worth a century of ingredient juxtapositions.*

SZECHUAN SHRIMP

WITH CHILI AND GARLIC SAUCE

Another one of my all-time favorite shellfish dishes also shows great culinary creativity—but this burst of invention must have happened long ago and far away.

Have you ever noticed, in Chinese restaurants, the marvelous texture of shrimp in stir-fry dishes? Nothing rubbery or mushy here. Instead, there's a crisp kind of chew—I often say the shrimp "pop" or "explode" in your mouth. For years, it was a mystery to me how this small textural miracle was achieved.

Then, about twenty years ago, I came across an article about Chinese restaurant cooking, which, first of all, delighted me by acknowledging this shrimp phenomenon, and then thrilled me by explaining how to do it! The Chinese call it salt leaching, and it simply involves sprinkling shelled shrimp with a large quantity of salt, letting them soak awhile, washing the salt off, and repeating the process a few times. The salt removes water from the shrimp (just as it does with eggplant or cucumber)—leaving behind a firmer-textured, "crunchier" shrimp, which I find utterly captivating. And don't worry that this process may dry out the shrimp. For after the salt leaching the shrimp are cooked very briefly in deep oil—which leaves them fantastically juicy, as well as crunchy.

And here's another technical surprise: though we've all been dutifully stir-frying our ingredients for years, in our dutifully purchased woks, Chinese chefs for centuries have been doing it a different way. For many so-called stir-fried dishes, the chefs first heat 4 cups of hot oil in a wok to about 375 degrees. Then, many of the ingredients in the "stir-fry" get an initial deep-fry; it usually takes no more than 30 to 60 seconds to cook the food. The ingredients are removed from the oil, drained on towels, and kept waiting for the other ingredients to catch up. When all the deep frying is done, either most of the deep oil is spilled out of the wok or another wok is heated with a little oil. In go garlic, ginger, scallions, et cetera, along with the ingredients that have been deep fried. A quick toss with the elements that make up the sauce (soy sauce, hoisin sauce, oyster sauce, and so on), and the "stir-fry" is complete.

If you want to test my theory out, by all means do it with the following dish. It was one of my immediate favorites when I discovered Szechuan food in the early 1970s, and it remains so today. The only problem is that now I have to make it myself: Szechuan restaurants have declined so in quality that what I usually get is a gloppy, supersweet, lurid orange mess. Here's one case where your home Chinese food will be much better than a restaurant's!

SZECHUAN SHRIMP
WITH CHILI AND GARLIC SAUCE

The collision of garlic, chili, ginger, scallion, and shrimp in this great recipe makes one of my favorite composite flavors in the whole Chinese repertory. It's all robed in a delicious reddish sauce that relies on a Chinese product called chili paste with garlic, which is easy to find in any Chinese market; I particularly like the brand called Lee Kum Kee. Another essential element couldn't be less exotic: the chili sauce called for in this recipe is, believe it or not, Heinz, the stuff in the supermarket that's almost like ketchup. The name *ketchup* actually is derived from an old South Chinese name for a popular condiment, and in this century Chinese chefs have avidly taken to the Western-style tomato preparation that borrowed its name.

SERVES 4 AS PART OF A CHINESE DINNER

1 pound medium shrimp

4 teaspoons salt

2 tablespoons hoisin sauce

2 tablespoons chili sauce (see above)

2 teaspoons shao hsing (or dry sherry)

1 teaspoon thin soy sauce

1 teaspoon fish sauce

1 teaspoon chili paste with garlic

1/2 teaspoon sesame oil

1/2 teaspoon hot chili oil

1/2 teaspoon sugar

1/2 teaspoon MSG (optional)

4 cups peanut oil

2 tablespoons finely minced fresh gingerroot

3 tablespoons finely minced garlic

1/2 cup minced scallion (about 4 fat scallions, white and green parts)

3 dried red chilies

Cilantro leaves for garnish (if desired)

1. Peel, devein, and butterfly the shrimp. Sprinkle with 1 teaspoon of the salt, and allow to stand for ½ hour.

2. During this time, prepare the sauce: mix together the hoisin sauce, chili sauce, shao hsing, soy sauce, fish sauce, chili paste, sesame oil, hot chili oil, sugar, and MSG (if desired). Reserve.

3. When you are ready to cook, bring the peanut oil to 375 degrees in a wok.

4. Thoroughly wash the salt off the shrimp with running cold water. Add another teaspoon of salt to the shrimp, mix, let stand for 30 seconds, and wash off the salt. Repeat this procedure twice more. The final time, drain well but do not dry—let some water cling to the shrimp.

5. Immerse ½ of the shrimp in the hot oil, and cook until just past translucent (20 seconds or so). (See photo A.) Remove the shrimp to paper towels. Add the remaining shrimp. The oil will not be as hot, so this portion of shrimp may need 30 seconds to finish cooking. Remove them to paper towels.

6. Drain all but 2 tablespoons of the oil from the wok. Over high heat, stir-fry the ginger, garlic, scallions, and dried chilies for 1 minute. (See photo B.) Add the reserved shrimp, and toss well to blend. (See photo C.) Add the reserved sauce, and stir to coat the shrimp. (See photo D.) Turn the dish (see photo E) out onto a platter, garnish with cilantro leaves, if desired, and serve immediately.

High Heat: Another Key to Authentic Chinese Stir-Fries

Another reason why homemade Chinese food tastes like, well, homemade Chinese food, is that home ranges can't crank up the BTUs like Chinese restaurant ranges can. You need a roaring inferno, my friends, to make your stir-fry taste authentic.

If you don't have one, however—and most of us don't—there are a few things you can do to make the most of the heat you have.

1. Deep-fry as many of your bulky ingredients (vegetables, fish, meat) as possible, then hold them on paper towels.

2. When you are ready to stir-fry, place your wok over the highest heat your range can muster at least 5 minutes before cooking.

3. Add a little oil to the wok by dripping it down the sides; let it smoke before adding the food.

4. The most important thing of all: don't crowd the wok! If you put too much food in at the same time, the temperature in the wok falls, and the food is steamed rather than fried. If your wok is not very large, and if your heat source is not very powerful, you may have to put as little as 1 cup of ingredients in the wok at a time to ensure an authentic Chinese taste. Sometimes, you may have to break a dish into four equal parts, and stir-fry them four times, in order to get enough to serve four people. It's worth the trouble!

Criteria for Quality (for Stir-Fries in General)

- Are the ingredients perfectly cooked? (meats should be tender, fish shouldn't be overcooked, vegetables should be just cooked)
- Do the ingredients seem "fried"? or do they seem steamed? (they shouldn't seem steamed)
- Is the sauce of a pleasing consistency? (sauce that's gloppy and sauce that's too thin are common pitfalls)
- Is there just enough sauce? (quantities of sauce may vary, but too much is usually not a good thing)
- Are the flavors harmonious? (a common problem is flavor that overwhelms the main ingredients of the dish)
- Is the dish too salty? too sweet? too oily?

When

This dish is for four people—but that's only if other dishes are served alongside it, in typical Chinese fashion. I like to serve this one with dishes that offer some contrast—such as a stir-fry of Chinese greens (American broccoli will do just fine), a spicy stir-fry of chicken with a brownish sauce, perhaps a whole deep-fried fish with a black bean sauce. Bowls of steamed rice would be an appropriate accompaniment.

In Your Glass

The very strong flavors of chili and garlic make this a difficult dish for wine. Something on the sweet side and low in alcohol (like white Zinfandel) will do—but I'd much rather give my corkscrew a rest and simply pass icy bottles of Tsingtao beer.

CRAB CAKES

Many sins have been committed in the name of crab cakes (except in Maryland, where restaurant crab cakes are often at least very good). Across the country I have been served a disturbingly high percentage of woeful, fishy, heavy, uncrabby clumps when I order crab cakes. There's just no excuse for this—because crab cakes are really very easy to make.

Here are the key factors in making great ones.

Choice of Crabmeat. The leading culprit in the ruination of crab cakes is bad crabmeat. What I expect from a crab cake is a mouthful of sweet, fresh-tasting, plump lumps of Maryland blue crab; all too often, what I get instead is a mouthful of fishy, stringy meat.

As I see it, you really have only two shopping choices:

1. Cook up a batch of blue crabs yourself, and extract the meat.

2. Buy the very expensive, refrigerated tins of fresh crabmeat (this will cost you about $20 a pound). You can find them at better fish markets.

Now, if you're going the latter route—as most people, including me, usually do—you'll have several grades of refrigerated tins to choose from. I used to insist on lump meat only—large white chunks from the body of the crab, the most expensive grade. But a friend in Baltimore pointed out to me that crab cakes made solely from lump crabmeat are harder to bind together; if, instead, you use half lump crabmeat and half backfin crabmeat—a less expensive grade, with smaller pieces—the cake holds together better, and the flavor is not affected at all. And this is now the way I like to make crab cakes. Saves a few bucks, also.

Other Flavorings. Another culprit in the bad crab cake plague is too much competing flavor. To me, crab cakes, above all—far above all—have to taste crabby. The flavor competition you often see includes mustard, Worcestershire sauce, Maryland crab seasoning, and, worst of all, minced bell pepper. I have no problem with minute doses of the first three—as long as they're used to provoke the crab flavor, not overwhelm it. But I've had so many crab cakes that taste like green pepper cakes, not crab cakes, that I have struck all bell peppers from my crab cake kitchen.

What do I use?

1. Salt—and I like to apply it directly to the crabmeat before I mix anything else in, because this intensifies the crab flavor.

2. A tiny amount of Maryland crab seasoning (Old Bay is good and nationally available; J.O. is hard to find outside Maryland, but I like it better). Don't go past a pinch!

3. Fresh lemon juice—which piques the crab flavor.

4. Melted butter—which also makes the crabs taste crabbier.

If you're a fanatic, you may also want to consider using the mustard-colored goop from fresh-cooked Maryland blue crabs and a heavily reduced crab stock made from fresh crabs. Nothing boosts the crab flavor like these two. You will need to buy fresh, live crabs however. If you wish to undertake all of the trouble—I think it's worth it, though you can make excellent crab cakes without these two ingredients—read all about it in "Secret Formula for the Best Crab Cakes Ever," page 157.

The Binding. Here's yet another way in which crab cakes often get murdered: cooks keep the cakes together (and the ingredients costs down) by spilling into the cakes an ungodly amount of bread crumbs, usually from a can. This turns a magically held together mound of pure crab into a sodden, heavy disk with severely compromised crab flavor.

Now, I must confess that in Baltimore many chefs do use bread crumbs and egg to hold their cakes together—but, with their instinctive, Maryland-bred sense of proportion, they use just enough to bind, not enough to turn the cake heavy. Still, I can sometimes taste the bread crumbs in these cakes, and I find the crumbs give the cakes a kind of gumminess that's not to my liking.

What alternatives are there?—for it is clear that crabmeat by itself won't hold together; something needs to be added if you're going to make a "cake."

Well, there is an alternative tradition in Baltimore crab circles: soaked white bread. This yields an entirely different texture: these crab cakes are lighter, more airy, perhaps more French in feel. Not everyone prefers this texture. But I love it.

And I've loved it even more since I discovered a trick that was published by Michael Tucker, the actor and fine amateur chef, who has Baltimore in his background: use Wonder bread! Yes, it's true—this insubstantial bread virtually melts away in the cooking process. It performs its task of holding things together, then gracefully exits the scene.

I've thrown in a few wrinkles of my own. I use a little more bread and egg than Tucker does, and I soak the bread briefly in a little white wine—which, once again, piques the crab flavor, doesn't compete with it. And I follow standard Maryland practice by using some mayonnaise as well to hold everything together.

The Shape of the Cake. In the Maryland tradition, crab cakes are more like crab balls; they like them high, domed, approximately the size of a tennis ball (or a little smaller). But I find that a lot of crabby flavor is created by browning the outside of the cake—and a thick ball has less external area than a thinner patty. Now, I'm not talking too thin—but my ideal crab cake looks like a large, fat hamburger. This shape increases the amount of crab filling that comes in contact with the heat of the frying pan—thereby increasing the flavor.

The Cooking Process. If you have a crab cake that's threatening to fall apart, broiling is the best method; simply putting your cake under overhead heat will least disturb it.

If you have a crab cake that couldn't be blown apart by a bomb (one of those bread-crumb jobs), you might want to consider deep frying, which gives a wonderfully flavorful exterior. But it's hard to keep a light cake together in the deep oil.

So my preferred method for crab cakes—which are just holding together as they hit the fire—is pan frying. And I find that the most flavorful medium for frying the cakes in the pan is lard—which adds an intriguing extra flavor that most people won't be able to identify. They'll be too busy swooning, anyway.

Crab Cakes Forever?

Surprisingly, the name crab cake *doesn't go back very far. The cakes themselves have been a tradition in Maryland for a very long time—but the first appearance in print of the term* crab cake *was in 1939, in Crosby Gaige's* New York World's Fair Cook Book. *They were called, of course,* Baltimore Crab Cakes.

PERFECT MARYLAND CRAB CAKES

Time is a key factor as well in perfect cakes. Try to mix everything together a few hours before cooking the cakes. And, after they're cooked, let them sit for 5 to 10 minutes before serving; this also intensifies the flavor.

MAKES 12 CRAB CAKES, ENOUGH FOR 6 MAIN-COURSE SERVINGS

8 slices Wonder bread

3 tablespoons dry white wine

4 cups backfin crabmeat from a refrigerated tin

4 cups jumbo lump crabmeat from a refrigerated tin

Maryland crab seasoning, to taste

4 eggs, beaten

1 tablespoon fresh lemon juice

1/4 cup melted unsalted butter

8 tablespoons thick mayonnaise (like Hellmann's)

Lard

Vegetable oil

1. Trim the crusts from the bread; discard, or reserve for another use. Tear the remaining bread into little pieces (about 20 pieces per slice); handle the bread lightly, so the pieces remain fluffy and don't flatten out. Place the bread pieces in a bowl, and sprinkle them with the wine; toss lightly to distribute the wine evenly.

2. Pick over the backfin and the jumbo lump crabmeat to remove any bits of shell. In a large mixing bowl, toss together the backfin and jumbo lump crabmeat. Season to taste with salt and with Maryland crab seasoning (see page 154 for more flavoring options). Add the soaked bread, beaten eggs, lemon juice, and melted butter; toss lightly, making sure to keep the crab lumps whole. Add the mayonnaise, and toss the mixture gently with your hands, distributing the mayonnaise evenly. Taste again for seasoning, if desired (if you don't want to taste raw egg, you can sauté a bit of the mixture in butter). For even better flavor, allow the mixture to sit in the refrigerator for a few hours.

3. When you are ready to cook, place a large, heavy-bottomed sauté pan over medium-high heat; the pan should have enough room for 4 crab cakes. Add enough lard and vegetable oil (in fifty-fifty proportion) to create a 1-inch depth of oil. When the oil is medium-hot, quickly shape ⅓ of the crab mixture with your hands into 4 cakes, each roughly the size and shape of a large hamburger. Gently place the cakes in the oil, making sure to preserve their shapes. Fry for 3 to 4 minutes, or until the cakes are just golden on one side. Flip them carefully with a spatula, and fry on the other side for 3 to 4 minutes. After about 8 minutes, the cakes should be golden brown on all sides and heated through (you want the pieces of bread inside to virtually disappear). Remove the 4 crab cakes from the pan, and place them on paper towels. Repeat twice, until 12 crab cakes are cooked.

Secret Formula for the Best Crab Cakes Ever (But It Takes a Bit of Trouble)

If the be-all and end-all of great crab cakes is great crab flavor, you can make the best crab cakes ever by extracting additional flavor from fresh, live crabs. This, of course, turns a five-minute prep into a one-hour prep—not to mention the time your shopping expedition in pursuit of live crabs will take. But if you really believe that life is a matter of taste, you simply haven't lived until you've tasted these souped-up cakes.

To add extra crab flavor to the Perfect Maryland Crab Cakes, you must buy (in addition to your tins of crabmeat) a dozen live Maryland blue crabs (the larger the better). Put about 2 cups of water in a wide pot that's large enough to hold the crabs; bring the water to a boil. Add the crabs all at once, cover tightly, and boil for about 12 minutes, or until the shells are bright red and the crabmeat is cooked. Remove the crabs from the water. Spill out and reserve the cooking water.

When the crabs have cooled enough to handle, tear off the claws and legs, then flip the crabs onto their red backs. You'll see an "apron," with a "spoke" running down the middle of the white "belly." Insert a knifepoint under the spoke, and lift it up. Bend it back like a pop-top, tearing it off at the top of the shell. This will leave a seam where the back meets the body of the crab; open the crab at that seam, peeling the red back away from the body. You will now have two pieces: a red, almost-empty back and the meat-laden body (as well as some claws and legs).

The most important thing you can do right now is extract all the mustard-colored matter that's the equivalent of a lobster's tomalley; it is this goop that makes your crab cakes taste insanely crabby! You'll find it lurking in the red back (including the recesses at the pointy corners) and in the central cavity of the meat-laden body. When you've removed every bit of it (as well as the orange roe, in case you have females), blend the goop (and the roe) with the tinned crabmeat at the beginning of step 2. Then proceed with the recipe. (Note: You may also remove the meat from the claws and body, and substitute it for some of the tinned meat that's called for in the recipe. But this is not necessary.)

For even more flavor, there's one more thing you can do. Place the pot in which you cooked the crabs over high heat. When it's hot, return the crab shells (and claws and legs) to the pot (either stripped of meat, which you can save for another use, or full of meat), and stir them over the high heat for 5 minutes. Now return the crab cooking water to the pot, and boil until it's reduced to about 1/4 cup. Add this concentrate to your crab cake mixture—and the flavor will astound you!

Criteria for Quality

- Above all—is the crab cake crabby?
- Are there big lumps of crabmeat inside? (as opposed to shreds and strings)
- Is it light? does it just hold together?
- Is the exterior golden brown—not too dark and not too light?

When

I love crab cakes as a dinnertime main course in the summer—along with corn, coleslaw, and French fries. But crab cakes make a delicious main course any time of year; I like two per person.

You can also serve one crab cake per person as a dinnertime first course, or put 'em on buns for a delicious lunch.

The one way I don't like crab cakes is gussied up—the whole panoply of salsas, beurres blancs, squeeze-tube squiggles, et cetera. Never, ever forget: crab cakes are about crabs!

In Your Glass

I love crisp, light, graceful, low-alcohol white wines with crab cakes—even those that have a touch of sweetness will be delicious. My old favorite, dry German Riesling, is ideal here: look for labels that say QbA, QbA Trocken, QbA Halbtrocken, Kabinett, Kabinett Trocken, Kabinett Halbtrocken, Spätlese Trocken, or Spätlese Halbtrocken.

Or drink a good beer!

DOVER SOLE

Some people get all misty over Dover's white cliffs. Forget the cliffs. The white *fillets* of Dover—now there's something to cry about.

This is, perhaps, the single most delicious fish in the world. Cooked whole, in butter, all crispy brown on the outside, firm and sweet within—you may not yet know what I'm talking about, but I assure you that once you've had it, you'll do anything to have it again.

Now, because some profit-minded fish people know this, you'll also cry over the expense of this fish. A Dover sole at the fish market, weighing perhaps ¾ of a pound—a not-enormous portion for one person—will cost you $15. If you're feeding four people, that's sixty bucks before you've bought a dinner roll. At a restaurant, $35 per individual portion is not unusual.

Last, I cry because Dover sole is hard to find here, especially in good condition. Why? Because it does not exist in American waters. It swims near Dover, on the south coast of England, in the English Channel, the North Sea, and the Bay of Biscay; it is sometimes seen in the Mediterranean as well. That's it. So if you're lucky enough to find Dover sole in America, it was flown in from Europe . . . adding to its expense. And because it came from so far, you have to be very careful in buying it: make sure that it's fresh, that its eyes are clear and not sunken, and that its flesh is firm and does not smell fishy.

Now, unfortunately, you're going to have to work extra hard to make sure of something else, too. For the sad fact of the matter is this: there are people in this country who will sell you an expensive fish and tell you it's Dover sole . . . when it's not Dover sole at all! In fact, chances are what you're getting is not even sole of any kind!

Let's look at the basics. Sole belongs to the family Soleidae. It is a dextral flatfish—which means that if you hold it in your hands, point its nose forward, and turn it like a dinner plate on its edge, you'll find both eyes on the right side of the fish. The species of sole that's found in European waters is usually *Solea solea,* or Dover sole. *Solea solea* can have different names, but most people know it by the name the English devised for the fish that was caught near Dover. There are a few true soles in the world other than *Solea solea,* including a couple found in Asian waters.

Now, where does America fit in? Well, here's the real tragedy: nowhere. That's right. With a few freakish, noncommercial exceptions, there are no true members of the sole family in American waters.

All right. I can live with that. There are jet transport planes, and dry ice, and splurge budgets for special occasions. But what really gets me mad is that fish sellers here cause all kinds of confusion because they know that you know that Dover sole has this exalted reputation—and they think that you *won't* know the difference if they substitute something else for it.

The deception starts with the very word *sole.* Why is this word used so widely in American fish markets and on restaurant menus? Because, once again, the sellers are counting on you going gaga over the name, and on you opening your pocketbook wider, because the name *sole* suggests Dover sole.

Usually what's labeled "sole" in America—whether it's called gray sole, lemon sole, fillet of sole, or whatever—is flounder. The slim ichthyological basis for this is that flounder, fluke, and scores of other American fish belong to a very large international group of fish, including sole, that's called flatfish. These fish, obviously, are not round or thick but flat. They all begin life with one left eye and one right eye, and all undergo the eventual migration of one eye to join the other on one side of the head. As I told you before, all Dover sole have eyes on the right side; if someone tries to sell you a left-eyed flatfish and calls it Dover sole, you know right there that you're being had. And watch out especially on the West Coast, where clever fish namers have officially called a type of Pacific flounder Dover sole; if you say, "That's not Dover sole," they can officially answer, "Yes, it is." They'd be right, but you'd still be frustrated.

But, Dave, you're wondering—does all this make any difference? Should I really care whether the fishmonger sells me true sole, Dover sole, or some fine, fresh substitute like flounder?

You bet your bait you should. I like flounder and fluke (another flatfish) well enough—but they aren't sole. Two things, for me, make Dover sole stand apart from all other flatfish.

1. The texture. Dover sole has amazing resiliency for a thin fillet of whitefish; when cooked just right, it actually offers some springy resistance to your bite. At the same moment, paradoxically, it's fatty, tender, even creamy. No other fish chews like this.

2. The taste. And no other fish tastes quite like this, though the taste is not as distinct as the texture. But there are an uncommon richness here, a hint of sweetness, and a depth that begin to suggest the flavor of shellfish.

Okay. I hope I've convinced you to go out of your way to find the real thing, the real Dover sole. So in case you're willing to go along with my obsession—how do you know which one is the true Dover sole? Here are the main characteristics.

The True Dover Sole . . .

1. is a fairly small fish, usually measuring from 12 to 16 inches the long way, and usually weighing considerably less than a pound.

2. is not especially tapered or pointy at its front end, as many fish are; instead, it seems like an elongated oval that is very rounded at the front end.

3. features a square-looking tail.

4. has two eyes on its *right* side.

5. is colored anywhere from gray to brown on its top side, with dark blotches; the underside is a pale beige.

6. has a black spot near the rear of the upper fin.

Now, when it comes to cooking Dover sole, I take the simple road. Oh, I know that there are hundreds of recipes in the French classical repertoire for elaborate sole dishes, many of which feature stuffed and rolled sole. And they can be delicious. But they can't compete with the pleasure of a whole sole, simply cooked in butter, served brown and sizzling at the table, on the bone—where the lucky diner, rather than quickly popping a few boneless bites in the mouth, has the joy of slowly dismantling this miraculous fish over the course of many pleasurable minutes (I'd never cut it short of thirty).

The true Dover sole, front and back

WHOLE SAUTÉED DOVER SOLE

It is not difficult to sauté a whole Dover sole in the classic method. The trickiest part is pulling away the dark skin from the top side of the fish—but you can always have your fishmonger do this for you.

MAKES 2 MAIN-COURSE SERVINGS

2 whole Dover sole, gutted and scaled, each about 12 ounces after gutting

2 tablespoons milk

Flour for dredging (preferably instant flour)

8 tablespoons clarified unsalted butter (see "Clarified Butter" below)

2 tablespoons unsalted butter

2 tablespoons chopped parsley

Lemon wedges

Parsley sprigs

1. With a pair of scissors cut off the dorsal and anal fins. Make a slit in the skin at the tail end on the dark side of the fish, and, using a towel for a better grip, pull the skin off, pulling in the direction of the head. When you get to the gills, cut the skin off neatly, and leave the head covered.

2. Sprinkle the fish on both sides with about 2 tablespoons of milk. Season with salt and pepper.

3. Dredge the fish on both sides in a pan of flour; shake off the excess.

4. Let the fish dry on a rack for 10 minutes.

5. If you have a sauté pan that's large enough to hold both fish, pour all the clarified butter into the pan over medium-high heat. If you don't have a pan this large, divide the butter between 2 smaller pans. When the butter is very hot, add the fish, skinned side down. Using a spatula, check after 1 minute to make sure it is not sticking, and cook for 3 minutes on this side. It should be golden brown. Turn the fish over, and cook it for 3 more minutes. Then remove the fish to 2 dinner plates, and wipe out one pan.

6. Add the 2 tablespoons of butter to the pan, and heat it until the butter foams. Pour the butter over the fish. Sprinkle with chopped parsley, garnish the plates with lemon wedges and parsley sprigs, and serve immediately.

Clarified Butter

Clarified butter at a high temperature doesn't turn unattractively brown or black; by clarifying the butter, you have separated out the milk solids, which burn over high heat.

To clarify butter, gently melt at least 1 stick of butter in a small pot. After a few moments, you will have three layers: a layer of white foam on top, a large layer of clear yellow liquid in the middle, and a layer of milky residue way at the bottom of the pot. To retrieve the clarified butter, first spoon off the foam from the surface. Then carefully pour the clear yellow liquid in one motion into a cup or bowl; do not let the milky residue at the bottom flow into the now-clarified butter.

Use immediately, or save for weeks, covered, in the refrigerator.

Why the Milk?

The milk soaks into the fish and helps the flour stick. It is the adhered flour that gives the fish its wonderfully crisp exterior. And, as many chefs have discovered, instant flour—like Wondra—really is wondrous in creating crisp exteriors on panfried items.

Eating a Whole Fish

The excitement that eating a whole fish engenders in me is the adult counterpart of the excitement I felt about eating a whole lobster when I was ten years old. Is it the same for everyone? Apparently not. What's odd to me is that many Americans who love to sit down in front of a whole lobster and do what it takes to get at all the succulent meat will not consider doing the same with a whole fish. I don't know why, but I do know that these people are missing something really special.

For starters, whole fish simply taste better than fish fillets. Meat cooked close to the bone, and clinging to it, is much more delicious than detached meat. Furthermore, the whole fish offers a wide variety of tastes and textures; fillets are monochromatic, whole fish are kaleidoscopic.

Then there's the ritual aspect. Just as in lobster eating, there's something supremely satisfying in sitting down to a whole entity, close to its form in a natural state, and systematically working your way through it. It's a rhythm thing. Eating a fillet has no rhythm at all; you just go from one end to the other. Eating a whole fish is something you orchestrate.

If you're not used to the process, of course, you may be concerned that it's tricky—but it's really not. Just remember that you use your knife (a wide one is recommended) to lift the fillet away from the bone; you do this by running the knife between the fillet and bone. You do this on one side, eat that fillet, then lift the bone away to reveal the other fillet. There are fine points, but don't be afraid to discover them on your own—everything else is basically an improvisation!

Criteria for Quality (for Whole, Sautéed Dover Sole)

- Is the fish fresh?
- Is the meat neither underdone (still translucent) nor overdone (turning soft and mushy)?
- Is the meat firm and resilient?
- Are the edges and exteriors of the fish golden brown, not blackened?
- Is there some crunch on the outside?
- Is there enough foaming butter to cover the fish? is there too much? (it shouldn't seem greasy)

When

To me, a whole sautéed Dover sole is the ideal main course for an elegant lunch: it gives you a significant gastronomic experience without weighing you down. I also wouldn't sneer at it as a main course for a light dinner or—on Trencherman's Night Out—as a fish course before a heavier meat course! Any way you cut it, don't cut it—it has to be one whole fish per person, otherwise the experience is compromised. Serve with boiled potatoes, lightly buttered and parsleyed.

In Your Glass

Whole sautéed Dover sole has a few pitfalls for wine, easily avoided. The fish is delicate in flavor, so I think the delicacy of white wine is the best accompaniment. However, there are plenty of white wines in the market that are far from delicate: America's favorite white, for example, California Chardonnay, is likely to overpower the poor critter with its combination of fruit, oak, alcohol, and sweetness. What's really needed is a dry white wine that has body (to stand up to the texture) but not so much overt character that it will drown out the subtle fish. Where to turn? For me, this, finally, is the perfect place to wheel out an aged white Burgundy. Yes, it's Chardonnay—but the right white Burgundy features Chardonnay handled with surpassing delicacy. A ten-year-old premier cru from Meursault, Chassagne-Montrachet, Puligny-Montrachet, or Chablis will have diminished fruit (good!) and lots of subtle earthy-stony-minerally character. This should blend seamlessly with the taste of the fish.

SINGAPORE CHILI CRAB

You may remember the story in the papers a few years ago about the brutal official caning of a young American who had had the temerity to despoil a Singapore wall with graffiti. Shortly after that event, I went on a gastronomic journey to this tiny city-state at the southern tip of the Malay Peninsula, making very sure to leave my spray-paint cans home.

I'd heard, of course, that Singapore was a great food city, and I was clearly planning to make the most of it. But who knew which laws I'd be violating in the unrestrained pursuit of pleasure? Are there ordinances about tucking your napkin into your shirt? Fines for spilling your sauce on the tablecloth? Jail sentences for (gasp) using your chopsticks at the wrong end?

The answer is no. Food is an exception to some of the grim rules of Singapore, perhaps the only socially acceptable form of pleasure. The Singaporean food scene is even on the raucous side; though you'll find many sedate, luxurious, high-end dining venues in Singapore, the most exciting food of all is served at sprawling, teeming street food centers called food courts. And as you wander around such dazzling places as Newton Circus, you'll learn the ultimate secret about the disorderliness of Singaporean food: it's not one uniform cuisine at all but a messy, thrilling blend of three entirely discrete cuisines. Look over there: a man is twirling stretchy breads, as in India, preparing them for dips in a chicken curry. Right across the way a man is pulling fresh rice noodles, as in China, on their long march towards a soy-drenched union with stir-fried shrimp and bok choy. And, before you return to your table, don't miss the Malay chef combining the candlenuts and coconut milk of his indigenous cuisine with chunks of beef to make a marvelous *rendang*.

These ethnic elements have been simmering in this part of the world for centuries. But when the British arrived in 1819—it was Sir Thomas Stamford Raffles who realized that his countrymen could build Singapore into a great trading post—they weren't about to aid the movement towards culinary fusion. For though it's true that Raffles brought many more Indians to Singapore from another British colonial outpost, and in that way added more spice to the melting pot, the Brits were fundamentally afraid that all of these groups—Malays, Chinese, and Indians—might unite and rebel against their colonial masters. Therefore, Raffles decreed that all ethnic groups must live in separate residential neighborhoods. The result was that each culture and each cuisine was preserved intact. And today you still do see some culinary segregation—Indian restaurants, Chinese restaurants, Malay restaurants, a gastronomic ordering that seems in step with modern Singaporean regimentation.

But no amount of governmental regulation—then or now—could keep the culinary ideas apart forever. Over five hundred years ago things had already begun to merge gastronomically, deliciously. In the fifteenth century a large contingent of Chinese men settled near what is now Singapore and began to marry local Malay women. These intermarriages established a new ethnic subgroup that became known as Straits Chinese. It is said that the Malay wife taught the Chinese husband to like curries and slowly simmered dishes, and showed him how to cook with fiery chilies, coriander, cumin, cardamom, and velvety smooth coconut milk. He, in turn, taught her how to use rice noodles and Chinese vegetables, fermented soy and bean paste, bamboo shoots, and ginger. And he showed her how to use a wok to stir-fry. The women in this group were known as *Nonya*s and, since the cooking was largely left to them, the cooking style—based on the blending of the intense, fragrant Malay food with the more subtle flavors of Chinese cooking—became known as Nonya.

Another type of ethnic blending has resulted in chili crab—a remarkable dish in which big hunks of fresh crab, in the shell, are sautéed and thrown together with a spicy, sweet, sour tomato sauce. It is a deliriously delicious dish that makes me happy every time I eat it, because—in addition to its great taste—it reminds me that legislators can't legislate food; if cultures want to merge, they'll merge. Textbooks refer to it as not Chinese, Malay, Indian, or Nonya; it is called Singaporean, as are a number of other hybrid dishes. Furthermore, I defy anyone to pass petty laws about local cleanliness while eating chili crab; no matter how repressive and regulated Singapore may appear, when chili crab is served, everyone rolls up his (or her) sleeves and gets permissibly dirty.

The Great Chili Crab Debates

One of the first questions you'll be asked in Singapore is if you've ever tasted chili crab. If you say no, be prepared to hear a long list of suggested restaurants—a list that will be contradicted by your concierge, who's got his own list.

Then there's the discussion as to whether the local, smaller blue swimmer crabs are sweeter than the big crabs from Sri Lanka, traditionally used for the dish. Once that's settled, you'll have to listen to arguments for flavoring the sauce with chili sauce from a jar or with homemade chili purée. It's not over, of course—for then there'll be the debate about thickening the dish with cornstarch or with egg.

As you'll discover, when it comes to controversy, chili crab is the Singaporean equivalent of bouillabaisse, cassoulet, and paella.

SINGAPORE CHILI CRAB

This version of Singapore chili crab was inspired by a class I attended in Singapore, given by Violet Oon, Singapore's most famous cooking teacher. You won't, of course, be able to use the crabs they use in Singapore—but our large West Coast Dungeness crabs are most like theirs. The dish could also be made with Maryland blue crabs, or even with frozen king crab legs from Alaska.

MAKES 4 TO 6 SERVINGS

2 large live Dungeness crabs, each about 1 1/4 to 1 1/2 pounds

10 to 12 fresh, medium-hot red chilies, stemmed, seeded, and chopped

2 tablespoons minced garlic

2 tablespoons minced shallots

1 tablespoons finely grated gingerroot

3 tablespoons vegetable oil, plus additional

1 1/2 cups water

1 tablespoon Asian fish sauce, such as nam pla

3/4 cup Heinz chili sauce

2 tablespoons fresh lime juice

1 tablespoon cornstarch combined with 2 tablespoons water

2 large eggs, lightly beaten

3 tablespoons sliced scallion for garnish

1. In a large pot of boiling salted water, add the crabs and cook them for about 1 minute, or until they're no longer moving. Drain them, and set them aside until they are cool enough to handle.

2. To clean the crabs, pull off the top shells; pull and twist off the aprons; remove the gills. Separate the large claws, but leave the legs intact. With a sharp knife, cut the crabs into quarters.

3. In a mortar with a pestle, or a small food processor, pound or process the chilies, garlic, shallots, and ginger with a little oil if necessary to make a paste.

4. Heat a wok over moderately high heat. Add 3 tablespoons of oil, and heat until hot. Add the chili and garlic paste, and stir-fry for 1 minute. Add the crabs, and stir-fry for 2 to 3 minutes. Add the water, fish sauce, chili sauce, and lime juice. Bring to a boil, and simmer, covered, for 7 minutes. Transfer the crabs to a bowl.

5. Bring the sauce in the wok to a boil. Stir the cornstarch mixture, and add it to the wok. Simmer until it is thickened. Reduce the heat to low, and gradually add the eggs in a stream, whisking. Return the crabs to the wok, and coat them with sauce.

6. Transfer the crabs with their sauce to a serving platter, and garnish with scallion.

How to Serve

Eating Singapore Chili Crab is a messy, hands-on affair, and silverware just doesn't cut it (so to speak). Cracking the claws with anything at hand (including your teeth), sucking, and slurping are all part of the scene. Just provide finger bowls, nutcrackers for any stubborn shells, bowls for the wreckage, and some good crusty bread to sop up the sauce. That's right—in the multicultural enclave of Singapore, they sometimes use bread (even white bread!) for sauce sopping.

Criteria for Quality

- Are the crabs perfectly cooked? (not overcooked)
- Is the dish filled with big, abundant hunks of them?
- Does the sauce have layers of flavor?
- In addition to the heat, can you taste the *flavor* of the chilies?

When

Singapore Chili Crab is a great addition to any meal that already includes other Asian dishes. If you're making, say, a Chinese dinner, and have two or three main courses that you're planning to serve together on platters, a platter of Singapore Chili Crab would be a great addition. Likewise if you're planning a tabletop of Thai, Vietnamese, or multi-culti main courses.

In Your Glass

Well, the national beer of Singapore is Tiger—since Singapore was once overrun with tigers and was named for tigers. Never mind that the last tiger seen in the city was shot under the barroom at Raffles a hundred years ago. The beer with its name—or any other crisp lager—makes a fine accompaniment to Singapore Chili Crab.

PAELLA

Like many of the world's great multi-ingredient dishes—e.g., choucroute, minestrone, cassoulet, gumbo—paella provokes never-ending debate. We know that paella is a rice dish, often yellow in color, and contains a plethora of other ingredients—fish, meats, vegetables. But what is the classic paella? Well, no one really knows that, of course—for there is no "classic" version of paella, or of any of these legendary dishes.

However, each of these dishes does have a classic *profile*—that is, a range of elements that are right in the dish and a range of elements that would be wrong. To me, the essence of paella is in the following four considerations.

The Rice-to-Stuff Proportion. Above all, paella is a *rice* dish; when Spaniards eat it, it is the rice that they find most interesting. In America, paella falls into that group of transplanted dishes that focus too heavily on the proteins around the star ingredient. Paella in American restaurants usually features lousy, uninteresting rice upon which piles of shellfish, chicken, and sausage take up space; to add insult to injury, the proteins aren't often of high quality or perfectly cooked. The chef's main statement is that he's generous enough to throw a lot of "stuff" onto your rice.

The Rice Itself. Don't think "pilaf" when you think about paella; the texture of the rice in a well-made paella is not fluffy. Thinking "risotto" will get you closer to the original—for though a proper paella is not quite as wet and creamy as an Italian risotto, it tends in that direction. Paella rice glistens invitingly with oil, and the grains, though not clumpy, more or less adhere to one another. To achieve the authentic look and feel, you should use short-grained Valencian rice, called *granza.* If you can't find it, an Italian rice intended for risotto—like Arborio—will make a good substitute.

The Stuff. As long as the rice is perfectly cooked, the question of "which stuff" goes into a paella doesn't concern me that much; many different paella helpers are used in Spain. When I make paella, I usually include some variety of shellfish (I especially like tiny clams and mussels in my paella). I like to include pieces of chicken as well (preferably the more moist and flavorful dark meat), and I'm always excited by slices of chorizo, the great paprika-spangled pork sausage of Spain. I hasten to point out, however, that adding these meats to a shellfish paella is a source of great controversy. In Valencia, they remain purists; paellas are seafood paellas, meat paellas, or vegetable paellas. Mixtures will be made for visitors who expect them—which means that the seafood-chorizo paella is "tourist food." But I must confess that, though I'm usually a stickler for regional authenticity, I find this is one case where the evolved, international version of a local dish is also delicious.

There's another explanation for the appearance of shellfish with pork in the same dish. Some believe that it dates back to the 1490s, when many Jews were expelled from Spain. Jews were allowed to remain at that time if they renounced their Judaism—and what better way to proclaim one's renunciation than to include both shellfish and pork in paella? Now, I'm not renouncing anything—but I do believe the mixture of shellfish sweetness and rich porky flavor to be utterly delicious.

Other Flavorings. The Arabs brought saffron to Spain, as well as rice, and today people always think of paella as saffron-flavored rice. In Valencia, however, saffron is not always used; orange-colored paella (as opposed to yellow-colored paella), or even black paella (from squid ink) is perfectly acceptable. In American restaurants, the rice is almost always yellow—but, unfortunately, it's often cheap turmeric masquerading as expensive saffron that makes it so. Saffron is a pleasant addition to paella, and, if I'm feeling flush, I use it.

A paella spice that's even more commonly used than saffron in Spain is sweet Spanish paprika; it gives paella an attractive orange color. I try to find quality Spanish paprika and often use it in paella, even alongside saffron. I also couldn't dream of a paella that didn't use garlic, olive oil, and a terrific stock to flavor the rice.

There are two other important considerations when making paella: the pan to use and what fire to put it over.

The traditional paella pan, made of metal, is round, wide, and quite flat; standard ones are about 1½ feet in diameter, though they can be smaller or much, much larger. Spaniards feel that this pan is essential to the moist, traditional texture of paella.

Originally, paella was cooked in the open air, over wood fires. To this day, many Valencian men take it on as a pleasant chore to cook paella outside, over fire, usually on Sunday. However, modern life being what it is, most Spaniards go the more convenient route of cooking paella in the kitchen—usually on top of the stove for the initial simmer, then in the oven for the last 10 minutes.

The Original Paella

The origins of paella are shrouded in antiquity. But this much is clear. Rice came to Spain in the eighth century, brought from the Middle East by the conquering Arabs (hundreds of years before rice appeared in Italy!). The east coast of Spain became the center of Spanish rice production, in the Mediterranean province of Valencia. Some enterprising cook there—we don't know in which century—decided to combine rice with a few ingredients that were locally abundant. Rabbit was surely one; Spain, in fact, was so overrun by rabbits that the name España itself comes from a Carthaginian word for "rabbit." Valencia was also crawling with snails, ancient paella's second most important ingredient. And, despite thousands of restaurants today putting peas in their paellas, the first ones appear to have been greened instead by snips of string beans.

So there you have it: rice, rabbit, snails, string beans. The Ur-paella.

Buying a Paella Pan

If you want to cook paella the traditional way, in a traditional paella pan, you can mail-order a good pan from

Cerámica de España: *7700 N.W. Fifty-fourth Street, Miami, FL 33166 tel: 305-597-9161 fax: 305-591-0989*

They sell paella pans in either stainless steel or iron and in a wide range of sizes. For the paella recipe here, I recommend the 13 1/2-inch stainless steel pan (reference VC6PLZ).

The best way to simulate a traditional paella would be to place your paella pan on top of a smoky wood fire in a covered grill; when a recipe calls for covering the pan, simply cover the grill.

As you know, convenience is not one of my highest priorities in approaching a dish—I want *great* food above all! But I once stumbled upon an utterly nontraditional paella method—it uses a wok!—that yielded absolutely scrumptious and authentic-tasting results. It has become my favorite home paella.

A MODERN VERSION OF AN ANCIENT PAELLA: SAFFRON RICE WITH CHICKEN, SHRIMP, STRING BEANS, AND SNAILS

This version of paella, based on a recipe I devised for a book I wrote on matching wine with food, requires no open fire and no paella pan. All you need is a range top and a wok—this paella doesn't even go in the oven! I once served it to Penelope Casas, doyenne of Spanish cookbook writers in America, who was amazed that such results could be achieved this way. Later on, I served it to Lou Broman, the wonderful head of the Wines from Spain office in America who died way too young; I'll never forget Lou calling it the best paella he'd ever tasted. Its ingredients are based on what we know of the Ur-paella—except that I've substituted chicken for the less available rabbit. If you want to be historical, by all means change the chicken back to ½ pound of boned rabbit.

MAKES 4 MAIN-COURSE SERVINGS

1/2 pound medium-size shrimps, about 12

1/2 teaspoon freshly ground coarse black pepper

1 tablespoon Spanish extra-virgin olive oil

2 large chicken thighs, skin on, boned, each cut in quarters

2 ounces chorizo, sliced thin

2 large shallots, chopped

3 medium garlic cloves, chopped

2 ounces string beans, cut in 1/2-inch lengths

1 cup Spanish short-grained rice (or use Italian short-grained rice)

1/2 cup very finely minced fresh parsley leaves

2 cups rich chicken stock

1/2 teaspoon saffron threads

1 teaspoon sweet Spanish paprika

12 large canned snails

1 large red pepper, roasted, peeled, and seeded (optional)

1. Butterfly each shrimp by cutting along the back, through the shell, to remove the black vein. Rinse, then spread each shrimp wide open, leaving the shell on. Sprinkle with salt and the freshly ground pepper. Set aside for ½ hour.

2. In a large, heavy pan with a tight-fitting lid—prefer-ably a large wok—heat the olive oil over medium-high heat. Season the chicken thighs well with salt and pepper, then add them to the hot oil, skin side down. Cook for 2 minutes, or until the skin just begins to brown. Add the chorizo slices, and toss them with the chicken. Cook for 1 minute. Add the shallots, garlic, and string beans. Mix well. Add the rice and half of the parsley, stirring to coat the rice thoroughly with oil. Add the chicken stock, saffron, and paprika. Stir well. Bring the mixture to a boil, reduce the heat, cover, and simmer for 15 minutes.

3. Lift the cover, embed the shrimp in the top part of the rice, then scatter the snails around the shrimp. If you are using the red pepper, cut it into 8 strips and arrange it in the rice in a decorative pattern. Cover, and cook for 10 minutes more, or until almost all the liquid has been absorbed and the rice is just cooked.

4. Serve at the table out of the cooking vessel, sprinkling the portions with the remaining parsley.

Criteria for Quality

- *Is the rice the star of the dish?*
- *Is the rice moist and glistening?*
- *Is it al dente?*
- *Is it loaded with flavor?*
- *Have cheap saffron substitutes (like turmeric) been avoided?*
- *Are the supporting players harmonious together?*
- *Have they been cooked just right (not overcooked)?*

When

Paella in Spain is a main-course event, and I strongly urge you to make it the centerpiece of a dinner party or family meal. If you're making a one-course meal, a green salad with a few Spanish touches (olives, peppers, and chickpeas, perhaps) and a good loaf of bread would round things out perfectly.

Of course, you could also make your paella an in-between course in a fancier meal. Start with, say, a Spanish-accented opener—like asparagus with sherry-vinegar mayonnaise or an assortment of Spanish-style hams. Serve smaller portions of paella as a kind of pasta course; the recipe given here will serve 8 in this way. Then go on to a main course, like roast lamb or roast pork. Very Spanish, very delicious.

In Your Glass

I'd wager that most of the paella served in this country is served in the presence of sangria. This pitcher of wine and fruit is also served sometimes in Spain, and, to tell you the truth, I'm rather fond of the match. Just make sure to stick to Spanish tradition here: your sangria should be made with red wine. In Spain, there is no such thing as white sangria. (Turn page for recipe.)

I do, however, prefer a good bottle of wine with paella—and, once again, the color is red. In Spain, white wine is almost never drunk with paella. The wine of choice is a young, fruity, mirthful red.

Which brings us to a wine distribution problem in America. The paella type of red wine in Spain can be called vinos jovenes *(young wines) or* sin crianza *(no aging). In other words, only the youngest, simplest red wines are drunk with this dish. But since these wines are inexpensive, American importers rarely bother bringing them into our country. So it's hard to find a Spanish wine in the United States that goes perfectly with paella. Look, instead, for young Beaujolais from France, young Novello from Italy (a Beaujolais Nouveau–type wine made in many Italian regions), or young, inexpensive Shiraz from Australia.*

Sangria for Paella

If you do choose to serve sangria with paella, make sure that it's made with lively, fruity, young red wine and that it's not too sweet.

MAKES 3 TO 6 SERVINGS

1 bottle Beaujolais Nouveau from the most recent
    vintage, or young Beaujolais

1 orange

1 lime

1/2 lemon

3 tablespoons Grand Marnier

1 tablespoon superfine sugar

Ice cubes

6 ounces soda water

1. *Pour the wine into a large pitcher. Wash the fruits, cut them into thin slices, and add them to the pitcher. Add the Grand Marnier and sugar. Marinate in the refrigerator for at least a few hours, preferably overnight.*

2. *When you are ready to serve, fill up the pitcher with ice cubes, add the soda water, and stir well. Serve with a wooden spoon in the pitcher.*

THE AMAZING FOOD OF SPAIN

One of my great loves—and I think a nation often overlooked as a travel destination by Americans—is Spain. The first night I ever hit Madrid—and got taken around to what seemed like a few dozen tapas bars, each serving delicious little plates—I knew that something was happening here that no wan paella in the United States had ever prepared me for. Even the tapas bars that started opening in the United States in the 1980s couldn't prepare you for the true taste and spirit of Spain.

The quality that's most salient, and leaves the strongest mark on the food, is sociability: Spain is a country that, even more than France or Italy, loves to live life in public. Most nights, year-round (particularly in the South), streets are crowded with Spaniards eating, drinking, laughing, flirting, arguing, singing. Glasses of sherry (called copitas*) are continually being filled and downed, and small plates of food are being passed everywhere. Out of this environment come tastes that are compact, concentrated, and vivid; one slice of Spanish sausage on a plate is all you need to make your palate reverberate for minutes—until the compact, concentrated, and vivid sip of Fino sherry you take prepares you for the next taste of food.*

Spain is on its own time when it comes to food. That first tapas crawl I took in Madrid started at about 8:00 P.M.—the time most Americans are finishing dinner. It went on for two hours, but these were just the preappetizer appetizers; we sat down at a restaurant for dinner at about 10:30! Many subsequent experiences have demonstrated the point: if you arrive at 10:00 P.M. you'll be a lonely American in the restaurant. People start arriving at 10:30, but the crowd doesn't really hit until 11:00 P.M. Lunch is no different. I realized this on my first visit to sherry country, in the South, when I paid a visit to a bodega—"before lunch," as they said. They seemed a little surprised when I showed up at 11:00 A.M., but they graciously gave me a tour of every-

thing—for a good four hours. I was feeling more than a little peckish, but it wasn't until 3:30 or so that they suggested we go to a tapas bar for some fried seafood. It was delicious, and I thought that was lunch . . . until we showed up at a fancy restaurant for a full-course lunch at 4:30.

How do they do this, day after day? How do they finish dinner at 1:00 A.M. and get ready for work the next day? I'm not really sure—but I know it has something to do with letting the pleasure of dining drive your life, not letting the crushing pressure of other responsibilities dictate that you grab a hamburger on the run. Spanish food, in Spain, satisfies the hunger for quick, intense, vivid bites (at the prelunch or predinner tapas bars) and the hunger for slow, focused, luxuriant dining (at the more formal restaurants or around the family dining table). And it satisfies those dual hungers twice a day, every day. To do just one or the other in the United States, as we almost always do, and to do them at the wrong time, robs the Spanish dining experience of its essential rhythms and, for me at least, changes the way I perceive the food.

Another important reason for the different taste of Spanish food in America is the unavailability of Spanish ingredients. This is a cuisine that is driven by the high quality of local products—and the products that are the very most exciting are not available in the United States. Never feel comfortable again in a comparison of hams from around the world until you've tasted Jabugo, the amazing ham of southwest Spain. Produced from a special breed of black-nailed, acorn-munching pig, it is simply the greatest ham I have ever tasted: sweet, silky, nutty, earthy, haunting. The U.S. government has always made it hard for artisanal foreign hams to show up here, and Spanish ham is no exception. This is a shame—because Americans have no idea that Spain is the greatest cured-pork nation on earth.

But the joys of Spain go beyond turf—for surf is outstanding as well. Will you forgive me one more superlative? Spain—particularly along the northern Atlantic coast, but also near Cádiz in the South, and off the Mediterranean coast in the East—has the greatest seafood I've ever tasted. The variety of fish and shellfish coming out of these waters is unsurpassed, and much of it (particularly the shellfish) has a sweetness that I've rarely experienced elsewhere. Even the oysters—which I've been lucky enough to taste hauled right out of the fjordlike rías of Galicia, the source of the world's greatest shellfish—are the only oysters in the world that compare to Brittany's.

Another surprise in Spain is the great variety of regional cuisine.

The first region I visited in Spain, after a stopover in Madrid, was Catalonia, the region around Barcelona—where I was haughtily told that the Castilians (in the center of Spain) roast; the Andalusians (in the south of Spain) fry; but the Catalans (in the northeast corner) cook.

They needn't have been so dismissive of those central roasters; simple restaurants throughout the heart of Spain roasting legs of baby lamb and whole suckling pigs regularly turn out some of the best lamb and pork I've ever tasted. It is true that cooking in Andalusia can be a little greasy and a little casual—but the range of dishes there combining fabulous tomatoes, peppers, and other produce with the exotic culinary vestiges of Arab occupation make for a terrifically exciting regional cuisine.

As for Catalan cuisine—well, it is fabulous. The part of Spain that's closest to France has a few cuisines that seem more, well, French, in their elaborateness, precision, attention to detail, elegance, and creativity. Near Catalonia is the Basque region, which many feel—the Catalans will hate me for this—has the best cooking in all of Spain.

Along the way there are regional styles of cooking all over the country that will take your breath away, and regional dishes almost no one in the United States has heard of. I'll never forget the fabada *of Asturias, along the north coast—a rich stew made from very large white beans, brimming with secret parts of pigs and an embarrassment of flavor. The* morcilla, *or blood sausage, made in Burgos, a little south of Asturias, is firm textured, sweetly spiced, absolutely wonderful—and supplies one of the pillars for an astounding hot red pepper and* morcilla *soup that is traditional in the Rioja region. And the Galician twist on* cocido—*a dish interpreted as a modest chickpea, meat, and vegetable soup in most parts of Spain—results here in an enormous platter of cured meats and vegetables piled as high as the ceiling, a joyous antidote to the gray days and witchlike spookiness of Spain's rain-swept northwestern corner.*

MOUSSAKA

Moussaka is a fabulous layered casserole from the eastern Mediterranean—perhaps my favorite casserole in the world—that combines two of the region's top ingredients, eggplant and lamb.

I always think of it as a kind of Coptic version of lasagna al forno: instead of pasta layers, you have eggplant layers; instead of meatballs or sausages, you have ground lamb; instead of gooey mozzarella on top, you have a béchamel sauce. Additionally, there are other ingredients that make the dish taste oh-so-Greek to me: olive oil, oregano, and the kind of tomato sauce that could never be Italian, flavored as it so prominently is with cinnamon and red wine vinegar.

Of course, what I call oh-so-Greek may be oh-so-Turkish to someone else—for the fact of the matter is that this dish has long been in dispute between the two countries, a squabble as explosive as the one over Cyprus. Who owns moussaka? Where did it originate? Greece or Turkey?

My own position on the matter is: I don't care. I grew up eating moussaka in Greek restaurants, so I do tend to think of it as Greek. However, fabulous Turkish places are now opening all over our country—and perhaps this generation of restaurants will sway my allegiance. Ultimately, it makes little difference; I don't care if it's Greek moussaka or Turkish moussaka as long as it's *good* moussaka.

And that's where the real problem comes in.

I wouldn't say that moussaka is riding high, reputation-wise, these days. Having become the flagship dish of Greek cuisine throughout the world, it has been abused by lazy chefs everywhere for generations now. This is the case even in Greece. I recently went through every Greek cookbook I could read and found little enthusiasm for the dish; Greek cookbook writers seem to include it because they have to.

Here are the main moussaka problems:

- It tastes tired.
- The topping is thick and heavy.
- The moussaka is drowning in tomato sauce.
- It's too oily.

The last one is the biggest problem. The slices of eggplant have to soften through cooking before they're layered in the casserole, and the traditional way to do this is to sauté the slices in olive oil. Well, eggplant is a sponge—and those slices absorb the oil like crazy. A few years back, when I was discovering the fabulous possibilities of whole eggplants baked in the oven, I realized that one of those possibilities is moussaka. If you simply cook your whole eggplant at 375 degrees for about half an hour, it will be perfectly softened and moussaka-ready. At that point, cut it into ½-inch slices! Then, if you like, you can briefly sauté the slices in a little oil to give them a slight caramelization on the outside.

MOUSSAKA

See if you don't agree that this is the lightest, least oily, least tomatoey, most eggplanty, most refined moussaka that you've ever tasted.

MAKES ABOUT 15 SERVINGS

4 large eggplants, about 1 1/2 pounds each

6 tablespoons Greek olive oil, plus a little for coating the eggplants

4 medium onions, chopped

6 garlic cloves, chopped

One 28-ounce can crushed tomatoes in tomato purée

1/4 cup fresh parsley, minced

2 teaspoons dried oregano

1/2 teaspoon ground cinnamon

2 tablespoons red wine vinegar

2 pounds ground lamb

1/2 cup dry white wine

4 pinches freshly grated nutmeg

6 tablespoons unsalted butter

4 tablespoons flour

2 cups hot, scalded milk

White pepper

4 eggs

10 tablespoons fresh bread crumbs

1 cup grated Kefalotyri cheese (or substitute pecorino Romano)

1. Prick the eggplants several times with a fork. Rub a little olive oil into their skins. On a large baking sheet, roast the eggplants in a 375-degree oven until they are soft, 30 to 35 minutes, turning frequently to prevent charring.

2. Cool the eggplants, and cut them into round slices that are ½ inch thick.

3. In a sauté pan heat 4 tablespoons olive oil over high heat, and brown the eggplant slices lightly on each side. You'll need to do this in batches, adding a little of the oil each time. Drain the eggplant on paper towels, and sprinkle with salt.

4. Prepare the tomato sauce: In a saucepan heat 1 tablespoon olive oil over medium heat. Add 1 chopped onion and 2 chopped garlic cloves, and sauté them until they are tender.

5. Add the tomatoes and their purée to the saucepan, squeezing the tomatoes with your hands into coarse chunks. Add the parsley, oregano, cinnamon, and vinegar. Stir well. Bring the sauce to a boil, reduce it to a simmer, and cook, uncovered, for 25 minutes. Reserve.

6. Prepare the lamb: Heat 1 tablespoon of olive oil in a large sauté pan over medium-high heat. Add the remaining onions and garlic. Sauté them for 5 minutes. Add the lamb, in stages if necessary, and brown it well, breaking up the pieces with a wooden spoon.

7. When the lamb is nicely browned, add the wine, bring it to a boil, and cook until the wine has nearly evaporated.

8. Season the meat with salt, pepper, and 2 pinches of nutmeg. Stir in 1 cup of the reserved tomato sauce. Bring it to a boil, reduce the heat, and simmer for 1 hour.

9. Prepare the béchamel: In a large saucepan melt 4 tablespoons of the butter over medium-low heat, and gradually whisk in the flour. Cook for 2 minutes, whisking constantly. Do not let the roux brown. Add the hot milk all at once, and whisk rapidly to combine. Bring the sauce to a slow boil, whisking constantly. Reduce the heat, and simmer the sauce for 25 minutes, stirring frequently, until it is smooth and thickened. Season with salt, white pepper, and the remaining nutmeg. Let it cool slightly.

10. Beat the eggs well in a mixing bowl, and whisk in a spoonful of béchamel. Whisk in the remaining béchamel in a thin stream, and adjust the seasoning, if needed.

11. Preheat the oven to 350 degrees.

12. Assemble the moussaka: Sprinkle 2 tablespoons of bread crumbs across the bottom of a large baking dish (18 × 8 × 3 inches), and cover the crumbs evenly with half the eggplant slices. Drain as much oil from the lamb mixture as possible, and spread the meat over the eggplant layer. Top the meat with half of the cheese, then with half the remaining bread crumbs. Place the remaining eggplant slices on top of the bread crumbs, then the béchamel sauce, the remaining cheese, and the remaining bread crumbs in even layers. Dot the top generously with the remaining butter.

13. Bake for 45 minutes. The top of the moussaka should be well browned. If it's not, brown it briefly under a broiler. When the moussaka is cooked, let it cool slightly—about 15 minutes—then cut it into 3-inch squares to serve. Serve with extra tomato sauce, if desired.

On Greek Olive Oil

Though I've done everything I can to reduce the oiliness of moussaka, I wouldn't want you to leave the oil out entirely! This is especially true if you're using Greek olive oil.

Greek olive oil makes Greek food taste Greek. Much of it is green, like the oil of Tuscany—but it often tastes, of all things, like olives. I've enjoyed especially Greek olive oil made from the Krononeiko olive (an especially good one is the Peloponnesian Agoureleo). Not only are Greek olive oils great oils, but they represent, perhaps, the best value in the whole olive oil marketplace.

On Greek Cheese

If you're using grated cheese in a Greek dish, you might as well do it the Greek way—use Kefalotyri, a hard, yellow, sheep's-milk cheese that's also made in Cyprus and Syria. Tyri means "cheese" in Greek, and kephalo (like cephalo-) means "head"; no, this is not headcheese, but it probably earned its moniker by being larger than the small village cheeses. After dry salting and three months of maturation, it's a pretty sharp, salty product—perfect for grating.

Another typical Greek cheese is Mizithra (usually sheep's milk), which is made from the whey left over after feta cheese is made from the curds (Italian ricotta is also a whey cheese). Mizithra is made in a variety of ways: soft, medium, firm, fresh, aged, low fat, full fat. If you want to use it as a grating cheese, look for the hard, salty variety usually called Skliri (hard) Mizithra. The best Mizithra comes from Crete.

If you don't have access to Greek cheeses, any dry, aged, hard Italian sheep's-milk cheese (called pecorino) will be a fine grating substitute.

Criteria for Quality

- Is it oily and heavy? (it shouldn't be—there should be a taste of Greek olive oil about it, but the lighter the moussaka feels on the palate, the better it is)
- Does it taste of eggplant?
- Does it taste of lamb?
- Does it taste of cinnamon? (a subtle taste is best)
- Are the tomatoes kept to a minimum?
- Is it brown and puffy on top?
- Do the layers meld into a soft, sensuous, mouth-caressing whole?

When

I'm used to eating moussaka as a main course in a Greek meal. Start with cold, nonmeat Greek meze (like taramasalata, feta with kalamata olives, large white beans with olive oil, skordalia, et cetera), then move on to your main-course casserole. The Turks sometimes like to add potatoes to moussaka, but I prefer to serve roasted potatoes with olive oil and lemon on the side.

In Your Glass

You'll never catch me drinking anything other than Retsina with moussaka. This bane of wine connoisseurs everywhere earns its disdained position by dint of an additive—pine resin—that dates back to antiquity as a flavoring for wine. Those who hate it say it makes the wine taste like turpentine. But if you're used to it, you'll agree that food tastes a whole lot more Greek when it's served with Retsina. Think of it as an extra spice, or herb, that you get to mix with your food.

   I know that this confession'll earn me the undying enmity of wine geeks everywhere. But better Greek than geek.

CHOUCROUTE GARNIE

The great Alsatian specialty choucroute garnie is gastronomic heaven for me: a steaming platter of exquisitely flavored sauerkraut, topped by an assortment of sausages and other cured or smoked meats. After a first course of raw French oysters, my last meal on earth would indubitably feature choucroute garnie as the main course.

Ironically, it took me years of travel to France before I even noticed this miracle of informal cooking. During my heaviest French travel years, the 1980s, I was bewitched by two- and three-star restaurants, the top of the gastronomic heap, places where you'd never see choucroute garnie in a million years. Well, it wasn't hard to be bewitched when the American dollar bought ten francs, and two Americans could dine on the world's most expensive food in the world's most luxurious settings for less than a hundred dollars.

One day a Parisian friend took me for *une choucroute* at one of the hundreds of Parisian spots where the dish is available; until then, I'd had no idea that Paris is crawling with choucroute. I was, of course, bowled over by it. I'm especially hot for choucroute in France because never once—I mean this: never once!—have I had anything like real French choucroute in a restaurant in the United States.

And it's not for lack of trying! Here are the "domestic" choucroute problems:

1. In typical American fashion, we take a wonderful peasant dish and, unlike the tasteful peasants who created it, focus on the flashy protein part of the dish. What we have historically failed to understand is that pasta is about pasta, not meatballs! Pizza is about pizza, not pepperoni! Paella is about rice, not shellfish toppings! Remember: choucroute is about sauerkraut, not about the meats that top it. The full name of the dish is choucroute garnie, or "garnished sauerkraut." That says a lot: the meat that *we* tend to focus on is perceived by the Alsatians as a *garnish* for the main event—which, of course, is the sauerkraut.

2. Ah, the sauerkraut. This is the outstanding problem in America. In Alsace, every fall, tons of cabbage heads are sliced and salted to make the new sauerkraut for the year; great care is paid to the process, and great sauerkraut comes out of it. Here in America, the process is not seasonal, much more commercial . . . and really mediocre sauerkraut comes out of it. What's the difference between the two? The largest problem is that American producers don't shred the cabbage correctly: ours is thick cut, and sometimes irregular in its cut, as if it went through a huge industrial machine while the "mechanics" were on a coffee break. Sauerkraut in Alsace (and Paris) is always wonderfully thin and delicate—sort of like capelli d'angeli to our fettuccine. In such a potentially heavy dish as choucroute garnie, this makes all the difference in the world; the French cut of sauerkraut brings an utterly surprising lightness to choucroute garnie that Alsatians find essential.

3. Finally, when it comes to the garnie—I find the meats they use in France much more interesting than the meats we use here. Granted, a real choucroute garnie in France will have sausage in it that looks something like hot dogs (*saucisses de Strasbourg*)—but these will usually be accompanied by a range of other, more interesting sausages, with coarser textures and porkier flavors. Additionally, many choucroutes in France offer cured and smoked pork cuts that are either difficult or impossible to find here.

Now for the good news. First of all, choucroute garnie is actually an extremely easy dish to make—so there'll be no cooking problems to prevent you from serving a great one at home. The only problems are shopping problems—but I'm about to arm you with the information you need to find the best possible ingredients in America!

SHOPPING FOR SAUERKRAUT

Do not, under any circumstances, buy sauerkraut in a can when making choucroute! This most readily available form of sauerkraut is limp, watery, cabbagey, old tasting.

The next widely available option is fine: plastic bags of sauerkraut that you'll find in the refrigerator case of the supermarket. Though the sauerkraut in these bags is cut American style—coarsely—the product is fresh, usually has a good crunch, and picks up flavors nicely.

Even better, if you can find it, is "loose" sauerkraut, out of a barrel. You will need to investigate the German–central European grocery possibilities in your area; many of these Old World delis carry barrels of fresh sauerkraut. In my experience, you won't find much improvement here in the cut of the sauerkraut—it's *still* too thick—but the flavor of this sauerkraut is usually more sour, more salty, more palate stimulating than the flavor of the sauerkraut in the refrigerator-case bags.

Now for the big news. *After much searching, I have located a sauerkraut product, available in America, that approximates the thin-cut, delicate sauerkraut of Alsace!* I hesitate to get your hopes up, because I'm sure it's not *widely* available here. I will give you the name and phone number of the store where I buy it, and I know the store will ship you some—but I'm not sure how many phone calls it will take to wipe them out of their supply (maybe just a few). In any event, the product is an aluminum-foil pouch from Germany called Mildes Wein Sauerkraut (mild wine sauerkraut) manufactured in Neuss am Rhein by a company named Leuchtenberg. If you purchase it, you will see exactly what I mean by a thinner, more delicate cut. Furthermore, despite the fact that it sits on a shelf—no refrigeration is needed!—the product seems remarkably fresh, both in texture and in taste. The only shortcoming is that it's sauerkraut that has already been cooked, and you have to like the flavor the producers have given it. I do, as a matter of fact: slightly winy and sour. But it's not exactly like starting from scratch and building your own flavor.

Nevertheless, Leuchtenberg Mildes Wein Sauerkraut has become my only choice for homemade choucroute. I buy it in New York City, at the German grocery–butcher shop called Schaller & Weber. The store is found at 1654 Second Avenue (right near Eighty-sixth Street, in what used to be a great German and central European neighborhood called Yorkville). There is a mail-order business, and the phone number is 212-879-3047. Pouches of this sauerkraut weighing 500 grams (a little over a pound) cost $2.59 each, and there is a minimum mail-order charge of $35.00 at the store. But don't despair—you can beef up (or pork up) your order by also buying many of the meats you'll need for choucroute garnie (see opposite).

If you do acquire and use this sauerkraut salvation of American choucroute lovers, do not soak it before cooking (see the instructions in the recipe).

SHOPPING FOR THE MEATS

You can, of course, make a choucroute garnie with any meats that you fancy. If your only shopping source is a supermarket, you're not out of luck. Good hot dogs are fine, but an even better choice from the standard supermarket is kielbasa, or Polish sausage, cut into chunks about 4 inches long. The supermarket may also provide whole chunks of bacon, which you can cut into thick slices (about ⅜ inch) for inclusion in choucroute. Slices of smoked ham or pork chops may also be found at the supermarket. For me, a good choucroute should feature at least three or four different kinds of sausage and/or meats. But the more the merrier; for a big crowd, and a big splurge, I've "garnished" my choucroute with up to a dozen different sausages/meats.

No matter where you're buying from, here's a range of "garnishing" options for choucroute.

Sausages (these are the ones most commonly available in the United States)

Hot dogs
Kielbasa
Bratwurst (usually white in this country, though in Germany "bratwurst" signifies sausages of any color intended for browning)
Weisswurst (the finest white sausage; a Munich specialty made of veal and flavored with lemon rind)
Bauernwurst (a thick, pinkish red sausage)
Knockwurst (an even thicker, pinkish red sausage, something like a superfat, garlicky hot dog)
Bloodwurst (blood sausage, a German version of boudin noir)

Bacon (buy bacon in chunks and cut it into slices approximately ⅜ inch thick; to garnish the choucroute, do not use presliced bacon in a package—because it's so thin, it will cook away to nothing)

Lightly cured bacon, unsmoked
Lightly cured bacon, lightly smoked
Salted pork belly (this comes from the same part of the pig as bacon, but it gets a brining—like corned beef; it tastes practically like fresh meat and is delicious. At German butcher shops, they call it *Bauchfleisch.*)

Poultry (some French chefs like to mix pieces of fatty birds into their choucroutes)

Cooked goose or duck
Confit of goose or duck
Smoked goose or duck

Other

Cured pig knuckles (called *jarret de porc* in France)
Smoked ham hocks (a little too smoky for French tastes)
Smoked veal tongue (a great one is available from Schaller & Weber)
Liver dumplings

You're ready for one more consideration before you get started—for there is great controversy in Alsace concerning the proper cooking time for choucroute garnie.

The long-cooking school contends that choucroute is best when the meats have simmered with the sauerkraut for quite a while—say, two or three hours—so that the meat flavor permeates the sauerkraut. Another advantage of long cooking is that the sauerkraut picks up more fat from the meat and the result is an unctuous, almost creamy texture.

The short cookers believe that cooking sauerkraut this long makes it heavier, less attractive, and less digestible. They sacrifice a little meaty flavor in the sauerkraut to obtain a lighter, cleaner finished product.

I must say that I'm pretty much on the latter side—it is the totally unexpected lightness of choucroute in France that makes it such a delight. However, an hour of heat sure brings out a great deal of flavor. . . .

Choucroute garnie

CHOUCROUTE GARNIE

To me, this recipe is a very happy compromise between the short-cook school and the long-cook school; it yields plenty of cooked-in flavor, yet the sauerkraut retains a little fresh-tasting crunch. By all means, cook it longer if you prefer. (I have to admit that this choucroute is outrageous when it's re-heated the next day!) Remember that if you are using fresh sauerkraut (either from a refrigerated bag or loose from a barrel), you will have to give it a brief soak in water to remove the excess sourness; if you've been lucky enough to obtain the Leuchtenberg Mildes Wein Sauerkraut, do not presoak it. The meat choice in this recipe is up to you; use whatever you find on your shopping mission. This recipe yields enough sauerkraut for six hearty eaters, and—if they're really hearty—you're going to need anywhere from 4 to 6 pounds of meat altogether to make them happy (this should yield some leftovers). This amount does not include the ⅓ cup of chopped bacon, which can, if you like, come from a supermarket package of thin-sliced bacon.

MAKES 6 SERVINGS

5 pounds fresh sauerkraut, either from refrigerated plastic bags or loose from a barrel (or Leuchtenberg Mildes Wein Sauerkraut in an aluminum-foil pouch)

1/3 cup chopped bacon (you can use thin slices of supermarket bacon)

3 cloves garlic, chopped

1/2 bottle dry white wine (preferably Riesling from Alsace)

2 tablespoons juniper berries, lightly crushed with a heavy cleaver

1 teaspoon whole black peppercorns

4 cloves

4 to 6 pounds assorted sausages, cured meats, smoked meats, et cetera (see page 181 for a list of possible meats)

1. If you are using fresh sauerkraut, immerse it in a large bowl filled with cold water. Soak for 15 minutes. If you are using Leuchtenberg Mildes Wein Sauerkraut, eliminate this step.

2. Place the chopped bacon in a heavy, ovenproof pot over high heat. Sauté for 1 minute. Turn heat to medium-low, add the garlic, and sauté for another minute.

3. Preheat the oven to 325 degrees.

4. If you are using fresh sauerkraut, remove it from the water and squeeze it dry, reserving 1 cup of the soaking water. If you are using Leuchtenberg sauerkraut, simply open the pouches. Add the sauerkraut to the pot. Stir well to blend with the bacon. If you are using fresh sauerkraut, add the reserved cup of soaking water; if you are using Leuchtenberg sauerkraut, add 1 cup of tap water. Add the white wine, juniper berries, pepper-corns, and cloves. Bring to a boil on top of the stove, and boil until the liquid has almost evaporated (20 to 30 minutes).

5. Embed the meats in the sauerkraut, cover the pot, and cook in the oven until the meats are hot, about 30 minutes. Serve on a large platter; the sauerkraut should cover the bottom of it, and the meats should "garnish" the sauerkraut on top.

Criteria for Quality (some of these will be hard to satisfy with American ingredients)

- *Is the sauerkraut the point of the dish?*
- *Is there a copious ratio of sauerkraut to "garnish"?*
- *Is the sauerkraut light? lacy? a little crunchy?*
- *Is the sauerkraut a little sour but not unattractively so?*
- *Is the sauerkraut well flavored with meat juices but not unattractively fatty?*
- *Are the meats varied and interesting?*
- *Are the meats cooked right (i.e., hot, not withered, juicy)?*

When

Though I have, on occasion, had choucroute garnie for lunch—in fact, it makes a splendid family lunch on Sunday—it certainly is going to slow you down for the rest of your working day. For me, choucroute garnie is a fabulous dinner— particularly when you have plenty of time to savor it and to sit around digesting it. Don't hurry through a choucroute— before, during, or after.

As you know, I like to precede choucroute with a platter of raw oysters; if you want to be more American about it, any platter of raw or cold cooked shellfish would be a great start. With the choucroute, serve some boiled potatoes (preferably yellow ones) with a little butter, coarse salt, and parsley, and a hunk of French country bread (some whole wheat in the bread, making it a little dark, would not be inappropriate). You probably won't need much more than a simple fruit dish for dessert.

In Your Glass

The Alsatian wine of choice for choucroute is widely thought to be Gewurztraminer—that intensely flavored, litchilike Alsatian oddity that's actually very difficult to match with food. To the Alsatians, Gewurz's strong character completely overwhelms the beloved flavors of their beloved dish. No—the local wine they drink with choucroute garnie is Riesling.

Unfortunately, wine-geek Americans who know this make another huge mistake in selecting wine for choucroute. Assuming that Alsatians drink top-quality Alsatian Riesling with their choucroute, American sommeliers are always going on about grand cru this and grand cru that when recommending choucroute wine—wines that are likely to cost at least $50 in a restaurant. The French would be appalled. The Riesling you want for choucroute is light, simple, everyday, not weighed down by expensive extract, not burdened with dish-overwhelming fruit, just a good, clean, well-behaved, crisp drink with enough acidity both to match the sauerkraut and to cut through the richness of the meats. If you've spent over $15 for your choucroute-bound Alsatian Riesling at a retail shop, you've spent too much. The only type of higher-priced Riesling I like for choucroute is older Riesling; if I have a choice between a fruity young one at $10 and the same wine from five years ago at $20, I'll go for the latter since I really like with choucroute the petrol-like flavors that a little age brings to Riesling.

By the way, prices have gone nuts in Alsace over the last few years. One producer who has kept the cost of his basic Riesling down—and who continues to make it in the crisp, food-loving style I like—is Trimbach, whose basic Riesling shouldn't cost more than $12 at a wine shop. It's a great choucroute choice. Of course, if you go for Trimbach's fabulous Cuvée Frédéric Émile, you're up to $35; and if you opt for his Clos Ste. Hune—perhaps my favorite Riesling in all of Alsace—you're approaching $100 a bottle. Strangely enough, I wouldn't turn aged versions of either of these impeccably balanced wines down as choucroute partners.

At the other end of the socioeconomic spectrum, you could always drink a beer—which is just great with choucroute! I'm not enamored of the Alsatian beers available in this country, so I'd look for something in a similar style—perhaps something made here to maximize freshness. I recently discovered a microbrew from Long Island called Southampton Lager that is, to me, the best-tasting, hoppy German-style lager available in this country. It's well worth seeking out, with choucroute or without. And my favorite beer for food, wheat beer—particularly from Belgium or Germany—would be an ideal choucroute partner.

LEARNING TO LOVE GERMAN FOOD

To get truly excited about sauerkraut, you have to throw yourself into the northern European aesthetic; basically, you have to love the food of Germany. It's not easy for everyone; somehow, appreciating and respecting the soul food of the Mediterranean, or of southeast Asia, comes more easily to many Americans.

I suppose I have a few advantages in this regard. For one thing, my father's father, David Rosengarten, was born in Hamburg; so when I search for my roots, they definitely include celery roots and parsnips.

Second, I've long been partial to the glories of wine *from northern Europe. Many people who regularly watch* Taste *have noticed that the white wine I choose for food more than any other is dry German wine; this is confusing, outside Germany, because of the near-universal perception that German wine is sweet. But once you've spent time in Deutschland, you know that most people there wouldn't be caught dead drinking sweet wine with their meals; almost three-quarters of the wine produced in Germany is dry, and it goes brilliantly with food.*

But northern wine appreciation also led me to northern food appreciation. For the most important food revelations came to me in wine country, in the homes of wine makers, where I was lucky enough to experience some family-style German dining. Germany is another case of a culture's spirit having great impact on its food and the way we think about that food. It's curious that when we Americans conjure up images of French wine makers, we tend to think of ruddy-faced, beret-topped compagnards *in Beaujolais sitting under a tree with cheese, baguettes, and bottles of wine; our hearts are warmed, and we can't wait for the next hunk of* bleu de Bresse. *When we think of Italy, the hats change and the cheeses change, but it's basically the same guys sitting there in our minds' picnic spot. When we turn to Germany, however, the picture changes; Germany is more associated with cars than it is with food, and the romance of the imagined setting diminishes, like a Mercedes coming off the* Autobahn *and into a grimy industrial town with a fifteen-mile-per-hour zone. Dine with any country family in Germany, however—such as my great friends the Selbachs, in Zeltingen, in the spectacular Mosel River Valley—and you'll find the same type of country people you'd find in France or Italy, with hearts as big as their vineyards. It will change the way you think about northern European food, forever flush you with warmth the moment the idea of sausage or sauerkraut or roast duck or red cabbage arises.*

BOEUF BOURGUIGNON

Boeuf bourguignon is one of the great dishes of regional French cooking, and when you taste it today—no matter how jaded your palate is—you can't help but be reminded that there are certain verities in the gastronomic world, certain ancient formulae that need no rewriting. In the 1980s, as I descended into the Quagmire of Misguided Creativity, I went without boeuf bourguignon for many years; I'm back to it now, happily so, serving it at wintertime dinner parties with regularity. And people love it.

What is boeuf bourguignon? Actually, the name I'm using for the dish has become widely accepted—but it's not technically correct. Literally, *boeuf bourguignon* means "Burgundy beef"—and those who are sticklers for accuracy will tell you that the name should be applied only to dishes that contain beef that is actually raised in Burgundy. It is worth making this distinction, because the Burgundy region of eastern central France is home to the strain of cattle called Charolais—one of the greatest beef cattle of the world.

The sticklers would go on to point out that the dish we're discussing here, since it includes no beef from Burgundy, should actually be called boeuf à la Bourguignonne—or "beef in the style of Burgundy." This means chunks of beef stewed in red wine (guess which one) with bits of cured pork or bacon, small white onions, and mushrooms. It's the skill of the stewing that makes the difference in this great dish; I think it actually makes little difference whether you use a great beef like Charolais or not. And I know it makes no difference (or any sense) when you use a great Burgundy wine—what a waste of wonderful wine!

Here, then, is what you want in the stew pot, ingredient by ingredient.

The Beef. Stews are often ruined by the wrong cut of beef. In order for the meat in a long-cooked stew to remain tender, it has to begin with a good deal of fat in it. This means that "round" beef—like top round or bottom round—is not a good choice for the stew pot, because of its relative leanness. Chuck is my favorite choice—nicely marbled beef that's a little too chewy to be enjoyed when it's fast-cooked but absolutely delicious after a long, slow stew. Don't be foolish and hold out for beef from some pedigreed animal, like Charolais. Don't be foolish and insist on prime meat. And don't be insane and buy an expensive cut—like sirloin or filet mignon—for the stew pot.

The only other beef issue concerns the way you cut the meat. For me, bigger is better when it comes to boeuf bourguignon. The very best one I've ever eaten was at my favorite restaurant in Burgundy, a one-star in Dijon called Thibert. There, the chef used *joues de boeuf*—beef cheeks—and they appeared on the plate in hunks as big as fists. They were glorious. You probably won't be able to find beef cheeks here, but you certainly will be able to cut your chuck into hunks that are at least 2 inches square.

The Wine. There is a long tradition in Burgundy of naming dishes after the region's most famous red wines—as in the chicken stew coq au Chambertin. I once did an extensive survey in Burgundy to see if anyone had actually put the $100-a-bottle Chambertin in a stew pot. I couldn't find a chef who had ever done it—or even a chef who actually had any evidence of anyone ever doing it! The subtleties of great wine simply get lost in the sauce. My rule of thumb for cooking with wine: don't use any wine that you wouldn't drink in cooking—on the other hand, don't use any wine that you really want to drink!

I must confess that I really want to drink most red Burgundy—it's my favorite wine on earth. It's also among the most expensive, even at the lower levels. So when I make boeuf bourguignon, I usually avoid real red Burgundy. Burgundy's made from the Pinot Noir grape and, though Pinot Noirs from other parts of the world don't taste exactly like Burgundy, they are good cooking stand-ins for the real thing (something inexpensive like Napa Ridge Pinot Noir from California would be just fine). Frankly, almost any decent red'll do. The one kind of red I'd avoid would be the kind that has strong character from another grape variety; something that tastes intensely of Cabernet Sauvignon or Syrah could make the stew taste a little un-Burgundian. But not very much.

The Pork. The question here is: do you like smokiness? Bacon is always cured, but it's not necessarily smoked. If you like a good dose of smokiness, use smoky slab bacon from a specialty butcher for boeuf bourguignon. I like a little less smokiness than that, so I simmer the slab bacon for three minutes to reduce the smokiness. If you like even less smoke (and prefer to pick up bacon at the supermarket), you can use commercial bacon, the presliced kind. If you like even less smokiness, you can simmer the commercial bacon in water. And if you like no smokiness whatsoever, you can purchase unsmoked bacon (such as the Italian pancetta) or other types of cured pork (such as fatback or salt pork).

The Onions. Little pearl onions add a very typically Burgundian touch to this dish; buy fresh ones that are no more than an inch in diameter (I like to use the smallest ones I can find because they're more delectable to bite). Be careful in peeling them, because you want them to remain whole in the stew (e.g., don't cut a slit on the side of the onion to remove the peel). After peeling, you could just toss the onions in the stew pot, but the following recipe gives you a much better way to handle them: you brown the onions in butter, with a little sugar, *before* tossing them in the pot.

The Mushrooms. The relatively boring white mushrooms available in every supermarket are actually the traditional mushrooms to use in this dish! That's because this type of cultivated mushroom was developed in France—in Paris, in fact, hence the name champignon de Paris. I stick to tradition when I make boeuf bourguignon—that's what you do when you make comfort food, with old, emotional associations—but I certainly wouldn't hold it against you if you wanted to try tossing some great wild mushrooms (like morels, or chanterelles, or cèpes) into the pot in place of the champignons de Paris. I might even do it myself someday.

Beyond the ingredients, there's technique. Marinating the beef gives it a much deeper flavor. Browning the beef in bacon fat adds great flavor to the stew. Skimming fat from the stew while it's cooking adds elegance. Treating the onions and mushrooms separately adds lots of texture interest. Thickening the sauce with beurre manié is a handy French technique.

Most important, though, is cooking the stew for a long time over low heat. The great beef cheeks they serve at Thibert are put in the oven at night as the chefs leave the restaurant, then served at dinner the next night. If you wish to emulate that, use large chunks of beef, turn the heat down to about 215 degrees, and braise to your heart's content. But whatever you do, don't dare cook any higher than 275 degrees or for less than three hours—otherwise you risk tough pieces of beef.

BOEUF À LA BOURGUIGNONNE WITH HEART-SHAPED CROUTONS

This wonderful recipe was contributed to *Taste* by Georgia Downard, the culinary director of Food Network. As you know, I'm not partial to messing around with boeuf bourguignon—but Georgia told me that when she learned the dish, years ago, at a cooking school in Paris, they suggested garnishing it with delightful, parsley-rimmed toasted breads that were cut in the shape of hearts. They're pretty and delicious—and have made this boeuf bourguignon one of my top choices for a Valentine's Day menu.

MAKES 6 MAIN-COURSE SERVINGS

3 cups dry red wine

2 cups beef stock (you may use canned beef broth)

1/4 cup Marc de Bourgogne (or 2 tablespoons brandy plus 2 tablespoons grappa, or 1/4 cup brandy)

1 large onion, peeled and cut in quarters

2 carrots, peeled and cut in large chunks

4 garlic cloves, peeled and sliced

12 parsley stems

1 teaspoon dried thyme

1 teaspoon dried rosemary

10 black peppercorns

4 whole cloves

4 allspice berries

1 bay leaf

3 pounds fatty beef chuck, cut into 2-inch pieces

1/2 pound slab bacon

6 tablespoons unsalted butter (plus 1 tablespoon softened unsalted butter, plus 3 tablespoons melted unsalted butter)

1 tablespoon olive oil

1 tablespoon tomato paste

1 pound pearl onions, carefully peeled

Pinch of sugar

1 pound white mushrooms, cleaned (use the smallest ones you can find)

1 tablespoon flour

6 slices firm white bread, crusts removed, cut into 6 heart shapes

1/4 cup very finely minced fresh parsley leaves (no stems)

1. In a large bowl, combine the red wine, beef stock, brandy, onion, carrots, garlic, parsley stems, thyme, rosemary, peppercorns, cloves, allspice, and bay leaf. Stir well to blend. Add the beef, and stir. Refrigerate, covered, overnight.

2. The next day drain the beef, reserving the marinade and vegetables separately. Pat the beef dry with towels, and season it well with salt and pepper.

3. Preheat the oven to 275 degrees.

4. Remove the outer rind of the bacon. Cut the remaining slab the long way into ¼-inch-thick slices; then cut these slices into lardons that are ½ inch long. Cover the lardons and the rind with cold water, bring to a boil, turn down the heat, and simmer for 3 minutes. Remove the lardons and rind, reserving both.

5. Add 2 tablespoons of butter and 1 tablespoon of olive oil to a large Dutch oven set over medium heat. Dry off the lardons, add them to the Dutch oven, and cook, stirring often, until they are golden. With a slotted spoon transfer the lardons to paper towels to drain.

6. In the same Dutch oven, over high heat, brown the drained and dried-off beef in the remaining bacon fat, in batches so the meat browns evenly. When you are done, pour off all but 1 tablespoon of fat. Return all of the browned beef to the pot.

7. Add the vegetable-and-herb mixture reserved from the marinade, and cook over medium-high heat, stirring, for 5 minutes.

8. Add the reserved marinade liquid, tomato paste, lardons, and reserved bacon rind. Bring the liquid to a boil, and taste it for seasoning. Cook in the oven, covered, for 3 hours.

9. After 3 hours, remove and discard the large chunks of onion, carrot, and parsley stem. Skim the fat from the stew.

10. Make the vegetable garnish: Place the pearl onions in a skillet, cover them with water, add 1 tablespoon of butter, the sugar, and salt and pepper to taste. Simmer the onions over medium-high heat until they are almost tender. Raise heat to high, and reduce the cooking liquid to 2 tablespoons. Continue to cook the onions, shaking the pan over the heat, until the onions are golden brown and glazed.

11. In another skillet set over medium-high heat, melt 3 tablespoons of butter; add the mushrooms and salt and pepper to taste. Cook the mushrooms, tossing often, for 7 minutes, or until they are golden brown.

12. Meanwhile, prepare the beurre manié: Cream together the tablespoon of softened butter with the tablespoon of flour. Roll the mixture into pieces the size of peas.

13. Add the cooked onions and mushrooms to the stew. Bring the liquid to a simmer, and add enough beurre manié, bit by bit, stirring constantly, to lightly thicken the sauce.

14. Make the croutons: Brush both sides of the bread with a total of 3 tablespoons of melted butter, arrange them on a baking sheet, and bake them in a 400-degree oven until they are golden brown. Dip the edges of the bread in the stew pot to moisten, then in parsley to coat.

15. Divide the boeuf bourguignon among 6 dinner plates, and garnish each with a heart-shaped crouton. Serve immediately.

Burgundy

Burgundy is one of my favorite places in France to visit. Driving on the back road that winds through the great Côte d'Or, or golden slope of vineyards, is an experience not to be missed. There they are, one after another: Chambertin, Le Musigny, Bonnes Mares, Romanée-Conti, La Tâche, Le Corton. You step out of your car, amidst these unmarked fields, and feel as if you're standing at the center of the gastronomic universe.

But Burgundy is not just wine. It is revered for great game, fabulous cheeses, the famous Charolais beef, the best escargots in France, plump Bresse chickens, and, of course, Dijon mustard. In addition to this, Burgundy has some of the best restaurants in France: L'Espérance (in St.-Père-sous-Vézelay), A la Côte St.-Jacques (in Joigny), Côte d'Or (in Saulieu), La Mère Blanc (in Vonnas), Lameloise (in Chagny)—and, my favorite, a mere one-star among these three-star big boys, Thibert in Dijon. The great French gastronome Brillat-Savarin chose well to be born in Burgundy in 1755.

A Great Boeuf Bourguignon Side Dish

In Burgundy, the usual starch accompaniment to boeuf bourguignon is a simple dish of boiled potatoes—maybe with a little butter and parsley. I, however, in recent years, have started serving something more complicated alongside the stew . . . and loving it! It is one of the great unknown regional dishes of France: a potato gratin called tartiflette.

I discovered tartiflette about ten years ago, when, after having wrapped up a wine-tasting tour of Burgundy, I traveled a few miles east to the beautiful lakeside town of Annecy, in the French département called Haute-Savoie. There are some very famous restaurants in Annecy, which was why I went there—but I got the biggest gastronomic thrills from a group of bistros in the old section of the town. Why? Because they all specialize in this great dish I'd never heard of before.

What distinguishes tartiflette from all other potato gratins is the cheese they use in Annecy: Reblochon, a famous local cheese, which is served from cheese carts all over France and is much loved. But never had I heard of chefs actually cooking with this deeply flavored cow's-milk cheese . . . until I encountered tartiflette. I almost knew it as soon as I walked into my first tartiflette bistro, because the whole place reeked of strong cheese. This may be hell for some, but for me it was heaven.

Happily, tartiflette is not a complicated dish to make, and the following recipe will enable you to come pretty close to the Annecy original. However, Reblochon is difficult to find on these shores—even if you do find it, chances are it won't be ripe enough. Therefore, I've played around with cheeses that are available in the United States and discovered that any fairly smelly cheese will give you a good tartiflette facsimile. Look especially for the washed-rind cheeses of France (but don't use the rind): Livarot, Muenster, Epoisses. In my tests, a combination of cheeses used together came the closest to the Reblochon taste: 1 firmly packed cup of rindless Livarot mixed with 1/2 firmly packed cup of the English cheese Wynendale (again no rind).

When the runny ooze of this dish meets the runny brown sauce of the boeuf bourguignon, you'll know why eastern France is considered by so many to be a gourmand's paradise.

Tartiflette
(Gratin of Potatoes with Strong Cheese)

MAKES 6 SERVINGS

6 ounces good-quality bacon, cut into slices 1/4 inch thick, then into lardons 1/2 inch wide

9 ounces large white button mushrooms, cleaned and sliced 1/4 inch thick

4 tablespoons unsalted butter, softened

2 1/2 pounds waxy potatoes, peeled and sliced 1/8 inch thick

1 1/2 cups firmly packed, crumbled strong cheese (see headnote)

2 cups heavy cream, heated

1. Preheat the oven to 300 degrees.

2. In a skillet, sauté the lardons over medium-high heat until they are lightly crisp and brown, about 5 minutes. Remove the bacon with a slotted spoon to paper towels.

3. Discard all but 1 tablespoon of the bacon fat from the skillet. Reheat, add the mushrooms, and sauté until lightly brown (about 5 minutes); season well with salt and pepper.

4. Generously butter a shallow 9 1/2-by-13-inch baking dish with 2 tablespoon of butter. Toss the potato slices with a generous amount of salt and pepper, and arrange half in a layer in the baking dish. Sprinkle with all of the bacon, then with all of the mushrooms. Top with half of the cheese, and season again with salt and pepper. Top with the remaining potatoes, and pour enough cream over the top to barely cover the potatoes (you may not need the full 2 cups). Dot with the remaining butter.

5. Bake until the potatoes are tender (about 60 minutes).

6. Remove the baking dish from the oven, dot with the remaining cheese, and continue to bake, checking frequently so the cheese doesn't burn, until the cheese is melted, browned, and bubbly (about 10 minutes more).

7. Let sit, covered with foil, for 10 to 15 minutes before serving.

Criteria for Quality

- Is the meat tender?
- Is the stew deeply flavorful?
- Are the mushrooms and onions whole, with texture, not decomposed?
- Is the sauce winy but not too winy?
- Is the sauce limpid and bright, not muddy and dull?
- Is the sauce thickened just so—neither too thin nor too thick?

When

Boeuf bourguignon is a perfect main-course dish, particularly on a winter's night. Some kind of Burgundian salad (like greens tossed with sizzled chicken livers) first, then the stew, then a few cheeses, then a fruit tart add up to my idea of heaven in February.

In Your Glass

There are many possibilities for wine with boeuf bourguignon—and many surprises.

First of all, the most obvious wine to drink with the dish—red Burgundy—turns out to be one of the least successful choices. I once sat down with Anne Willan, who runs a cooking school in Burgundy, and tasted through a wide range of wines with boeuf bourguignon. We liked none of the red Burgundies with the dish—because red Burgundy is a delicate, subtle thing, and this hearty stew rides roughshod over it. I imagine that if you spent a lot of money on a young grand cru from the Côtes de Nuits in a great vintage—a young Chambertin, say—it would probably have the stuffing to stand up to the dish. But I think its subtlety would be robbed by the rich sauce, and I'd rather save a wine like that for a simple roast.

We found that rich but well-balanced young reds did best of all. There's a wide range of these in the world, but the wines of the Côtes du Rhône—just south of Burgundy—scored the biggest hits at our table. Once again, there's no need to break the bank and buy the very best. But young Crozes-Hermitage, or Gigondas, or even Côtes-du-Rhône Villages, from good producers in great vintages, will go spectacularly well with boeuf bourguignon.

The biggest surprise of our tasting was the white ringer we threw in: it was a Pinot Blanc (a Burgundian grape) made in California, and it was extremely smooth with the stew. I've often noticed that long-cooked meat likes rich white wine—so, if you're white wine inclined, don't hesitate to serve a weighty one with boeuf bourguignon (just make sure it's low on fruitiness and sweetness, as many California Chardonnays aren't).

JERKED CHICKEN

Every once in a while, a food or wine comes along that causes a stir *just because of its name.* Some years back, for example, Americans wanted to drink Pouilly-Fuissé—perhaps because they thought they knew how to pronounce its name. Typically, it doesn't matter if the item in question tastes good or not; the entertainment value of the name's the point.

I'm tempted to include jerked chicken in this category of meretricious "name" foods; there's something funny, almost naughty about the moniker of this Jamaican specialty, and one reason people order it so much is that they have a good time just saying the name. However, in this case, the food behind the name is delicious—astonishingly delicious even, based as it is on a number of ingredients that grow profusely in Jamaica. I'm not sure the dish would have received the same notoriety had it been called marinated Jamaican chicken, but I like to think it would have.

Nobody knows the origins of the name, but there are theories. There was a Spanish word—*charqui*—that denoted the Peruvian Indian method of preserving beef by sun-drying it. Maybe *jerk* comes from that, some hypothesize. Then there's the theory that the name comes from the constant turning of the meat—or "jerking" it. Others believe that the *jerk* in jerk is what you do when you pull the meat off the bone after it's cooked. To make things even more complicated, some call it *jerked* chicken and some call it *jerk* chicken. Me? I say: "Doan worry, *mon*—it's jest jerk!"

It is also Jamaica's most famous dish—and the Caribbean equivalent of southern BBQ. It is meat that has been flavored—and in jerk, it's intensely flavored—then smoked over wood to give it an earthy quality. Jerk began in Jamaica when runaway slaves, called Maroons, took to the hills trying to escape the British. They needed to eat, of course, so while they were being hunted, they hunted also—and what they hunted mostly were small wild boars. They could have eaten them all on the spot, but, not being sure they'd catch any the next week, they developed a means of preserving them with salt, Scotch bonnet chili peppers, and, especially, allspice.

Why allspice, of all things? Simple. It's indigenous to Jamaica, where it is called pimento. The name is somewhat confusing to us. Jamaican pimento (allspice) is not the red-bell-pepper kind of pimiento that gets stuffed in an olive. Nor is Jamaican allspice a mix of spices. It is the fruit of the pimento tree, a berry the size of a large peppercorn or a small pea. When it's dried it becomes one of the world's most fragrant spices—a spice that does, in fact, seem to suggest "all" spices (or at least nutmeg, mace, and cinnamon).

Over the centuries in Jamaica, boar gave way to pork, and jerked pork became the most popular jerked dish. No more, however. In modern times, jerked chicken is the jerk of choice in Jamaica. And all over the island, but particularly near Boston Beach, you will find the air thick with smoke from jerk shacks—octagonal or circular structures with telephone poles in the center supporting simple roofs.

When you're ready to "jerk" some chicken at *your* shack, there are two crucial parts of the process that will require some decisions.

1. HOW TO FLAVOR THE CHICKEN

You can flavor your jerk in three different ways.

A Dry Rub. This sprinkle of spices, to me, doesn't penetrate the chicken well enough—though I would consider applying some "jerk seasoning" to the chicken towards the end of cooking.

A Paste. Better than a dry rub. This is, in fact, the traditional way to flavor the meat. You will see on the market today a number of jarred jerk pastes, just waiting for the turn of a lid to facilitate your jerk. However, I find that a thick paste, once again, does not provide maximum penetration of the meat.

A Marinade. A two-day soak in a jerk marinade is the best way to powerfully flavor your jerk (see the recipe).

2. HOW TO COOK THE CHICKEN

Originally the wild boar, slathered with salt and spices, were probably wrapped in leaves and placed in a hole in the ground filled with hot stones. But if you want to cook authentic jerk, you don't have to do that—because, over time, the jerk climbed out of the ground and onto a slow fire of green wood. And this being Jamaica, home of allspice, the wood of choice, of course, was allspice, or pimento, wood! The wood gives off lots of smoke, and that smoky flavor became an essential part of the jerk experience. Today, in some Jamaican jerk shacks, the meat is cooked over pimento wood in converted steel drums—the kind they use to make music as well as dinner!

Obviously, in the United States there's not going to be a lot of steel drum action, or a lot of pimento wood. So jerked chicken is one of those dishes that's hard to reproduce here exactly. However, it seems to me that many of the restaurants in the United States that have helped build the jerked chicken craze have not done enough to reproduce the taste of Jamaica. They slather their chicken with a little paste out of a jar, then slap it on a grill or place it under a broiler. But where's the smoke? No smoke, no jerk!

To get the smoke thing going, all you need is a piece of equipment I often tout for the home cook—the stove-top smoker from the Max Burton Company in Tacoma, Washington (it costs under $50, and you can call 800-272-8603 to order one). It's a simple box that, after being filled with soaked wood chips, just sits on top of your range, holding and flavoring the meat. The Burton Smoker creates the smokiest flavor in the shortest amount of time, which is why I favor it. But it has another advantage as well for lots of modern Americans—you can use it in city apartments, where you have no access to the great outdoors.

Of course, if you do have outdoor space, you can always use an outdoor grill as a smoker. Just light your charcoal (actual charcoal chunks are preferable to briquettes), and let it burn until it is covered with a fine ash. Soak some wood chips (hardwood) in water for about twenty minutes. When the coals are ready, rake them over to one side of the grill bed. Put the wood chips on the coals, and when they begin to smoke, oil the rack, put it in place, and put the chicken on the rack on the side away from the coals. Cover the griller, and smoke away.

Either way, you will have great smoky jerk flavor. But there are two more things you need to do if you want absolutely fabulous jerk.

First of all, the smoking process—particularly if you're using the Burton Smoker—doesn't necessarily give the meat a browned, crispy exterior. So, after the chicken "smokes," you need to place it over (or under) very high heat for a few moments. You can do this on an outdoor grill, in a ridged grill pan on the stove top, or under a broiler.

Second, your cooked chicken could use some kind of glaze to make it superyummy at the table. My solution is to mix together a finishing sauce and glaze the cooked chicken pieces with it just before serving.

Jerk Confusion in Jamaica

The whole jerk concept had always been somewhat elusive to me—but I assumed that on my first trip to Jamaica, after a dedicated jerk fest across the island, I'd come away with the definitive story. Not so. Every single time I had jerk in Jamaica, there was something completely distinct about the version I was eating. For example:

- *Some jerks were dry.*
- *Some jerks were moist.*
- *Some jerks had soggy skin.*
- *Some jerks had crisp skin.*
- *Some jerks were marinated for a few hours.*
- *Some jerks were marinated for four days.*
- *Some jerks were served with basically no sauce, paste, or condiment.*
- *Some jerks were served with a thin, runny "jerk" sauce.*
- *Some jerks were served with a thicker "jerk" sauce that had chopped-up stuff in it.*
- *Some jerks were served with a "jerk" sauce that was like grainy mustard in texture.*
- *Some jerks were covered with their "sauce."*
- *Some jerks had their "sauce" on the side.*
- *Some jerks were painted with a sweet "jerk" glaze.*

After so many jerks, I decided that my *ideal Jamaican jerk would be long marinated, moist, crispy skinned, and served with a sweet glaze.*

JERKED CHICKEN

Proper jerked chicken is hot-hot-hot. In Jamaica, it is made with another great indigenous Jamaican ingredient: the Scotch bonnet chili, one of the hottest peppers in the world. Fresh Scotch bonnets are sometimes difficult to find here, so in the following recipe I've substituted a hot sauce made from them. If you find some fresh Scotch bonnets, of course—and if you can take them—by all means throw some in your food processor when blending the marinade. If you use about a dozen of them, you can fly to Jamaica without an airplane. Another choice you'll need to make concerns the chicken: Which part should you use? Jerk can be made with all chicken parts, but I prefer the thighs (my favorite chicken part). Next question: bone-in thighs or boneless thighs? They're both good. If you're having the kind of dignified party at which your guests will be sitting down with knife and fork, boneless may be better. But if you're trying to foment a little mayhem, there's no better way than telling your guests to pick up their jerked chicken in their hands and start nibbling on the bones.

MAKES 8 SERVINGS

For the marinade:

1 cup vegetable oil

2 tablespoons Caribbean hot sauce (I prefer West
    Indies Creole Hot Pepper Sauce [see note]
    use more or less according to taste)

8 tablespoons coarsely chopped garlic

6 tablespoons freshly grated gingerroot

4 tablespoons minced scallions

4 tablespoons Myers's rum

3 tablespoons molasses

3 tablespoons lime juice

3 tablespoons balsamic vinegar

1 tablespoon dark brown sugar

1 tablespoon ground allspice

1 teaspoon dried thyme leaves

1/2 teaspoon ground cinnamon

1/2 teaspoon freshly ground nutmeg

1/4 teaspoon ground cloves

2 teaspoons freshly ground black pepper

1 teaspoon salt

16 chicken thighs (bone in or boneless)

For the finishing sauce:

3/4 cup chicken stock

1/2 cup molasses

1/4 cup balsamic vinegar

3 tablespoons dark brown sugar

2 tablespoons lime juice

2 cloves garlic, smashed

1 tablespoon black peppercorns, coarsely crushed

1 tablespoon whole allspice, coarsely crushed

Hot sauce to taste (I like about 1 tablespoon)

1. Put all the marinade ingredients in a food processor, and purée until smooth.

2. Pierce the chicken thighs with the tip of a knife to make many tiny holes. Rub the marinade into the chicken, and refrigerate it in a tightly wrapped bowl for forty-eight hours.

3. When you are ready to cook, prepare a smoker. If you are using the Burton Smoker (see page 193), soak a handful of wood chips (I use hickory) in water for 20 minutes. Place them in the smoker, and put the smoker over medium-high heat on your range. Let the chips smolder for 3 to 4 minutes. Remove the chicken from the marinade, and dry it off. Place a drip pan on the wood chips, then brush the smoker rack with oil, and place it on top of the drip pan. Arrange the chicken on the rack, cover the unit, and smoke for about 20 minutes, or until the chicken is almost cooked through. Remove the chicken. You may hold the chicken on a platter, covered, for up to 1 hour.

4. Prepare the finishing sauce: Place the chicken stock, molasses, vinegar, sugar, lime juice, and garlic in a small, heavy saucepan. Reduce over high heat, watching constantly so that the sauce doesn't boil over. Stir occasionally. After 10 minutes, add the black pepper and allspice. Remove from heat when the sauce has reduced to ¾ cup (about ½ hour all together). Strain. Add hot sauce, if desired. Reserve.

5. When you are ready to serve, brown the chicken over a hot fire, on a very hot ridged grill pan, or under the broiler. When the chicken is done, brush it with the finishing sauce, coating lightly on both sides, and serve immediately.

NOTE: The West Indies Creole Hot Pepper Sauce, made in Dominica, West Indies, for over fifty years from Scotch bonnets and papayas, is available from Mo Hotta–Mo Betta in San Luis Obispo, California. You can mail-order the sauce by calling 800-462-3220.

Cuban Black Beans: A Great Side Dish for Jerked Chicken

In Jamaica, you're likely to eat all kinds of island vegetables, grains, and beans with your jerked chicken. But I customarily serve mine with the finest pot of black beans I know; it's a great recipe that comes from a very funky Cuban lunch spot, Margon, just around the corner from Food Network. When they finally gave me the recipe, I was amazed to discover that it had a few "convenience" products in it—like chicken bouillon cubes and Goya's packets of spices. I thought about substituting chicken stock and home-ground achiote seeds . . . for about twelve seconds. Then I decided to leave this great recipe alone, no matter what it calls for.

Cuban Black Beans Margon

MAKES 16 SERVINGS

2 pounds dried black beans
4 tablespoons olive oil
2 1/2 cups finely minced onion (about 2 large onions)
8 large cloves garlic, chopped
1/2 cup cilantro, chopped
3 tablespoons cider vinegar

2 Knorr chicken bouillon cubes
2 envelopes Sazón Goya with cilantro and achiote (4 teaspoons)
2 tablespoons tomato paste
2 1/2 cups finely minced red bell pepper (about 2 large ones)

1. Pick through the beans to remove any foreign objects. Rinse the beans, then soak them in water overnight.

2. Drain the beans, cover them with 12 cups fresh water, and boil until tender, about 1 hour, adding more water if necessary.

3. Heat the oil in a large pot. Add the onion, garlic, cilantro, vinegar, bouillon cubes, Goya seasoning, tomato paste, and red pepper. Sauté for 5 minutes.

4. Add the beans and their liquid to the pot. Bring to a boil, and simmer for 45 to 60 minutes, or until the mixture has the consistency of a thick soup. Taste for seasoning, and serve.

Jerked Chicken Salad with Jicama, Peppers, and Lime Vinaigrette

A Jerked Chicken Appetizer

After taping my jerked chicken show, we had lots of leftover jerked chicken—so I recycled the leftovers into the following great first-course salad. Nowadays, I sometimes make jerked chicken just to get to this salad! Of course, you don't have to go to all that trouble—the salad's a bright, delicious appetizer if you substitute any type of chicken strips, or even if you leave the chicken out.

Jerked Chicken Salad with Jicama, Peppers, and Lime Vinaigrette

MAKES 8 FIRST-COURSE SERVINGS

6 tablespoons freshly squeezed lime juice

4 teaspoons grated lime zest

2 tablespoons honey

4 to 5 teaspoons West Indies Creole Hot Pepper Sauce (more or less according to heat preference; substitute another medium-thick Caribbean red hot sauce if desired)

6 tablespoons vegetable oil

3 garlic cloves, finely minced

16 jerked chicken thighs at room temperature (see the preceding recipe, and choose the boneless thigh option)

3 cups long, thin julienne strips of jicama

3 cups each long, thin julienne strips of red and yellow bell pepper

6 medium tomatoes, quartered, seeded, and cut into thin julienne strips

1 to 3 tablespoons finely minced fresh chilies (depending on your heat preference)

3/4 cup minced cilantro

3 avocados, peeled and cut into thin slices

1. Place the lime juice and 1 teaspoon of the lime zest in a mixing bowl. Whisk in the honey, hot sauce, and oil until the dressing is smooth. Add the minced garlic. Season to taste with salt and pepper. Reserve.

2. Cut the boneless chicken thighs into strips (about 10 strips per thigh). In a large mixing bowl, toss together the chicken strips, jicama, red and yellow bell pepper, tomatoes, chilies, cilantro, and the remaining 3 teaspoons of lime zest. Toss with the dressing. Check for seasoning. Gently fold in the avocado slices.

3. Divide among 8 dinner plates, and serve.

A Simpler Finishing Sauce

If you prefer to pour your finishing sauce out of a bottle (and save yourself a little time), there's a terrific Jamaican product that makes a perfect substitute for the finishing sauce in my recipe. It's called Pickapeppa sauce, and it's made in Shooters Hill, Manchester, Jamaica, from mangoes, raisins, and tamarind, among other things. It's available at many supermarkets, but if you can't find it near you there's a store in Pound Ridge, New York, called Scott's Corner Market (914-764-5736) that will ship bottles anywhere. Make sure to get the brown sauce marked "original flavour." To use it in this dish, combine 3/4 cup of it with 2 tablespoons dark brown sugar, 1 tablespoon ground allspice, and 1 tablespoon freshly ground black pepper. No cooking is needed; now you're ready to dip that jerk right in the sauce.

Chicken's Not the Only Jerk

The marinade I use for jerked chicken can be used for a wide range of other foods. Let common sense guide you as you adjust the marination time and the smoking-grilling time.

- Meats (like pork, beef, lamb) can be marinated just as long as the chicken.
- If you want your meat rare, obviously the smoking-grilling time will be shorter.
- If you want your meat well done, the smoking-grilling time will be longer.
- Fish is also a great option (jerked lobster is popular in Jamaica, but jerking's also great for shrimp and for whole fish). Here, both the marination time and the cooking time should be shorter than for chicken (marinate fish for half a day, smoke-grill for 10 minutes).

Criteria for Quality

- Is the jerk intensely flavored with Jamaican-style spices (e.g., allspice)?
- Is the jerk smoky?
- Is the jerk spicy-hot?
- Is the jerk juicy within, browned without?

When

Here's my ideal jerk scenario: a patio party near the outdoor grill on a warm summer night. If you've already smoked your jerk in the Burton Smoker in the kitchen, all you have to do outside is build a hot fire and throw your mostly cooked pieces of chicken on it for just a few minutes to brown. And if it is a large party, why not marinate and smoke a number of other meats as well? Jerked pork chops, jerked beef ribs, jerked rabbit—you can jerk anything you want. Bring out a pot of black beans, some fluffy rice, an array of salsas, salads, condiments—and you've got one merry time on your hands.

But you don't have to wait for this ideal occasion to make your jerk. I love it too as a quiet, indoor family main course for dinner.

In Your Glass

If you haven't cranked up the chili level to way beyond the Minimum Daily Adult Requirement, the usual array of vinous hot-food dousers will serve: inexpensive sparkling wine, white Zinfandel, fruity young red wine. However, the only thing "red" that I really crave with jerked chicken is Red Stripe—the refreshing beer of Jamaica that's readily available in the United States. If you can't find it, substitute a light Mexican beer or Rolling Rock.

ALLA FRANCESE DISHES

In the Italian-American restaurants that furnished my first "ethnic" dining experiences, I used to eat dishes named *alla francese* all the time. To be more accurate, I used to taste alla francese dishes all the time that were ordered by my mom—for this was one of her favorite preparations in the world. Veal francese, shrimp francese, and, especially—for my mom was crazy about birds—chicken francese. Lovely slices of meat, sautéed to light gold in a delicate batter (sometimes flavored with grated cheese), served with a wisp of winy sauce sometimes accented with lemon—francese dishes, at their best, can offer a startling harmony of subtle flavors. A good "francese" is one of the world's best-balanced main-course treats.

In a recent fit of nostalgia, I wanted to go back and re-create the great "francese" dishes of my youth—which, with the passage of time, were seeming better to me every year. Moreover, I wanted to make them at home for my kids. So I started marauding Italian cookbooks for ideas. *Niente.* No mention of alla francese. Okay . . . maybe I was looking at the wrong cookbooks. Maybe I was checking actual Italian cookbooks, as in "the food of Italy." Maybe I forgot that nobody in Italy makes alla francese dishes—for these dishes are definitely Italian-American creations, like spaghetti and meatballs, like veal parmigiana, like pasta primavera.

So I then looked at my collection of very specifically Italian-American cookbooks. *Niente* again. Authors who were documenting Italian food in America were leaving out a dish that for decades appeared on the menus of every red-checkered-tablecloth restaurant in America! And after I discussed on television this lacuna in the literature, I got scores of letters from people telling me that they too couldn't find alla francese recipes in print!

Why? Why are these dishes being ignored? I have a theory.

I think alla francese got invented at a time when Italian restaurants in America were feeling distinctly inferior to French restaurants. The 1939 World's Fair in New York spun off a French restaurant called Le Pavillon—which became wildly popular and wildly fashionable and wildly influential. Suddenly, Italian red sauce on everything didn't seem so chic. So somebody—and I think his or her name is now lost in the sands of time—created a veal cutlet dish that had no tomato sauce and no blanket of heavy melted cheese. It seemed lighter . . . whiter . . . more elegant . . . more French. It may have been triggered in the inventor's mind by an old Neapolitan dish called artichokes alla francese, which was prepared by dipping artichoke hearts in batter, deep-frying them, and serving them with lemon. In any event, the *alla francese* name stuck—and was no doubt helpful in attracting World War II–era diners who suddenly believed that all things French were *très, très chic.*

The great irony today, of course, is that the tables have completely turned. *Italian* food is now chic in America. French food is about as chic as a pound of butter. Italian food is thought of as light and healthful; French food is thought of as heavy and bad for you. Why would any self-respecting Italian cookbook author today want to put the French curse on one of his or her dishes by calling it alla francese?—or even admit that there was a time when the Italians had to suck up to the French?

Well, I love this dish, and I refuse to omit it from my lineup or to call it anything else. Tell your friends who have fond memories of Little Italy: alla francese has now gone into print.

First, there is one other piece of unpleasant business we must clear up: a lot of the alla francese recipes being served out there today in old-fashioned Italian-American restaurants don't *deserve* to go into print. Like many long-standing, old-time dishes, this one is being abused by the contemporary generation of restaurateurs. Here are the problems I often encounter:

- The meat is soggy and/or pasty.
- The meat is oily and/or buttery.
- The meat is burned.
- The meat is dry.
- The sauce is heavy.
- The sauce is bland.
- The sauce is too sour.

The following recipes come to grips with all the "francese" problems. The first recipe is simple as can be, showing you the fundamental francese techniques; it doesn't even include lemon or cheese and is amazingly delicious for such a simple preparation. The second recipe has more steps, more ingredients—and, correspondingly, more layers of flavor. It is, quite frankly, the most delicious alla francese dish I have ever tasted.

SIMPLE CHICKEN FRANCESE

What really distinguishes the alla francese dishes is the light, golden coating that the slices of meat receive. But there is some controversy about the best way to achieve this coating. This much is certain: bread crumbs are *out* (the coating they create is more Milanese—actually more Germanic—not francese). That leaves it up to flour and egg—but which one gets applied to the meat first? When I make simple francese, I like to dust the cutlets in flour first, then dip them in egg; golden, comforting egg on the outside really captures the soft, gentle soul of this dish.

MAKES 2 SERVINGS

1/2 pound boneless, skinless chicken breast
6 tablespoons butter
Flour for dredging

1 egg, beaten well
1 cup dry white wine

1. Cut the chicken breast into 6 pieces of roughly equal size. Place the pieces between sheets of wax paper, and pound with a mallet until they're thin. Season with salt and pepper.

2. Add 4 tablespoons of the butter to a sauté pan large enough to hold the 6 cutlets in a single layer. Melt the butter over medium-high heat; when the foaming starts to subside, the butter is ready.

3. While the butter is heating, place the flour on a wide plate. Place each chicken cutlet in the flour, and coat lightly. Place the beaten egg in a wide, shallow bowl. Dip the floured cutlets in the egg. Remove them, making sure to let the excess egg drip off, and add them immediately to the foaming butter.

4. Sauté the cutlets, turning once, until they are golden on the outside, just cooked on the inside (about 2 minutes per side). Remove the cutlets, and hold them in a single layer.

5. Spill the butter out of the sauté pan. Return the pan to high heat. Add the white wine, and reduce it to ½ cup. Turn the heat to very low. Swirl in the remaining 2 tablespoons of butter until the sauce is thickened. Taste for seasoning. Add the reserved cutlets to the pan, turning them until they're coated with the sauce. Divide the cutlets between 2 dinner plates, pour the remaining sauce over them, and serve immediately.

CHICKEN FRANCESE WITH LEMON AND PECORINO

This more complicated version of the dish gets such frills as lemon, pecorino cheese, and parsley. In this variation, the cutlets get dipped first in cheesy egg, then in flour. But the essential gentleness of the francese style still comes through. I hope you like this lemon sauce as much as I do; by avoiding lemon *juice,* and by cooking *slices* of lemon in wine, you end up with a lemony-tasting sauce that's not unattractively sour.

MAKES 2 SERVINGS

1/2 pound boneless, skinless chicken breast

2 heaping tablespoons finely grated pecorino cheese (no lumps)

4 tablespoons very finely chopped parsley leaves

1 jumbo egg, beaten well

Flour for dredging

1/4 cup olive oil

1/4 cup dry white wine

1 cup chicken stock

6 thin, round slices of lemon, seeds removed

2 tablespoons butter

1. Cut the chicken breast into 6 pieces of roughly equal size. Place the pieces between sheets of wax paper, and pound with a mallet until they're thin. Season with salt and pepper.

2. Place the cheese and 2 tablespoons of the parsley in a wide, shallow bowl. Slowly add the beaten egg, whisking until it's smoothly incorporated. Place the flour on a wide plate. Dip the cutlets in the egg mixture. Remove them, making sure to let the excess egg drip off. Place each cutlet in the flour, and coat lightly. Remove the cutlets from the flour, and hold them in a single layer (on a platter or on a counter).

3. Add the olive oil to 2 sauté pans, each large enough to hold 3 cutlets in a single layer. Place over medium-high heat. When the oil is hot, add the cutlets. Sauté, turning once, until the cutlets are golden on the outside, just cooked on the inside (about 2 minutes per side). Remove the cutlets, and hold them in a single layer.

4. Spill the oil out of the sauté pans. Return the pans to high heat. Add 2 tablespoons of white wine to each pan, and reduce it to 1 tablespoon in each pan. Divide the stock and the lemon slices between the pans. Boil for 5 minutes, then remove the lemon slices. Keep boiling the sauce (another moment or two), until it's reduced in each pan to ¼ cup. Turn the heat to very low.

Swirl a tablespoon of butter into each pan until the sauce is thickened. Taste for seasoning. Add 3 reserved cutlets to each pan, turning them until they're coated with the sauce. Divide the cutlets between 2 dinner plates, pour the remaining sauce over them, sprinkle with the remaining 2 tablespoons of parsley, and serve immediately.

Another Naming Theory

After the Taste *show on alla francese dishes aired, a New York chef who viewed it told me his theory of the name of the dish. Very often in Italian restaurants, he said, the cutlets are dipped in flour first, then in egg, then placed immediately in the pan. The chef pointed out that only one other famous dish gets an egg dip before going in a pan—French toast! So the namers, he reasoned, were actually making a reference to a breakfast dish—which is itself misnamed!*

Which Meat to Francesify?

I guess I'm my mother's son: my favorite meat for alla francese dishes is chicken breast.

This is a surprising predilection for me, in several ways. First of all, when it comes to Italianate cutlet dishes, I'm all for veal. Other meats, to me, often seem second best, as if the cook is using a cost-cutting substitute. And veal—particularly very expensive veal scallops—works very well in alla francese dishes. But somehow, for me, this particular Italianate cutlet dish tastes best when the coating surrounds the softness and tenderness of chicken, not veal.

Another surprising element here, for me, is chicken breast. *I normally have trouble understanding why Americans vastly prefer this relatively tasteless, ever-threatening-to-be-dry chicken part. Most of the rest of the world prefers chicken thighs, and so do I. However, once again, alla francese provokes anomalies; the very blandness of the meat plays perfectly into the essential delicacy of the dish.*

Of course, it doesn't really hurt that chicken is a fairly economical solution. There are a few other good-tasting economical solutions. Turkey cutlets sound very un-Italian—but, in reality, tacchino *is used quite often in Italy, particularly around Bologna. And if you want to give the dish a slightly heartier, chewier character, pork cutlets also work very well.*

The one other option that you often see is shellfish. Shrimp alla Francese is a very popular restaurant variation, and I like to make it myself, using either of the two francese recipes I've given here. Just remember to shell, devein, butterfly, and flatten the shrimp before coating and cooking them; the attached halves of a butterflied shrimp function as a single fillet. If you can find six very large shrimp that weigh a total of 1/2 pound, you can work directly from the chicken recipes, treating each flattened shrimp as one "cutlet." Two diners get three shrimp "cutlets" each.

Criteria for Quality

- *Are the cutlets golden and gauzy on the outside—not browned, greasy, soggy, or pasty?*
- *Are the cutlets juicy inside, just done, not dry and overcooked?*
- *Is the sauce medium-light, just thick enough to cling delicately to the cutlets?*
- *Is the sauce unattractively harsh with uncooked wine? unattractively sour with lemon juice?*
- *Does any one flavor—such as cheese, wine, or lemon—stand out? (it shouldn't)*
- *Does the dish create an impression of lightness? (it should)*

When

Dishes alla francese are remarkably useful to meal planners. They're great as the main courses for light lunches or light dinners (particularly in warmer weather) that feature only one course (with just a sauté of garlicky greens on the side). However, because of their lightness, they also are very useful if you're planning a multicourse Italian meal. I could easily see, for example, going from a light seafood salad as an opening course to a pasta with a vegetable sauce to a chicken francese course to a substantial main course involving red meat. I could also see going to bed right after this . . . very happily, I might add.

In Your Glass

I like white wine for dishes alla francese, and there are two key factors to keep in mind:

1. *The subtle flavors call for a subtly flavored wine that won't overpower the food.*
2. *The acid in alla francese dishes (from the lemon, or the wine reduction, or both) calls for a high-acid wine.*

Italy is not the world's best place for high-acid wines, since there's usually a good deal of sunshine at harvesttime. However, Italy's a spectacular place for "subtle" white wines. To me, dishes like these are perfect for these underachieving Italian whites—as long as they come from cool vintages that allowed the retention of acidity. Soave and Verdicchio are two easy-to-find wines that may be just right.

Your odds, however, are higher if you choose wines that are always crisply acidic. Despite the abuse it takes from wine writers, the low-alcohol Tuscan wine called Galestro is light, refreshing, ever crisp, and very easy to match with food; it washes down francese dishes extremely well. And the similarly light Vermentino, from Liguria, is another unrespected white wine that will earn your respect next to these dishes.

BARBECUED RIBS

You are about to discover a miraculous recipe that will deliver all the wonder of true barbecued ribs to your kitchen. Everyone always thought that you just couldn't make a facsimile of the real thing in a regular old oven. However, I have figured out a way!

Before I tell it all to you, let's talk a little barbecue. I can't state this strongly enough: *there is no greater indigenous food treasure in America than barbecue,* that fabulous meaty miracle lovingly prepared from the Carolina coast straight through the South into Texas, and north to such great barbecue centers as St. Louis and Kansas City. When I first stood in line at Sonny Bryan's in Dallas (circa 1985), smelling the smoke pouring out of the smokestacks, then carrying my tray of succulent brisket to an outdoor table, then devouring every meaty morsel, this New York boy knew he was on to Something Big. And when I took Alain Ducasse, the great French chef, for his first taste of barbecue and watched him licking his fingers, muttering, "*Je l'adore! Je l'adore!*" . . . I knew that this could be . . . no, this *must* be . . . *the* Great American Dish.

It also causes Great American Confusion. Where I come from, "Do you want to have a barbecue?" means "Do you want to cook some hot dogs and hamburgers over charcoal briquettes in the backyard?" The meaning is virtually the same on the West Coast. But in the Barbecue Belt, the meaning of *barbecue* couldn't be more different. There, *barbecue* is meat that gets cooked, indirectly, by wood smoke, in a covered "pit," at about 210 degrees, over the course of fifteen, sixteen, or seventeen hours. The result is sublime: juicy, tender, smoke-scented meat that, at its best, is not falling off the bone but coyly, seductively waiting for you to tear it off.

However, there's even confusion right there in the Barbecue Belt—because barbecue is the closest we come in the United States to the ontological condition of great European dishes like cassoulet or paella: no one knows exactly what they are in their ideal states; everyone has a different opinion.

Here are some of the leading barbecue controversies.

Which Meat? Pork is the reigning King of Barbecue, with strongholds in the Southeast, Kansas City, and St. Louis. And when you see barbecue attempted out of the Barbecue Belt—at good places in, say, Chicago or L.A., or in national chains like Tony Roma's—it's usually pork ribs or pork baby back ribs that are being cooked.

But there are strongholds of other meats as well. Texas is the leading iconoclast; oh sure, you can find pork there . . . but you'd better be ready to fight if you don't order at least some kind of beef. Lamb has its devotees as well, particularly around Owensboro, Kentucky. And, all over the country, you'll find barbecue chefs working their magic on sausages (usually called links) and on chicken.

How to Flavor It? Opinions vary widely about how to flavor barbecue. Some chefs like to marinate the meat before cooking it. Some chefs like to apply a thin film of flavored liquid—called a wet mop (because it's "mopped" on)—to the meat *while* it's cooking. Some chefs like to flavor the meat only with a dry mixture of spices, called a dry rub—which can be applied early in the cooking, midway through, or at the very end. Last, some chefs—especially in Texas—prefer to let you taste nothing other than meat and smoke; Texas barbecue is austere. Of course, even in Texas you can slather some barbecue sauce on at the table . . .

How to Sauce It? This is a raging controversy all by itself. First of all, most of us Northern boys have always misunderstood barbecue sauce. It is, truly, a sauce—that is, something to be applied to the meat at the table. It is not supposed to be slathered on the meat during cooking—especially since most barbecue sauces contain sugar, and the sauce will burn if you cook it. (It is permissible, however, if your heat's not too high, to slather it on for the last few minutes of cooking.)

But now it gets really sticky—for every region in barbecueland has a different taste in its barbecue sauce. The one that serves as the model for all that supermarket stuff across the country is Kansas City–style sauce: red, tomatoey, sweet, thick, a little smoky. Texas-style sauce is also red, but less red. Also less thick and less sweet. Over in the Carolinas, everything changes—several times. In the western part of North Carolina, the sauce is still tomatoey, but more of a sweet-and-sour kind of thing, with lots of vinegar in it. East of Raleigh, however, the tomato drops out entirely—and what you get is a thin, vinegary sauce. Move a little south, like to South Carolina, and the thickness comes back into the sauce—this time supplied by mustard! And these are just the *major* variations!

But I must confess that I love barbecue more than I love barbecue sauce. The latter, it seems to me, is sometimes just a way to mask poor examples of the former. When a slab of ribs is perfectly cooked, seductively smoked, a little crisp on the outside, primordially tender within—who needs barbecue sauce?

Finally, How to Serve It? It only gets more complicated from here. The type of barbecue served across the country outside the Barbecue Belt is usually slabs of pork ribs, preslathered with sauce in the kitchen. But inside the Belt, preslathering is not the norm (especially not in Texas); your meat at real barbecue joints may come to the table unslathered, awaiting the precision of your perfect self-slathering.

But there's more confusion—because not every locality serves something you can pick up in your hands, like ribs. Much of the barbecue in the Carolinas, for example, is made from pork shoulder . . . and that pork is cut up, in some fashion, mixed with barbecue sauce, and served on white bread or rolls as a sandwich! Even the cut-up, however, has its controversies. Do you want your pork chopped or hand-pulled apart? Do you want the crispy outside of the barbecue or the moister inside meat? Perhaps a combination?

The good news about traveling through the Barbecue Belt is this: for almost no money and certainly no fuss, you can always get some of America's greatest regional food. Moreover, you can shape your standards for barbecue here—which will always impel you to higher and higher barbecue thrills back in your hometown, where you can influence your local barbecue masters to come closer to the original product.

The bad news has always been this: unless you were willing to invest a lot of money in a smoking pit, to spend a lot of time learning the techniques, and to stay up all night watching your firebox as your meat slowly cooked, there wasn't a lot you could do to emulate authentic barbecue at home.

Until now! I came up with the following method for ribs while I was developing recipes for a *Taste* show on spareribs. I wanted a method that anyone could use in his or her home oven, without expensive equipment. The model I had in mind was the great platter of dry-rub ribs I was served in Memphis, Tennessee. Now, when people in Memphis say "the King," they're usually referring to a guy who swiveled his hips. Not me. I'm referring to a guy who dry-rubbed his ribs. My king is Charlie Vergos, and when I go to Memphis to visit the royal palace, it's not Graceland that makes me doff my cap but Charlie Vergos's Rendezvous on South Second Street. To me, this is Barbecue Ground Zero, the best ribs you'll ever taste in your life. Obviously, I was setting my standards high.

The easy part of my recipe development was creating a delicious dry rub. A little trickier was cooking the ribs in just the right way, for just the right length of time, in order to get that crispy-outside, tender-inside. But hardest of all was finding a way to infuse the ribs with smoke flavor (and I refuse to use liquid smoke).

Well, the smoky answer turned out to be quite simple—with the aid of a small, inexpensive unit called the Max Burton Stove Top Smoker (made in Tacoma, Washington, and available by calling 800-272-8603). It's a little metal box in which you place soaked wood chips. Over the chips you place food on a rack, and the box is covered tightly with a metal sheet. When you put the box over heat, on top of your range, the chips smoke, and the food picks up a great smoke flavor. The problem for authentic barbecue is that you wouldn't want to keep the box over direct heat for many hours, because the chips would burn and turn acrid. But if you just pop the smoker in the oven, the chips in the bottom will stop smoking!

So . . . my solution involves moving the box back and forth from stove top to oven: short sojourns on the stove top to keep the wood smoldering, long stretches in the oven to give the meat the time it needs to tenderize.

When I brought my recipe to the Food Network kitchen and they tried it out, I was nervous as could be—especially since one of our terrific chefs is from Memphis. Imagine how happy I was when Marie said, "This is almost exactly like Charlie Vergos's!" Now imagine how happy you, your family, and your guests will be.

Barbecued Dry-Rub Ribs, Memphis Style

Okay. I'm not saying this is the most convenient recipe in the world. First of all, you need one of those Burton Smokers to make it (see ordering info above). In fact, you might even need two of them—because one smoker yields just one rack of ribs, barely enough for two people. Then you need to make sure of your oven temperature (215 degrees) with an oven thermometer (inexpensive, though, and available at any housewares store). After you know the temperature, you have to leave about 6 hours for cooking the ribs. All in all this adds up to more than the usual amount of trouble. However, (1) the cooking process itself is quite simple and positively foolproof; and (2) the ribs you will turn out by following this recipe are guaranteed to make you a local hero. You will achieve that rare plateau of rib perfection on which the meat is not falling off the bone (that would be too wet and soft) but, instead, agrees to come away from the bone at your merest nibble. You will also experience the thrill of the Memphis dry-rub effect, wherein caked-on spices, neither too dry nor too wet, set your mouth atingle. Oh, go ahead. Bite the bullet: put a weekend aside for this dish, and know rib heaven forevermore.

MAKES 1 RACK OF RIBS, ENOUGH FOR 2 MODEST PORTIONS

2 tablespoons sweet paprika

1 tablespoon Old Bay seasoning

1 1/2 teaspoons chili powder*

1 1/2 teaspoons granulated brown sugar

1 1/2 teaspoons freshly ground black pepper

3/4 teaspoon garlic powder

3/4 teaspoon onion powder

A slab of spareribs, 2 1/2 to 3 pounds

4 cups of wood chips (hickory, mesquite, et cetera)

1 tablespoon white vinegar

1/2 teaspoon salt

1. Mix together the paprika, Old Bay seasoning, chili powder, sugar, black pepper, garlic powder, and onion powder in a bowl. Rub half the mixture all over the slab of spareribs. Reserve the other half of the dry-rub mix.

2. Heat the oven to 215 degrees. While the oven is warming, soak the wood chips in cold water to cover (for about 20 minutes).

3. Remove the chips from the water, and spread them evenly in the base of the smoker. Place the smoker, uncovered, on top of two stove-top burners set at medium-high heat. Let the wood chips smoke for about 3 minutes. Then place the slab of ribs on the smoker tray, place the tray over the wood chips, and cover the smoker tightly with its lid. Turn the heat down to medium, and leave the smoker on the burners for 5 minutes. Then transfer the smoker to the oven, placing it on the oven floor.

4. After the ribs have been in the oven for 1½ hours, remove the smoker, and once again place it over two burners set at medium heat for 5 minutes. Return the smoker to the oven floor.

5. After the ribs have been in the oven another 1½ hours, remove the smoker, and once again place it over

two burners set at medium heat for 5 minutes. Return the smoker to the oven floor.

6. After the ribs have been in the oven for 1 hour more, remove the smoker from the oven. Carefully lift up the tray holding the ribs, and pour off the liquid that has accumulated in the tray, reserving it. Return the tray with ribs, uncovered and out of the smoker, to the middle portion of the oven, and cook for 1 hour more.

7. While the ribs are cooking, degrease the reserved cooking liquid, and measure 2 tablespoons of it into a bowl. If you don't have 2 tablespoons, make up the difference with water. Add the vinegar, and blend well. Reserve. Add the salt to the remaining dry-rub mix, and blend well. Reserve.

8. Remove the ribs from the oven, and brush the top sides with the cooking liquid–vinegar mixture. Then sprinkle the salted dry-rub mix evenly over the top sides of the ribs. Return to the middle portion of the oven, and cook uncovered 1 hour more (a grand total of 6 hours).

9. Remove the ribs from the oven. Let stand for 15 minutes. Carve into individual ribs, and serve.

*It's best if you use a high-quality chili powder—preferably one with a smoky flavor. My favorite for this recipe is Smoked Jalapeno Flakes made by Chile Today, Hot Tamale in North Brunswick, New Jersey.

No Barbecue Sauce?

These fabulous ribs would not be eaten in Memphis with a barbecue sauce (that's the "dry-rub" thing they do there). However, if it's just not ribs to you without barbecue sauce, by all means open or make your favorite one and slather away at the table.

Great Corn Bread to Go with Your Ribs

Now that you've gone to the trouble of making a dead-ringer facsimile of Southern barbecue, it's time for a dead-ringer facsimile of Southern side dishes like corn bread, right? Wrong. For the best corn bread I've ever tasted was not in the South at all—but at a theme park of a barbecue restaurant in New York City called Virgil's. There, you'll find good food that'll never pass the authenticity test. But I gotta tell you that their individual loaves of corn bread—moist, sweet, and loaded with corn kernels, cheese, scallions, and cilantro as only a Yankee could do—are absolutely wonderful. Here's the recipe.

Damned Good Yankee Corn Bread

MAKES 10 MINILOAVES

1 1/2 cups yellow cornmeal

1 2/3 cups sifted flour

2/3 cup sugar

1 1/2 teaspoons salt

1 tablespoon baking powder

1 teaspoon baking soda

8 tablespoons melted butter

1 1/2 cups buttermilk

1/2 cup milk

2 beaten eggs

Tabasco to taste

4 ounces warm corn kernels

3 ounces grated cheddar cheese

1/4 cup chopped scallions

2 tablespoons chopped cilantro

1. *Preheat the oven to 425 degrees.*

2. *In a bowl combine the cornmeal, flour, sugar, salt, baking powder, and baking soda*

3. *In another bowl whisk together the melted butter, buttermilk, milk, beaten eggs, and Tabasco to taste. Add the dry ingredients, and just combine. Then fold in the corn*

kernels, cheddar cheese, scallions, and cilantro.

4. *Pour the mixture into buttered loaf pans 1 1/2 by 1 1/2 by 3 inches, filling them 2/3 full. Bake for 20 minutes, or until the bread is golden brown and a skewer inserted in the center comes out clean. Serve warm or at room temperature.*

Great Coleslaw to Go with Your Ribs

I'm passionate about coleslaw—but I'm also improvisational. I blend my coleslaw by my eye, not by a book—and I urge you to do the same. Here are the key elements.

1. *The most important factor for me in great coleslaw is the cut of the cabbage. The thinner the shredding, the better the coleslaw. That's why I like to cut my cabbage on a mandoline. If you don't have a mandoline, get fanatic about making very fine shreds with a very sharp knife. Remember: capelli d'angeli, not fettuccine.*

2. *I hate runny coleslaw—so I always make the slaw at the last minute. And it is mayonnaise—usually Hellmann's mayonnaise out of a jar—that gives the coleslaw the body I'm looking for.*

3. *After I mix in the mayo, however, I start to thin the*

slaw out a little bit (because mayo alone would be too thick). For this I use cider vinegar; add it slowly, until the coleslaw is just the consistency you like.

4. *The vinegar will turn the coleslaw a little sour, so a little sugar is needed for balance. Sprinkle in instant-dissolving sugar, and stir until you have the perfect sweet-and-sour ratio.*

5. *The only other flavor I like in my coleslaw is celery seed. Add some, along with salt and freshly ground pepper, and you've got it made.*

Criteria for Quality

- *Are the ribs not falling off the bone but willing to come away from it as you nudge them with your teeth?*
- *Are the ribs caked with palate-tingling spices—neither too dry nor too wet?*
- *Are the ribs slightly crunchy on the outside?*
- *Is the meat moist?*

When

Anytime! In my ultimate fantasy, I've got four Burton Smokers, and I'm serving ribs at an outdoor party along with all kinds of meats I'm cooking on the grill, and mountains of corn bread, and tubs of slaw, and crocks of baked beans, and a few kegs of beer. A country band is playing, and I'm saying "yee-hah!" a lot.

In Your Glass

Hold the beer for a moment—there are some wines I really enjoy with barbecued ribs. The category is hearty, young, purply, strong-tasting reds. Make sure the wines aren't more than two years old, at which point the fruit starts modulating into something more subtle—the last thing you want for a rib mate! Look for young Zinfandel from California, young Rhône-style reds from California, and particularly young and relatively inexpensive Shiraz from Australia (this stuff can cost you, but don't spend over $15 a bottle). In the latter group, young Shiraz from Rosemount Estate is always a rollicking rib wine as is young Shiraz from Banrock Station.

You want rollick? You can't go wrong with beer—unless it's beer that's too serious, too strong, too bitter. I actually like a wide range of beers with ribs—from simple Mexican lagers through German Weizenbiers to stronger European lagers (as long as they're well behaved and not too hoppy, like Grolsch) to well-balanced American microbrews in the English style (like Atlantic Amber from Norwalk, Connecticut).

There is one wacky American specialty beer, however, that I particularly love with ribs: it's called Cave Creek Chili Beer, and, believe it or not, it comes with a fresh green chili right in the bottle (okay, it's not a ship or a worm, but it's still pretty cool). I'd enjoy this bottle of beer just for the novelty—but the producers have gone to the trouble to make the beer around the chili pretty darned good as well. Seek it out!

4

MY FAVORITE DESSERTS

FRUIT SALADS—FRUIT SOUPS—
FRUIT TARTS—TARTE TATIN—APPLE PIE—
ICED FRUIT DESSERTS: GRANITAS,
SORBETS, AND SHERBETS—
CHOCOLATE CHIP COOKIES—
MOLTEN CHOCOLATE CAKE—TIRAMISÙ—
CRÈME BRÛLÉE—
PECAN PIE—PUMPKIN PIE

I firmly believe that the world is divided into cooks who love making dessert and cooks who love making everything else. The two practices come from different parts of the brain, it would seem. Dessert cooks and bakers are like scientists; they follow a formula, often placing something in the oven and waiting patiently for their precision to pay off. Sauce makers, fish grillers, meat sautéers, and salad tossers, by contrast, are like painters; they participate more in the final stages of the process, improvising madly from moment to moment in direct response to what they're seeing and smelling.

Apollo must have been a baker, and Dionysus a short-order cook. I've always leaned towards the Dionysian myself. The most troubling words in all of gastronomy for me are "Do not open the oven door!" If I'm not touching, prodding, poking, sniffing, appraising—right up to the last minute—I don't feel as if I'm "cooking." Nevertheless, I, like the rest of humanity, find that a little sweet at the end of a meal brings things to a natural close. I'm always trying to find desserts that are alluring without being technically demanding; I'm not a big one for complicated pastries and fancy cake decorating. I tend to prefer desserts that I can make quickly at the last moment, that have, as their greatest goods, integrity and freshness of ingredients.

If you feel as I do, you'll find lots of terrific home-cooking ideas in the following three categories of simple dessert making.

──────────── FRUIT DESSERTS ────────────

Time and time again, it is fruit that I turn to when dessert rolls around. All of those fancy cakes and confections that we associate with European cooking are rarely consumed by Europeans for dessert. It is much more typical on that great gastronomic continent—particularly around the Mediterranean—to finish a meal simply, with only a piece of raw, unconverted, perfectly ripe fruit.

I often do the same. But sometimes I go further—because good as good fruit is just by itself, the right window dressing can make it taste better still. I love uncooked fruit with light and tangy sauces, sometimes fortified with a racy splash of wine or liqueur. I'm nuts about uncooked and cooked fruit with various dairy products—butter, cream, crème fraîche, ice cream. And I truly believe that nothing makes a better marriage with pastry than meltingly tender, flavor-concentrated cooked fruit.

Here, then, are a few simple ideas for taking supreme advantage of fruit at dessert time.

FRUIT SALADS

I'd always believed that fruit salad was something pedestrian—something served at boarding school or picked up hastily at the deli. But that was before I had my first fruit salad in Paris, at an elegant restaurant—where the fruits resembled jewels more than berries and the tingling "dressing" for the "salad" drew out every ounce of fruity flavor. These days, elegant fruit salad is my number-one solution when there's absolutely no time to think about dessert for a dinner party. Just remember the following fruit salad rules.

Use Impeccably Fresh Fruit. There's nowhere to hide in a well-made fruit salad! Lots of kitchens and stores slough their worst fruits into fruit salad; that's why the dish has become debased. Don't allow any fruit into your fruit salad that you're not proud of!

Cut the Fruit into Attractive Shapes. Common sense is your guide here. Generally speaking, thin sliced is better than thick sliced. And try to make cuts that suggest the original fruits. For example, apples seem more like apples when they're in thin, skin-on slices rather than thick, skin-off chunks; grapes seem more like grapes when they're simply cut in half rather than diced; kiwis seem more like kiwis if your slices are round and preserve the pretty seed pattern.

Make the Salad no More Than 30 Minutes Before Serving. Lots of fruit salads fail simply because they're made too far in advance. Two problems occur as they sit: (1) the fruit starts to seem waterlogged, mushy, less fresh; and (2) juice leaks out of the fruit, turning the whole creation watery.

Make Sure the "Dressing" Has Perfect Ratios of Sweet and Sour. Too much sugar, and the salad tastes oppressive; too much lemon juice, and the salad tastes stingingly tart. Taste as you add these ingredients; when you hit the perfect sweet-sour ratio, you'll know it. The ratio varies from salad to salad, because the fruits themselves vary. The following recipe is only a suggestion.

Add a Little Filip of Flavor to the "Dressing." Liqueurs really come in handy here, particularly flavored brandies and eaux-de-vie. My absolute favorite one for fruit salad is Grand Marnier, an orange-flavored cognac from France; through some magical alchemy, it always makes the fruit taste fruitier, fresher, more French—without imposing too much of its own personality.

Serve the Salad on a Dinner Plate. We've all grown up being served "fruit cocktail" in heavy glass dishes on stems—the kind of glass that lacks delicacy, the kind that shows the hard seams of its factory manufacture. At diners, all kinds of foods get placed in these receptacles: shrimp cocktail, Jell-O, pudding, et cetera. But one of the things in France that changed my mind about fruit salad was the elegant presentation: I saw fruit salads laid out beautifully on large, exquisite dinner plates, made by such houses as Ginori and Villeroy & Boch. Celebrate your fruit salad! You don't have to arrange the fruits symmetrically . . . but do give them a great plate. You may either spread them out across the plate or attractively mound them in some way in the middle.

Garnish the Salad Attractively. The best and easiest garnish for a fruit salad is mint leaves. You can also pick out a few perfect fruits (like raspberries) and arrange them symmetrically around your asymmetric salad. Another possibility is highly colored fruit purée (made from, say, mangoes or raspberries), which you use like paint to make a design (you might do this with a squeeze bottle).

(Clockwise from upper left) red fruits, purple-blue fruits, green fruits, orange-yellow fruits

Selecting Fruits for Fruit Salad

The exact composition of your fruit salad is completely at the mercy of the season and of your local market. Never try to include a particular type of fruit just because you must have that fruit; if it's January, it's likely that you won't find salad-worthy peaches, no matter how much you want to include them. Instead, respond to what you see when you're shopping.

I always include at least five different fruits in my fruit salads; the variety keeps things interesting. I try to look for a range of tastes and textures as well. Most important by far is a range of colors: as I stand in the market plotting my strategy, many of my decisions are made with respect to the salad's ultimate color scheme.

Here are the major color groups, along with some of my favorite fruits. When I make a fruit salad, I try to select at least one item from each group. I present them here with slicing and presentation preferences.

Red: strawberries (thin slices the long way); raspberries (whole); watermelon (thin triangles); red cherries (pitted and cut in half).

Purple-Blue: purple grapes (seeded and cut in half from pole to pole); plums (crescent slices, skin on); blueberries (whole).

Green: green grapes (seeded and cut in half from pole to pole); kiwis (peeled and sliced into thin rounds).

Orange-Yellow: peaches (crescent slices with red tinge from pit area, skin off); nectarines (same, but maybe with skin on); melons (tiny balls); bananas (thin slices from small bananas).

Yellow-White: apples (thin crescent slices, skin on); pears (thin slices, skin off); star fruit (thin, star-shaped slices); Mt. Rainier cherries (pitted and cut in half); pineapples (little triangles).

In addition, I always include at least one member of the citrus family—usually oranges, but sometimes grapefruit, tangerines, et cetera. The best way to cut citrus fruits is to cut away the rind with a very sharp knife, making sure to shave off all the white pith as well. Then cut out individual sections of fruit. Sink the knife in just next to the white membrane line of a section, then into the white membrane line on the other side of the section. By completely cutting around the section, you end up with a peeled citrus section, free from rough membrane.

Yellow-white fruits (left), orange-yellow fruits (right)

ELEGANT FRUIT SALAD

Some cooks like to prepare a simple syrup (equal parts sugar and water boiled down together) for fruit salad because granulated sugar can be a little "crunchy" when tossed directly into the mixing bowl. I find, however, that if you let the salad sit for 10 minutes after you've tossed in the sugar, the sugar "melts" into the fruit juice. You can also use instant-dissolving sugar.

MAKES 6 SERVINGS

6 cups assorted sliced fruit (see opposite)

4 tablespoons granulated sugar

5 tablespoons freshly squeezed lemon juice

4 tablespoons Grand Marnier

Fresh mint leaves for garnish

Place the fruit in a large mixing bowl. Sprinkle with the sugar, and toss lightly. Add the lemon juice and Grand Marnier, and toss again. Let sit for 10 to 30 minutes, either on a counter (if you like a warmer salad) or in the refrigerator (if you like a colder salad). Divide among 6 dinner plates. Garnish with mint leaves, and serve immediately.

Something Extra

If you wish to take a fruit salad in a slightly more baroque direction, you can ladle a dollop of flavored crème fraîche on top. Don't do this if you're seeking lightness (as on a hot summer day); do do it if you're seeking enrichment (as on a cold winter's day). Here's a simple, delicious recipe.

Vanilla Crème Fraîche

MAKES ENOUGH FOR 6 FRUIT SALADS

8 ounces crème fraîche

1/4 cup sugar

2 teaspoons vanilla extract

Blend the ingredients together in a mixing bowl. May be served immediately or held for a few days in the refrigerator.

Criteria for Quality
- *Is the fruit fresh?*
- *Is the fruit varied in every way (color, taste, texture, shape)?*
- *Is the balance of sweet and sour correct?*
- *Is the salad correct in consistency—not too watery, not too dry, not too sugary-thick?*

In Your Glass
Only a wine of surpassing lightness could accompany fruit salad. So why not pick one of the lightest wines of all—sparkling wine? Of course, your bubbly is going to need enough sugar to stand up to the fruity sweetness, and enough acidity to stand up to the lemon juice. My perfect solution is sparkling Moscato from Piemonte in northwest Italy—in the form of either Asti or, even better (and a little more expensive), Moscato d'Asti.

(Clockwise from top right) Honeydew Melon, Pearl Tapioca, and Coconut Milk Soup; Simple Fruit Soup with Grand Marnier; Zuppi di Frutta; Fruit Soup with Lightly Jellied Orange Broth

FRUIT SOUPS

My other quick-fix salvation at dessert time is fruit soup. Actually, the way I—along with a lot of trendy restaurant chefs—prepare it doesn't really make it a "soup" in the traditional sense. No fruit is cooked to prepare this kind of fruit soup; raw fruit is simply placed in a wide, shallow soup bowl with a soupy liquid. You might say it's more like a wet fruit salad than it is like a soup. Great! That makes it easier on the cook. But its ease of preparation hasn't stopped a lot of big-deal restaurants from serving it. In fact, at the very finest restaurants in France and the United States—the kind that offer you dessert in "courses" (sometimes as many as four or five dessert courses)—I am often served some sort of raw fruit soup as my dessert "appetizer." This course-by-course thing is not how I serve fruit soup at home; usually, just a perfumed bowl of this marvelous stuff is quite enough dessert for me, my family, and guests.

To make a great fruit soup, pay heed to the same criteria that create a great fruit salad. Freshness and quality of ingredients are paramount. You should cut the fruit into delicate, attractive shapes. And the proportions of sugar and acid, once again, are crucial.

Fruit soup has one additional requirement: the "dressing" of the fruit salad, which here becomes the "soup," must be sufficiently balanced and delicious on its own that diners can sip it just by itself with a soup spoon.

Here are some of my favorite fruit soups—which I serve for either the most informal family dinners or the fanciest dinner parties.

SIMPLE FRUIT SOUP WITH GRAND MARNIER

This one is so much like a fruit salad, it actually is the fruit salad on page 217 converted into a fruit soup. To serve it, you can either plate it completely in the kitchen, as the recipe suggests, or serve the bowls to your guests with just the fruit salad in them, then ladle the "soup" from a tureen over the fruit in each bowl at the table.

MAKES 6 SERVINGS

8 tablespoons sugar
10 tablespoons lemon juice
1/2 cup Grand Marnier

6 cups fruit salad (see preceding recipe)
Fresh mint leaves for garnish

1. Place the sugar, lemon juice, and Grand Marnier in a mixing bowl. Whisk until well blended. Let sit for 15 minutes.

2. Divide the fruit salad among 6 wide, shallow soup bowls. Ladle the Grand Marnier mixture over the fruit, and serve immediately, garnished with the mint leaves.

FRUIT SOUP WITH LIGHTLY JELLIED ORANGE BROTH

One of the greatest fruit soups I ever had was at a brilliant two-star (which later became a three-star) restaurant in Veyrier-du-Lac, near Annecy in eastern France: Auberge de l'Éridan. The chef created a fabulous citrus broth, which was enriched with gelatin and chilled in such a way that it became medium-thick without any thickeners! I've done a good job, I think, of reproducing the remarkable texture and flavors of that soup. Just remember: as the soup chills in the refrigerator, its texture will keep changing. It will go from thin through medium and medium-thick to, ultimately, aspic. It's up to you to pull it from the refrigerator when it reaches the texture you like (I like it medium-thick). It's hard to predict exactly how long the process will take, but the texture I like is usually reached after about an hour. Then, you'll spoon it over fruit that sits in a wide, shallow soup bowl. I've left the fruit choice up to you. If you like, you can once again use 1 cup per person of the Elegant Fruit Salad on page 217. Or you can use any combination of fruit and flavors that you prefer. My all-time favorite permutation will not be to everyone's liking, but the one time I served it half of my guests were dazzled (the other half left the table). I purchased in Chinatown a whole durian—the notorious, cheesy, impossibly stinky fruit of southeast Asia—scooped its noxious but custardy flesh into the center of bowls, and surrounded the durian with this lightly jellied orange broth. Outstanding! A more generally acceptable custardy fruit that's also delicious in this soup is cherimoya.

MAKES 6 SERVINGS

4 tablespoons sugar
1 1/2 cups orange juice, strained and chilled
2 tablespoons powdered gelatin
1/4 cup Grand Marnier

6 cups fruit salad, chopped fruit, or large pieces of soft
    fruit (like durian or cherimoya)
Mint chiffonade for garnish

1. In a saucepan mix together the sugar and orange juice.
2. Sprinkle the gelatin over the surface evenly. Let it sit for 2 minutes.
3. Bring the juice gently to a boil, stirring.
4. As soon as it boils, remove from heat and add the Grand Marnier. Put it in the refrigerator, and chill for about 1 hour, until thick but not gelled.
5. Place the fruit in wide, shallow soup bowls, and spoon the gelatin mixture over all. Garnish, if desired, with mint chiffonade.

ZUPPA DI FRUTTA

Here's another simple recipe that brings amazing rewards for a minimum of fuss. Its basis is the serendipitous discovery I made in my kitchen one day—don't ask me how—that cream and grappa, in the presence of a little sugar, go cosmically together. This fruit soup features raw, undressed fruit—it's really quite austere. You could put the fruit in some type of syrup or "dressing," if you prefer. But I like the simplicity of this recipe. And you can plate it in such a way that each bowl ends up looking something like a Miró painting.

MAKES 6 SERVINGS

2 cups heavy cream

5 tablespoons plus 1 teaspoon sugar

4 teaspoons grappa, or more to taste

1 medium plum

1 medium nectarine

1 medium orange, sectioned

3 large strawberries

18 blueberries

1. Mix together the cream, sugar, and grappa. Blend well. Divide the cream mixture among 6 shallow bowls.
2. Slice the plum and nectarine into 6 slices each. Divide the slices and orange sections among the 6 bowls.

3. Cut the strawberries in half, and divide the halves among the 6 bowls. Place 3 blueberries in each bowl, and serve.

HONEYDEW MELON, PEARL TAPIOCA, AND COCONUT MILK SOUP

This simple fruit soup is my staple dessert in New York's Chinatown, whenever I go for dim sum. But there's no reason you can't serve it at any dinner, plain or fancy. It's as satisfying as it is refreshing.

MAKES 4 SERVINGS

4 ounces large pearl tapioca (available in Chinese groceries)

About 2 cups canned, unsweetened coconut milk

2 to 4 tablespoons sugar

1 1/2 cups small honeydew melon balls

1. Soak the tapioca in 2 cups of water overnight.
2. Drain the tapioca, add it to a heavy saucepan, and cover with 3 cups fresh water. Bring the water to a boil, reduce heat to low, and cook gently for 30 minutes. The tapioca should be quite soft, and much of the water should have been absorbed. Let the tapioca cool in the water for 20 minutes.

3. Add the coconut milk to the tapioca and water; the soup should have the consistency of fairly thick cream. Add sugar to taste. Add the melon balls. Chill if desired (for a few hours), or serve immediately by ladling into wide, shallow soup bowls.

A Beautiful Garnish: Edible Flowers

If you're preparing fruit soup for a fancy dinner, you might want to consider topping it with an edible flower garnish. One small, perfect, brightly colored beauty on each soup will do the trick: chamomile, citrus, lavender, peach, and mimosa flowers are all leading contenders.

Criteria for Quality

- Is the fruit in peak condition?
- Is the soup attractively presented?
- Is there a proper ratio of sweet to sour?
- Is the "broth" delectable all by itself?

In Your Glass

As with fruit salads, my top choice here is sweet sparkling wine. You can serve either the sweet Moscatos from Piemonte that I recommend for fruit salad or the sweet wines of Champagne—labeled, confusingly, either extra dry or demi-sec (such as the delicious Veuve Clicquot Demi-Sec).

FRUIT TARTS

When I feel like creating a dessert that's more complicated—but not too complicated—the first thing I think about is the fruit tart. There are manifold permutations of the fruit tart, of course—but I like the kind that captured my imagination in Paris many years ago: a shallow shell of light, crumbly pastry (made wide enough for a family or small enough for one person), filled with a flavored pastry cream, topped with gorgeous pieces of uncooked fruit, which sparkle (like jewels) under a thin jam glaze. These tarts have no pastry on top—the stunning arrangement of fruit is the top—and are sometimes presented out of their baking tins (if you bake them in false-bottom tins).

Once you understand the basic four elements of the fruit tart, you can go on to a whole universe of fruit tart variations.

1. THE TART SHELL

The hardest part, for those without a white thumb, is the pastry itself. But if you follow these directions carefully, you should have no trouble.

In classical French pastry practice, the most common doughs for tart shells are *pâte brisée sucrée* (a flour-sugar-butter combination that Julia Child translates as "sweet short paste") and *pâte sablée* (which adds egg to the basic mix and is translated as "sugar crust"). The dough I favor for fruit tarts not only adds egg to the flour-sugar-butter combination but adds a little heavy cream as well. The result is buttery, rich, tender—and surpassingly light at the same time.

BASIC TART SHELL

MAKES ONE 9½-INCH TART OR SIX 4-INCH INDIVIDUAL TARTS

1 egg

2 tablespoons heavy cream

1 3/4 cups all-purpose flour

2 tablespoons sugar

12 tablespoons (1 1/2 sticks) unsalted butter, chilled
    and cubed

1. In a bowl, beat the egg and cream together well.

2. Sift the flour into the bowl of a standing electric mixer, like a KitchenAid (or, if you are not using a mixer, into a large mixing bowl). Place the sugar and butter in the bowl with the flour.

3. If you are using an electric mixer, select the paddle attachment, and mix the flour-sugar-butter until it resembles coarse, uncooked oatmeal. You can do the same, quickly, in a Cuisinart. If you are not using either, mix the flour-sugar-butter together by hand, working quickly so the butter doesn't melt. Be careful not to overmix.

4. Pour the egg mixture into the flour, and combine by hand, forming it into a ball. The dough should still be slightly crumbly at this point. If it's too crumbly to hold together, add a little more cream. Wrap the ball of dough in plastic wrap, and chill it for 1 hour.

5. Remove the dough from the refrigerator, unwrap it, and, on a lightly floured surface, roll it out to ⅛-inch thickness. Fit it across the bottom and up the sides of a buttered 10-inch tart pan (or four 4-inch pans). You may use regular pans or pans with removable bottoms. Trim off the excess dough (by rolling a pin right across the top of the tart pan), prick the bottom of the dough all over with a fork, cover it in plastic wrap, and return it to the refrigerator. Chill for at least 30 minutes.

6. Preheat the oven to 350 degrees.

7. Remove the plastic wrap, line the tart with parchment paper, wax paper, or foil, and fill it with pie weights (or dried beans). Bake for 15 minutes. Remove the weights and paper, and bake for 15 minutes more, or until the pastry is golden. If you are using a regular pan, place the pan on the counter. Let it cool on a rack. If you are using a false-bottom pan, unmold the tart, and place it on a rack.

2. THE PASTRY CREAM

This is one of those marvelous French inventions that has made the world a better place. Traditionally called *crème pâtissière,* it is a not-too-thick custard made with egg yolks that serves as the anchor for the fruit in a fruit tart. The following one is a little less finicky than most, since it's stabilized with cornstarch; it is flavored with vanilla—but the whole world of pastry-cream flavorings (grated citrus rind, flavored liqueurs, chocolate) is open to you if you wish to improvise.

BASIC PASTRY CREAM

MAKES 1¼ CUPS PASTRY CREAM (ENOUGH FOR ONE LARGE TART)

1/2 cup whole milk
1/2 cup heavy cream
1 fresh vanilla bean
2 tablespoons sugar

2 egg yolks
2 tablespoons cornstarch
1/2 tablespoon softened butter

1. Put the milk and cream in a heavy, medium-size saucepan, and place over medium-high heat. Split the vanilla bean lengthwise, and scrape the seeds into the milk and cream. Put the rest of the bean and 1 tablespoon of sugar into the milk-cream mixture, stir, and bring the liquid to a boil. Reduce heat immediately, and simmer slowly for 1 minute. Remove from heat.

2. In a bowl stir together the egg yolks, the remaining 1 tablespoon of sugar, and the cornstarch. Add 1½ tablespoons of the warm milk-cream mixture, and whisk to eliminate any lumps.

3. Off the heat, slowly whisk the egg mixture into the warm milk-cream mixture in the saucepan. Return the mixture to gentle heat, and whisk rapidly until the liquid thickens. Stir in the butter.

4. Remove from heat, and pour the pastry cream into a bowl set over ice water. When the pastry cream is cool, pass through a medium-fine strainer, cover the surface with plastic wrap, and refrigerate. Pastry cream will keep, refrigerated, up to 5 days.

3. THE FRUIT

Fruit for fruit tarts, as for fruit salads and for fruit soups, must be in gorgeous condition—perhaps even more so here, since in a fruit tart the fruit is symmetrically lined up in a kind of fruit showcase across the top.

Your first decision is a fundamental one: do you want to make a tart with one kind of fruit only, or with a mixture of fruits? Mixtures can be very beautiful: mixed fruits in concentric circles, mixed fruits in quadrants, mixed fruits with a raspberry standing next to a blueberry standing next to a raspberry, et cetera. For me, however, tarts devoted to one fruit only somehow seem more "serious," and they are the kind I usually make.

Choices are endless, but they can be divided into two categories.

Whole Fruits. Some of my favorite fruit tarts are made with berries: raspberries (even golden raspberries), blueberries, blackberries, loganberries, et cetera. You simply line up the small, uncooked berries in a neat arrangement on top of the tart. Small strawberries—such as the wild ones the French call *fraises de bois*—make great tart toppers. Regular strawberries can sometimes be a little too large, so I choose the smallest ones available—or cut larger ones in half at the equator and use only the pointy part of the strawberry at the opposite end from the stem. Grapes are another whole-fruit choice, though pastry chefs sometimes like to cut these in half as well.

Sliced Fruits. With sliced fruits, your mandate is to create one pleasing shape from the fruit you use (e.g., you're making a kiwi tart, and all your peeled kiwis are cut into thin rounds with similar proportions). Slices are laid on top of the tart flat side down. Whether they overlap, barely touch, or don't touch at all is up to you—though crammed fruit on top of a tart is much more classic than sparse fruit on top of a tart. Round, small stone fruits—such as peaches, nectarines, plums, et cetera—are often cut into thin crescent shapes. When it comes to larger fruits—like melons and pineapples—you're on your own in shape creation.

4. THE GLAZE

A glaze—which is simply jelly, jam, or preserves cooked with a little water until it becomes thin and spreadable—adds zest, luster, brilliance to the top of a fruit tart; it turns something that looks homemade into something that looks like it came from a French pastry shop. You can serve a fruit tart with no glaze, but it may look a little dull.

I must point out that some pastry chefs like to glaze a tart to death, covering every square millimeter with a thick layer of the stuff. I don't like that; I prefer a lighter touch, just dabbing the glaze on the fruit to produce a subtle, jewel-like sparkle.

A glaze can have one other function in a tart. If you are not going to serve your fruit tart right away, paint the inside of your cooked and cooled tart shell with a thin layer of glaze a few minutes before adding the pastry cream. This will prevent the shell from turning soggy if it has to sit for a few hours under a layer of pastry cream.

Which jelly, jam, or preserve should you use? For tarts that seem to require a yellow-orange glaze (like peach tarts), I prefer apricot. For tarts that seem to require a reddish glaze, I prefer red currant. If you're using jam or preserves, you'll have to strain them before placing them in a saucepan or after cooking them; if you're using jelly, the mixture is already clear and needs no straining.

BASIC GLAZE FOR FRUIT TARTS

MAKES ¹/₂ CUP GLAZE

1/2 cup jelly, jam, or preserves (if jam or preserves, make sure to strain first through a sieve)
2 tablespoons water

1. Place the jelly, jam, or preserves in a small saucepan over medium-high heat. Add the water, bring to a boil, stir to blend, lower heat, and simmer for 2 minutes.

2. Let the glaze cool a bit, but use it while it's still warm, before the glaze gels again. It should be runny enough to drip off a pastry brush onto the fruit.

5. ASSEMBLY

Now that you have the four basics down pat, you're ready for the assembly of your tart. The following instructions apply to one 9½-inch tart, but common sense will guide you if, instead, you're making four individual tarts (usually 3 to 4 inches across).

1. If you're not planning to serve your tart immediately, use a pastry brush to seal the bottom of the pastry with a thin layer of glaze.

2. Spoon approximately 1 cup of pastry cream into your tart shell. Using a rubber spatula or a pastry spreader, smooth it out on top. The pastry cream should come most of the way up the sides of your shallow shell.

3. Art time: Arrange your fruit as beautifully and symmetrically as possible on top of the pastry cream (which acts as an anchor).

4. Working with a pastry brush, dab the fruit with a light layer of glaze until you have a sparkling veneer.

I'm absolutely serious about the ease of tart making; once you know the basics, you don't really need a specific recipe. It's all about improvisation. However, if you've never made one before and feel you need a little hand-holding, here's a specific recipe.

BLACK AND BLUEBERRY TART

MAKES ONE 9¹/₂-INCH TART

One 9 1/2-inch cooked tart shell (see "Basic Tart Shell")
1 cup pastry cream (see "Basic Pastry Cream")
1 pint blackberries

1/2 pint blueberries
1/4 cup black currant glaze

1. Fill the tart shell with the pastry cream.
2. Make 2 concentric rings of blackberries around the perimeter of the tart.

3. Fill in the center of the tart with blueberries.
4. Glaze the tops of the berries lightly with black currant glaze.

And just for variety's sake, here's another specific tart recipe—one that I devised about ten years ago for *Food & Wine* magazine. Actually, this recipe has quite a few deviations from the "basic" recipes I've given here. The pastry is a bit different. Less pastry cream is used, giving more focus to the fruit. The glaze is a bit sweeter. And the fruit itself is marinated in a sweet wine from the south of France.

MELON TART WITH MUSCAT DE BEAUMES DE VENISE

MAKES ONE 9¹/₂-INCH TART

1 small melon, such as cantaloupe or honeydew, peeled, seeded, and sliced thin
2/3 cup Muscat de Beaumes de Venise, plus 2 tablespoons
8 tablespoons granulated sugar
1 1/2 cups sifted flour
1/2 teaspoon salt

8 tablespoons chilled sweet butter, cut into bits
1 whole egg, plus 2 egg yolks
1/4 cup milk
1/2 cup apricot jam
1/2 to 2/3 cup pastry cream (see page 224)
Mint for garnish

1. Arrange the melon in a shallow dish. In a bowl combine the Muscat and 5 tablespoons of the sugar. Pour over the melon, and chill for 24 hours. Drain.

2. Prepare the pastry: In a bowl combine the flour and 1 tablespoon of sugar with the salt. Add the butter, and blend until the mixture resembles coarse meal. In another bowl whisk together the egg and milk. Add the flour mixture, and knead with your fingers until the mixture resembles coarse oatmeal. Form it into a rough ball. Chill, covered, for 2 hours.

3. Preheat the oven to 350 degrees.

4. Roll out the dough into a ⅛-inch thick round on a floured surface. Place the dough onto a 10-inch tart pan with a removable bottom. Prick the pastry shell all over with a fork, and cover it with a sheet of buttered wax paper. Fill the shell with dried beans, and place it in the preheated oven for 8 minutes. Remove the beans, prick again with a fork, and bake for another 10 minutes or so, or until the tart is golden brown. Let it cool on a rack. Remove, unmold.

5. Prepare the apricot glaze: In a small, heavy saucepan, combine the apricot jam with 1 tablespoon of sugar and 2 tablespoons of Muscat. Bring it to a boil, and boil for 1 minute. Strain.

6. To assemble: Brush a thin layer of the hot glaze over the bottom of the tart shell. Then place a thin layer of pastry cream. Arrange the melon slices over the pastry cream. Warm the remaining glaze, and brush it over the melon slices. Let the tart rest for at least 15 minutes.

7. Garnish the center of the tart with mint leaves. Include a mint leaf with each serving. If desired, serve a chilled glass of the melon marinade with the tart.

My Favorite Service of Tarts

When I'm preparing a large dinner party and I've decided on fruit tarts, I love to make an array of small, individual tarts—each one with a different kind of fruit. Then, at dessert time, I take a huge silver tray, place a large doily (or a series of overlapping doilies) on it, and top it with, say, a dozen tarts—making sure that the green of the kiwi, the red of the raspberry, and the yellow-orange of the peach are juxtaposed for maximum color effect. It looks like a display case from Fauchon, and it never fails to draw oohs and ahs.

Criteria for Quality

- Are the proportions of the basic elements correct: thin pastry, just enough pastry cream to support the fruit, enough fruit to grab center stage?
- Is the pastry light and crumbly?
- Is the pastry soggy? (it shouldn't be)
- Is the pastry cream too thick? (it shouldn't be)
- Is the pastry cream balanced in flavor? (not too sweet, and just enough "extra" flavor to make an impression)
- Is the fruit pristine?
- Is there the right amount of glaze? (just enough to make the fruit sparkle, not enough to form a sweet, sticky layer)
- Is the overall impression one of lightness and freshness?

In Your Glass

There are many good dessert wine options for fruit tarts. Remember, however, the overriding dessert wine rule: the wine should be a little sweeter than the dessert (otherwise it will taste thin and acid).

Once again, sweet sparkling wine loves fruit—and an Asti, a Moscato d'Asti, or a sweet Champagne would work well here. But because a tart has more body than a fruit salad—after all, both pastry and pastry cream are involved—the wine can be correspondingly richer. You can move from airy bubbles to dense, still wine without any trouble.

Which still wine? My choice, first of all, would be those still dessert wines that are of the "white" wine variety; "red" dessert wines (such as port) and "brown" dessert wines (such as sweet sherry) don't have the delicacy to partner fruit tarts perfectly. Second, I would avoid those dessert wines not known for bracing acidity (like Sauternes, or Hungarian Tokay); lively acid's important here to match the acidity of whichever fruit you're using.

My top choice, therefore, would be the sweet-and-crisp late-harvest Rieslings of Germany. Some Ausleses will be sweet enough, depending on the wine and depending on your tart. Beerenausleses and Trockenbeerenausleses will always be sweet enough. Best of all, perhaps, would be German Eiswein—which features so much acidity alongside its prodigious sweetness that your teeth may throb.

All of these German wines are expensive. But you can find delicious equivalents from American wineries. Look for late-harvest Rieslings from California, Washington, and New York State. Designations differ from winery to winery, but try to find a wine that has at least 6 percent residual sugar. And if your heart is set on Eiswein—or ice wine, as we say in these parts—but the pocketbook's a problem, look either for the vins de glacière from Bonny Doon in California or the ice wine from Inniskillin in, of all places, Ontario, Canada.

TARTE TATIN

With tarte Tatin, we move into the realm of the cooked fruit tart. Tarte Tatin is one of the great desserts of all time. In fact, now you know the menu for my last meal on earth (should I get to choose): raw oysters (see Chapter One), choucroute garnie (see Chapter Three), and tarte Tatin (stay right where you are) for dessert.

Tarte Tatin is an upside-down apple tart (the caramelized apples cook on the bottom, the pastry cooks on the top) that was invented at the dawn of the twentieth century by Fanny Tatin. She was the elder of two sisters who owned the Hôtel de la Gare in a small town south of Orléans in the Loire Valley. The sisters called the dish la Tarte des Demoiselles Tatin. The renowned gastronome Curnonsky discovered the tarte at their restaurant and brought it back to Paris in 1926—where it has been a bistro classic ever since.

I will never forget the ideal tarte Tatin, the one that I had at a small auberge in Villers-sur-Mer, a French seaside town—but this sea was the English Channel, and this town was in Normandy, where cooks know a thing or two about apples. Caramelization, crisp and flaky pastry—all the essentials were superbly in place. But the thing I loved about this tarte Tatin so much was its geometric irregularity. This was no perfect circle, all measured, tucked in, fluted, standing at one level. It was up and down like a map of the Massif Central, all hills and valleys, spread out like a pizza flung by a pizza man on his first day on the job. Remember: this is not fine cuisine. Tarte Tatin is not an elegant dish, not a creation of symmetry and perfection. The ideal tarte Tatin is as rustic as can be.

Too many restaurants making tarte Tatin today forget that. Tarte Tatins come out every night looking pretty, molded, and rounded—but the apples have no texture (they've been cooked to mush) and the pastry has no soul. The price of great tarte Tatin is vigilance—the kind of vigilance that's very easy for a home cook to supply. Tarte Tatin is the ultimate touchy-feely dish. As you caramelize the apples, you must make sure the heat is distributed evenly so the sugar browns to a deep mahogany without burning. This is tarte Tatin, not tarte brûlée; if it burns it will be bitter. Conversely, don't make the mistake of taking the pan off the heat too soon. You want a dark brown bottom that crisps to a crackling crunch. So you have to hover over the pan, poke at it, play with it, cajole it. Nobody, anywhere, on any kind of range can assume the apples will cook absolutely evenly. Over the course of the twenty minutes or so that these apples are cooking, you have to keep moving the pan around. You will see a particular area begin to bubble. That's a hot spot. Move the pan around to get the hot spot going in another part. Keep it moving. And baste the tops of the apples with the caramel. It will improve the flavor and keep you amused while you constantly watch and create hot spots evenly across the bottom of the pan.

To reward myself for such labor-intensive work, I always allow myself to evade pastry-making duty when I prepare tarte Tatin. Most cookbooks call for a pâte brisée, and some call for homemade puff pastry. Since my dream tarte Tatin in Normandy had flaky, buttery puff pastry, I always opt for the latter. But I buy it, frozen, at the fancy grocery store. There are some really good products available today—like Dufour—and I always feel that if I'm being a vigilant maniac with my apples, I deserve a break with my pastry. Be careful, however—for there are frozen puff pastries out there made with vegetable shortening, not butter. You don't want those.

My favorite apple for tarte Tatin is the Golden Delicious (no relation to the Red Delicious, which I do not recommend for cooking). The Golden Delicious is a low-acid apple, which makes it great for cooking—because apples that are low in acidity tend to hold their shape better.

One more thing before you get started: timing is crucial. A tarte Tatin is absolutely at its best, in my opinion, when it's still warm, taken out of the oven maybe half an hour before serving. They don't do it that way in restaurants anymore. Most pastry chefs create pies, tarts, and cakes early in the day . . . then they knock off in the afternoon, hours before dessert is served. This is bad for tarte Tatin. It gets soggy, mushy, monochromatic by the time it's eaten. This is just another reason why tarte Tatin is a perfect dish to master and serve at home—or in a sleepy, low-volume inn on the coast of Normandy.

TARTE TATIN

MAKES 6 SERVINGS

6 large apples, preferably Golden Delicious
Juice of 1 lemon
1 1/2 cups granulated sugar

6 tablespoons butter
Approximately 14 ounces store-bought puff pastry

1. Peel the apples, cut them in quarters, remove the cores (cutting each quarter at the core so it has a "flat" side), and toss the quarters in a large bowl with the lemon juice and ½ cup of the sugar. Let it rest for ½ hour.

2. Melt 4 tablespoons of the butter in a round, 10-inch cast-iron skillet over medium-high heat. Cover with the remaining cup of sugar, sprinkled over the butter in an even layer. Add a few tablespoons of the apple marinating juice to the pan, and cook the butter-sugar mixture over medium-low heat for 15 minutes carefully, so as not to burn it. Spread around any dark spots that appear. The color should be a rich brown.

3. Add the apple quarters to the pan, arranging them in a decorative pattern, rounded side down. Top the apples with the remaining 2 tablespoons of butter, cut into little bits.

4. Cook the apples over medium heat for approximately 20 minutes, occasionally spooning the bubbling liquid over the apples. This part of the recipe takes almost constant surveillance. In a few minutes, you will begin to see brown caramel bubbling up in the part of the pan over direct heat. Immediately shift the pan, so that other, nonbrowned parts go over the direct heat. Over 20 minutes, you may have to shift the pan a dozen times or more to get things evenly browned. The apples are ready when the liquid in the pan has turned to a thick, dark tan ooze. The apples should still be slightly resilient. Do not allow the apples to get entirely soft or the liquid to turn dark brown. This part of the tarte Tatin can be prepared hours in advance, or you can proceed immediately with the rest of the recipe.

5. Preheat the oven to 375 degrees.

6. Flour a work surface, and place the sheet of puff pastry on it. Working quickly, roll out the pastry until it is slightly larger than the interior of the apple pan. Lay it over the apples, tucking any protruding edges under the apples in the pan. Place the pan in the oven, and cook for approximately 30 minutes, or until the puff pastry has risen and cooked. The pastry should be dry and flaky (check inside the pastry to make sure that's so).

7. Remove from the oven, and let the tarte rest for a few minutes. Place a large, round platter over the tarte, and flip it over, releasing the tarte from the pan. The browned apples will be on top, the pastry on the bottom. You may serve it hot, if desired . . . but my preference is to serve this tarte warm, about half an hour after cooking. You can also serve it room temperature, or cold. Serve with Vanilla Crème Fraîche, if desired (see page 217).

Tarte Tatin

A Great American Tarte Tatin

I thought I would never see it. Mushy tarte Tatin after mushy tarte Tatin in American restaurants had led me into utter despair: I was sure that I'd never find a great tarte Tatin in America.

Then it happened. I was sitting at The Ivy recently, in Los Angeles, when a friend said, "You've gotta try the tarte Tatin here." In trendy California? In a restaurant that makes a specialty of pizza, pasta, and Cajun food? I assessed the odds and did all I could to prevent the order. But my friend persisted . . . and he was right. The Ivy's tarte Tatin is the only one I've ever had in America that comes close to the texture and joy of good ones in France.

QUINCE TARTE TATIN

When quince is in season—October and November, just when I start thinking tarte Tatin thoughts—I sometimes use it instead of apple for tarte Tatin. Why? Well, it seems a logical innovation to me: it tastes very much like apple in the finished product, except that it has a slightly more tropical, more exotic character.

MAKES 8 TO 10 SERVINGS

1 cup sugar
1 tablespoon water
1 teaspoon lemon juice

4 ounces (1 stick) butter, cut into tablespoons
8 quinces, peeled, cored, and quartered
14 ounces store-bought puff pastry

1. Preheat the oven to 400 degrees.

2. In a heavy, 10-inch, cast-iron pan combine the sugar, water, and lemon juice. Cook over medium heat until the mixture is caramelized to a nut brown color, stirring occasionally.

3. Off the heat, let the caramel cool for 1 minute, then add the butter. Return to heat, and stir to melt the butter.

4. Beginning at the center, add the quince quarters like spokes of a wheel. If you have leftover pieces, cut them in half and lay them in between and on top.

5. Cook the quince over medium heat for 15 minutes, rotating the pan frequently to avoid burning.

6. Roll out the pastry until it is slightly larger than the interior of the pan. Place it on top of the fruit, tucking in the edges. Put the tarte in the oven, and cook it for another 25 minutes, or until the pastry is golden and cooked through.

7. When the tarte is done, remove it from the oven and let it rest for 5 minutes. Then invert a serving platter on top, and turn over the pan and platter together quickly to transfer the tarte to the platter. If desired, serve with Vanilla Crème Fraîche on the side (see page 217).

Tarte Tatin Tips

1. *Use Golden Delicious apples. Some other apples will give off too much water or get too soft.*

2. *While the caramel is cooking, sweep around the inside of the pan one time with a wet pastry brush so the sugar doesn't recrystallize.*

3. *Make sure the caramel doesn't get too dark. The consequence of that mistake will be a bitter caramel.*

4. *While you are cooking the apples (or quinces) on top of the stove, move the pan around on the burner so all the slices of fruit cook evenly.*

5. *Puff pastry often looks cooked on the outside when it's still raw inside. Make sure your pastry is cooked through completely before removing it from the oven.*

Criteria for Quality

- *Do the apples retain some chew? (they shouldn't be mush)*
- *Is there a slightly crackling, golden brown glaze on top? (it shouldn't be sticky-hard, but it shouldn't be nonexistent)*
- *Is the glaze bitter? (it shouldn't be)*
- *Are the apples appropriately sweet-tart?*
- *Is the pastry crisp, flaky, buttery?*
- *Does the whole tarte seem rustic? (it shouldn't seem symmetrical, molded, or seamless)*

In Your Glass

A wide range of dessert wines will go with tarte Tatin, just as long as the wine's a little sweeter than the dessert.

Once again, however, my top choice wold be late-harvest Riesling—late for the extra blast of sugar that helps the wine meet the dish's richness, Riesling for the inherent acidity of the grape, which helps the wine cut through the dish's richness.

APPLE PIE

The classic American version of a cooked apple tart, I suppose, is apple pie—which also happens to be one of my favorite desserts on earth. Sure it's much heavier than French fruit tarts; it has a double crust, which means there's also pastry over the top of the fruit. And the flavoring is bolder, which means the natural flavor of the fruit is compromised somewhat by the add-on flavors of cinnamon and other spices. But when I'm thinking Apple Pie, none of these things is a flaw. They are, in fact, the very wholesome, emotional, traditional American features that make apple pie taste so good in the first place. Here's a catalog of key apple pie elements for the home baker—what can go wrong, and what needs to go right.

The Apples. Once again—as for tarte Tatin—my apple of choice is the Golden Delicious. In this dish, there's even a kind of poetic justice in using it, because the Golden Delicious is out-and-out American. It was the result of an accidental cross-pollination between two other golden varieties and was first discovered on a West Virginia farm in 1914. Whatever its history, it cooks to a beautiful, firm texture, adds lots of perfumy apple flavor, and supplies a great deal of natural sugar (allowing you to add a little less of the cane stuff).

Texture of the Filling. Here's where many an apple pie goes awry. Some pies feature a heavy, gooey paste all over and around the apples; this is the too-thick-filling error. Some pies feature apples that are barely held together by a runny little juice, causing the fruit to slip-slide away; this is the too-thin-filling error. A perfect Apple Pie, to me, features apple slices that are just held together by a medium-textured golden runoff. The way to achieve this is to mix your apples, before putting them in the pie, with the perfect amount of flour: about ½ cup of flour to 3 pounds of apples.

Flavor of the Filling. Though I fully accept the apple-flavor diminution that comes with the addition of sweet spices to apple pie, I never allow it to go too far. I've had apple pies that tasted like garage sales of spice collections. I prefer to use cinnamon only—and not too much of it, at that. If you keep the sugar down and brighten everything with a good dose of lemon juice, you should end up with a delicious, superappley apple pie.

The Crust. Here's where apple pies show the greatest degree of divergence. The variations are too numerous to mention, so I will merely describe my ideal apple pie crust: so flaky you can watch it crack into layers; so buttery the layers never seem dry, and the wholesome flavor makes you cry. Now, you'll read all kinds of opinions about the shortening you need to achieve such a splendid crust. Propaganda from the butter advocates, the Crisco advocates, the lard advocates. My ideal crust is made of butter and lard, in a proportion of 4:1.

The greatest apple pie I ever tasted was baked by an outstanding shop just west of New York's Times Square called the Little Pie Company. I'd done many an apple pie experiment of my own, but nothing I ever made could compare with their masterpiece. Because life is short, I simply got the recipe from them and made it my apple pie, whenever an apple pie was called for. With their gracious permission, I am able to bring you a version of that recipe here.

Here are a few of the features that make it stand out:

1. The pastry is made with a mixture of regular flour and cake flour, which makes it softer.

2. The pastry is made with a little vinegar, which provokes the flavor of the crust.

3. Most important, the pastry is made with—hold on to your hats—cheddar cheese! Now, I know that at first this may sound to you—as it did to me—like some kind of tricked-up, ultra-Americana shopping-mall nonsense. But I think one bite will convince you (it helps that you don't taste the cheese).

4. The proportions of this pie are heartwarmingly mammoth. The Little Pie Company mounds the apples high, and the finished look is positively domelike.

SUMPTUOUS APPLE PIE WITH CHEDDAR CHEESE CRUST

MAKES 8 SERVINGS

For the cheddar dough:

1 1/4 cups unbleached all-purpose flour

1/4 cup cake flour

1/4 teaspoon salt

8 tablespoons unsalted butter, frozen solid, slightly thawed

2 tablespoons lard or vegetable shortening, frozen solid, slightly thawed

1 cup lightly packed grated New York extrasharp Cheddar cheese

2 teaspoons white wine vinegar mixed with 1/3 cup very cold water

For the apple filling:

6 to 7 large Golden Delicious apples (3 pounds), peeled, cored, and sliced into 1/16-inch-thick slices

2 tablespoons freshly squeezed lemon juice

1 1/4 cups sugar, plus additional for sprinkling

1/2 cup unbleached all-purpose flour

3/4 teaspoon cinnamon

3/8 teaspoon salt

2 tablespoons unsalted butter, softened

1 egg beaten with 1 tablespoon cold water, for glaze

1. Make the dough: In the work bowl of a food processor fitted with a metal blade, combine the flours and salt.

2. Cut the butter and lard into small pieces, add them to the work bowl, and process for 5 seconds.

3. Add the cheese, and pulse on-off 2 times to mix.

4. With the motor running, pour in just enough vinegar mixture in a slow, steady stream for the dough to form a loose ball.

5. Turn the dough out onto a work surface. Specks of butter and cheese will be visible. Shape the dough into

a disk, wrap it in plastic wrap, and chill it for at least 2 hours or overnight before using.

6. When you are ready to cook, preheat the oven to 425 degrees.

7. Toss the sliced apples gently with the lemon juice. Whisk together 1¼ cups sugar, flour, cinnamon, and salt, add them to the apple slices, and toss gently to coat evenly.

8. Divide the dough into 2 unequal pieces, making the piece for the top crust slightly larger. On a lightly floured work surface, roll the smaller piece into an 11-inch round. Line a 9-inch pie plate with the bottom crust, and fill it with apples. Using your hands, shape the apples into a firmly packed mound that's higher in the center than at the sides; dot with butter. Trim the edges of the bottom crust with scissors to a ¼-inch overhang.

9. Roll out the remaining dough to an 11-inch round, and arrange it over the filling. Trim the edges of the top crust to a ¾-inch overhang. Fold the top crust under the edge of the bottom crust, and flute the edges decoratively, pressing them together with your thumb and forefinger. Cut three 1¾-inch slashes in the center of the top crust.

10. Bake the pie in the lower third of the oven for 20 minutes. Reduce the oven temperature to 375 degrees, and continue to bake for 30 minutes more. Remove from the oven.

11. Brush the top with egg glaze, sprinkle with additional sugar, and return to the oven for 10 more minutes, or until the pastry is golden brown and the juices are bubbling. Cool for at least 1 hour before serving (you may serve the pie slightly warm or at room temperature).

As American as Apple Pie

People say that there is nothing more American than apple pie. The fact of the matter is that apple pie was popular in England long before there was an America. However, there's this to be said for us Yanks: we have become the world's largest apple-producing nation and, as such, may justly claim bragging rights to this great dessert. After all . . . self-promotion is as American as apple pie.

Criteria for Quality

- *Is the pastry golden, light, buttery, flaky—not sodden, heavy, or crumbly?*
- *Does the pie seem crammed with apples, brimming with goodness—not deflated or meager?*
- *Are the apples just held together by a golden ooze that's neither too thick nor too thin?*
- *Is the pie just sweet enough? (I especially dislike overly sweet apple pie)*
- *Are the spices used with restraint, allowing the flavor of the apples to come through?*

In Your Glass

Once again, a wide range of dessert wines—just as long as the wine's a little bit sweeter than the dessert—will do nicely with this wine-friendly pie.

But I must be honest with you. Drinking wine with apple pie—even though America is blessed with wonderful dessert wines—seems like a violation of the spirit of apple pie. Oh, I know Mom enjoys a glass every now and then—but somehow a cuppa joe seems a lot more appropriate than a stem of Riesling. Now, don't get me wrong: I usually subscribe to the European coffee school, which holds that coffee should be drunk after dessert, not with it. But this is one case where the Europeans just don't get a vote. It's an American thing, buddy.

ICED FRUIT DESSERTS: GRANITAS, SORBETS, AND SHERBETS

Another favorite fruit option of mine for dessert is iced fruit in the form of granitas, sorbets, and sherbets—which are really a lot easier to make than you may think.

I know, I know—right away you're fretting about the bother of fancy machines to create iced desserts. In case you are, I've got good news for you on two fronts:

1. To make granitas (perhaps my favorite of the three main types of iced desserts) you need no equipment whatsoever, aside from your freezer.

2. Once you bite the bullet and invest in an ice-cream-making machine to make sorbets and sherbets, dessert making becomes supereasy—because your machine does most of the work!

There's always a good deal of confusion about iced dessert terminology, so here are the essential differences among the three kinds.

Granitas are ices made with water, sugar, and flavorings (in this case fruit juice). I use the Italian name—granita—because it's extremely popular there (sold by street vendors and ice-cream shops). You'll see it in France as well, however, where it's called *granité.* The best way to make granitas is to place your flavored liquid in a flat baking pan (prechilled), then place that pan in the freezer. Now, if you just left the pan in the freezer, you'd have, after a few hours, a solid chunk of ice. That's not what you want; the desired end product is soft, flaky shards of ice that can be eaten spoonful by spoonful— something like a lightly packed snowball. This is extremely easy to achieve: simply remove the pan from the freezer every ½ hour, and break up the congealing granita with a fork. Return it to the freezer (with the fork resting in the pan to keep it cold), and get ready for your next ½-hour breakup. After about 2 hours, your granita should have the right consistency. Serve it up in dessert goblets.

Sorbets are much smoother iced desserts. They are typically made with fruit juice or puréed fruit, sweetened with sugar, and sometimes flavored with other things (such as liqueurs). These days, hardly a high-end restaurant in France or America is without a beautifully presented assortment of fruit sorbets at dessert time. You need an ice-cream machine to make them—but once you have one (and they can be had for as little as $65), sorbets are amazingly easy to make. You simply blend together a flavor you like (some recipe suggestions follow), then pour the liquid in the machine and follow the manufacturer's instructions. When your sorbets are ready, you can serve them in either dessert goblets or bowls—or you can form them into oval quenelles, shaping them with two tablespoons that have been dipped in hot water, and present the quenelles arranged on fancy dinner plates (appropriately garnished with fruit and mint leaves).

Sherbets are just about the same as sorbets—in fact, the names are sometimes used interchangeably. However, some people who specify sherbet mean by that name a sorbetlike mixture that has had some dairy product (milk, cream, or even egg whites) added to it. Obviously, this type of sherbet will be a little richer and creamier than a sorbet. Making sherbet is the same as making sorbet: you blend a mixture, buy a machine, and follow the manufacturer's instructions.

Here are some of my favorite iced fruit desserts that I've devised, and gathered from other sources, over the years.

LEMON GRANITA

MAKES 4 SERVINGS

6 tablespoons sugar
1/3 cup lemon juice

1 teaspoon finely grated lemon zest

1. In a saucepan combine the sugar with 1½ cups water; bring it just to a boil over medium heat, stirring until the sugar dissolves.
2. Remove the pan from the heat, leave it to cool, then refrigerate it until cold.
3. Stir in the lemon juice and zest. Pour the lemon syrup into a square metal cake pan, and place it in the freezer. Freeze for 2 hours in all, removing the pan from the freezer every 30 minutes, stirring and scraping with a metal fork until the ice crystals break up. After 2 hours, the granita will resemble snow.
4. Scrape the granita into 4 dessert goblets, and serve immediately.

Espresso Granita

One of my favorite granitas is not made from fruit at all but from coffee. Espresso granita is wildly popular all over Italy—as a great late-afternoon pick-me-up in a Roman café (sometimes with whipped cream on top), as breakfast in Sicily, as a snack anywhere and anytime. It is made in the freezer exactly like other granitas. Simply brew yourself some espresso, sweeten it to your taste (or not at all), and freeze away. Astonishingly good in the summertime.

MANGO SORBET

MAKES 4 SERVINGS

1 mango, peeled and pitted
1/2 cup sugar

1 tablespoon lemon juice
Pinch of salt

1. Place the mango flesh in a food processor, and make a smooth purée.
2. In a bowl, mix the purée with 1 cup of hot water, the sugar, lemon juice, and the salt. Taste, and add sugar if desired.
3. Put the bowl in the refrigerator to chill.
4. Put the chilled purée in an ice-cream maker and freeze, following the manufacturer's instructions.

GRAPEFRUIT HONEY SORBET

MAKES 6 SERVINGS

1/2 cup honey
2 cups grapefruit juice

1. Warm the honey in a saucepan over medium heat until it is just heated through.
2. Add ¼ cup of the grapefruit juice, and mix together thoroughly. Pour into a bowl, and add the remaining juice. Taste, and add sugar if desired.

3. Chill the mixture in the refrigerator.
4. Put the chilled mixture in an ice-cream maker and freeze, following the manufacturer's instructions.

DRIED APRICOT SORBET

This sorbet, taken from a recipe by Julia Child's old collaborator Simone Beck, is a little more complicated than most sorbets—but eminently worth the trouble.

MAKES 12 SERVINGS

3/4 cup granulated sugar
3/4 cup packed dark brown sugar
3/4 pound dried apricots

3 to 4 strips lemon zest
1 cup dry white wine
1/2 cup fresh lemon juice

1. Put the sugars and 2½ cups water in a medium saucepan, and bring them to a boil. Cook until the sugars dissolve.
2. Add the apricots and lemon zest, and simmer until the apricots are soft (20 to 30 minutes). Let the mixture

cool slightly.
3. Put the mixture in the bowl of a food processor with the wine and lemon juice, and process to a purée.
4. Put the chilled mixture in an ice-cream maker and freeze, following the manufacturer's instructions.

PINEAPPLE SHERBET

MAKES 4 SERVINGS

1 1/4 cups pineapple purée (see note)
1/2 cup sugar

1 tablespoon lemon juice
1 egg white (or 2 tablespoons heavy cream)

1. In a bowl mix together the pineapple purée, sugar, lemon juice, and 1 cup of hot water. Taste, and adjust the lemon-sugar balance if necessary.

2. In another bowl beat the egg white just until it starts to foam—do not allow it to become stiff. Mix the beaten egg white into the other ingredients, and chill in the refrigerator. (If you are using heavy cream, simply mix the cream into the other ingredients and chill.)

3. Put the chilled mixture in an ice-cream maker and freeze, following the manufacturer's instructions.

NOTE: To obtain 1¼ cups pineapple purée, simply remove the peel, the core, and the "eyes" from a small, fresh pineapple. Place the pulp in a blender or food processor, and purée. Measure out 1¼ cups. You could do the same with canned pineapple chunks, but the flavor won't be as good.

Criteria for Quality

- *For granitas: Are they soft enough?*
- *For granitas: Are they light?*
- *For sorbets: Are they smooth, free from lumps?*
- *For sherbets: Are they rich?*
- *For all iced fruit desserts: Is the flavor of the fruit that's used very intense? very specific?*
- *For all iced fruit desserts: Is the balance of sugar and acid just right?*

In Your Glass

Wine is not necessary with iced fruit desserts, which are almost liquids themselves. If you insist, however, on a glass of something—particularly if a celebration is under way—a sweet sparkling wine would be the best choice.

CHOCOLATE DESSERTS

When it comes to all-time favorite dessert categories, my runner-up is chocolate desserts. Why? Once again, as with fruit desserts, chocolate desserts can be extremely easy to make. More important—as with fruit—I'm insane for the basic ingredient. If you have great chocolate, you practically don't need to do anything with it; it speaks volumes all by itself. However, once again, as with fruit, a little manipulation by the home cook can sometimes raise the basic ingredient to an even higher level.

But chocolate, as a basic ingredient, is much more confusing than fruit. At the market, for example, one can easily intuit one's way to a great piece of fruit just by looking, smelling, touching; this would be impossible with chocolate, which is always wrapped and packaged. Furthermore, it's even difficult to get a handle on what chocolate is. Fruit is fruit—but what on earth is chocolate?

Since it's always a good idea for cooks to understand what they're working with, let's take a look at the chocolate basics before proceeding to some of my favorite chocolate desserts.

To organize your thinking about the creation of chocolate, visualize global chocolate production as a three-tier system.

The first tier is the plantation level, devoted to the growing, harvesting, drying, fermenting, and shipping of cacao seeds, which will ultimately become chocolate. These seeds grow in large, bumpy pods, which grow on cacao trees. The cacao trees are native to Mexico, but since the nineteenth century their cultivation has spread to many regions of the world that fall within twenty degrees of the equator: parts of the West Indies, Brazil, Venezuela, West Africa, Madagascar, Sri Lanka, and the Philippines, among other places.

The second tier is the chocolate factory, where dried cocoa seeds are received (after fermentation, technically, they switch names from cacao to cocoa) and are converted into big blocks of what is recognizably chocolate. These chocolate factories may be found in Switzerland, Belgium, France, England, America, and other places. Some of them have names that are very well known to chocolate fanatics: Valrhona, Callebaut, et cetera. Factories all use a chocolate-making process that is fairly standard in its basic procedures.

Roasting. Cocoa seeds are roasted in very large ovens, at temperatures that range from 100 to 150 degrees Celsius. This is an important step in bringing out the chocolate flavor. Too little roasting, and the flavor is insipid; too much, and the resulting chocolate will have a bitter, unpleasant taste.

Winnowing the Shells. A winnowing machine then cracks open the seeds, revealing little morsels inside that are called nibs. The husks that surrounded the nibs are blown away by the machine. Nibs from various sources are blended at this point to reach the desired house taste; as many as ten sources may be used.

Grinding. Another machine then grinds the blended nibs, under heat. The result is a liquefied product known as chocolate liquor, though it has no alcoholic content. With no or very few additions, this chocolate liquor can be solidified into bars that are known as baker's chocolate. This is very pure stuff, but to the human palate it's too pure; further additions are needed before the product starts tasting like great chocolate.

Extracting the Cocoa Butter. The factories take a giant step towards great chocolate when they put the chocolate liquor under hydraulic pressure. Now the liquor is separated into two items: cocoa butter and cocoa solids. During this process, approximately 53 percent of the original chocolate liquor becomes milky cocoa butter, the fatty part of the liquor. When this cocoa butter is solidified, it becomes the main ingredient of white chocolate. The approximately 47 percent of the liquor that's left behind—the part with the chocolate flavor—is called cocoa solids. When pulverized, these solids give us cocoa powder. But most important, when these cocoa solids are blended back with some of the cocoa butter, along with sugar, you have reached the condition of chocolate. Of course, many variations of basic "chocolate" are possible: extrabittersweet, bittersweet, semisweet, sweet. Generally speaking, as you go from extrabittersweet chocolate to sweet chocolate, the ratio of cocoa butter increases, as does the amount of added sugar.

Making Milk Chocolate. Chocolate fanatics prefer their chocolate dark, and there is evidence that even in the wimpy U.S. market a general consumer preference for dark chocolate is growing. But in the land of Hershey's Kisses, we sure love our milk chocolate: chocolate to which the manufacturers have added powdered milk (sometimes condensed milk). Milk chocolate is lighter in color, less chocolaty, and sweeter than dark chocolate.

Refining and Conching. These two processes improve the texture of the new chocolate, which has a coarse, gritty feel in the mouth at this stage. In refining, the chocolate is ground by three to five steel rollers down to tiny, microscopic bits. This makes for a much smoother mouth feel. Rodolphe Lindt, in the nineteenth century, took it one step further; he invented conching machines (so named because they looked like shells), which smooth the chocolate further in rectangular troughs or round drums. According to Thierry Meuret of Godiva Chocolate, however, the main purpose of conching is not to improve texture. "In conching," he says, "the agitation of the chocolate under high temperature evaporates the chocolate's acid into the air, which dramatically improves its flavor."

Tempering. Throughout most of the chocolate-making process, the chocolate has been kept quite hot, not far from the boiling point. In tempering, the temperature is manipulated—hot to cool (down to about 84 degrees) and up to hot again. The purpose is to stabilize the cocoa butter crystals in the chocolate so they won't melt later on and become grainy again.

Finally, the chocolate is ready. Most factories prepare it in ten-pound bars. Before being shipped, the chocolate usually is aged for a few weeks—or longer for great dark chocolate—to improve flavor.

Please note: When you're making chocolate desserts, it will most likely be chocolate from this second tier that you'll be using—big blocks of bittersweet chocolate, semisweet chocolate, et cetera.

Now the third tier kicks in—the producers of chocolate candies or chocolate confections. Their products—the kinds of exquisite finished candies you see in fancy chocolate stores—will not be the raw ingredients for your chocolate desserts. But you may well pick up a pound or so to place on a fancy dinner table after the regular dessert has been cleared!

It is important to realize that few of the chocolate companies famous for high-quality chocolate candies—like Godiva, Neuhaus, et cetera—make their own chocolate. They are third-tier producers, having purchased their chocolate from second-tier chocolate manufacturers. The same applies, of course, to the many small artisans around the world who craft exquisite little confections; essentially, they are candy makers, not chocolate makers. *Candy,* in fact, is a technical term in the chocolate world: it refers to the confections that are made from chocolate by a third-tier producer after the chocolate itself is made by a second-tier manufacturer.

The candy maker has, at his disposal, a very wide range of tricks to convert chocolate into exquisite confections. He adds things like butter and cream to the basic manufactured chocolate he has received. He creates fillings for candies, which can be chocolate mixed with cream, or chocolate mixed with nuts or fruit or liqueur, or many other possibilities. He coats fillings with a spreading chocolate called *couverture,* which he has made from second-tier chocolate blocks. He can create fanciful chocolates—Santas, bunnies, mice, et cetera. He can color his chocolates or "garnish" them with swirls, dots, curlicues, et cetera. The possibilities are endless.

Categories of Chocolate for Chocolate Desserts
When you shop for dessert-bound chocolate, you'll be confronted with a wide variety of possibilities. For most chocolate desserts, you should use blocks of chocolate that come from second-tier chocolate producers. Here are some of the forms you'll most likely see that chocolate in.

__Baker's Chocolate.__ This is pure chocolate liquor hardened into bars, with no sugar, milk, or extra cocoa butter added. It is very bitter and not to the taste of many people. It is also called baking chocolate, bitter chocolate, and unsweetened chocolate.

__Bittersweet Chocolate.__ Here, the purity of chocolate liquor gets diluted. Sugar, flavorings (like vanilla), and lecithin (an emulsifier) are all added to the chocolate liquor, which, by law, must account for 35 percent of the finished bittersweet chocolate. The finished product is dark and quite bitter.

__Milk Chocolate.__ This is a different animal entirely—since milk (usually powdered, sometimes condensed) is added. The chocolate is much lighter in color and much less chocolaty. American milk chocolate must contain only 10 percent chocolate liquor.

__White Chocolate.__ Because this product contains none of the cocoa solids, many refuse to call this chocolate at all. But it is mostly cocoa butter from cacao beans, with a little sugar, milk, vanilla, and lecithin added.

Which of these chocolate blocks should you use? It all depends on how much you like the "real" chocolate flavor—which is "dark," earthy, mysterious, not at all sweet and obvious. Chocolate geeks—the equivalents of snobby wine geeks—disdain milk chocolate and insist on chocolate with the highest levels of chocolate liquor. Sometimes, they insist that the cocoa solids part of the chocolate liquor be especially high—75 percent cocoa solids seems to be the current fashionable ratio. I'm sympathetic to this position—but I'm also a cook, and I find that it's bittersweet chocolate that seems to work best in the widest range of chocolate desserts.

My Favorite Producer of Chocolate for Chocolate Desserts

There are many wonderful blocks of chocolate out there for making desserts. For a long time, my favorite was the chocolate produced in southern France, Valrhona—and I still love it and use it frequently. However, something new appeared on the radar screen a few years ago that has completely captivated me. It's called El Rey, and it's made by a family company in Venezuela—a country that's famous for its first-tier chocolate production because some of the world's greatest cacao beans are grown there. El Rey, however, is reversing the Venezuelan tradition of shipping those beans abroad; the company is now holding on to the beans and has become a second-tier producer as well. El Rey has imported European machinery and know-how, and now makes a chocolate that, to me, has the purest, deepest chocolate taste you can find anywhere. El Rey chocolate is available through a firm in Brookfield, Connecticut, called Simpson & Vail (tel.: 800-282-TEAS; fax: 203-775-0462). You can mail-order extrabitter chocolate, bitter chocolate (my favorite for most dessert uses), dark milk chocolate, or white chocolate. Fourteen-ounce packages cost $8.50 each; 1-kilogram packages (2.2 pounds) are $17.00 each; 3-kilogram packages (6.6 pounds) are $48.00 each.

Recipe testing with my chief tester, Shelly Thomas

CHOCOLATE CHIP COOKIES

The chocolate chip cookie is undoubtedly my favorite cookie of all—but I gained even greater respect for it about ten years ago at a restaurant in Manhattan.

It was a place newly opened by David Liederman—yes, that David, the cookie genius behind David's Cookies, the cookies that fueled us all in the late seventies and early eighties. Before David's Cookies exploded into fabulous success, David had never typecast himself as a cookie man. French food, in fact, was his real love—and, in pursuit of it, he had spent many years in France dining in, even cooking in, top French restaurants. One of his favorites (and mine) was L'Ami Louis, the old-fashioned Paris bistro where roast chicken and garlic potatoes are brought nigh unto godliness. In the late 1980s, David decided to open a similar restaurant in New York. He called it Chez Louis—to make sure the reference was clear—and included on the menu many of the dishes for which the Parisian L'Ami Louis was famous.

However, he knew well that this was a restaurant in America and very cleverly put an American spin on many of the French details. One such "spin" concerned the platter of giveaway pastries that is de rigueur in a fine French restaurant after the desserts are finished. David offered no delicate petits fours at Chez Louis; instead, your table was graced with a platter of warm, chewy, meltingly chocolaty chocolate chip cookies. Not only was it a master culinary stroke, but it made everyone see chocolate chip cookies in a new light. Suddenly, the chocolate chip cookie was no longer an after-school snack with milk in front of the TV! Through the same strategy employed by the Dadaists in putting ordinary objects in museums—the chocolate chip cookie was a work of art! An American treasure! And so it has been for me ever since.

But connoisseurs' cookie or not, the chocolate chip cookie is undoubtedly America's favorite cookie as well. Remarkably, it hasn't been with us that long at all—only since 1930. It all happened in Whitman, Massachusetts, where one Ruth Wakefield ran an establishment called the Toll House Inn in an eighteenth-century tollhouse halfway between Boston and New Bedford. She was making butter cookies one day—or so the story goes—and had the sudden inspiration to chop up a bar of Nestlé's semisweet chocolate and add the "chips" to the cookies. Apparently, she expected the chocolate to melt in the cookies. But . . . eureka! . . . the chocolate chips held their shape, and something new was under the sun. At first she called her creation the chocolate crunch cookie. Later, she called it the Toll House cookie. Still later, it was Nestlé that called—asking if it could print her recipe on the paper that wrapped its bars of chocolate. Ruth said yes. Finally, in 1939, Nestlé made it really easy for Americans: it started to market prechipped chocolate chips expressly for the making of these cookies.

Now, I have nothing whatsoever against Nestlé. They make a fine everyday chocolate. But ever since the apotheosis of the chocolate chip cookie at Chez Louis, I don't want my cookie to be "everyday." And that's why I say:

1. Make your own chips for chocolate chip cookies by cutting up bars of chocolate (did you ever notice that "chips" in the bag sometimes have a grayish "bloom" on them, indicating that they're less than fresh?).

2. Make those chips out of great chocolate (using either bittersweet or semisweet bars): El Rey from Venezuela, Valrhona from France, Callebaut from Belgium, or something of that caliber.

Beyond that, there are a multitude of chocolate chip cookie "issues" that you'll have to grapple with before deciding how to proceed in the kitchen.

Crisp or Soft? The two poles here are (1) the kind of very crisp, crumbly cookies that come out of a supermarket bag; and (2) the kind of soft, melting cookies that come right out of the oven. In most cases, I prefer the latter. The sooner you eat the cookies, the softer they will be; the longer you wait, the crisper they will be. Another factor is butter: lots of it promotes crispness.

Light or Dense? Do you like them delicately textured, as most crisp cookies are? Or do you like them heavy and chewy, as many of the softer cookies are? If you prefer the latter, as I do, you'll find that the use of brown sugar and molasses helps to achieve your favorite texture.

Light or Dark in Color? Brown sugar is also a factor in this choice: less of it (or none of it) makes a lighter-colored cookie; more of it makes a darker-colored cookie. Length of baking time is another factor here—just keep in mind that the longer they cook and the darker they get, the more your cookies will be on the dry-crumbly side.

Thin or Thick? The standard chocolate chip cookie we all grew up with was of an in-between thickness. Then came the revisionists—making wide, flat ones, with an almost French delicacy, and also making wide, superthick ones (à la David's Cookies), which make you feel like an American. I like both kinds . . . but if I had to choose, I'd be an American, damnit.

Chippy or Chunky? David also turned everyone on to the concept of bigger chunks of chocolate in the cookie. I must say, my taste has been forever changed by this—I find it difficult to go back to weeny chips. And if you're using great chocolate for your massive chunks, then you've got something spectacular that Ruth Wakefield never dreamed of.

Chips Alone or Chips with Other Stuff? There are lots of variations out there today—nuts (particularly macadamia), raisins, coconut, Lord knows what else (at least I haven't seen sun-dried-tomato chocolate chip cookies). But, though I recognize the possibility of good flavor synergy between chips and some other things, I'm pretty much a chips-alone man. Even a good complementary nut—like the walnut—takes away from the textural thrill that occurs when you bite into the chocolate part of your chocolate chip cookie.

Here are two different chocolate chip cookies that demonstrate the two poles of chocolate chip cookie possibility. I love them both—though I must confess that the chockablock bulk of cookie number 2 is certainly the peak experience for me.

THIN AND CRISP CHOCOLATE CHIP COOKIES

Everything in this recipe—the mixing with an electric blender, the use of white sugar only, the large amount of butter, the relatively small size of the cookie—is designed to contribute to a crisp texture.

2 sticks unsalted butter, softened (plus a little extra for greasing the cookie sheet)

2 cups granulated sugar

4 large eggs

2 teaspoons vanilla extract

2 2/3 cups all-purpose flour

2 teaspoons baking powder

1/2 teaspoon salt

2 cups of chocolate "chips" cut from bars of bittersweet or semisweet chocolate

1. Preheat the oven to 350 degrees.

2. In a bowl beat the butter with the sugar until they are thoroughly blended. Add the eggs, one at a time, and the vanilla extract; beat until light and fluffy. (Note: You may beat the mixture with a wooden spoon by hand, but I get a crisper finished product when I use a hand-held electric rotary beater.)

3. In a bowl, sift together the flour, baking powder, and salt. Working slowly, with a wooden spoon, beat the flour mixture into the butter mixture. Blend in the chocolate chips. Chill in the refrigerator for 1 hour.

4. When you are ready to bake, grease a cookie sheet with butter. Drop heaping teaspoonfuls of the dough onto the sheet, placing them 2 inches apart. Bake until the cookies are golden brown around the edges, about 18 minutes.

5. Remove the cookies from the cookie sheet, and cool them on a rack.

SOFT AND CHEWY CHOCOLATE CHUNK COOKIES

And here, everything tilts towards the opposite effect: brown sugar and molasses for chewiness, huge chunks of chocolate for heft, bigger balls of dough and a shorter cooking time so the finished product will be less crisp.

2 1/4 cups all-purpose flour

1/4 teaspoon baking soda

2 sticks unsalted butter, softened (plus a little extra for greasing the cookie sheet)

1 cup white granulated sugar

1/2 cup light brown sugar

1 tablespoon molasses

1 teaspoon vanilla extract

1 tablespoon heavy cream

1 egg, beaten

2 cups chocolate chunks cut from bars of bittersweet or semisweet chocolate, each chunk about 1/2 inch square

1. Preheat the oven to 350 degrees.

2. In a mixing bowl, combine the flour and baking soda. Set aside.

3. In another bowl, cream together the butter, sugars, molasses, vanilla, cream, and egg. Beat until just blended.

4. Add the flour mixture to the batter and combine. Stir in the chocolate chunks. Chill the dough until it is firm (at least 1 hour).

5. When you are ready to cook, grease a cookie sheet with butter. Working quickly, form the dough into Ping-Pong-size balls, and place them on the sheet 3 inches apart. Bake until they are just golden (10 to 12 minutes).

6. Remove the cookies from the cookie sheet, place them on a rack, and let them cool for at least a few minutes. But remember: the sooner you eat them, the softer they will be!

Criteria for Quality

For thin and crisp chocolate chip cookies:

- *Are they thin and crisp?*
- *Are they buttery?*
- *Do they avoid sawdustlike dryness?*
- *Are they just sweet enough?*
- *Do they have the flavor of great chocolate?*

For soft and chewy chocolate chunk cookies:

- *Are they soft?*
- *Are they relatively chewy?*
- *Are they just sweet enough?*
- *Do they have enormous chocolate chunks?*
- *Do they have the flavor of great chocolate?*

In Your Glass

Come on. Milk.

MOLTEN CHOCOLATE CAKE

Here is a chocolate dessert that truly is high end . . . and the really great thing about it is that it takes no more time, trouble, or skill than other, humbler treats.

The molten chocolate cake took New York by storm in the late 1980s, when Jean-Georges Vongerichten—French born, but now one of America's most creative chefs—was in a fury of invention at the now-defunct Lafayette restaurant. At dessert time there, diners received small, individual chocolate cakes that looked conventional enough. However, as the forks penetrated through the warm, firm exteriors of the cakes, reaching the centers, one thing became quite clear: each cake had a runny chocolate middle, that, like a fried egg's yolk inside a circle of solidified white, could be stabbed with a fork and made to ooze over all. It was new, and it was devastatingly sexy. Soon, chefs all over the country were copying it.

You too can be devastatingly sexy at your next dinner party—or at least your dessert can. Just make sure to use the best chocolate imaginable (see ordering instructions for El Rey on page 244). And be very careful with the degree of doneness—if you bake the cake even a little too long, it won't have the molten lava center that is its very raison d'être.

INDIVIDUAL MOLTEN CHOCOLATE CAKES

This recipe is based on the original Vongerichten creation—though I've taken the liberty of adding even a little more chocolate to the dish, just to make sure the volcano's not dormant.

MAKES 6 SERVINGS

7 1/2 ounces imported bittersweet chocolate
   (preferably El Rey or Valrhona), coarsely chopped
11 tablespoons unsalted butter, cut in large pieces
3 large eggs

3 large egg yolks
1/4 cup plus 2 tablespoons white granulated sugar
5 tablespoons all-purpose flour, sifted

1. Preheat the oven to 325 degrees.
2. Butter and flour six 6-ounce custard cups.
3. Place 5½ ounces of the chocolate and the butter in a metal bowl, and set it over a pan of simmering water. Stir until melted and smooth. Cool slightly.
4. Using a standing electric mixer with the whisk attachment, beat the eggs, yolks, and sugar at medium-high speed until they are pale and thick, about 10 minutes.
5. Reduce the speed, and gradually mix in the flour.
6. Add the chocolate mixture to the flour mixture, and continue to beat until thick and glossy, about 5 minutes.

7. Divide half the mixture among the prepared custard cups. Divide the remaining 2 ounces of coarsely chopped chocolate among them, placing the chunks in the very center of the chocolate mixture (there should be about 1 tablespoon of chopped chocolate per custard cup). Then top with the rest of the chocolate batter.
8. Bake until the cake is set around the edges but the center jiggles slightly when the cup is moved, about 12 minutes. Cool slightly (no more than 5 minutes).
9. Run a sharp knife around the edges of the cups. Turn the cakes out onto plates, and serve.

Saucing and Garnishing the Cake

This dish is really delicious just as it is; you can simply unmold the cakes onto plates, serve them with no sauce, no garnish, and watch your guests create all the sauce and visual excitement they need by plunging their forks into the centers of the cakes.

Some chefs, however, like to take things a bit further by offering something white and creamy along with the dark chocolate. The simplest choice—and one that's very popular—is vanilla ice cream; top your warm chocolate cake with an oval of ice cream the moment before serving it, and watch the white part ooze over the oozier dark brown part. Yum. Another saucing option is crème anglaise, a medium-thin custard sauce, poured all around the chocolate cake. And, if you want to make that a bit more elaborate, you can spread some crème anglaise on each plate, then melt some chocolate with a little butter in a saucepan and pour it into a pastry tube. Then, starting at the center of the plates, "draw" four or five concentric circles with thin streams of chocolate emanating out to the edge of each plate. Next, using a toothpick, draw lines from the center to the edge, dragging the chocolate through the crème anglaise to form a spiderweb pattern. Finally, unmold the cakes on top of the spiderwebs, and impress the heck out of your diners.

One other option I like—this one purely a garnish—is to place a pretty paper doily over a large white dinner plate. Sprinkle good powdered cocoa over the doily, then very carefully remove it—leaving the doily pattern on the plate in cocoa powder. Very carefully unmold the chocolate cake onto the center of the plate, and, once again, you've got one of those big-deal-restaurant visual stunners.

Last, if you'd like to supply a little extra visual appeal—but don't feel like going to any trouble at all—just sprinkle a little confectioners' sugar through a sieve right on top of the cake.

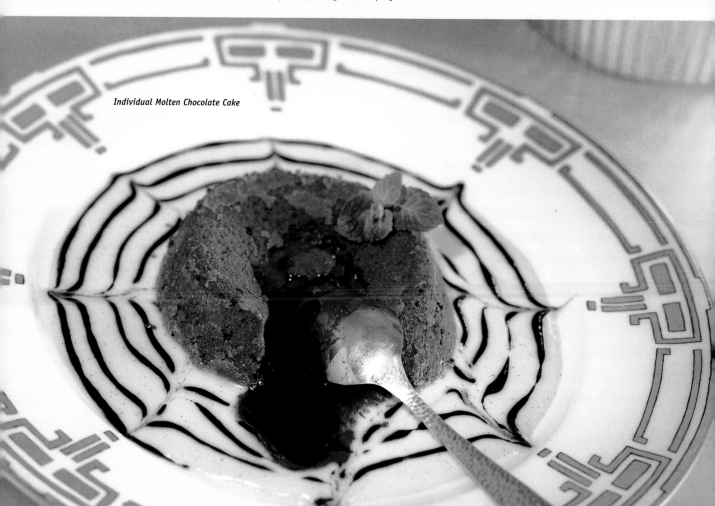

Individual Molten Chocolate Cake

EATING DESSERT WITH A SPOON

The first time I ever sat down at a restaurant table in France, I was bombarded with so many surprising differences in dining customs—as well as so many large revelations in food quality—that it was difficult to take notice of everything at once. However, I will never forget the glaring difference I observed when the table was prepared for dessert.

After the main-course dishes and silverware were cleared away, the waiter gave each diner a spoon. It was exactly like an oval spoon that's normally used for soup, except this one was twice the standard size. When I saw it, I assumed some large bowl of something soupy—pudding, perhaps?—was on its way.

So when they served the apple tart, I patiently waited until they brought me my fork . . . until I noticed that the French people in my party were merrily scooping up the tart with their outsize spoons. I figured they were jumping the gun. But no pudding followed, of course . . . and no mistake had been made.

I discovered right then and there that the French like to eat dessert—any dessert—with a spoon. It may seem like no major cultural divider to you, but after hundreds and hundreds of other meals in France, I have come to the conclusion that the choice of silverware for dessert actually means a great deal. We Americans guiltily eye the pie, the tart, the chocolate cake and, with hard-won self-control, apply our precision-instrument forks to the task at hand. We topple off a corner here, scratch out a fuzzy morsel there, safely restrained by the inability of a fork— usually a smaller device at that, called a dessert fork!—to carry a sizable payload.

The French are different, God bless them. Just as trying on a pair of too-small pants makes you feel large, using a too-large spoon makes you feel small. In fact, I believe the precise mechanism at play at the French table is the regression of the spoon bearer to the condition of childhood. Now, what's a small child going to do with a large spoon in his or her hand? Fill it up, of course . . . and innocently savor what has been scooped. For the French adult knows that once he or she is playing a child at table, it would be absurd to start counting calories or grams of fat.

Oh, go ahead. Try it. Eat a chocolate cake with a big old spoon. See if it doesn't taste a whole lot better . . . and if you don't leave the table a whole lot happier, and a whole lot younger.

—————————— OTHER DESSERTS ——————————

Fruit and chocolate do seem to dominate my dessert table. But here's a roundup of the other sweets that also keep popping up on my menus—some fancy, some funky, some from great international traditions, some from the good old U.S. of A.

TIRAMISÙ

This Italian dessert—made with espresso-dipped ladyfingers, creamy mascarpone, whipped cream, eggs, a little chocolate, and some kind of alcoholic kicker—has taken America absolutely by storm. Twenty years ago no Italian restaurants or cookbooks in America even hinted at its existence . . . then the wave hit, about ten years ago, and it's still sweeping over us. Tiramisù is the beef Wellington of the nineties. Despite all this, I like it.

The name literally means "pick me up," because the espresso is supposed to give you a little lift. Perhaps it does, but what's indisputably getting a lift is the income of Italian restaurants. They love to serve this dessert because, in addition to making people happy and being inexpensive, it's really easy to prepare. It doesn't require the talents of a fancy pastry chef. In fact, it doesn't require any kind of pastry chef at all, or much talent: there's no pastry making involved, just the combination of some well-chosen ingredients. You don't even have to cook it!

Where did it come from, this Italianate confectionery sensation? And why did no one know about it until yesterday? Concerning these questions, there is much debate.

According to Lorenza de' Medici, the great Tuscan chef and cooking teacher, the dish originated in Tuscany, in Siena, where it was called *zuppa del duca,* or duke's soup. Then, she says, it migrated to Florence, also in her beloved Tuscany, and became very popular in the nineteenth century among the many English people who came to live in the city at that time.

Others, however, are not so sure. Some call Milan the place of origin, and their argument is bolstered by the fact that Milan's province, Lombardy, is the birthplace of mascarpone. Then there are those persistent "Venice" theorists, who claim that tiramisù was invented a long time ago there. I even came across one source, recently, that claims the dish was invented by a chef at the restaurant Toula in Treviso, near Venice . . . a mere twenty years ago! If this one is true, it would certainly explain why this dish has risen to prominence only recently.

Whatever the source, tiramisù is here to stay. What bothers me more than not knowing its origins, I'm sorry to say, is knowing too well what's being served out there under the name of tiramisù. Pitfalls abound. But fear not: it is a really simple dessert to make, and it will come out beautifully if you follow a few simple guidelines.

First, the Ladyfinger-dunking Thing. The ladyfingers must absorb some flavor from the espresso dunking liquid (freshly made espresso only, please!). But the danger lies in letting the ladyfingers absorb too much; they'll get soggy and start to fall apart. Dip, don't dunk. You dip each ladyfinger on two sides, and the dipping of each should take no longer than a total of two seconds.

Second: Mascarpone, Heavy Cream, Eggs. These are potentially leaden ingredients, but combined properly they can make a light and airy cream. You are instructed to whip the cream, to beat the egg whites, and to fold everything together with egg-yolk-enriched mascarpone. Just be sure not to overfold and deflate the air you've beaten in. Remember, this dish is called "pick me up," not "lay me down."

Third: Don't Serve the Dish the Second You've Put It All Together. But don't serve it the next day either. Just let it rest in the refrigerator for a couple of hours. The airy cream will firm up, the ladyfingers will absorb their coffee liquid more evenly, and the whole dessert will cool to a refreshing temperature. About 3 hours is ideal. By the next day, the ladyfingers may become soggy and the flavors may begin to fade.

Remember: This is not a slimming dessert, no matter how you slice it. But do slice it small, to maximize damage control, and you will end your meal with a delightful pick-me-up.

TIRAMISÙ

I love the flavors of coffee and chocolate together—so my version of tiramisù goes a little heavier on the chocolate than most. I find that the addition of chocolate liqueur to the coffee soak—it's usually brandy that's used—gives more flavor to the dish. And I'm nuts about the texture extra added by chocolate-covered coffee beans as a garnish.

MAKES 12 SERVINGS

7 eggs, separated
8 tablespoons sugar
1 pound mascarpone
5 tablespoons chocolate liqueur (see note)
3/4 cup heavy cream

1 cup espresso, cooled
35 ladyfingers (preferably imported Italian Savoiardi)
2 ounces bittersweet chocolate shavings
40 chocolate-covered espresso beans

1. In a large bowl beat together the egg yolks, sugar, and mascarpone. Mix until smooth. Beat in 3 tablespoons of the chocolate liqueur.
2. In a separate bowl, beat the heavy cream into stiff peaks.
3. In a third bowl, beat the egg whites until stiff.
4. Mix 1/3 of the whipped cream into the mascarpone mixture, then gently fold in the rest.
5. Mix 1/3 of the egg whites into the mascarpone mixture, then gently fold in the rest to make a mousse.
6. In a wide bowl, put the coffee and remaining chocolate liqueur. Dip half of the ladyfingers quickly, one side at a time, into the coffee liquid, then lay them across the bottom of a 9-by-13-inch baking dish.
7. Spread half the mousse over the ladyfingers, and sprinkle with half the chocolate shavings.
8. Dip the rest of the ladyfingers in the coffee mixture, and add them to the baking dish in a single layer on top of the mascarpone mousse. Cover the second layer of ladyfingers with the rest of the mousse, and sprinkle with the rest of the chocolate shavings.
9. Cut the chocolate-covered coffee beans in half, and decoratively arrange them on top of the tiramisù.
10. Chill in the refrigerator for 3 hours, covered, to set.
11. Cut into 3-by-4-inch portions and serve.

NOTE: You can easily make your own chocolate liqueur by combining 4 tablespoons Hershey's syrup and 4 teaspoons brandy.

Mascarpone

There is a twelfth-century document from Lake Como, not too far from Milan, indicating that what they called mascarpone then was actually like ricotta cheese. Today's mascarpone is somewhere between crème fraîche, sour cream, and American cream cheese. Some say it's an example of the type of cheese called triple cream, but in truth it is not a cheese at all. It is more accurately described by Steve Jenkins in his book Cheese Primer as a "cow's cream dairy product," since no starter or rennet is used in its production; lemon juice is what helps it to coagulate. He adds that all brands are excellent, even the versions made here in America. Just be sure it has no lumps and is very fresh. Use it right away; because of its low sodium content mascarpone is highly perishable.

Chocolate-covered Coffee Beans

Chocolate-covered coffee beans are available at gourmet specialty shops, candy stores, and some espresso bars.

Raw Eggs

The eggs in this dish are not cooked, so there is some small chance of salmonella poisoning. Be sure your eggs are fresh and come from a reputable grocer.

Freeze It

The cookbook author Patricia Wells recommends freezing tiramisù and serving it as a frozen dessert. Though it's no longer tiramisù, in its own way this is pretty wonderful. The freezing strategy is also a good way to handle leftovers.

Criteria for Quality

- Do the ladyfingers retain some texture? or are they a soft, insipid mass from overdunking? (they shouldn't be)
- Is there a wonderful paradox created: soothing creaminess but airy lightness?
- Does it taste fresh?
- Is it sweetened just enough? (it shouldn't be too sweet)
- Does the flavor and bitterness of coffee come through?
- Is there a subtle chocolate undertone?
- Was the alcohol used in moderation? (there shouldn't be an alcohol "burn")

In Your Glass

I like tiramisù with a rich, brown-colored wine that's a little sweeter than the food. Brown southern Italian Muscats, Marsalas, and Malvasias are possibilities here, as well as sweet madeiras (Malmseys) and rich tawny ports.

CRÈME BRÛLÉE

Another dish I love making for dessert is crème brûlée, the little bowl of custard with a crackling "burnt" sugar crust. It's classic, simple, delicious—much of its deliciousness, in fact, comes from its classic simplicity—and, best of all for home cooks, it's extremely easy to make. Are you seeing a pattern here? I'm sure you've recognized this dish as very typical Rosengarten dessert food.

The dish's name would lead you to believe it's French, and so would millions of Frenchmen. But if you believe them, you'll be infuriating millions of Spaniards—particularly those who live in Catalonia, a corner of Spain very close to France. For in that stellar gastronomic region, there is a classic dish called *crema Catalana,* which, for all intents and purposes, is crème brûlée. Whenever the French and Spanish take a break from slugging it out over the ownership of mayonnaise, they love arguing about this one.

Amazingly, however, it may be the case that neither country owns the bragging rights to crème brûlée. Even more amazingly, international culinary consensus usually attributes the dish to that shining star of gastronomy, that jewel of cuisine, this dyspeptic isle, this . . . England? You could look it up. Many say that crème brûlée was born when an English chef accidentally burned a custard he'd sprinkled with sugar. Undaunted—and fully assuming the mantle of first culinary spin doctor—he passed it off as an original creation, dubbing it burnt cream. People loved it (of course, anything might seem welcome after a steady diet of trifle and spotted dick). And where did this plucky chef change the course of culinary history? Cambridge University, it appears; some old cookbooks even refer to a dish called Cambridge cream.

So how did this English dish get a French name around the world? Some say that an American— the first American foodie, in fact—may have been responsible for that. Thomas Jefferson, who loved the dish, spent a good deal of time in France and probably encountered the dish in Paris—where the French had already appropriated it, and literally translated "burnt cream" into *crème brûlée.* Now, Jefferson spoke with lots of influential people in the Anglo world—often about food!—and was never reluctant to flash his French. So the theory goes that Jefferson always referred to this dish by its French name and, before long, American and English people were doing the same. We know for sure that by the end of the nineteenth century the dish was always called crème brûlée in England.

But the international wheel spins again—for it was an Italian who took this old dish, which wasn't exactly a mass-market sensation in the midtwentieth century, and turned it into one of the most popular desserts at high-end restaurants around the world in the 1980s.

I'm speaking, of course, of Sirio Maccioni, the owner of New York's legendary Le Cirque—where part of the legend stems from the kitchen's great version of crème brûlée. Why was it so good? The real reason, I believe, was nothing more than consistency of effort (the custard itself had a great consistency, too!). I remember a day, back in the early 1980s, when I happened to be interviewing Sirio at Le Cirque. A new chef in the kitchen had just inherited the responsibility of turning out the crème brûlée. Sirio stopped the interview when a dish of it came out for approval. And I'll never forget this; I wish I'd had my camera. He said, "Excuse me, please," and he started to tap the crust all over the top surface. He was like a doctor listening to a heart. He did everything but call for a stethoscope. At last he was satisfied that the dish was perfect, and the chef returned to the kitchen a happy man.

What was Sirio looking for, exactly? I can't say with precision what his standards were, but I'd be glad to tell you mine.

The Burnt Sugar Crust. The crust must be crisp, browned, but definitely not charred; charred sugar is bitter. It must be firm, crackling, crunchy—firm enough so that if you tap on it lightly with your spoon, it will make a noise, as if you're tapping on a hard cookie. But it's very important that this firm crust be thin . . . not a thick sheet of brown glass! It should remind you in thickness and texture of a sheet of ice over a cold northern lake that you've decided not to skate on—because the ice is too thin!

The Consistency of the Custard. I've had crème brûlées featuring thick, dense custards in which you could stand up your spoon. I've had crème brûlées featuring very runny custards, more like a custard sauce than a custard—which is closer to what I favor. Neither extreme works for me. But if you can create a custard that is just past the runny sauce stage—a thickened runny sauce, let's say—then I'll call it a great crème brûlée.

The Temperature of the Custard and Crust. Of course, the consistency of the custard has a great deal to do with its serving temperature. My ideal texture can't be achieved when the custard is right out of the refrigerator; it stands up too firmly then. A properly runny crème brûlée can be hot, and it can be warm to room temperature. It is, in fact, room-temperature custard that I prefer. The crust should be room temperature too.

The Depth of the Custard in Its Dish. This is a crucial element in crème brûlée. I often see it served in fairly narrow, fairly tall ramekins, like chocolate pudding dishes. When it's served this way, there's a tiny ratio of "brûlée" to "crème," and a thick wad of custard making up most of the dish. Wrong, say I! Crème brûlée should feature a wide, shallow layer of custard with a high ratio of crackling top to custard. Look for six-ounce, wide, low, shallow, oval or round dishes, similar to gratin dishes. Oval ones are about 7 inches long, and round ones are about 5 inches in diameter. Each diner gets his or her own dish. In specialty kitchenware shops, they call these dishes, appropriately enough, crème brûlée dishes.

(Clockwise from lower left) crème brûlée that's too light, crème brûlée that's just right, crème brûlée that's too dark

The Flavor of the Custard—and Flavorings. Classic crème brûlée tastes of eggs, cream, and vanilla. These simple ingredients, when handled correctly, add up to a heartwarmingly delicious flavor; my only caveats here would be to use enough vanilla, and make sure not to use too much sugar. Should you add anything else to crème brûlée? Purists get up in arms about this one; I know many creative kitchen types who would modernize flan at the drop of a raisin but would never dream of disturbing the classic balance of crème brûlée. I'm in deep sympathy with these people, because I find crème brûlée perfect in its classic formulation. However, I'm not fully one of them—since I have also enjoyed, from time to time, a jazzed-up crème brûlée that has been jazzed up in just the right way.

CLASSIC CRÈME BRÛLÉE

Classic crème brûlée is not a difficult dish to make, but to get it right you have to start with the best ingredients. Fresh eggs. Real vanilla pods (good extract's fine, but good fresh beans are always better). Above all, great cream (if you can find a little boutique dairy turning out rich, profound cream, that would be ideal).

MAKES 6 SERVINGS

4 cups heavy cream
2 vanilla beans, split in half lengthwise
2 strips lemon zest
8 large egg yolks

Pinch of salt
3/4 cup granulated white sugar, plus 6 tablespoons for topping

1. Preheat the oven to 300 degrees.
2. Put the cream in a saucepan, and scrape the vanilla bean seeds into it with the tip of a knife. Add the scraped-out vanilla beans and lemon zest, and bring the cream to just under a boil. Lower the heat, and heat gently for 5 minutes. Remove from heat, and cover for 15 minutes.
3. In a large bowl whisk together the egg yolks, salt, and sugar until they are well blended and slightly thickened.
4. Remove the vanilla pods from the cream. Warm it until it is almost simmering. Pour the cream into the egg mixture slowly, in a thin stream, whisking all the time, until the mixture is well blended. Strain the custard into a pitcher or large measuring cup with a spout.
5. Choose six-ounce crème brûlée dishes (definitely wide and shallow, either oval or round). Divide the custard mixture among them evenly. Place the dishes in a roasting pan, and fill the pan with enough simmering water to come halfway up the sides of the dishes. Bake in the oven until the custard is just set but still jiggles slightly in the center (this can be anywhere from 40 minutes for very loose crème brûlée to 60 minutes for firmer).
6. Remove the dishes from the pan, and let them cool to room temperature.
7. Before serving, evenly sprinkle 1 tablespoon of sugar on top of each dish in a thin layer. Set the dishes on a baking sheet, and position the sheet 4 inches under a broiler to caramelize the sugar. Watch carefully. It should take between 30 and 60 seconds. Alternately, use a propane torch (see "Ways to 'Brûlée,'" below).
8. Let the dishes cool slightly, and serve.

Ways to "Brûlée"

Most home cooks "brûlée" their custard under a hot broiler. This method works well, if you take a few precautions. The biggest danger is burning the custard; you want it to be dark brown but not super–dark brown. Watch the dishes carefully. Rotate them if they're not burning evenly (an even brown is the ideal). If they are developing burn spots, put tiny pieces of aluminum foil over the darkest spots and continue to broil the rest.

There are other ways to "brûlée" at home. Some cooks like to use what is essentially a branding iron (called, confusingly, a salamander, the same name used for the intense overhead broiler units found in restaurant kitchens). You heat the iron (which should be the same shape and size as the top of your brûlée dish), then "brand" the custard by holding the very hot iron 1/8 inch from the sugar. Much easier, however, is a propane blowtorch; just turn it on, and direct the flame to your crème brûlée. It gives you fabulous control, enabling you to "brûlée" your custard very evenly. Williams Sonoma (800-541-2233) sells a handy small one for $34.

BANANA CRÈME BRÛLÉE

This was my first "creative" brûlée; I created it for an article in the February 1986 *Bon Appétit.* I justified the departure from "pure" crème brûlée because the bananas seem to gently reinforce the taste of the vanilla, not to fight against it. This recipe features another crème brûlée variation: the custard is served cold, under a hot crust. The best way to achieve this, if you're using a broiler, is to place the dishes on a bed of ice while you're broiling them (if you're using a torch, the ice is not necessary as long as you take the custards straight from the refrigerator).

MAKES 6 SERVINGS

1 tablespoon unsalted butter

3 bananas, peeled and coarsely chopped

6 tablespoons granulated white sugar

Juice of 1/4 lemon

3 tablespoons Spanish brandy

3 cups heavy cream

1 vanilla bean

8 egg yolks

12 teaspoons light brown sugar

1. Preheat the oven to 300 degrees.

2. Over medium heat, melt the butter in a sauté pan. Add the bananas, and sprinkle with 1 tablespoon of white sugar. Stir well to blend the sugar and butter. Cook, stirring occasionally, for 5 minutes. The bananas should be lightly caramelized.

3. Mash the bananas with the back of a wooden spoon. Add the lemon juice to the mixture, raise the heat to high, add the brandy, and boil for 1 minute. Remove from heat, divide among 6 wide, shallow crème brûlée dishes, and let cool.

4. Place the heavy cream in a saucepan. Split the vanilla bean lengthwise, and scrape the seeds into the cream with the tip of a knife. Add the scraped-out vanilla bean, and bring the cream just to a boil, then remove from heat. Reserve.

5. Place the egg yolks and 5 tablespoons of white sugar in the top of a double boiler. Whisk them together, then stir over simmering water until the mixture becomes fairly thick (about 15 minutes).

6. Strain the reserved cream into the eggs, and stir the mixture over simmering water for 10 minutes. Remove from heat, and ladle over the cooled banana purée in the 6 dishes.

7. Place the dishes in a roasting pan, and fill the pan with enough hot water to come halfway up the sides of the dishes. Bake in the oven for 40 minutes. Remove the dishes from the pan, and chill them for at least 3 hours.

8. When you are ready to serve, sprinkle 2 teaspoons of light brown sugar over each dish, distributing evenly. Place the dishes on a bed of cracked ice in a roasting pan, and position the pan under a broiler until the sugar caramelizes. (Or use a propane torch.) Watch carefully, and move the dishes around so the sugar browns evenly but doesn't char.

9. Remove and serve while the crust is still hot.

Criteria for Quality

- *Is the crust dark brown, but not super–dark brown or charred?*
- *Is the crust evenly browned?*
- *Is the crust brittle? (it should be)*
- *Is the crust thin? (it should be)*
- *Is there a high ratio of crust to custard? (there should be a wide, shallow portion of custard topped by a wide crust of burnt sugar)*
- *Is the custard silky?*
- *Is the custard attractively runny? (not too runny)*
- *Can you taste the vanilla in the custard?*

In Your Glass

There are many brown dessert wines and "white" dessert wines (actually yellow or orange) that work very well with crème brûlée—as long as the wine's a little sweeter than the dessert. One of my favorite wines for crème brûlée is Sauternes, from the Bordeaux region of France. Sauternes, which can be a little bitter, tastes best with desserts that have a little bitterness in them (like the burned part of this one).

PECAN PIE
(The Search for Satisfaction)

As you are probably well aware, I don't have many culinary prejudices. But I must 'fess up that I have never been able to understand the attraction of a dessert that tastes like pure sugar, that features big, sticky, clumped-together nuts, that actually makes your *teeth* stick together, and that offers very little flavor return for all that chompin' work.

Pecan pie. A very American dessert—there's nothing like it anywhere else in the world. And maybe it took a non-American perspective to get me interested.

A few years back I met Umberto Eco, the great Italian novelist (author of *The Name of the Rose* among other works) and professor of semiotics and structuralism. He's also known for being a world-class eater. When we met at a book party in New York, he shared his impressions of American food with me—and he remarked that America has contributed two (but only two) dishes to world cuisine: the Reuben sandwich and pecan pie.

I like the Reuben sandwich well enough. But pecan pie? And I thought to myself: if this Bolognese structuralist has taken a shine to this weird, sticky thing, maybe I'd better go into my kitchen, deconstruct it, and see if I can come up with a version that pleases me. So . . . using my usual quality-improving principle of starting with the highest-quality ingredients, I looked into the nuts themselves.

The pecan (southerners say "puh-CONN," not "PEE-can" or "pee-CAN") is a great American phenomenon. It is a native American nut, a product of the hickory tree. There are many different kinds of hickory nuts, but the pecan is the most popular. The pecan that you buy in the supermarket, however, is probably not the finest example.

There are about four hundred different kinds of pecans . . . from tiny ones to wide and fat ones. Once you get into the subject, you'll discover that there are lots of pecan producers out there willing to sell you specific types of pecans, with specific names—and that you'll have some flavor and texture preferences among the different types. You'll discover the Seedling pecan, which is the original American nut, not a hybrid. You'll find varieties with Native American names, such as the Choctaw, the Mohawk, and the Cheyenne. You'll find the Western Schley, which has a shell that's extremely easy to crack. And you'll find the so-called improved varieties—a group that includes my favorite pecan of all, the Desirable. After experimenting with about a dozen different types, I decided that the Desirable has, well, the most desirable flavor and texture for pecan pie.

Now, whichever nut you choose, keep in mind that freshness matters; with such a high fat content (pecans are 60 to 70 percent fat), these little guys can turn rancid very quickly. When you store them, store them in a cool place—even the refrigerator or freezer. And one other handling tip: always toast your pecans (whether making pie or just eating them straight). Put them in a pan in a single layer, then into a 350-degree oven for 10 minutes or so. Stir them every few minutes, and don't let them brown. You'll be amazed how this simple process brightens their flavor and improves their texture.

Now you've got the best nuts, fresh and toasted. Are you at the gates of pecan pie heaven? Not yet—because a classic-recipe pecan pie made from these great nuts will still be sticky and clunky.

So I deconstructed further. In fact, I blew those pecans to smithereens—in my food processor. For one night it came to me in a dream: if you make a nutty powder out of those great pecans, you may get all that great pecan flavor in your pecan pie but none of the heaviness of whole nuts. I was elated! Visions of smooth pecan pie flooded my imagination. No big, dense, awkward, sticky nuts to chew through. A whole new concept! Why, they'd even name this pie after me; Umberto Eco would give it the Name of the Rosengarten.

And then reality intruded. When I made my pecan pie with 100 percent ground nuts, it seemed insipid. You may not believe this, but I began to feel nostalgic for the clunky crunch of the nut.

So I went back to the drawing board—and dang it if I didn't crack that nut, solve that problem, right there on the second try. The answer is this: you make pecan pie with half ground nuts and half whole nuts. I want you to make this pie too; I'm betting that whether you're a pecan pie lover ("Why would anyone want to mess with the classic recipe?") or a pecan pie hater ("Why would anyone want to salvage this disaster?"), you're going to love this new, improved pecan pie.

PECAN PIE

See if this sleek, modern version of pecan pie doesn't deliver all the traditional flavor, with a much more appealing texture.

MAKES ONE 9-INCH PIE

For the crust:

1 1/4 cups all-purpose flour

2 tablespoons confectioners' sugar

1/2 teaspoon salt

8 tablespoons cold unsalted butter, cut into bits

2 tablespoons cold vegetable shortening (like Crisco), cut into bits

1 large egg, separated

Ice water

For the filling:

6 tablespoons unsalted butter

1 cup firmly packed dark brown sugar

1/2 teaspoon salt

3 large eggs

3/4 cup light corn syrup

1 tablespoon vanilla extract

1 cup finely ground pecans

1 cup coarsely chopped pecans

1. For the crust: In a bowl combine the flour, sugar, salt, butter, and shortening, and blend the mixture with your hands until it resembles coarse meal. In a clear measuring cup combine the egg white (reserving the yolk) and enough ice water to measure a total of ¼ cup. Add the liquid ingredients to the dry ingredients, and combine until a dough forms. Shape the dough into a ball, flatten it into a 4-inch disk, dust it lightly with flour, wrap it tightly in plastic wrap, and chill it in the refrigerator for 1 hour.

2. On a lightly floured surface, roll out the dough into a round that's approximately ⅛ inch thick and 13 inches in diameter. Transfer the dough to a 9-inch pie plate, preferably glass. Press the dough into the corners of the plate. Trim the outer edges of the dough so there is an even, ½-inch overhang. Tuck the overhang under the dough that's sitting on the edge of the pie plate and, working with your fingers, flute the edge of the dough (you don't have to do this, but it looks nice). Chill for 1 hour more.

3. Preheat the oven to 400 degrees.

4. Prick the bottom and sides of the shell with a fork. Fit the shell with a round of wax paper, and weight it with rice or beans. Bake for 15 minutes. Remove the paper, and bake for an additional 10 minutes. In a small bowl whisk together the remaining egg yolk with ⅛ teaspoon water, and brush the bottom and sides of the shell with the mixture. Return the shell to the oven, and bake for 1 minute more (this will prevent the crust from getting soggy).

5. Lower heat in the oven to 275 degrees.

6. Make the filling: In a bowl set over simmering water, melt the butter. Remove the bowl from the heat, and whisk in the sugar, salt, eggs, one at a time, corn syrup, and vanilla. Return the bowl to the heat, and stir until the mixture is shiny and quite warm to the touch (about

130 degrees). Add the ground pecans and the chopped pecans.

7. Return the partially cooked pie crust to the oven to warm it (putting a warm filling in a warm crust also helps to prevent sogginess). Remove the shell from the oven after 5 minutes, and fill it evenly with the pecan mixture. Bake in the oven for 50 to 60 minutes, or until the center feels set but still slightly soft. Cool at least 4 hours.

The Native American Connection

The word pecan is a Native American word. It comes from either the Cree word pakan or the Algonquin word paccan; both of these mean "nut with a hard shell to crack." It's not unreasonable that we get our word for pecan from the Native Americans, since the nut was so important to them. Early Spanish and French explorers have written that some Native American tribes planned their yearly migrations around the harvesting of these nuts—taking to the road after all the nuts had been gathered. Then they would live on them, almost exclusively, for the winter. Fortunately, pecans are unusually nutritious.

Criteria for Quality

- Does the pie have all the wonderful brown flavors of pecans, caramel, butterscotch, et cetera—without feeling impossibly heavy and sticky on your palate?
- Do the pecans have some crunch?
- Does the pie fall short of cloyingly sweet? (it should)
- Is the crust, at least, flaky and light?

In Your Glass

Because of the brown, sticky, treacly quality of pecan pie, this is a perfect opportunity to break out one of those brown, sticky, treacly dessert wines (which often are astounding values). You know the type: aged tawny port, Malmsey madeira, Pedro Ximénez sherry, dried Moscato wines from southern Italy. On TV, I chose to drink a New World brown one with my pie—because one of the finest brown dessert wines in the world is Australian Muscat.

PUMPKIN PIE
(The Further Search for Satisfaction)

I saved the biggest confession for last: I hate pumpkin pie.

Mind you, I don't hate pumpkin. Pumpkin is one of man's earliest cultivated vegetables—it might have been as early as 7000 B.C. that the natives of the Tamaulipas mountains in Mexico started raising their gourds—and its subtle, haunting, fascinating flavor has been incorporated into cuisines all around the world.

My problem with pumpkin pie, primarily, has to do with the subjugation of the pumpkin. All of those "sweet" spices, like cinnamon and nutmeg, that are used so liberally in most recipes completely overwhelm pumpkin's subtlety. Add to this the texture problem: a fruit that actually has quite a fascinating chew is puréed to death in pumpkin pie, leaving a pap that seems most suitable for people without teeth. To top it off, approximately 88 million of these things are baked in America every Thanksgiving from canned pumpkin pie filling—which has the least chance of all of capturing pumpkin flavor and texture.

I speculate that much of America's taste for pumpkin pie has to do with America's thirst for tradition. Since we don't have a lot of historic food traditions—compared with Europeans and Asians, who are rolling in them—we like to embrace those few we do have. And all of the foods we associate with the Puritan tradition of Thanksgiving are right up at the top of our limited national culinary tradition list.

Now, it is true that the Native Americans taught the Puritans in New England how to grow and cook pumpkins. And it is almost certain that some form of pumpkin was consumed by them together at whichever feast, or feasts, became the working prototype for "Thanksgiving dinner." But my research indicates that what we call pumpkin pie today was certainly not an option in 1620. Apparently, the most likely form of "pumpkin pie" that everybody shared was a dish the Native Americans showed the Puritans how to make: you scoop out the flesh of a pumpkin, mix it with milk, honey, and spices, pour it all back in the pumpkin shell, and bake the whole shebang for six hours.

When I heard about that, I said, "Aha! I could learn to love pumpkin pie!" And I set out to create a modern version of that old Native American dish that would finally enable me, at Thanksgiving dessert time, to escape being Scrooge way before the Christmas decorations are up.

I scored. What I like to call "Original" Pumpkin Pie is now one of my favorite desserts of all. I created a wonderfully velvety base custard out of egg yolks and cream. I flavored it with maple syrup, which gives the dish a fabulous New England–like flavor. Most important, I mixed the custard with sugary chunks of pumpkin flesh—creating a real pumpkin chew in the custard, and a deeper pumpkin flavor. And this flavor is further developed by cooking the custard right inside hollowed-out pumpkins.

There is, however, one problem with this dish: you simply cannot make it year-round. The type of pumpkin the dish requires—small ones, called "sugar" pumpkins in the trade—are available only in October and November. That's the bad news. The good news is

1. Halloween and Thanksgiving are when you'd most like to make this dessert anyway.

2. If you hoard pumpkins in October and keep them in a cool place, they will last at least until Christmas, and probably beyond that.

There's no excuse, then, not to start a new tradition in your household.

"ORIGINAL" PUMPKIN PIE
(PUMPKIN CUSTARDS IN THE SHELL)

MAKES 6 SERVINGS

6 small sugar pumpkins, about 1 pound each
2 tablespoons melted butter
6 tablespoons white granulated sugar
4 1/2 cups heavy cream

1 1/2 cups maple syrup
12 egg yolks
1 tablespoon brown sugar

1. Preheat the oven to 325 degrees.

2. Cut the tops off the pumpkins and reserve. Scoop out the seeds of the pumpkins, leaving a tidy cavity in each. Brush the cavities with melted butter, and sprinkle with 2 tablespoons of the white sugar, coating the insides evenly.

3. Cover the pumpkins with the reserved tops, and place them in the oven. Cook until the pumpkin flesh is fairly soft, about 35 minutes. Remove from the oven and let cool.

4. Cutting around the inside of the pumpkins with a sharp knife, and, using some of the flesh from the cut-off tops, remove about ¼ cup of cooked pumpkin flesh from each pumpkin. The whole pumpkins left behind should have evenly shaped cavities. Sprinkle the cut-out pumpkin flesh with 2 tablespoons of white sugar, and divide the remaining 2 tablespoons of white sugar among the 6 pumpkin cavities, sprinkling evenly.

5. Place the heavy cream in a heavy saucepan, and blend in the maple syrup. Cook over medium-high heat until the mixture is almost boiling. Beat the egg yolks in a large bowl, then very slowly stir in the hot cream mixture. Add to it the cut-out and sugared pumpkin flesh. Divide the egg yolk–pumpkin mixture among the cooked pumpkin shells, and top each pumpkin with its lid. Place the pumpkins in a roasting pan, then pour hot water in the pan to a depth of 1 inch. Place the pan in the oven, and cook until the custard is barely set, about 1 hour and 15 minutes. Towards the end of this time—15 minutes or so before the pumpkins are ready—remove the lids, sprinkle the custards with brown sugar, and cook for the final 15 minutes without the lids. When done, the custards should still be slightly runny.

6. Serve the pumpkins with their lids. They may be served immediately, but a half-hour rest is better. Or you may chill them and serve them the next day.

While I was working with pumpkin—trying desperately to come up with a pumpkin dessert to serve at Thanksgiving time that I myself feel like eating—I also stumbled upon the idea of a pumpkin crumble. It's a mix of pumpkin chunks, apples, raisins, bourbon, and spices that is a sophisticated evocation of the flavors in pumpkin pie. And the crunchy oat flour–brown sugar topping supplies the kind of textural interest that I find so sorely lacking in the traditional pumpkin pie.

PUMPKIN CRUMBLE WITH APPLES, RAISINS, AND BOURBON

Here's another great alternative to "traditional" pumpkin pie.

MAKES 8 SERVINGS

One 2- to 2 1/2-pound pumpkin, cut in 2-inch-square chunks (rind on)

2 large Golden Delicious apples, about 1 pound

1/2 cup granulated sugar

Juice of 1 lemon

1 1/2 sticks unsalted butter

1/4 cup bourbon

2 tablespoons raisins

1/4 teaspoon allspice

1/2 teaspoon cardamom

3/4 cup quick-cooking oats

3/4 cup all-purpose flour

3/4 cup lightly packed light brown sugar

1. Preheat the oven to 375 degrees.

2. Place the pumpkin chunks in a roasting pan, and pour in water to a depth of ¼ inch. Cover tightly with foil. Place in the oven, and cook for 30 minutes, or until the pumpkin is just tender. Remove from the oven, cut away the rind and stringy flesh, and cut the pumpkin flesh into slices about 2 inches long and ½ inch thick.

3. While the pumpkin is cooking, peel and core the apples, and cut each apple into 16 slices. Toss the slices with the granulated sugar and lemon juice. Heat ½ stick of butter in a heavy saucepan over medium-high heat, until it melts and starts to sizzle. Add the apple slices. Stir well. Add the bourbon, raisins, all-spice, and cardamom. As soon as the mixture comes to a boil, lower the heat, cover, and simmer for 20 minutes. Then add the cooked pumpkin. Turn off the heat.

4. Make the topping: In a large mixing bowl, combine the oats, flour, and brown sugar. Cut the remaining stick of butter into 16 or so pieces, and knead it into the oat mixture until you have lumps the size of small peas. Do not overwork it.

5. Butter the bottom of a 12-inch oval casserole. Spread the pumpkin and apple mixture out in it, and top with an even layer of the oat mixture. Place under a broiler until the top is sizzling brown, 2 to 3 minutes. Let rest for 5 minutes, and serve.

In Your Glass

The mild flavor of pumpkin, by itself, can find happiness with a wide variety of wines. However, in desserts pumpkin usually gets paired with a ton of sugar and a bevy of strong-flavored spices. These will be your chief determinants when it comes to wine.

The two pumpkin desserts described here have less sugar and fewer strong flavorings than is the norm. However, both dishes exhibit a brown quality, shall we say: maple sugar and burnt sugar in the custard, bourbon and brown sugar in the crumble. With either, I would choose a brown, treacly dessert wine—such as Malmsey madeira, tawny port, or a sweet Oloroso sherry.

5

WINE . . . AND OTHER GOOD THINGS
TO DRINK WITH FOOD

MATCHING WINE WITH FOOD—
TWELVE WINES I ALWAYS RELY ON—
A FEW OTHER WINES—
BEER—BRANDY—OTHER SPIRITS—
COFFEE—TEA—BOTTLED WATER

Though I'll defend to the death the proposition that my dad was the Ur-foodie, you'll never catch me boasting about the sophistication of what we drank in the 1950s with our Ur-food. The most typical beverage on the Rosengarten table was ice water, in a glass pitcher that I was always given the responsibility of prepping for mealtime. Occasionally, Dad would break out a beer—pretty good stuff usually, like Heineken or Beck's—but nothing esoteric. And if company was coming and Dad was doing his big lobster fra diavolo production number, you could always count on a bottle or two of Soave Bolla. Beyond this, the well was dry.

Obviously things have changed—for me, and for our gastronomic culture in general. They haven't changed so much for my dad, by the way, who still demands ice water in every restaurant we visit, and who always tells me that the only aroma he gets from the Pinot Noir, or Sauvignon Blanc, or Gewurztraminer I'm forcing him to sniff is "wine." But the food world has moved on, and these days millions of Americans are getting lots of pleasure out a wide range of beverages we never drank before, or out of more sophisticated versions of beverages we always drank before.

Unfortunately—improved as things are—they are far from perfect in the world of American drinking. Lots of products have been introduced to us in forms that deviate from their classic forms. Lots of Americans have been taught to drink these products in ways that deviate from the classic ways in which they're drunk. Commerce is usually to blame, and the upshot is that many of us are not getting maximum enjoyment out of what's currently in our glasses and cups.

Here's a drink-by-drink look at what you might be drinking with your food, and my in-depth ravings on the subject of what you need to know to have a better drinking life at your table.

WINE

Well, I'll state it point-blank: I have bucketfuls of problems with the ways in which wine is consumed in America. In almost every way, it seems to me, we've been taught to drink exactly the kind of wine that doesn't go with food. And having wine with your food, as far as I'm concerned, is the only reason to have wine at all.

How did this happen to us? It's sure not that way in Europe, where wine is usually treated as just another element that belongs on a table set for a proper meal. There's no more fuss about the wine than there is about the bread, the butter, the cheese, the sausage, et cetera. They're all in the same ontological category. Oh, every once in a while someone will break out a bottle that deserves special attention or go to a restaurant that features unusual older wines. For the most part, however, Europeans are just drinking the recently fermented juice of grapes that were grown in a vineyard not too far away.

Here in America, many people have the notion that you're supposed to worship this stuff. You're supposed to "know" all about wine in order to select one, you're supposed to flash your erudition at the wine steward in the restaurant, and you're supposed to develop a sense of inferiority if you haven't memorized a vintage chart or two.

What out-and-out nonsense!

Here are the leading areas of insanity concerning wine in America.

The Question of Expense. It is widely taken for granted in America that expensive wine is more desirable than inexpensive wine. Sure it is—if your desire is to flaunt how much money you have to burn. But real wine drinkers—those who prefer a good glass of wine with every meal, rather than those who get their pleasure out of hoarding prestigious labels—usually prefer something simple and inexpensive as a steady diet. Expensive wine, when it's young, has too much "stuff" in it to make it widely attractive with food; expensive wine, when it's old, has a great deal of subtlety and nuance—which means that many foods threaten to overwhelm it. I say: find cheap wines you like, and never underestimate their considerable charms.

The Question of Vintage. All wine regions of the world produce wine in every year, or what wine people call every vintage. People who live in these regions are accustomed to drinking the wine of each and every vintage with their food. This year the wine's a little different from the way it was last year, which is a little different from the way it was the year before that. But nobody gets bent out of shape about insisting on wine only from the "best" years.

Americans, however—particularly American wine writers—do. I can't tell you how many delicious wines I've been able to buy and drink, at fair prices, because other wine-drinking Americans had been advised by wine writers to ignore the horrible vintages in which these delicious wines were made.

You know what wine writers mean by "great" vintages? They mean those hot years (lots of sun) that produced wines either high in tannin or high in alcohol—or both. Wine makers, working with the heavyweight grapes from these years—and sensing that the wine writers are about to go nuts and drive up the price of the vintage—make matters worse by loading these wines down with new oak, which brings even higher wine-writer ratings and makes the wines even more difficult for normal people to drink. (A Napa Valley wine maker once said to me, "I love it when I get killer grapes in here, so I can really slap the boards on 'em.")

Now, there is a smidgen of validity in all this insanity. It does happen to be the case that "great" vintages can produce wines with a greater chance of longevity. But that would interest you only if you had perfect cellar conditions, a bundle of money, and twenty or thirty years of patience. The reality, for the rest of us, is that "great" vintages produce wines that are much more difficult to drink when they're young. Me—I like to buy "off" vintages for near-term consumption. And I do this not only because they're cheaper; these vintages are also responsible, generally, for wines that go more easily with food.

This is especially true when it comes to white wine. Whenever I hear that Burgundy, for example, has had a "great" year, producing fat, rich white wines that will last a decade, I stay away from even the cheap white wines in that vintage. Give me lean years for white wine—rainy years that enabled the grapes to retain much of the acidity that makes white wine so good with seafood. You don't put sugar on oysters, do you? You put lemon juice on oysters, shrimp, lobster, sole, et cetera—and I also put white wines from "bad" years on them. Yum.

The Question of Varietal. *Varietal* is winespeak for "grape variety"—the exact type of grape that is used, or blended with other grape varieties, to make a specific wine. Red Burgundy, for example, is made from the Pinot Noir variety. Vouvray is made from the Chenin Blanc variety. Chianti is made from a blend of varieties that has a preponderance of the Sangiovese variety in it. There are hundreds of grape varieties used by wine makers around the world to make wine; each old wine-making region has a choice few, and each new wine-making region has many to choose from.

So which of these varietals have American wine drinkers deemed the best? That's an easy one. Look in any wine magazine to see which varietals get the press. Read any wine store ad to see which varietals get the biggest push. Ask any beverage manager at any restaurant which varietals sell the most. The answers will be the same, time and again: Chardonnay for white wine, Cabernet Sauvignon for red wine. These are the varietals that cause the most consumer excitement in America, fetch the highest prices, and, presumably, are thought to be the best in the world.

But are these two varietals the best?

Here's the way I see it. When Americans—consumers and future wine makers alike—started to get interested in wine in the 1960s and 1970s, the textbooks they read on the subject were telling them that the world's greatest white wine was white Burgundy, from France, and the world's greatest red wine was red Bordeaux, also from France. The white Burgundy they were referring to is made from 100 percent Chardonnay grapes; red Bordeaux is made from a blend of grape varieties, but it is usually Cabernet Sauvignon that predominates. These details were indelible; a whole generation grew up believing that Chardonnay and Cabernet Sauvignon were the top of the oenological heap. This generation led future American generations into wine, and many of the new drinkers accepted the varietal dogma from the old drinkers.

But to me, they've all got it wrong.

The textbooks that gave pride of place to Chardonnay and Cabernet were written by wine geeks— those dedicated to the old-fashioned romance of wine, the boys' club from the nineteenth century, the privileged few who get to taste the most expensive wines from their own cellars, from their friends' cellars, or through the largesse of wine makers who want them to perpetuate the old myths.

Now, Chardonnay in Burgundy can make one of the richest white wines in the world, and one of the few that can age well. But the vast preponderance of Chardonnays made around the world today—and that includes some Burgundian Chardonnays—are heavy, oafish, too sweet, obvious, overoaked, high in alcohol, headed nowhere, and positively awful with food. Cabernet Sauvignon in Bordeaux can make one of the most complex red wines in the world, and one that can age extremely well. But the vast preponderance of Cabernet Sauvignons made around the world today—and that includes some from Bordeaux—are too tannic, too high in alcohol, one-dimensional, dull, bitter, not able to age well, and positively awful with food.

Doesn't it bother you just a little bit that the two varietals that almost every American has heard of, and the two varietals that most American wine drinkers covet, are two of the worst varietals in the world for matching with food? But the marketers continue to market these two as if they were brands, making what hay they can out of their name recognition. And these irresponsible marketers have never once asked themselves, What would happen to wine in America if we marketed wine that actually tasted good with food? The desire for a quick buck always prevents that question.

And every time another Chard or Cab is purchased in a restaurant by someone who thinks these varietals are what he or she should be drinking, I say to myself, "There goes another potential wine drinker, who'll be back to Bud or Diet Pepsi before too much more money is wasted on this stuff."

The Question of Components. Which elements of wine are most appreciated by American wine drinkers? Judging by the kinds of wines that sell, and by the descriptions of the best wines in wine journals, one would have to conclude that the following components in wine are the most attractive:

Low acidity
Sweetness
High alcohol
Lots of wood flavor from oak barrels
Tannin (a bitter substance that is thought to help red wine age)

Speaking particularly of the last three elements, a wine collector in California once told me: "I know a wine is good when it hurts." It hurts me to hear this—because all five of the "prized" elements listed contribute to bad matches with food.

To me, these should be the elements that wine drinkers prize:

High acidity
Dryness
Low alcohol
Little or moderate oak
Little tannin (except in red wines destined to age, and then the tannins should be soft and cushioned with lots of fruit)

This is the list that counts if you want your wine to go with your food.

I do. Read on.

Matching Wine with Food

It seems to me that more attention is not paid to wine as an accompaniment to food because many people are intimidated by the whole subject of matching wine with food. We all think it's much easier to just say "Chardonnay" in a restaurant, or "Cabernet"—and to accept the congratulations of one's table-mates—than it is to consider any of the other options out there.

We think this, in part, because the advice we've read on matching wine with food has never gotten us any closer to exciting matches than simply saying "Chardonnay" or "Cabernet" has.

Here are the most popular schools of thought on matching wine with food—each one deeply flawed.

COLOR CODING

It's the most basic rule of all: white wine with fish, red wine with meat. But it makes no sense. Anyone who has enjoyed Beaujolais with tuna, or California Sauvignon Blanc with lamb stew, knows that this advice just doesn't stand up. It may have some limited applicability, but it's no principle to build a system on.

White wine with red meat (lamb stew)

VARIETAL MATCHING

About twenty years ago, wine writers started recommending specific varietals for certain foods. What do you drink with lobster? "Chardonnay," they'd answer in chorus. Never mind asking what type of lobster dish was being prepared. And never mind the fact that Chardonnay can be either a thin refreshment of 11 percent alcohol, grown in a cold summer in a northern French town, that lands on your palate like lemon juice, or a rich 15 percent alcohol blockbuster, grown in the sweltering desert of California's Central Valley, that lands on your palate like a Mack truck. Not all Chardonnay is the same; not all dishes prepared with a common ingredient are the same. But I can tell you that all generalizing varietal responses are the same: hogwash.

FLAVOR MATCHING

With this strategy, we get a little closer to something helpful—but not awfully close. The theory is that the sophisticated flavors of food and the sophisticated flavors of wine must line up for a good match to be made. Some sommelier somewhere will tell you, in deathly earnest, that "the grassiness of the Sauvignon Blanc echoes perfectly the grassiness of the cilantro." And of this reasoning are matches born every day.

The amusing accident of Sauvignon Blanc and cilantro both being described as "grassy"—though neither one actually tastes like grass—can lead to some correspondence of a low order. But these flavor intersections never contribute heavily, in my opinion, to the success or failure of matches.

COMPONENT MATCHING

So what's it all about, then?

To me, the practice of matching wine with food comes down to a consideration of what I call the basic components of wine and food. By components, I mean those very simple sensations that you experience on your tongue—as opposed to the more complex sensations (like the taste of truffles or the taste of raspberries) that are facilitated by the olfactory nerve in your nose (try tasting raspberries when your nose is blocked by a cold).

Here are the chief components of food that are perceived on the tongue:

Saltiness
Sweetness
Bitterness
Sourness
Heat (as in chilies)

Here are the chief components of wine that are perceived on the tongue:

Sweetness
Sourness
Alcohol (which feels "hot" on your tongue)
Tannin (which feels astringent on your tongue)

Oakiness (which feels astringent on your tongue)

Fruitiness (which feels ample on your tongue)

If you learn how the components interact, you'll be matching like a master in no time. Here are some of the permutations of the various food and wine components.

FOOD COMPONENTS

Saltiness. When food is *salty,* it doesn't go well with table wines that are either high in alcohol or very oaky. It does, however, go nicely with wines that are high in acid . . . and cold wine also seems to be refreshing with salty food. Last, a bit of sweetness in wine can play nicely against salt. So if, for example, I'm serving smoked salmon—a salty food—I'll look for a low-alcohol, low-oak, high-acid, slightly sweet cold wine. Off-dry German Riesling, of course!

Salty food (smoked salmon) with low-alcohol, low oak, high-acid, slightly sweet cold wine

Sweetness. Sweetness in food makes sweet wine taste less sweet. If a main-course food is slightly sweet, a very dry wine will taste unattractively dry when drunk with it—so I like to drink slightly sweet wine with slightly sweet food. At dessert time, sweet food again will reduce the perceived sweetness of sweet wine. Since you want your dessert wine to taste sweet, I always make sure to find wine for dessert that's at least a little sweeter than the food.

Bitterness. The human palate tends to dislike bitterness in food—so the best thing a wine can do is reduce the perception of bitterness in food. Amazingly, bitter food—like meat charred by the grill or oil-cured olives—can taste less bitter when it's served with a wine that has some of the bitterness of tannin. Too much tannin, however, and the opposite effect takes place—it all tastes more bitter! So with your charred, black-and-blue lamb chops, choose a California Cabernet that you know to be moderately tannic.

Slightly bitter food (charred lamb chops) with tannic red wine

Sourness. We're often told not to drink wine with salad. Why? Because the acidity of the salad dressing supposedly is going to interfere with the balance of the wine. This is true, of course, if you have a perfectly balanced wine. But if you have a wine that is already a little too acidic—a sour little northern Pinot Noir, for example, from a cloudy vintage—it will positively blossom when served with an acidic salad. And the salad will taste less acid, too. Remember: acid food and acid wine are great together.

Acidic food (salad with vinaigrette) with acidic wine

Hot and spicy food (Thai fish) with sparkling wine

Heat. Spicy food is no great friend to wine. If the food is very spicy, no wine will taste like anything other than wet. When you get to lower levels of spiciness, wine does become possible—but I'd do my damnedest to avoid complex, subtle wine with spicy food at any level. The best general advice is to serve noncomplex bubbly (like inexpensive California sparkling wine) with spicy food, because the bubbles scrub the chili oil off your palate (just like beer does). And, if the dish seems appropriate, a little bit of sweetness in wine can be a nice counterpoint to spicy food.

WINE COMPONENTS

Sweetness. When wines you expect to be dry turn out to be a little sweet—like many California Chardonnays do—they are troublesome next to dishes requiring dry wines (sweet California Chardonnay would ruin a simply sautéed Dover sole). But if you know in advance that you have a slightly sweet wine in captivity, you can adjust the food to make the wine taste better. When you serve your fish with some kind of sweet sauce—like a mango–red bell pepper salsa—the sweetness in wine vanishes. It's an amazing transformation: when sweet wine meets sweet food, the wine tastes drier, better, more complex, more sophisticated. When it comes to dessert, the same thing is going to happen to your sweet dessert wine next to sweet food: it will diminish in perceived sweetness. This is why I always recommend making sure that your sweet dessert wine is a little sweeter than the dessert; that way, it will still taste like a sweet wine.

Sourness. I love wines with bracing acidity; they are among the most food-friendly wines of all. Acidic wines go beautifully with acidic foods (yes, you can serve wine with salad—as long as the wine's acidic!). Acidic wines are refreshing next to salty foods. And acidic wines are often just the thing to buzz-saw through rich foods (try acidic wines with cream sauces; acidic wines with fatty cold cuts, like prosciutto; acidic wines with a pile of hot sausages).

Alcohol. Most wines weigh in at about 12 percent alcohol. Generally speaking, food matching becomes easier as you dip below that level, and harder as you rise above that level. Low-alcohol wines (they go as low as 8 percent alcohol), which generally come from colder wine regions, are great with all light foods, sometimes perfect as foils to rich foods, and always at home with salty foods. High-alcohol wines (they go as high as 16 percent alcohol) are sometimes acceptable with very rich foods, but I find they make more trouble than they solve at the table.

Tannin. Tannin is a substance that serious young red wines pick up from grape skins, seeds, stems, and sometimes new oak barrels. Tannin is supposed to act as a preservative in red wine that's intended for aging. After many years in the bottle it smoothes out, but in a wine's youth it's unpleasantly astringent. Let's say you've got a young Cabernet that you're just dying to try, so that you can experience all those fruity flavors the wine won't have when it ages ten or twenty years. The problem, of course, is that while it's young it will be forbiddingly tannic. Stick to those foods with a little bitterness of their own. Now, if the wine's ferociously tannic, your gambit may backfire. But if the tannin level is moderate, the wine will taste smoothed out next to grilled meats (which are slightly bitter from the char), grilled vegetables, black oil-cured olives, and bitter greens mixed with traditional red wine foods (like the Orecchiette with Broccoli Rabe and Sausage on page 80). One food stands out above all as a tannin fighter: grilled eggplant. I'm not exactly sure why it happens, but whenever I want to taste a red wine prematurely, I serve it with grilled eggplant—and its tannin magically vanishes.

Tannic red wine with grilled eggplant

Oakiness. Allowing wine to ferment, or repose, in new oak barrels often adds to the wine a range of attractive flavors. A vanilla-like quality is the one most noticeable in white wines, and a spicelike quality (something like clove) is the one most noticeable in red wines. However, many wine makers overdo it—and the overoaked wines end up tasting too oaky (not necessarily a problem for food) and astringent (definitely a problem for food). I don't know of any foods that are specifically helped by oak. But salty foods can taste downright unpleasant next to the astringency of an overoaked wine, and an overoaked wine will seem clumsy next to foods that are naturally light (you wouldn't want a galumphing wood-bomb Chardonnay next to slices of fluke sashimi).

Big oaky wines with nothing

Fruitiness. This is Factor X when it comes to matching wine with food. It's not exactly a component, since fruitiness is most often evident as a flavor. But if a wine is fruity, you'll often feel it in your mouth as well; it will seem lush and ample (the Bordelais refer to the feeling as "baby fat"). Now, excess fruitiness in white wine, in my experience, is often a deficit; it impedes white wine from doing all those crisp, cut-through things that white wine is supposed to do. I always prefer white wines from areas that don't yield very fruity wines, from vintages that don't yield very fruity wines, and I prefer white wines that have had a few years in the bottle to lose their fruit. Red wine for me, however, is another story. I love a wine like Beaujolais—the fruitiest red of all—in its extreme youth; the red fruit acts like a cushion, enabling the wine to envelop a wide range of foods. Red wine with fish? As long as the wine's fruity. Red wine with salty foods? The fruit smoothes everything over. Red wine with sweet foods before dessert? The fruit almost yields an impression of sweetness, which enables it to partner some sweet foods. Red wine with spicy foods? Difficult (as is all wine with spicy food)—but the fruit sometimes makes it work. One of the great problems of wine distribution in this country is that not enough young, fruity red comes to the marketplace while it's still young and fruity. Distributors know that most Americans think red wine improves with age, so they're in no rush. But only a small percentage of red wine will be better in twenty years, and most red wine tastes dull at four to five years old—the precise age of most reds in our market. Whenever I see inexpensive, fruity reds that are just a year old, I snatch them up like nobody's business and drink them soon with food.

The Similarity Principle
Keep in mind that many matches work through the similarity principle:
1. *Sweet food makes sweet wine taste less sweet.*
2. *Acidic food makes acidic wine taste less acidic.*
3. *Bitter food makes slightly bitter wine taste less bitter.*

The Question of Age
A wine's age has a great deal to do with its ability to match food.

All brand-new wine tastes strongly of grapes—that is, young wine is fruity. I'm not crazy about this quality in young white wine, but simple, young, fruity red is a bonanza with food.

Many red wines—like Beaujolais—are intended to be drunk in this young, fruity stage, for that's when they taste best and go best with food. But some of the world's red wines—serious wines, like great Bordeaux, great Rhône wines, great Barolos, great Tuscan reds—go through a transformation with time that can make them better and that certainly changes their interaction with food. To visualize this metamorphosis, think of a fresh red apple. Cut it, and put it on the counter. What does it smell like? Apple, fruit, youth. Now leave that apple on the counter for a few months. What will it smell like? At some point it will reach a dried-up stage when it will smell like nothing—it becomes inert, neutral. Amazingly, this is what happens to red wine that's destined for long aging when it hits five years old or so. Wine people say it's "closed," or "dumb"; the wine's not saying anything at all. Now, if you leave that apple on the counter for a few months more, it starts to decompose—which finally brings some aroma back to the old fruit; most people, of course, don't find the aroma of rotting fruit attractive. But the miracle of aged red wine is that those third-level aromas and flavors of decomposition—which creep into a great red wine at anywhere from ten to twenty years of age—are perceived as beautiful, extraordinary, haunting! In great red wine, they usually take the olfactory form of truffles, mushrooms, earth, forest floor, even unmentionable parts of bodies. Very sexy stuff. And wine at this stage is gentle, rounded, and smooth to boot. I'd no longer serve it with the foods cut out for fruity young red wine; now it has become the ideal accompaniment to roast chicken, simple veal dishes, and rare red meat.

The white wine picture's not quite as pretty. Many whites are obnoxiously fruity in youth, then simply go nowhere with age (they start tasting oxidized, or sherrylike). A few whites that I don't crave in youth do develop nicely with age—like white Burgundies, particularly from the northern village of Chablis. I love ten-year-old Chablis, when the fruit has died off and been replaced by a steely, earthy, mineral-like character; this is ideal for austere fish dishes of all kinds. And German Rieslings, to me, have the happy property of being both food friendly in fruity youth and food friendly in old age (when the wine's flavors morph into something like petroleum—which, believe it or not, is attractive!).

"Difficult" Matches

The gastronomic literature is filled with foods that are supposed to be difficult for wine—but if you just use the basic logic of components, you can usually find a good match.

A perfect example of a food that's perceived as difficult is the artichoke. Most books don't tell you why artichokes cause trouble for wine, but the reason is that artichokes contain a chemical that makes everything you taste after tasting an artichoke taste sweet. This can really be a problem if you're serving a 1961 Château Margaux. However, if you find a wine that's forbiddingly dry—one that could use a little sweetness to soften it up—you're home free. I love the flavors of Tavel rosé but often find it dry to the point of austerity. No problem! I just create some kind of southern French artichoke dish to go with my southern French rosé.

Twelve Wines with Very Favorable Components that I Always Rely on for Food

Now it's time to get specific. If you want to improve your wine-and-food-matching odds immediately, simply take note of the dozen wines discussed in this section. Make them your wines. Buy them at stores. Look for them on restaurant wine lists. Some of them may be difficult to find, some may be easy—but they're all worth a special effort. Remember: there are lots of other good wines in the world . . . but these are the ones that will make you a matching wizard.

1. DRY GERMAN RIESLING

If you watch *Taste* with any regularity, you've undoubtedly noticed that the white wine I select for food more than any other is dry German Riesling. This is no accident. I believe it to be the most flexible white wine in the world for food—both for traditional food and for the new realm of creative world cuisine. Unfortunately, it is also one of the most misunderstood wines in the world; non-Germans always assume that German Riesling is sweet and precisely not what you should drink with dinner. So the situation is this: the best wine for food is considered to be the worst wine for food. Sounds like the rest of the American wine scene, doesn't it?

Another Riesling "problem" is the label; neophyte wine drinkers are often confused by the welter of information that's given on a German wine label. I admit that it can be daunting—but, with a little practice, you'll be able to read the label easily, and you'll even be thankful for the amount of precise information that it gives you.

If you're simply trying to pick wine for food, there are a few things on a German label you should virtually ignore, and a few things you should pay attention to.

Things to Ignore. Don't worry about the big name on the label, usually two words, which tells you the town and the vineyard. Bernkasteler Badstube, for example, means the Badstube vineyard in the town of Bernkastel (the *er* at the end of Bernkastel is like our *'s,* a possessive—"Bernkastel's Badstube"), but only geeks absolutely need this info.

Don't worry about the name of the wine producer right now; this also is a game for connoisseurs. And don't worry about any government classification numbers you might see on the label.

Things to Pay Attention To. First of all, for simplicity's sake, make sure the wine you're considering is a Riesling (there are other good grape varieties grown in Germany, but keeping track of them makes things much more complicated).

Next—and most important—you'll need to figure out the level of sweetness in the wine you're considering. There are a few German wines that are out-and-out sweet, which you should consider only as dessert wines. These will say Beerenauslese, Trockenbeerenauslese, or Eiswein on the label.

Beyond that, it gets trickier. To understand how to determine sweetness/dryness from a label, you have to understand a few things about grape picking and wine making.

Grapes can be picked at various levels of ripeness; they can be low in sugar (not too ripe) or high in sugar (very ripe). Vineyard owners sometimes opt for low ripeness, because they worry that the

German wine is ideal for sausages . . .
and about a thousand other things

weather may change and harm their grapes before the grapes have a chance to get more ripe. Whatever they do, it's really the wine makers who determine dryness/sweetness: they can choose to make dry wine by fermenting the grape juice until all the sugar has gone out of it (fermentation is actually the conversion of sugar to alcohol), or they can stop the fermentation so that the finished wine has more sugar and less alcohol (this is how sweet wine is made).

Now, the best German wines are designated on the label as QmP, or Qualitätswein mit Prädikat—quality wine with a description. That means the label will tell you (through a "description") roughly how ripe and sugary the grapes were at the time they were picked. If the description is "Kabinett," that means the grapes weren't too ripe. If the description is "Spätlese," that means the grapes were riper, with more sugar. If the description is "Auslese," that means the grapes were quite ripe and sugary.

However, just because the grapes were ripe and sugary, it's not necessarily the case that the wine's going to be sweet. Because, once again, wine makers can choose to convert that grape sugar into alcohol; the more that's converted, the drier the wine will be. How do you know? If the label says "Trocken," that means the wine maker decided to convert all, or almost all, of the sugar to alcohol; *Trocken* means "dry," and that's what Trocken wines are. If the label says "Halbtrocken"—or half dry—the wine in the bottle will be just a touch sweet, or off dry. If the label says neither Trocken nor Halbtrocken, the Germans call this wine *leiblich*—but they don't put "leiblich" on the label; they just know by the absence of Trocken or Halbtrocken that the wine's going to be on the sweet side.

Now, the really interesting thing is the interplay between the ripeness "description" words from the vineyard (Kabinett, Spätlese, Auslese) and the wine maker's fermentation words (Trocken, Halbtrocken). Here are the permutations.

Kabinett. A lightly sweet wine, not too high in alcohol (as low as 8 percent—because the wine maker stopped the fermentation to preserve some sugar).

Kabinett Halbtrocken. An off-dry wine, a little higher in alcohol (because the fermentation went longer, so more of the sugar would be converted into alcohol).

Kabinett Trocken. A dry wine, with the most alcohol of any Kabinett wine (though Kabinett Trocken, since there wasn't too much sugar in the grapes to begin with, rarely gets above 11 to 12 percent alcohol).

Spätlese. A medium-sweet wine, sweeter than Kabinett (because the grapes had more sugar). Low in alcohol.

Spätlese Halbtrocken. An off-dry wine, with more alcohol and body than either Spätlese or Kabinett Halbtrocken.

Spätlese Trocken. A dry wine that can have a fairly high alcohol level (like 12 to 13 percent).

Auslese. A rather sweet wine that sometimes is sweet enough to drink with dessert. Fairly low in alcohol.

Auslese Halbtrocken. An off-dry wine, with more alcohol and body than Auslese, Spätlese Halbtrocken, or Kabinett Halbtrocken.

Auslese Trocken. A rich, dry wine, which, from warmer German regions, can have as much alcohol as white Burgundy or California Chardonnay (in the realm of 13 to 14 percent).

Another term on the label you should pay attention to is the region from which the wine came. There are thirteen major German regions, and what you need to know is this:

1. Some of the crispest, lightest wine comes from the Mosel. There are decent dry wines made here, but the lightly sweet ones are even better.

2. Some of the richest, fattest wine comes from the Pfalz. Auslese Trockens from here can have the weight of the biggest dry white wines from anywhere.

3. The Rheingau and the Nahe are two regions producing wine that falls somewhere between the Mosel and the Pfalz in weight.

Moving past the label, you're probably wondering exactly what kinds of foods go well with dry German wines. Here's a short list.

Raw Shellfish and Cooked, Cold Shellfish. Absolutely dry is best here.

Fish Dishes . . . Particularly in Cream Sauce. Once again, dry is best—but a Mosel Spätlese Halbtrocken wouldn't be bad either.

Sushi. Superb! The light sweetness in the rice can blend perfectly with the light sweetness of off-dry German wines.

Chinese and Thai Food. No one type of wine can cover all the possibilities in these cuisines. But when I think wine for these foods, I think German first. The whole range of foods from light and savory up to heavy and rich can be accommodated by German wines: lightly steamed fish fillets with dry, light wines and Peking duck (with sweet hoisin sauce) with rich, off-dry ones.

Picnic Food. A wide range of cold meats, hams, salamis, cold poultry, pâtés, salads with mayonnaise or vinaigrette, sandwiches, et cetera go beautifully with dry German wines.

Fatty Meats. Meats traditionally served with sweet sauces—duck, goose, pork—are fabulous without sweet sauces, and with dry or off-dry German wine instead.

Vegetables. German wines can be thrilling with a wide range of wine-difficult vegetables: corn on the cob, asparagus, beets, and cauliflower.

Now, whose wine should you buy? There are hundreds of great producers in Germany today. But many of them run small operations . . . and when I tell you some of them, you may be frustrated at your inability to find their wines. Don't! Keep looking, and you may find something even better.

Producers I Like

Dönnhoff	Selbach-Oster
Müller-Catoir	Maximin Grünhaus
Neckerauer	Immich-Batterieberg
Lingenfelder	Heribert Kerpen
Dr. Loosen	Hans Wirsching

. . . and many, many more. Look especially for wines that have been imported by Terry Theise on the East Coast and Rudy Wiest on the West Coast.

One more word of advice. If your local wine shop is like mine, they may not even know what you're talking about when you ask for dry German wines. Try to educate them, and ask them to stock the Theise/Wiest wines. Or you can do an end run around your wine shop, and call a German mail-order specialist, like Bill Mayer, at The Age of Riesling in Berkeley, California (510-549-2444).

2. NEW ZEALAND SAUVIGNON BLANC

Wines made in France's Loire Valley from the grape variety called Sauvignon Blanc used to be some of my favorite white wines for food in the whole world. Grown in a cool climate, Sauvignon Blanc yields crisp, relatively low-alcohol whites with an unmistakable taste that is extremely attractive with food: this taste is variously called grassiness, herbaceousness, vegetal character, or, in France, *pipi du chat* (I don't have a cat, so I don't know what its *pipi* smells like exactly).

I say they *used* to be among my favorites—wines such as Sancerre and Pouilly-Fumé—because these days the wines have changed. Many of the growers seem to have been influenced by the clamoring of wine writers for grapes that are riper, wines that are richer—wines, in short, that don't go as well with food. Additionally, there is a perception in France—a correct one—that Americans don't like the herbaceous taste of Sauvignon Blanc. So, for that reason as well, many Loire Valley grape growers are now picking their Sauvignon Blanc grapes later, when the sun has burned out some of the varietal character (and made the wine much less crisp).

For a few years I was very depressed—because I couldn't find old-style Sauvignon Blanc on the market (examples from California are usually even less food friendly). Then I discovered New Zealand Sauvignon Blanc—particularly those wines made from grapes grown in the Marlborough region, near Blenheim, on the northern tip of New Zealand's South Island. Miraculous! These are wines that out-Sancerre Sancerre! They are blazingly varietal, crisp as a Granny Smith apple, relatively low in alcohol, and positively brilliant with food. Their one deficit, for some, is that they can be too varietal; those who don't like the real taste of Sauvignon Blanc sometimes compare the flavor of these wines with canned asparagus. But I'm not among them; I love this gooseberry-green character.

New Zealand Sauvignon Blanc is superb with oysters (especially fruity ones) and generally good with all shellfish. I especially like it with shellfish that has been flavored with garlic. It's a flexible wine with food that, because of its acidity, goes well with many different things—but its herbaceousness, of course, makes it an especially dynamic match with herb-accented dishes.

Some of the winery names I always look for are Selak's, Stoneleigh, and Palliser—but Marlborough Sauvignon Blanc is a category you can trust, one in which all the wines have a similar character. The one that stands out, of course, is the one that wine writers like the best—Cloudy Bay, which is usually richer and riper than the others. But the nature of the Marlborough is such that even this heavier wine is still remarkably graceful and a great choice for many foods (it is made beautifully and is absolutely delicious).

There are a few other pockets of Sauvignon Blanc—and its cousin grape, Sémillon—in the world today that make similarly crisp, food-loving wine. Australia's cooler regions can yield delicious Sauvignon Blanc and Sémillon. The Columbia Winery in Washington State has always made a crisp, grassy Sémillon. Best alternatives of all are the Sauvignon Blancs made around Cape Town, in South Africa; the one made by Mulderbosch, vintage in and vintage out, is one of my favorite Sauvignon Blancs for food anywhere in the world.

3. GALESTRO

Tuscany's Galestro is a light white wine that American wine snobs love to hate; there's not much to it, other than superquaffable, low-alcohol refreshment that goes extremely well with many foods. The Italians seem to have no problem with Galestro, consuming a sea of it every year. I particularly like it with lots of Italian things that have trouble with richer, fruitier Italian wines; it's a great wine for prosciutto, salami, antipasto in general, simple fish dishes, risotto, creamy pasta dishes, fried veal cutlets. It is, in fact, my everyday house pour when Italian food's on the menu.

Galestros from a number of producers are available in the United States; Antinori's Galestro is the most widely available, but I haven't found too many differences out there. The absolutely crucial thing, however, is to buy one young. In the year 2000, the 1998 will be way over the hill.

4. VINHO VERDE

Now here's a wine that is positively reviled by American wine snobs; admit you drink it, and lose all privileges at the club. Nevertheless, Vinho Verde can be one of the world's most delightful white wines for food—if you can only get over yourself.

Why don't the geeks like Vinho Verde? First of all, it's cheap—really cheap. It's about the only nonjug wine left in the world today that can sell for under $4 a bottle. Second, it's low in alcohol, light in body, high in acid—all the things that make wine geeks think of it as frivolous. (And, I must add, all the things that make it go so well, and so widely, with food.) Last, the geeks do have a point when it comes to the unacceptable condition of most Vinho Verde that's sold in this country.

In northern Portugal, where Vinho Verde is made, you can really understand why it's called green wine. It has nothing to do with color. They call it green because that's when you're supposed to drink it—when it's green, or young. It's so thrillingly acidic at this point that it even tastes "green" in your mouth. But the first horror of Vinho Verde in America is that you can hardly ever find the young stuff. If the Vinho Verde in your wine shop has a vintage date on it, it's likely to be at least two, maybe three years old. And, very often, there's no date at all—so you can't even tell how old this stuff is! The best Vinho Verde I ever had was at a bar in Oporto, out of a barrel, in October; I'm sure it had been made about ten minutes before I drank it, because it still had things floating in it. But it was great!

The second American Vinho Verde horror has to do with sweetness. In Portugal, Vinho Verde has none. But when they ship it to the American market, they add some sugar because they all know how sweet our American teeth are. This destroys the wine, turns it from crackling crisp to insipid candylike.

Lastly, Vinho Verde in Portugal is always *pétillant,* or lightly sparkling; that's a big part of its attractiveness for food. In the United States, due to a variety of factors, the wines are often less bubbly, less alive.

So . . . if you're to take my advice and put Vinho Verde on your regular wine shopping list, you're going to have to be a very clever shopper. Since it's so inexpensive, buy a single bottle of every brand you can find, taste each one, and see which comes closest to the real thing. Better yet, try to find a Portuguese wine-shop owner; you can do this by finding a Portuguese or Spanish neighborhood near your home. Forge a relationship with him. Tell him that you want Vinho Verde that's young, dry, crackling, *pétillant*—and that if you can find it, you'll buy cases of it every year. This usually brings results.

It is exactly what I do—sometimes from a Portuguese shop in New York called Oliveira, sometimes from a shop in Mineola, Long Island, sometimes from shops in Newark's Ironbound district (very Portuguese). Young Vinho Verde is my house wine every summer—the wine that was made just the October before, of course. I serve a lot of crabs, shrimps, lobster, clams, mussels in the summer—and most of these shells get consumed with Vinho Verde (or dry German Riesling). Vinho Verde is also spectacular with cold cuts and picnic food; it is my favorite wine, in fact, for prosciutto. And, of course, whenever there's a rich Iberian stew on the table—preferably seafood, but even light meats—Vinho Verde is one of my prime buzz-through options.

One caveat: do not let a shopkeeper talk you into buying a higher-priced version of Vinho Verde. There are some, made from the Alvarinho grape, that can cost as much as $20 a bottle. They are heavier, fruitier, more complex—and not at all like the food-loving Vinho Verde that I love.

5. TWO CRISP SPANISH WHITES

There are a few wines made in northern Spain that also, when young, have a remarkably crisp, refreshing character that's great by the pailful with all manner of seafood and salty food.

Just north of Portugal's Vinho Verde region is Spain's greatest seafood region, Galicia. The most prestigious Vinho Verde grape (but not the best for food) is grown there as well; in Spanish it's called Albariño. There has been a big marketing push in recent years to convince us that Galician Albariño is one of the world's most flexible wines for seafood. I've been there. I've tasted this wine. This wine was a friend of mine. This wine is no Vinho Verde (when it comes to automatically counting on it to go with food).

However, inland of the Albariño region another white wine is made that goes positively brilliantly with seafood. Because it's less fruity, less alcoholic, less sweet, more acidic than Albariño, it has gotten no attention at all from wine writers. But you can find it in America—as with Vinho Verde, make sure it's a young one you find—and the name of the wine is Ribeiro.

Another northern Spanish white you should go out of your way to find—but only if it's young—is the remarkably crisp, seafood-loving Basque wine called (in Basque) Getariako Txkolina (also known as Chacolí).

Both Ribeiro and Chacolí are imported into the United States by a great Boston-based Spanish importer named Jorge Ordoñez.

6. WHITE RIOJA

The Rioja region of northern Spain is world famous for its great red wine, which I love—but I always feel that its great white wine doesn't get enough respect. There's a reason for this: about twenty years ago most producers of Rioja Blanco responded to fashion and stopped producing their wine in the traditional way.

What did they think the market wouldn't like? Well, Spain is a wood-obsessed wine country, and the traditional white Rioja spent a lot of time in barrels—like five, ten, even fifteen years. In the process, the wine—in addition to picking up woody flavors—oxidized a bit, picking up sherrylike flavors along the way. Spanish producers looked all around the world, saw an emphasis being placed on fresh, fruity white wines fermented in stainless steel tanks, and moved Rioja Blanco in that direction.

Luckily, one producer, Murrieta, held its ground . . . and, happily, more producers today are coming back to the traditional method.

Now, Rioja Blanco is an unusual wine for me to love so much and to rely on so heavily for food. My basic position on overoaked whites is that the oak makes them very difficult to match with food in general. But Rioja Blanco, to me—though it's one of the most oaked white wines in the world—behaves entirely differently at the table than other oaky whites do. It may have something to do with the lovely acidity that Murrieta Rioja Blanco always has—but I swear to you that this is my favorite white wine in the world to call on when a white is needed to stand up to rich food. While every other wine chooser is reaching for his Chardonnay, I'm reaching for my Murrieta. I especially love it with anything in a cream sauce, which is a very tricky food for wine to match; old-fashioned Rioja Blanco, for me, is the world champion cream-sauce wine, the only one I know I can rely on every time.

Now, in this category, you're not looking for a young wine at all. Just the opposite. Happily, Murrieta is well equipped to satisfy you. In the 1980s, the "new" vintage of Murrieta Rioja Blanco that appeared on the market was usually about ten years old. They've modernized a bit, because the "new" vintage that now comes into our market is "only" five or six years old. But it still tastes just like traditional Rioja Blanco.

A few other whites from around the world achieve something of the same slightly oxidized, vanilla-laden taste. The best example, perhaps, is aged, high-level white Bordeaux. But not only are these wines heavier than white Rioja and a little harder to match with food, they also cost a great deal more. What's your choice: $150 for Laville-Haut-Brion or $12 for Murrieta Rioja Blanco?

7. CHABLIS

Real Chablis is one of my favorite white wines in the world. It is certainly my favorite expression of the Chardonnay grape, and probably my favorite high-ticket white made from any grape. But I'm speaking here of real Chablis; make sure you understand what that is before you buy any.

Real Chablis is produced in the small, cold, northern French town of Chablis, on the edge of the Burgundy region. Much more wine called Chablis is produced in the hot Central Valley of California and poured into huge, cheap jugs. The French government is outraged that we allow our wine producers to steal the name of a small French town that has painstakingly over centuries built a reputation for its wine. But our producers basically take the position that they can call their wine whatever the hell they want to call it. Case closed.

So don't you be fooled. If you want some cheap, fruity stuff for a big party, by all means buy California jugs of Chablis. But if you want one of the world's most reliable wines for food, make sure your Chablis label has French writing on it.

Beyond all that, Chablis is still a pretty confusing subject. Classically, Chablis is a crisp, high-acid white wine that is distinguished by the taste of minerals derived from the white, calcium-rich soil of Chablis. This earthy, minerally taste makes Chablis an ideal accompaniment to many traditional seafood dishes—and especially to raw oysters. To me, classic Chablis tastes like Chardonnay for grown-ups.

But a number of problems are preventing a lot of Chablis from tasting this way today. First of all, the Chablis producers have caught wind of the fact that Americans, and American wine writers, like bigger, riper, sweeter, less acidic, more alcoholic wines—so, like the Sauvignon Blanc producers of the Loire Valley, they are also sending us wine that tastes more American. Then, big fights go on in Chablis all the time about which vineyards deserve the name of Chablis; there has been much expansion in recent years of the legal vineyard area for Chablis wines, and—truth be told—not a lot of the new turf produces wine that tastes like Chablis. Last, a lot of producers these days, seeking a more "international" taste, ferment and/or age their Chablis in new oak—which definitely tramples on that old, minerally, Chablis-specific flavor.

This happens especially at the higher, more expensive levels of Chablis—Premier Cru Chablis and Grand Cru Chablis. But let's start lower down the ladder. If a wine is labeled simply "Chablis," that means it comes from just any old vineyard within the legal Chablis boundaries. If it's labeled "Premier Cru Chablis," that means it comes from one of about two dozen vineyards that the government has specified as of a higher quality ("first growth"). If it's labeled "Grand Cru Chablis," that means it comes from one of seven vineyards given the highest ranking of all ("great growth").

Now, if you want the traditional Chablis flavor—and a crisp white wine guaranteed to go with oysters like nobody's business—I recommend you start tasting wines labeled only "Chablis." Give them a few years for the young fruit to go away and the classic Chablis character to emerge—and avoid buying them in the warm vintages that all the wine writers and vintage charts are touting. Occasionally, premier crus from producers who don't like to use too much oak will also have the classic character: one I always like is the Premier Cru Chablis from the Fourchaume vineyard produced by Laroche (buy it from a medium-rated vintage; drink it at seven to ten years old).

Many other premier crus, however, and most of the grand crus, will give you another character entirely. These will be closer to what you're used to in Chardonnay: richer, rounder, with higher alcohol and more oak. The Chablis miracle is this: even with the more pampered treatment, big-deal, expensive Chablis wines still taste great. The soil and climate of the region are so good that even ham-handed, oaked-down Chablis still has grace, verve, refinement. I buy a limited quantity of "big" Chardonnay for some dining occasions—like a rich, white-meat stew such as *blanquette de veau*—and it's usually Grand Cru Chablis that I buy. The faves of the wine writers are usually wines produced by various members of the Dauvissat and Raveneau families—but I'm particularly partial to the slightly tighter wines of William Fèvre.

If you're buying Grand Cru Chablis, don't think of drinking it before it's seven or eight years old . . . and plan to give it ten to twelve years before it reaches its peak.

8. WHITE ZINFANDEL

Yes, I said white Zinfandel . . . and I said it proudly. My pride, however, is not in my taste for great wine. It's in my good sense in matching wine with food.

What is white Zinfandel? Well, Zinfandel is one of California's most interesting red wine grapes— but a few decades back not many Americans at all were interested in drinking it. So an enterprising winery—Sutter Home—took its surplus of Zinfandel grapes and made a lightly sweet rosé wine out of them. White Zinfandel—which is never white but usually a deep pink—was born.

The downside of white Zinfandel is that it doesn't have any Zinfandel flavor. In fact, it doesn't have too much flavor at all—just a mildly pleasant kind of generalized fruit quality. What really drives the wine snobs up the wall, however, is that it's a frankly off-dry wine.

And that, to me, is its virtue when I'm planning menus. There is a great deal of modern food that is on the sweet side—everything from Thai and Chinese food through New American concoctions with fruit to barbecued ribs with sweet barbecue sauces. I say: if the food is a little sweet, let the wine be a little sweet. And if the wine is a little sweet, let it be the very fresh, very clean, very accessible white Zinfandel.

Once again: drink it young! Because it's made in this country, it gets into the pipeline really quickly. Never drink white Zinfandel that's more than a year from the harvest. The producers I've liked the best have been Beringer and R. H. Phillips—but there's a lot of acceptable white Zin out there.

Remember: appropriateness with food is the point of wine!

9. BEAUJOLAIS
And now we have hit

1. Our first red wine
2. The only wine you really need on a desert island

Beaujolais with grilled Dover sole (or 'most anything!)

Beaujolais is the most flexible wine in the world. A great bottle of it from a great vintage can act like a serious red. A light bottle from a light vintage can act like a rollicking white (a Beaujolais producer once said to me that "Beaujolais is the only white wine in the world that happens to be red").

Beaujolais is made from Gamay grapes just north of Lyons, the town that many consider to be gastronomic ground zero (of France, which means of the world). When consumed young—as it almost always should be—Beaujolais is a party in a bottle: bouncy, merry, free from tannin, with a cornucopia of cherry-strawberry-banana fruit pouring out of it.

Because it has so much lighthearted fruit, I consider it to be the greatest red wine in the world for fish. But I also love it with picnic items, with sausages, with grilled meats, with roast chicken, with stews, with saucy Italian food, with salty Asian food . . . this list could go on forever. Remember: this is the most flexible wine in the world (especially when you serve it a little chilled). My gastronomic life would be unimaginable without Beaujolais always standing there, ready to step in and save the culinary day and give me boundless joy.

Of course, nothing is ever completely straightforward about wine—so there are a few further things you'll need to know about Beaujolais:

1. A little less than half of all Beaujolais produced these days is produced as Beaujolais Nouveau. This is a wine made from grapes picked in September (usually) that hits the market by late November of the same year. Two months later! Of course it tastes like fruit . . . it *is* fruit! Wine geeks especially hate Beaujolais Nouveau, because it has no promise whatsoever of aging into anything (it is a good idea to drink your Nouveau by summer). But this is the essence of what wine in Europe is all about: simple, unfussy, seasonal wine that you don't have to worship to enjoy.

2. The following spring (about eight months after the harvest, still a short time for red wine), the "regular" Beaujolais comes into the market. It doesn't say "Nouveau." It is a bit darker, richer, more substantial than the dizzyingly fruity Nouveau. But it still has the same essential character. I like to drink this stuff within a year of the harvest, no more than two.

3. These days, you're much more likely to see wine labeled "Beaujolais-Villages" than "Beaujolais." It's essentially the same stuff, with the same profile—but wine geeks get all excited by the fact that it comes from vineyards in approximately three dozen "villages" that the government has designated as higher in quality. Still, you should drink it within two years.

4. And for the highest quality, there are Beaujolais wines from ten very special villages. In fact, the villages are so special that these wines aren't called Beaujolais at all—they are named on the label, instead, for the villages that made them. This makes things pretty confusing for the novice, but you can always carry around a card with the ten names on it:

Brouilly	Regnié
Côtes de Brouilly	Saint-Amour
Chiroubles	Chénas
Fleurie	Morgon
Juliénas	Moulin-à-Vent

Most of these wines—collectively known as crus Beaujolais—are pretty much like Beaujolais-Villages, and I would use them in the same way. But keep in mind that the last three—Chénas, Morgon, and Moulin-à-Vent—are likely to be a little richer, darker, deeper. They may also be a little less explosively fruity in youth, and may carry a scratch of tannin. I usually avoid these three when they're very young, preferring to drink "lower-level" Beaujolais. Sometimes, however, they will afford you happy surprises; I've tasted wines from these three villages as old as ten years that had blossomed into delicious, Burgundy-like creations.

Beaujolais is a maze, producer-wise. Happily, one man has cornered the market and is responsible for a large portion of the Beaujolais that's shipped to America. His name is Georges Duboeuf—aka the Pope of Beaujolais—and he has kept very high standards of quality. You will find his wines—and all Beaujolais wines—to be among the last great values in the wine world. They provide a ton of flavor, great flexibility for food—and it's very hard to find a bottle that costs much over $10.

10. BARBERA

And this is my red wine staple for Italian food. Wines made in Piemonte from the Barbera grape have two properties that I love:

1. They are almost void, physiologically, of tannin.
2. They are among the most acidic red wines in the world.

The first point means that there's no tannin in Barbera to prevent good food matches—something very rare among red wines. And the second point means that Barbera is the red wine to choose when acidic food is on the table. There is no red wine better for tomato-sauce dishes. There is no red wine better for salads. And . . . the high acid means that Barbera can buzz-saw through rich foods as well. If you drink it young, as you should, the sheer amount of fruit will cushion the ride.

There is one Barbera confusion that is lately with us. A number of Piedmontese producers have decided that Barbera is indeed a noble grape—and have begun aging it in expensive barrels, raising its pedigree from friendly, everyday plonk to Wine of the World and charging a helluva lot more lire for it. These more "important" wines will not work with spaghetti puttanesca as well as my beloved simple Barbera. Look for Barberas that say Barbera d'Alba, Barbera d'Asti, or Barbera del Monferrato, refuse to spend more than $12 for them (the "new wave" Barberas can cost over $35), drink only vintages that are less than three years old (though Barbera can occasionally age)—and sit back and smile while others find their more expensive wines tripping all over their ravioli.

11. CALIFORNIA PINOT NOIR

One of the things that makes red wine reliable with food and widely flexible with food, is lots of yummy young fruit. If the wine is also low in tannin and alcohol, so much the better—so much more flexible will it be. California is a place where the hot sun and rich soil always conspire to load red wines with lots of fruit. The problem is that usually these wines also get loaded with tannin and alcohol, reducing their flexibility.

The great achievement of modern California Pinot Noir is that it enables you to enjoy all of that abundant, ripe California red fruit—without having to slog through a painful tannin field or too much alcohol. And this is why I'm always thinking about young California Pinot Noir for fish, for grilled meat, for vegetables, for picnics, for scads of things.

It wasn't ever thus. Just twenty years ago, most wine fanatics thought that the finicky grape of red Burgundy, Pinot Noir, could make great wine only in Burgundy. Attempts to make Pinot Noir in other parts of the world—especially in California—had failed miserably. Then, David Lett, who trained in California, made a few stunning Pinot Noirs in Oregon, just north of California. Suddenly, non-Burgundian

Pinot seemed a possibility. Next thing you knew, great Pinots starting popping up in New Zealand and Australia as well, and, occasionally, in other places.

Ironically, the place in the world today that most consistently gives Burgundian Pinot Noir a run for its money is the place that was so famous for Pinot Envy—California. It is my opinion that California Pinots today are even more reliable than those from Pinot's first successful American stomping ground, Oregon.

For food, all the usual rules apply here. Find California Pinot Noir that's very young; lots of the wonderful, food-friendly fruit will be gone when the wine gets past three years old. Respect the big-deal producers, making expensive wines that stand up to Burgundy's most expensive wines in blind tastings—like the incredible Williams Selyem of the Russian River Valley in Sonoma—but, when you have food in mind, pick the young cheapies (like Napa Ridge or Meridian, two sources for great-value, food-lovin' Pinot).

12. AUSTRALIAN SHIRAZ

There is one type of wine that would be extremely useful to menu planners but happens to be virtually absent from the international repertoire: off-dry red wine. Imagine: a lightly sweet red wine would be delicious with hamburgers that have ketchup, ribs that have barbecue sauce, Peking duck that has hoisin sauce, and all manner of Asian and multi-culti specialties dreamed up by modern chefs that feature a lick of sugar. Alas, no such wine exists.

Almost. The Syrah grape of France's Rhône Valley makes massive, wonderful dry wines in the south of France—and it does the same in Australia, where it's called Shiraz. But in Australia, a number of wineries produce an inexpensive version of Shiraz that is so plump with sweet young fruit it almost creates an impression of sweetness on the palate. To get this effect, you must never spend more than $15 for your Australian Shiraz, and you must always buy wine from the latest vintage (if it's fall 2000, look for wines from 2000—since Australia's in the Southern Hemisphere and wines are made there in March). Rosemount (in the Hunter Valley) and Peter Lehmann (in the Barossa Valley) are two wineries that get their young Shiraz wines into the American market fast . . . but there are many more. A great, recent discovery for me was Banrock Station.

A Few Other Wines You May Have Heard About . . . and How They Work with Food

The reputation of wine is a funny business. It is almost solely based on what wine geeks say about a type of wine, and rarely based on how it goes with food. Here are some wines that you may have heard great things about, some you may have heard horrible things about, and some you may have heard nothing about. My short descriptions tell you whether or not you need to hear anything further, if you're considering them for food.

CHAMPAGNE

I love some Champagnes with food . . . particularly Champagne that is older (like ten to fifteen years), is crisp and dry, and has lots of "bready" character. Most of the younger, nonvintage Champagnes, called Brut, are fine for aperitifs but not that widely flexible with food. I don't think that Champagne is as good with caviar, or with smoked salmon, as it's cracked up to be. But I do think it's brilliant with sushi, fried foods, soups, and egg dishes. And, though food's not necessarily involved, I can't imagine starting an important French dinner without a flute of this remarkable stuff.

By the way, in case you're asking . . . my favorite Champagne of all is Krug.

SHERRY

Real sherry from the south of Spain may surprise you. Some of it is brown, as many people expect, and some of it is sweet—but an awful lot of it is like white wine in color, is bone dry in flavor, and is astonishingly delicious with food. These lighter sherries are called either Finos or Manzanillas—and they are among my favorite meal starters. They're great with almonds, with olives, and with a wide range of Spanish tapas items. Try them with shellfish in garlic sauces, too. Look for Hidalgo Manzanilla and Lustau Fino.

CALIFORNIA CHARDONNAY

Well, there's no bigger success story in wine-sales circles than California Chardonnay—but there's probably no wine that's more of a turnoff for people like me who are serious about matching wine with food. Now, I'm not saying that there isn't a lot of good Chardonnay out there. Aside from the bubble-gum mass-market stuff, there are scores of boutique wines that are expertly made, brimming with wine-making pizzazz, deeply dimensional in flavor, et cetera. The problem is that so many of them have so much oak, or alcohol, or sweet-seeming fruit, that California Chardonnay is a very difficult category to rely on for food matching. I drink California Chardonnay—but mostly as an aperitif. That big fruit-and-oak explosion is a stimulating way to get any dinner party off the ground, as long as the food comes later. If forced to drink this stuff with food, I would usually choose sweetish savory dishes (like grilled fish with fruit salsas).

*The best role for California Chardonnay: with something a little sweet
(here, grilled fish with mango salsa)*

LONG ISLAND CHARDONNAY

You may not have heard much about this wine—but I constantly outrage my wine geek friends by telling them that I'd rather drink Long Island Chardonnay than California Chardonnay. Why? Well, it's lighter, higher in acid, drier, lower in alcohol—in short, more European in style and better with food. Some of my favorite producers are Palmer, Lenz, Sagpond, and Paumanok. I'm a big advocate of drinking local wine, and—since I live about seventy-five miles from these vineyards—I'd be a hypocrite if I drank Muscadet with my Long Island oysters rather than Long Island Chardonnay.

RETSINA

Oh, sure. Go explain this one to a wine geek. Retsina—an ancient Greek wine, flavored for centuries, and even now, with pine resin—is an immediate turnoff to wine snobs. Invariably, they find the taste of Retsina akin to turpentine. Me . . . I find it a taste that's absolutely essential in making Greek food taste Greek; I think of it as adding an extra spice. I hasten to point out that, in my opinion, most of the world's ethnic foods don't need to be drunk with the wines of their countries; French food doesn't require French wine, Italian food doesn't require Italian wine, et cetera. But I make an exception for Retsina. By the way, I somehow find Retsina attractive with virtually all savory Greek dishes.

RED BURGUNDY

Whenever people ask me what my favorite wine is, without blinking an eye I shoot back "red Burgundy." Well, it is—when it's great red Burgundy from France, and when it's served with the right food. But the reason it doesn't appear on my list of a dozen you-can't-go-wrong wines is that you can go wrong with red Burgundy.

For starters, there was a serious drop-off, a few decades back, in the quality of red Burgundy; the region as a whole has rebounded, but buying red Burgundy is still a minefield. It is the world's most expensive wine, on average, and it's still not hard to spend $40 for a bottle of something mediocre.

Second, it is true that red Burgundy is much more food friendly, across the board, than most other famous red wines; this is because—the Gallo brothers' ill-named "Hearty Burgundy" notwithstanding—real red Burgundy, made from Pinot Noir grapes, is one of the world's most delicate and harmonious red wines. But that virtue also leads to matching problems—since red wines today are being asked to partner a wide range of wild, strong-flavored dishes.

Nevertheless, I will always buy red Burgundy to have in my cellar—particularly because I have one fairly specific application in mind. It is my belief that when red meat is cooked rare—the way I like it—big, bold, rich, young, tannic wines are clumsy with it. A rare prime rib, for example, demands a more refined partner, preferably one with all the gentle and magical flavors of age. Red Burgundy—which never had too much tannin to begin with—becomes the most incredible senior citizen in the whole world of wine at fifteen or twenty years old. It is simply impossible to describe the convergence of mysterious flavors in an old Burgundy, though writers regularly haul out such images as fur, leather, Asian spices, human glands, boiled beets, and all kinds of other crazy verbal stabs.

Every time there's a red Burgundy vintage that has aging potential, I completely violate all of my prejudices in favor of young, simple wine, break open my piggy bank, and replenish the cellar with bottles that give me increased inspiration to live a few decades more.

There are far too many terrific Burgundy producers to cover that subject here; it deserves a whole volume by itself. But if I had to choose just one who's making age-worthy Burgundy—especially if you factor in value, because some of the most famous ones charge $600 a bottle for young Burgundy—I'd probably select the old, very traditional house of Pierre Bourée in Gevrey-Chambertin. To this day, the single greatest wine I ever tasted was a 1961 Latricières-Chambertin from Pierre Bourée—consumed in 1981, alongside (what else?) a rare prime rib of beef.

RED BORDEAUX

The other great contender for "world's greatest red wine" is red Bordeaux; it and red Burgundy are the great yin and yang of the wine world. And, let me state flat out that some of the most complex, most fascinating wines I've ever tasted have been old red Bordeaux.

That respect having been paid, I must confess that red Bordeaux is not one of my highest-odds propositions for food across the board. The type of red Bordeaux that's most widely food friendly is very young (like a year old), very fruity, simple red Bordeaux. But, as with so many other foreign wines, it's very rare to find young-enough examples of this in the United States; most Bordeaux come here when they're three years old.

The food problem with the famous, high-quality red Bordeaux wines—usually made from a predominance of Cabernet Sauvignon, though other related grapes can sometimes predominate—is that they're muscular and tannic in youth (hard for food), then they become dumb and austere at about five years old (also hard for food). Like red Burgundy, they are glorious in old age—but a great Bordeaux from a great vintage might take thirty or forty years to come around. And when they do, since they're usually bigger and richer than old red Burgundy, they're not as sure a thing for rare red meat.

In fairness, I must point out that I've had thousands of delicious matches with red Bordeaux over the years, and a great aged one is always welcome on my table.

CALIFORNIA CABERNET SAUVIGNON

Talk about tricky for food! These darlings of the tannin set—many bottles of which set out to outmuscle red Bordeaux—pack more mouth-assaulting power than almost any group of wines in the world. Sometimes, if the wine features a lush, velvet carpet of fruit, and if the tannin's relatively well behaved, you might find a young California Cab pleasantly gliding over your food. But the tannin-bomb potential is always there, so I choose to leave this wine off my most-wanted list. The final insult is that California Cab, to me, just hasn't demonstrated that it can reliably age into grandeur. Red Bordeaux, after thirty years, really does age into something else. But Cal Cab just gets less young—kind of like a fifty-something Malibu surf bum, still blond, only a little wrinkled, who hasn't learned too much that's new.

If, by the way, you are willing to send me a case of Caymus Special Selection Cabernet Sauvignon from Napa Valley, I'd be willing to eat these words in public (with a rare steak, of course).

WASHINGTON STATE CABERNET SAUVIGNON

In 1985 or so, I was on a panel of judges in Dallas (at the annual *Dallas Morning News* wine competition), and my task that time was judging American Cabernet Sauvignon (blind, of course). The usual array of harsh, one-dimensional, overextracted wanna-bes came my way—until one dark purple, bewitchingly complex, supernally balanced wine was set down. The other judges noticed it too. We all looked at each other in a what-the-hell-is-that? kind of way. Later, we found out. It was a 1983 Cabernet Sauvignon from a winery none of us had ever heard of: Quilceda Creek, in Washington State. When I got back to New York, I phoned them to order a case, and most of that case is still in my cellar, getting better year by year—just like great red Bordeaux.

Now, ultimately, I don't think that Washington State Cabernet Sauvignon is going to be any more flexible for a wide range of foods than red Bordeaux is. But I do think that when the smoke clears from the hype field of American wine making, it is going to become clear that the finest, longest-lived reds in the United States are being made in Washington State. If you like aging wine for an ultimate date at the table, I urge you to get some of these babies into your wine room. In addition to Quilceda Creek, you might want to buy into Leonetti Cellars, Woodward Canyon, Columbia, and the upper-echelon bottlings of Château Ste. Michelle.

BAROLO

Wine geeks often refer to Barolo, from the Piemonte region, as Italy's greatest red wine—and I guess that makes me a geek as well. If we're discussing that kind of expensive, medal-winning, stand-up-and-notice wine that takes aeons to come around in a wine cellar—as opposed to the simple, mirthful wines that I really drink all the time—I'd have to agree that it doesn't get any better than this in Italy.

Barolo is made from a grape that hasn't demonstrated too much in any other part of the world—Nebbiolo. Somehow, the combination of that grape and those Langhe hills creates a flavor in a properly aged Barolo that's different from, but almost as hypnotizing as, the flavor of Burgundy. The usual images here are roses, tar, and truffles—which is quite astonishing, since Barolo is made in exactly the world's greatest truffle region, right around the town of Alba.

The problem with Barolo, of course, is that it is fiercely tannic and unapproachable in youth—even though a new generation of Barolo producers has tried to soften it up. But this is a wine I never think about drinking before its fifteenth birthday—and, if I had my druthers, I'd be working on Barolos from the 1940s and 1950s right about now. However, if I could get my hands on an aged Barolo—which tastes specifically, spectacularly Italian—I'd do it up with rare meat dishes (just like Burgundy) or with any Italian meat dishes that are not too saucy. If you can get some white truffles in the picture, so much the better.

There are many terrific Barolo producers—but the one whose style appeals to me the most is Giuseppe Rinaldi.

RED RIOJA

You'd better hurry to buy some traditional red Rioja—because American wine writers are responding positively these days only to Riojas made in a big, international style, and more and more Rioja producers are switching over to that style. It's part of the McDonaldization of the world.

Traditional red Rioja is a thing of beauty. The best comparison is with aged red Burgundy: delicate, subtle, almost fragile stuff, amazing in its ability to spin such a powerful aroma off of such a thin wine. And make no mistake about it: since this is wood-crazy Spain, the aroma is of barrels. Oddly, it's

Sauternes with dessert that has a little rasp to it (here, butter cake with shaved coconut and walnuts)

American oak barrels that traditionally have been used, and the result of their interplay with the Tempranillo grape is something brimming with raisins, vanilla, and sweet spices.

One of the extraordinary things about traditional red Rioja is that it gets a lot of aging at the winery—so that when you buy it, it's almost like having a properly aged wine in your possession even before you've put it in your cellar. This means that most old-fashioned Rioja—particularly if it is designated Gran Reserva—can be purchased today and served with your rare meat tonight. Unless, of course, you've had the bad fortune to buy one of these wanna-be-Cabernet jobs.

Some producers sticking to their traditional guns are Muga, Cune, Murrieta, La Rioja Alta, and R. López de Heredía Viña Tondonia. Buy their wines and use them as you would any aged red wine—just don't expect a lot of food flexibility from them.

SAUTERNES

First of all, if you're like millions of other American wine drinkers, you might have a prejudice against sweet wines. "Oh, I've become more sophisticated about wine," I've heard many say. "I don't like sweet wine anymore." But the fact of the matter is that some of the world's greatest wines are sweet, and the world's greatest wine drinkers adore well-made sweet wines. Sweetness itself, for them, is simply not an issue; quality is.

Very sweet wines are extremely useful at the table; they are also known as dessert wines, and they go brilliantly with you-know-what.

The most famous dessert wine, perhaps, is Sauternes, made from rotten, shriveled-up grapes in the southern part of France's Bordeaux region. It brings torrents of knee-jerk enthusiasm from wine fanatics. I love it too—but only when it's paired with the right foods.

The problem is that menu planners indiscriminately throw Sauternes at a wide range of desserts. But Sauternes is a little different from most other golden dessert table wines. It is heavier than most, with higher alcohol, lower acidity, and an occasional scratch of bitterness. For these reasons, I always try to find a dessert that has a little roughness itself, in some ways, to stand up to the heft of Sauternes. A salty nut, perhaps. A flake of astringent coconut. A raspy quince that hasn't softened all the way. Anything with a little bit of edge, dessert-style.

Expensive Sauternes, like Château d'Yquem, is one of the most gloriously luscious wines in the world. But, for dessert, I find ultralate-harvest Rieslings from Germany, Austria, Washington, New York, and California to be generally more flexible.

BEER

I've been a beer lover for a very long time. So of course I was delighted to watch the resurgence, over the last decade, of American brewing—a phenomenon normally referred to as the microbrewery movement. However, one huge cloud, for me, has darkened the landscape: most of the American microbrewers seem to have chosen English ale as their model beer. What's wrong with that, you ask? Well, rather than selecting a beer style that's quieter, more harmonious—more flexible with food!—they have chosen a big, brassy, fruity style that is, in fact, quite a hard fit at the table. It's exactly like the early days of modern California wine making: "Let's make this stuff as big and obvious as possible so people will notice!"

In fact, I'm worried in general that beer people are taking the same road as wine people—the road that ignores food. Thankfully, we have gotten to the place where many American wine drinkers, even wine makers, are starting to ask real questions about wine with food. But beer lags behind in this regard. Some people even find it ludicrous to get serious about the discussion of beer with food. But I'm here to tell you that matching beer with food is every bit as complex, interesting, and rewarding as matching wine with food is.

It is a vast subject, actually, worthy of much research and theorizing. For now, I'll merely mention the five beer styles that I find most attractive for food.

WHEAT BEER

This is my out-and-out favorite beer for food, across the board. Variously called weiss beer, *Weizenbier, wit bier,* and *bière blanche,* wheat beer always includes a fairly high percentage of wheat in the brew (which means less barley than usual); most wheat beers are 30 to 40 percent wheat. This makes the beer taste lighter, more graceful, and more acidic. But wheat beer's no wimp when it comes to flavor. The yeast that's used in wheat beer brewing lends a spicy, clovelike, appley, sometimes bananalike flavor to the brew. And Belgian wheat beer makers push this further by actually adding some sympathetic flavorings to their beers.

I especially love the wheat beers from Belgium and Germany, though good ones are produced in other places (like Washington State and Austin, Texas). If you've never had one, you'll be amazed at how well they accommodate the whole range of light and spicy modern cuisine: sushi, Thai food, Chinese food, Indian food, even Mexican food. Then, they're also ideal for cutting through rich foods: I can't think of anything better, including wine, with a pile of sausages and sauerkraut. They're also splendid with other rich, meaty, Central European kinds of foods. Damned good around the barbecue, too.

FRUIT-FLAVORED BELGIAN LAMBICS

Belgium is, without question, the world's most intriguing beer country. You could spend decades classifying Belgian beer, because the subject is endlessly complicated. This much is clear: a lambic is a beer that, like wheat beer, has about 40 percent wheat in it—but, unlike wheat beer, or unlike most other beers in the world, is made by "spontaneous" fermentation (no extra yeast is added). Now, Belgian brewers sometimes take this a step further by adding to their already very light and graceful lambics the flavors of various fruits; cherry and raspberry are the most common ones.

So if you see Belgian Krïekenlambic (cherry beer) or Belgian Frambozenbier (raspberry beer), snap it up. You'll be amazed at how dry, crisp, subtle, and delicious these beers are. They are truly northern Champagne and, as such, deserve to be served in Champagne flutes. I'm crazy about them as aperitifs before dinner—but they also partner food in many of the same delightful ways that regular wheat beers do.

CZECH/BAVARIAN-STYLE LAGER

This style of beer, developed and refined in the Czech town of Pilsen—which is why the beer style is sometimes called Pilsener—is my favorite all-purpose beer style in the world (and that includes the purpose of sitting and watching a hockey game). At its best—and most of the common examples, like Beck's and Heineken, though good, are not Pilsener at its best—it is clean, golden, suffused with the unmistakable herbal aroma of hops and with the bracing, palate-clearing bitterness that hops can bring to a beer.

Not everyone likes the bitter backbone of a great Pilsener. But I find it delightful as a way of cutting through fatty foods. Sausages, pork, duck, goose, corned beef, pastrami—these are all fabulous with beer in this style.

Unfortunately, this is a style of beer that has not caught on with the American microbrewers. Why? I suspect it has something to do with the fact that lager—which means "to store"—takes up valuable storage space, while ale can go out the door as soon as it's brewed. Because ale is younger, it has more of the fruity, estery flavors of fermentation; because lager is older, it has more subtlety. This is another reason for lager's slow start here in America: the new beer drinkers are more immediately impressed by the high flavor profile of English-style ale.

I'm happy to report that a small Long Island brewery may contribute to a change in all this. It is called Southampton, and its beer is now available on tap in a few New York City restaurants, such as Drovers Tap Room. Southampton makes a startling lager—as crisp, clean, and hoppy as they come—which I hope will become a model for American microbrews.

Wheat beer

Fruit-flavored Belgian lambics

Czech/Bavarian-style lager

RICH ENGLISH-STYLE ALES

Okay. A few of the better-balanced rich ales being produced in America today can be relied upon to provide good refreshment next to hearty stews. For every twenty you try, however, you'll probably find only one that doesn't seem unnecessarily fruity, sweet, or over-the-top bitter. My favorite? It's brewed in Norwalk, Connecticut, and it's called Atlantic Amber.

SWEET, DARK BEERS

Sometimes, when beers are frankly and purposely sweet, I can warm up to them as dessert beers. Mackeson Stout is such a beer; it's brimming with wonderful chocolate-coffee flavors, and it's absolutely delicious next to dark desserts that aren't too sweet. I feel the same way about a rare, extraordinary, strong and sweet lager from Switzerland called Sammichlaus (brewed on only one day of the year, December 6).

Light Beer with Spicy Food

You could hardly call the group of water-light, practically flavorless Mexican beers that includes Corona, Tecate, and Pacífico Clara one of the world's great beer types. And yet, it does have its place—and its place is with chilies! Superspicy food clashes like crazy next to American microbrews, even next to only moderately hoppy lagers. But these wimpy beers are supereffective in putting out the fire—and making you want to reignite the fire so that you can enjoy putting it out again. Refreshment non pareil.

Rauchbier

Another beer type I like a great deal—though I rarely see it or get to drink it—is Rauchbier, or smoked beer, principally made in Germany. The smoke flavor happens to be great with all manner of spicy food—particularly hearty spicy food, like Mexican or Indian meats. It's also a knockout with barbecue.

Rich, English-style ales *Sweet, dark beers*

BRANDY

This is not really a drink that I consume with food—but it's hard for me to imagine a serious, pull-out-all-the-stops European dinner that doesn't include a drop of brandy after the food.

What is brandy? Well, it comes from a Dutch word for "burned wine." That's a colorful way of saying that wine is put over the fires of a pot still and distilled into a high-alcohol drink. Lots of other things get distilled in the world, of course: barley gets distilled into Scotch, potatoes used to get distilled into vodka, corn gets distilled into bourbon. But when it's wine that's getting distilled, the result is called brandy. And, somehow, its wine base makes it taste very appropriate after an evening of fine wines.

Here are my favorite brandies for postprandial sipping.

COGNAC

Cognac comes from the southwest of France, and it is normally considered to be the greatest of all brandies. But you know me by now: I don't give things normal consideration.

Cognac's extraordinary reputation rests on its delicacy and refinement; one is supposed to feel, when sipping cognac, that one is sipping the very soul of wine, somehow transformed into a 40-percent-alcohol spirit. And the strangest part is—I buy it! But—and this is a big but—only when the cognac in my glass is very old, very rare, and, I'm afraid, very expensive. The opening ante for cognac of this quality is usually $300 or $400 a bottle.

For me, the vast majority of cognac tastes just fine—but comes nowhere near providing the ethereal experience it's supposed to provide. Forty-dollar-a-bottle cognac tastes lighter than many other brandies, to be sure, and may hint of sublimity—but usually it just ends up being fairly uninteresting. One small producer whose cognacs taste like something special at less than $400 is Pierre Ferrand—but you'll still have to cough up $100 to $200 to check out his best stuff.

ARMAGNAC

Armagnac is a brandy that also is produced in the southwest of France, not too far from the Cognac region. However, there are easily discernible differences between the two.

In a word, Armagnac is richer. In more words, Armagnac is more powerful, more flavorful, more velvety, more immediately impressive. Most important, a $40 bottle of Armagnac will likely whip the stuffing out of a $40 bottle of cognac; one of Armagnac's most endearing qualities is that you can love it in any price range.

Of course, the cognac contingent will tell you that Armagnac's not as refined as cognac. It is an argument I know well, since it is precisely the kind of squawking I do over wines that are too powerful and muscular. But wine is different, it seems to me; wine is meant to go with food, and the more refined a glass of wine is the more widely it's going to marry well. Brandy is for sipping by itself—so why should it hold anything back? I go with the Gascons on this one: Armagnac is the iron fist in a velvet glove, and I love it.

*My favorite Spanish brandy
with proper size brandy glass*

SPANISH BRANDY

French brandy is usually considered to be the world's best brandy—but not everyone uttering this opinion has tasted Spanish brandy, from the sherry region in the south of Spain.

Leave all thoughts of delicacy behind when you approach this subject. The wood-loving Spaniards love to age their brandy in sherry barrels, and the result is an additional overlay of flavor that is anything but subtle. Furthermore, Spanish brandy producers are not adverse to letting their product show a little sweetness as well. In short, if you're used to the austerity of cognac, you may have a hard time getting into Spanish brandy.

I, personally, don't have a hard time at all getting into it, and it getting into me. You simply have to have an open mind as you sample it. I would wager that, in a blind tasting, most Americans would prefer Spanish brandy to either cognac or Armagnac. The fact that it's considerably less expensive is also a plus.

You will find a range of prices for Spanish brandy (none of them over $40 or so), and a range of styles as well. Some Spanish brandies are more in the delicate, cognac mold; my favorite of these is Conde de Osborne, in a weird bottle designed by Salvador Dalí for the house of Osborne. But most Spanish brandies are sweetish, rich, flavorful—and the one unquestionably at the top of this chart is Cardenal Mendoza, a virtual dessert of a brandy. It's my favorite.

GRAPPA

Grappa, from Italy, puts a slightly different spin on the brandy equation. It is made not from wine but from the skins, seeds, and stems left behind after grapes are crushed to make wine. This gives it a whole different character: fiery in spirit, earthy in taste. I love the taste of grappa, though I'm not sold on the fire. But if you taste around the more expensive grappas—usually made from the leftovers of some important wine, like Barolo—you may hit upon one that's smooth enough to enjoy. If you do, it's a bang-up finish to a great Italian meal.

Other countries make something like grappa as well. The most famous grappalike brandy is marc, from France. Marc (pronounced "mar") is made in exactly the same way as grappa, but it looks different: grappa is clear, marc is light brown (like cognac). There's often a taste difference as well: though they both exhibit that bewitching, earthy aroma, marc is often a little gentler, a little less fiery than grappa. In the United States, you can find a decent range of marcs from famous areas—e.g., marc de Champagne, marc de Bourgogne. But it's nothing like traveling around the wine regions of France and finding a marc with a slightly different nuance at every little appellation across the country ("Would you like to try our marc de Muscadet, monsieur?").

EAUX-DE-VIE

These clear spirits—"waters of life"—mark the borderline between wine-based brandies and distillates from other fruits. I say they're on the border, because some eaux-de-vie are made from wine and some eaux-de-vie are not.

My favorite eaux-de-vie are not; my favorites are made from fermented fruit in the great French gastronomic region of Alsace. These spirits may look like water, but they pack an incredible alcoholic punch, as well as an amazing amount of fruit flavor. It takes a leap of the imagination to understand that brandy comes from grapes; all it takes is a nose to understand that specific fruit eaux-de-vie come from specific fruits.

My favorite Alsatian eaux-de-vie are Poire William (which smells and tastes just like fresh pear); framboise (raspberry); fraise (strawberry); mirabelle (yellow plum); quetsch (blue plum); and mure (mulberry). I also once tasted a mint eau-de-vie in Alsace that was extraordinary.

I like to keep my eaux-de-vie in the freezer and serve them icy cold; they never freeze, but they do get extremely viscous. After a hearty Alsatian meal especially, I cannot think of a better after-dinner drink.

CALVADOS

And here we cross the grape line entirely. Calvados is always made from apples—never grapes—in the great apple region of France, Normandy. Is it brandy? If you define brandy as "burned wine," it isn't. But people usually call Calvados an apple brandy and usually include it in discussions of brandy.

One reason they do that, I suppose, is that it looks and tastes something like brandy. It is light brown in color, and its aromas suggest brandy mixed with a little fruit. I don't find Calvados overwhelmingly, or even appreciably, appley, but once you get used to the particular flavor it has, you will likely find yourself craving it. It is a little lighter, gentler, easier to take than most brandies—which is why you'll often hear young people at bars in Paris shouting to the bartender, "Un Calva! Un Calva!"

Why, I've been known to shout it myself on occasion.

The Brandy Glass

There is a great deal of silly information available about the drinking of brandy. Most of us have realized that heating brandy over a flame is a ridiculous practice that cooks a spirit you were intended to drink "raw" and have given our brandy warmers to charity.

But not everyone realizes that the oversize brandy sniffer is also a ridiculous invention. The theory is that it gives the brandy plenty of room in which to open up and reveal its aromas; the reality is that it dissipates the aromas of a drink that really needs no prodding. If you are choosing one type of special glass for brandy, make sure it's not fat and wide; look instead for something small and narrow that focuses the aromas. For an example, see the glass on page 307.

OTHER SPIRITS

Though I love wine and beer with my food . . . and occasionally, a little brandy after dinner . . . I am not a regular consumer of other forms of alcohol. However, there are a few gastronomic situations in which a little strange firewater makes a whole lot of sense. Here's my favorite hooch, the spirits that move me.

TEQUILA

I've got to admit it: I love the taste of tequila, the great distillate from the mountainous Jalisco state of Mexico. It strikes me as one of those mystical, ancient tastes of the world—not unlike the flavor of Mexican lime-slaked corn, and not a bad partner with it. I've also got to admit that tequila gives you one of the giddiest highs in the whole world of alcohol. Or so people tell me.

There is a good deal of confusion about tequila. For many years, I myself was not exempt from the prevailing condition. However, after a recent trip to Jalisco—and some very heavy (ahem) research—I've finally got it right. I think.

For starters, many believe that tequila is made from cactus—but it's not. It's made from agave, a spiny desert plant related to cactus. Now, in Mexico, there are over six hundred types of agave. Some of them are used in various parts of the country to make a spirit called mezcal. You could consider tequila one type of mezcal. Mezcal is usually oilier in texture and smokier in flavor than tequila—and is the one that contains the worm (or *gusano*) in the bottle (tequila never has a worm in the bottle). To make things more confusing still, agave—the plant from which mezcal and tequila both come—is itself sometimes called mezcal (in the following notes, *mezcal* will refer to the drink).

So what is tequila? Think of it in relation to mezcal as you would think of cognac in relation to brandy. Brandy is made in many parts of France; cognac is considered to be the finest brandy and is made only in the Cognac region. Mezcal is made in many parts of Mexico; tequila is considered to be the finest type of mezcal and is made in one region only.

The home of tequila is Jalisco, the state that boasts Guadalajara as its capital city. About forty miles to the west of Guadalajara is the small town of Tequila. Around it, producers of mezcal discovered a long time ago that a more refined drink can be produced from one type of agave in particular—*agave azul,* or the blue agave (so named for the tint of its spiky leaves). Today, the only agave allowed in the production of tequila is blue agave (this rule goes back only ten years or so).

Now, the usual simplification of the geographical situation is that tequila has to come from the area around the town of Tequila—and much of it does. In fact, however, if you wish to be completely accurate,

1. Some tequila is made in other parts of the state of Jalisco.

2. Some blue agave for tequila production is trucked into Jalisco from neighboring states.

3. The government allows a small quantity of tequila to be produced in three neighboring states (namely, Michoacán, Nayarit, and Guanajuato).

More confusion concerns the types of tequila available. Here are the three terms that are most important to know.

Blanco. This is the basic level of tequila, hardly aged at all before its release. Sometimes, a more refined version of blanco is called plata (or silver) by producers. Both look clear.

Reposado. This is tequila that has been aged for two to twelve months in large upright barrels. It is usually a little yellower than blanco or plata, and always more expensive.

Añejo. This is tequila that is aged up to six years in small barrels (what the French call *barriques*). It is darker still than reposado, and considerably more expensive.

Most Americans assume that añejo, owing to its expense and rarity, is the finest tequila of all. In one sense it is: some añejos taste almost like brandy and could be sipped slowly as fine after-dinner drinks. All that time in barrels makes them mellower and smoother, rounds off their rough edges, and removes much of the tequila-specific taste. Frankly, if I'm going to drink something in this way, I'd rather have an Armagnac.

I was amazed in Mexico to discover that real tequila geekos mostly like blanco, the basic tequila. Why? Because before any aging, tequila is most intense in what everyone calls the agave flavor—an earthy flavor, distantly related to grappa flavor, that's somewhat difficult to describe. But reposados can be rich in this flavor, too . . . and a little more rounded for their time in barrels.

Of course, the producer that you choose has everything to do with the ultimate quality of your drink. Many of the blancos from mass-market producers are rough and fiery, and not that intense in "the agave flavor." One reason for this is that a lot of cheap tequila is not 100 percent agave; there's much tequila made with a high percentage of sugarcane in the mix. If you're hell-bent on "the agave flavor," as I always am, make sure your tequila says "100% blue agave" on the label.

(Left to right) a filled tequilla glass; Don Julio, one of the best tequillas; bottled Sangrita; Sangrita in a tequilla glass (see page 313)

Then find a great producer. Here's a short list, with a few annotations, of my favorite producers.

El Jimador (makes a great, light blanco much favored at bars by Mexico's Gen X)
Chinaco
Patrón
Herradura (the one I most frequently drink in America—particularly Herradura reposado)
Don Julio (among the most expensive tequilas, and considered the best in Mexico; hard to find in the United States)
El Tesoro
Porfidio (the boutique tequila, now available in designer bottles going up to one long-aged añejo that costs $500!)

The two largest producers—Cuervo and Sauza—also make good tequilas at the upper limits of their product lines. Do, however, avoid anything designated "gold"—this is a cheap blanco, doctored with caramel to make it look more impressive, and fobbed off on easily impressed foreigners.

Drinking tequila brings its own set of misunderstandings. The margarita has become America's favorite cocktail, and that is the form in which most tequila is consumed in the United States. There are a lot of margaritas consumed in Mexico, as well—but mostly by foreigners. Many Americans don't realize that Mexicans themselves rarely touch margaritas.

However, if you wish to make a margarita that tastes as it might in Mexico, be sure to leave out the sweet stuff. Margaritas at American bars are sometimes thick with simple syrup and oppressively sweet. For a Mexican-style margarita, combine ⅓ tequila (good blanco or reposado), ⅓ fresh lime juice, and ⅓ orange liqueur (like Cointreau) in a cocktail shaker with lots of ice. Shake it like you mean it, then spill the elixir into a glass. I like my margarita on the rocks (I hate that frozen slush stuff) with a rim of salt. Salt, of course, would be a bad idea if I were drinking my margarita with a meal—but Mexicans would never drink a margarita with a meal, and I follow their aversion (they drink beer or wine with their food). If you want to add an authentic Mexican touch to your margarita, add a few drops of a liqueur called Damiana; it's made from a plant grown on the Baja Peninsula. If you can't find it, substitute something with a licorice taste—like Galliano.

So, without margaritas, how do Mexicans consume their beloved tequila? Straight up and in mass quantities, to be sure. Most of it is consumed before meals. It is usually served in narrow, disproportionately tall, small glasses, filled to the top. Though in the United States most tequila-shot drinkers follow a prescribed ritual of licking salt, shooting the tequila, then sucking a piece of lemon—in Mexico there is no graven-in-stone order of events. In fact, there's no lemon served with tequila! Only lime is used. I see people doing it all kinds of ways in Mexico—so I devised my own rhythm. I like to lick a little salt from my fingers, then take a sip of tequila (in Mexico, people don't shoot it; they sip it). I find that the salt intensifies the flavor of agave. Then, I like to wait ten seconds so I can fully savor the tequila taste. At that point, I suck on a little lime to clear the palate. It might take three or four of these sequences to down one small glass of tequila.

However, many Mexicans prefer to eschew entirely the salt-and-lime routine. Instead, they drink their tequila with a delicious side drink called sangrita. It is sold in bottles wherever tequila is sold, and is usually served in bars and restaurants alongside tequila, in the same kind of glass, whenever you order a tequila. What is it? Sangrita is a red, nonalcoholic drink made from tomatoes, fruit juice, sugar, and a little hot chili; imagine a spicy tomato juice with a little less body and a little more sugar, and you're pretty close. The usual way of drinking the two together is a sip of tequila, followed by a sip of sangrita—which mellows the tequila burn but complements, rather than wipes away, the agave flavor. It is now my favorite tequila accompaniment.

And hold the Doritos.

CACHACA

The next continent I want to roar through, gastronomically speaking, is South America—and cachaca (pronounced "ka-SHA-sa") is going to help me do it. It is a Brazilian rum distillate that is an essential ingredient in my favorite new drink: the caipirinha (pronounced "ky-per-EEN-ya"). I discovered caipirinhas at Brazilian-style steak houses (*churrascurias*)—and I now love them as cocktails before any south-of-the-border meal.

To make a caipirinha, you will need to find cachaca at a liquor store; if you're near a South American or Latino neighborhood, start your search there. Or call the importers of Pitú, a fine Brazilian brand of cachaca: EFCO Importers, in Jenkintown, Pennsylvania (215-885-8597).

Cut half a lime into small cubes, and place them in a cocktail shaker. Sprinkle the lime with a teaspoon of quick-dissolving sugar. Smash the lime with a pestle, spoon, or muddler; work it for a minute or two to release all the oils from the rind. Add a handful of cracked ice to the shaker, and pour 1½ ounces cachaca over all. Shake like crazy (at least 30 seconds). Then pour all into an old-fashioned glass, and garnish with a slice of lime.

The taste is amazingly refreshing, a limy call to action. And, as with tequila, the quality of intoxication is in a glass by itself.

OUZO/RAKI

All through Greece and the Middle East, anise-flavored distillates are much appreciated. They even turn up in Italy and the south of France, but in those places they are not as central to the dining experience.

In Greece, ouzo rules. It is the eponymous tipple of ouzerias, where delicious plates of appetizers—meze—are served alongside the viscous, clear spirit. Throughout the Middle East, each country has its own version; the one I've spent most time with is raki (pronounced "RAH-kuh"), the Turkish version. In all of these countries, a splash of the rich spirit is served in a glass, while ice and pitchers of water are placed on the side. You toss a few ice cubes into the glass, if desired, and cut the strong drink with a little water. The ouzo, or raki, turns milky white, and you're well on your way.

I have made more than a few mirthful meze parties with this milky mix. Just stuff a couple of grape leaves, purée some eggplant, wrap a few phyllo leaves, cloud up some ouzo—and watch your guests get very happy, very fast.

GIN

Though I generally eschew the great juniper-flavored spirit invented by the Dutch and refined by the British, there are two gastronomic situations in which I find it indispensable:

1. On a hot summer day, after work and just before a patio party, I have to have a gin and tonic made with Tanqueray gin and Schweppes tonic water.

2. Within five minutes of entering a steak house for some serious carnalizing, I have to have a dry martini in my hands—made with Bombay Sapphire gin and Boissieré dry vermouth. I ask the bartender to place some cracked ice in a shaker, to pour an ounce or so of vermouth over the ice, then to pour the vermouth into the drain (I'm almost in agreement with Winston Churchill that the addition of vermouth to a martini should consist of bowing once in the direction of France). Then the gin gets poured over the ice, and should be stirred—not shaken! Shaking, as they say, "bruises" the gin (the sober way to explain this is that too much water melts from the ice into the drink). The clear liquid is poured into a retro, very fifties martini glass, and either a twist of lemon rind or an olive is added. I'm of the olive school: I like big ones, green ones, unpitted ones, and three ones (or three, altogether).

SCOTCH

As soon as the baby boomers discovered single-malt Scotch—though I like to lead the pack, not follow it—I found myself caught in some huge quality undertow. "This is great stuff," I realized, and a small glass of a first-rate single malt sometimes replaces brandy for me as a postprandial treat.

I like to serve mine in cut-crystal tumblers I was given as a gift some years ago that were blown in Glasgow. My instinct is to serve it neat, like brandy, so you can fully appreciate the texture of the malt. But it's startling to learn that mavens in Scotland cut it with ice cubes, or even with water; they say you can smell it and taste it better that way.

As for regions and producers—well, I must confess that my heart's not in the Highlands. My favorite spot of all for Scotch production is the isle of Islay (pronounced, for some strange, apparently Scotch-induced reason, "EYE-luh"). This is the home of peaty Scotch, burnt with the smoky, iodinelike taste of local peat bogs. Laphroaig's the famous one, but I like Bowmore and Lagavulin even better. In fact, on my fortieth birthday—January 25, the same day as the great Scottish poet Robbie Burns—I bought a bottle of sixteen-year-old Lagavulin in England, and vowed to take a sip from it only on January 25 for the rest of my life. I'm taking very small sips every birthday, just in case . . .

Scotch from other places, however, can be awfully good too. I love Macallan from the Highlands, with its sherry-barrel taste—particularly the eighteen-year-old. And I'm a big fan of the Orkney Island distillery Highland Park, which also hits those sweet, seductive, sherrylike notes.

OTHER DRINKS

Coffee

I include coffee in this chapter in the same spirit that I include brandy: it is a traditional part of a great meal, but it is not traditional with the food.

This surprises many Americans. We who have been raised on cups o' java at the diner counter, with our apple pie—heck, even with our meat loaf—view with suspicion the European custom of drinking coffee after dessert, not during it.

I'm on the fence concerning this one. When I'm in Europe, I always do as the Europeans do—and doing so has helped me to see it from their perspective. I think they see the separation of dessert and coffee as paying respect to both dessert and coffee. Having them together, in their view, does a service to neither one. Furthermore, I suspect they feel about coffee as Italians do about the rampant use of Parmigiano-Reggiano on pasta: if you use it (grated cheese or coffee) every time, the food you're using it with (pasta or dessert) starts tasting the same all the time.

On the other hand, Americans have a point too. Coffee is good with a lot of desserts. What would apple pie be without it? And you can't deny the fabulous flavor synergy of chocolate and coffee.

Well, no matter when you drink your coffee (and I think we can all agree that a day must at least start with a cup of it), there are a few other coffee issues that need to be addressed.

Espresso or American Coffee? Life is a matter of taste, and so is this choice—but I have to tell you that since I started drinking espresso in Italy about a dozen years ago, I find it very hard indeed to make my taste go back to comparatively weak and insipid American coffee. Have you found espresso hard to take? Hold on; that may be because . . .

American Coffee Bars Serve Insanely Overextracted Espresso. The coffee issue is the same as the wine issue is the same as the microbrew issue: when we start to get excited about a great product from another culture, we overdo it, exaggerate it, nearly kill it by making it a parody of itself. American coffee roasters in those huge chain shops start by overroasting the coffee beans, until they're harsh and bitter—and then they brew the beans in such a way that maximum oil and bitterness are pulled out of them. This is madness! A great cup of espresso doesn't hurt! A great cup of espresso is deep in coffee flavor, a little bitter, a little acidic, beautifully balanced, with a lush texture and a velvety head of cocoa-colored foam (called *crema*). If you think you hate espresso, please keep going until you find somebody who makes it right (your first cup at the airport in Rome may change your whole life).

Flavored Coffee is an Abomination. I hope I'm not being too much of a purist for you—but once you get hooked on the wonderful flavor of great coffee, it's very difficult to get down the next cup of Almond Vanilla Hazelnut Mocha Surprise. Leave the flavors for dessert; give me coffee.

The Proliferation of Coffee Names at American Coffee Bars Is Way Out of Control. Sometimes, when I'm facing the big board at a coffee bar—which these days may look like the schedule of trains at Grand Central Station—I start thinking that Americans like coffee bars so much because ordering coffee allows them to express themselves through their orders. Why are we so obsessed with taking control? I'd rather just put myself in the hands of someone who knows how to make coffee and let him decide. In all fairness, however, I must point out that ordering coffee is easier for me than it is for most people: I just like it black and simple. If I feel like having a little foam in my brew, the furthest I'll ever go is to put just two words together and ask for an *espresso macchiato*—which means an espresso "stained" on top with a little foamed milk. And by the way—we consume a lot more foamed milk here, in many more ways, than they do in Italy. There, no one ever considers having milk in coffee after midday. Fewer options. More European. Better.

Which Beans to Buy? If you're buying coffee beans to brew your own coffee at home, you will once again be faced with a bewildering profusion of choices. Perhaps I can help by telling you my favorite beans: they are beans from Ethiopia, a country historians believe to be either the original source of coffee or near the original source of coffee. And if you get really lucky, you might find the superrich, winy, heady Ethiopian beans called Yergacheffe to take home with you.

How to Make Espresso at Home? This is a tricky one—since no home machine that I know of uses the high pressure that multi-thousand-dollar restaurant espresso machines use. This means that the water doesn't get pushed through the coffee beans for the right duration of time, and that the resulting brew is not rich and harmonious.

The best solution I've found for making espresso at home is buying one of those machines on the market that work only with preportioned packages of ground coffee. The people making these machines have labored to create a relatively low-cost solution to the espresso-at-home problem.

For years, my machine of choice was the Nespresso system—which employs little capsules of Nespresso coffee that cost about 40 cents each (call 800-562-1465 for machine and coffee details). The result, in my house, was always good espresso, with a reasonably thick *crema* of tan foam on top. The main problems were the temperature of the espresso in the cup (seldom hot enough) and the fact that this machine needs a regular and fairly complicated cleaning to keep it running well.

Then I discovered the Euromatik. It is made in Italy, and is generally much simpler to use. Furthermore, the espresso is hotter, the *crema* is thicker, and the espresso flavor is deeper *and* better balanced. Finally, the Euromatik is part of a consortium named E.S.E.—and the advantage here is that you can buy the coffee pods that the machine uses from any one of a dozen coffee-producing companies. The really good news is that one of them is Trieste-based Illy, one of my favorite coffee companies in the world. My Illy pods (available, along with Euromatik info, by calling 800 USA-ILLY) cost about 30 cents each, and are delicious.

Tea

Once again, tea is not something that I'm in the habit of drinking with my meals—except with Chinese food, particularly dim sum. However, it's in this chapter because I do drink it frequently with food—with toast at breakfast, perhaps, and especially at the wonderful collation that is late-afternoon tea. Don't mistake this for high tea—which is actually a kind of six o'clock supper eaten in England with tea. I'm talking about the four o'clock custom of sitting down to a restorative pot of tea, along with a few thin sandwiches, perhaps—and scones slathered with thick cream and strawberry jam.

Unfortunately, when I take afternoon tea at a fancy restaurant, hotel, or tearoom in this country, I usually find the American wine–microbrew–coffee problem all over again: the tea is overextracted! Why, I've seen cookbooks that call for five to six minutes of brewing tea leaves. This is an eternity! In my tea universe, boiling water—but water that has just come to the boil, otherwise its oxygen will be spent and the tea will taste "heavy"—is poured over tea leaves in a teapot and left there for precisely 2½ minutes. I find that no additional flavor gets extracted after this time period—but lots of additional tannin does. You may want the extra tannin if you're planning to douse your tea with milk, as they often do in England. But I'm a purist once again, and I like my tea straight, as they do on the Continent—or with a little bit of sugar when sweet foods are served with it.

One problem with extraction time is a technical teapot problem: many people pour a cup or two out of the pot, through a strainer, into a cup—and leave the tea leaves behind in the pot. When they pour the next round, the tea has steeped a very long time on those leaves and will be quite bitter. But there's a great solution for this problem: the Chatsford teapot. It comes with a mesh container that fits right into the pot. You put the tea in this container, steep the leaves for 2½ minutes—and then remove the container with the spent tea leaves! Your second, third, fourth, and fifth cups of tea will taste just as

The Chatsford teapot with mesh container

harmonious as your first. You can order the Chatsford pot by calling Upton Tea Imports in Hopkinton, Massachusetts, at 800-234-8327.

You'll also want to call this great company when you're ready to order some loose tea leaves. Their catalog of options is a delight just to read; you'll learn thousands of things every time you sit down with it about regions, tea plantations, grading practices, harvests, et cetera. By ordering frequently from Upton, I have discovered that the most famous tea, Darjeeling, can be brilliant—but is often an over-rated, overpriced disappointment. I have also discovered that another Indian tea, Assam—the rich and dark one that is often the backbone tea of English breakfast blends—is much more reliable, and alto-gether much more to my taste.

Bottled Water

Now, water is something I almost always drink with a meal—though not by itself. It usually stands on my table behind some other beverage; in fact, I know from experience that if I'm drinking a good deal of wine with dinner, I'll feel better when it's over if I'm also drinking a good deal of water.

I like water that's lightly fizzy more than still water, and more than water that's very fizzy. Perrier, for example, is a little painful to drink. When I'm in France, Badoit—a lightly fizzy mineral water—hits it just about right. In the United States, the most acceptable water to me that's widely available is San Pellegrino.

One thing that makes me—along with a lot of European waiters—laugh is the frequent American insistence on having bottled water in a glass with ice cubes. The great French wine man Alexis Lichine once told me that "Americans are born with freezers in their mouths." He was talking about our predilection for cold wine, but he would have been amused at the current water scene. Why do we spend unreasonable amounts of money on bottled water in restaurants, only to dilute it with melting chunks of water that came out of the tap? The texture that you paid so dearly for vanishes.

So do the subtleties of taste—the cleanness, the mineral notes—if you throw chunks of fruit in your water. I must confess that I do it too, sometimes, on a hot day, when I'm drinking water all by itself, and a slice of lime seems refreshing. But I dislike water with my meal that has citrus fruit in it.

AFTERWORD

HOW TO GET THE MOST OUT OF YOUR
GASTRONOMIC TRAVEL

It's truly wonderful getting the opportunity to see the world, to come face-to-face with multifarious food cultures. But—as I've learned through a great many disappointments—just getting off a plane in another country by no means guarantees that you will sensitize your taste to that country's cuisine, that you will go home with greater expertise. To do so, you're probably going to have to work hard to create a meaningful and authentic brush with the local food.

Here are the three main problems travelers encounter in breaking through to gastronomic authenticity—and some great ways to get around these problems.

Your Own Resolve. Sometimes you can be your own worst enemy in the quest for gastronomic authenticity. Traveling can be stressful—a different language, different customs, different attitudes. How tempting it is to grab a little comfort by eating something familiar when mealtime rolls around! I've known dedicated but stressed-out gastronomes who have gone so far as to succumb to McDonald's in other countries.

My dad's a perfect example. At home, in New York, he's as adventurous an eater as I've ever seen, eager to tackle a new ethnic cuisine at a different restaurant every night. But as soon as he hits the ground in Europe or Asia, he starts ordering bacon and eggs for breakfast. Later in the trip, he starts wondering if we have to have another Indian meal or another French meal, and starts talking longingly of hamburgers. His nostalgia and desire for known creature comforts get the better of him.

I'm tough on him, and I'm going to be tough on you. Put these temptations out of your mind! If you want to eat as you do at home . . . stay at home! Travel is your single greatest chance to understand the food of another country—but you will squander your chance if you don't completely dedicate yourself to the food of that country while you're there!

"All the time?" you ask. "At every meal?"

Yes! Yes! I strongly believe that only by throwing yourself into the gastronomic reality of a country can you understand from the inside (your insides) what the food of that country is really like. Eat the breakfast they eat. Eat the lunch they eat. Eat the dinner they eat. Eat these meals at the times they eat them. Eat between meals only as they do. Drink what they drink, when they drink it. Believe me, this works; after a week of following their schedule and habits, you will begin to have insights into that country's food that you would never have had otherwise.

Authentic Food Is Hard for Tourists to Find on the Road. Even if you're wholly devoted to avoiding the temptations of familiarity, you still may strike out in your quest for the real thing.

Keep these ten strategies and principles in mind:

1. Read everything you can about the food of the country in advance of your trip; that way, you'll know what you're looking for before you start looking (always a good idea). Your research should include books about the cuisine itself (like cookbooks) and travel guides that discuss the best restaurants. Be skeptical about these latter recommendations, however; I never go to book-recommended eating places unless the book fills me with confidence in the author or I've had a second positive opinion about a given place. But surveying the field in a book at least gives you the lay of the land. Another terrific type of book to get is a food dictionary; a company called Marling publishes a series of them, each of which translates into English all the food terms (and possible menu terminology) of a foreign country. And if you have a "research" personality, try to find recent magazine and newspaper articles (from publications you trust) that discuss restaurants in your travel destination. If you travel a lot (like I do) and are low-tech (like I am), you might want to start clipping articles out of periodicals and keeping them in a very simple file system (my office is littered with clipping-stuffed folders for many gastronomic destinations).

2. Before you leave, talk to as many people as possible who are gastronomically knowledgeable about the place you're going to. Ask trusted eating buddies if they've been there. If there's an author whose opinion you value, track him or her down; it's not that hard, and experts on foreign destinations are usually happy to share their knowledge. You can always make an approach through an author's publisher. I've gone further than this, at times: I've sent overseas letters to newspapers (food editors) and publishers (those houses I've noticed publishing cookbooks) in the country I'm going to, hoping to gather good restaurant tips. Another idea is to contact wineries. Let's say you're going to Paris—drop a note to, say, Château Margaux in Bordeaux or Domaine Faiveley in Burgundy, indicate that you're a great lover of that estate's wines, that you're going to Paris, and that you want to find the best current places for eating

well and enjoying your favorite wine. Most of the time, they will take your request seriously.

3. When you get to the country, spend a lot of time walking, talking, asking, listening. Think of yourself as an investigative reporter, working to uncover the real story on a country's food. I roam the streets restlessly, looking at as many menus as possible, peering into restaurants whenever possible; you get good at figuring out which places are appealing to locals (that's what you want). Talk to taxi drivers, the concierge at your hotel, people in shops, et cetera. "What's a great place for local specialties?" "Where do you really like to eat?" You'll develop skill at figuring out which people are willing to tell you what they really think; discovering who among them has good taste is a little harder, but I've never failed to learn something from visiting a restaurant recommended by a taxi driver.

4. Avoid tourist traps! Much of your research, unfortunately, will yield tired, obvious suggestions. You can train yourself to smell these places a mile away; think of the famous restaurants in your own city to which you'd never send a serious gastronomic pilgrim . . . and don't go to their equivalents overseas! In most cases, avoid the highest restaurant in town (especially if it revolves). If there's a "theme" connected to a restaurant—even the theme of "come celebrate our restaurant's glorious history"—you may be falling into the trap. Lots of places around the world were vital once but are now just living off of outdated guidebooks that don't bother to keep up with reality. When you visually inspect one of these places, even from the outside, you can usually sniff trouble: too much froufrou can indicate too little chow-chow.

5. Avoid buffets! You may be tempted to taste many different foods of a country at one sitting by doing the buffet thing. Don't. Buffets are usually set up for tourists, with touristic food—and the quality's not usually too high. Don't arrange trips to exotic countries that offer "lunch and dinner at the hotel"—because that usually means buffets. The one part of the world that is an exception to the no-buffet rule is Scandinavia; there, the locals really do eat smorgasbords, and the food really is authentic and delicious.

6. If you're really hunting for a country's most authentic food, don't make a steady diet of its most acclaimed big-deal restaurants. When I started traveling to France with great regularity in the early 1980s, I'd make reservations in advance for a two-star and a three-star restaurant every day. It was absurd! I learned a lot about the creative cuisine of France—but I shut myself out of France's real food, the wonderful bistro cooking. I was eating like an out-and-out tourist. Today, when I go to France, I'll allow myself an expensive restaurant meal once every two or three days.

7. When you get to your restaurant . . . order wisely! This is absolutely crucial; the education you come away with is completely contingent on the menu choices you make. The best advice is to be regional; take stock of where you are, and then go for as many local specialties as possible. In fact, if you're really intent on learning about the food of, say, Umbria, Catalonia, or Savoie . . . don't leave the area until you've tasted every specialty you've read about! In a specific restaurant, try to get a sense of what that restaurant's strengths are, and go in that direction; if it's a place specializing in grilled meats, don't order the one poached fish dish on the menu. Remember: don't order what you merely want to eat; that's what you do at home. Eating on the road is an educational mission; when I'm handed a menu in a foreign country, I never say, "What do I feel like today?" but always, "From which dish will I learn the most?" Last, you can get great ordering ideas from looking at the food on the tables of local diners; if you want the real thing around the world, use the reconnoiter-and-point technique whenever it's feasible.

8. Do whatever it takes to get into the homes of people who live in the country you're visiting (short of breaking in, of course). Before you leave on your trip, try to find a friend who has a friend at your destination; see if your friend can get the message through that you're looking for real food. Be in friend-making mode on your trip; chat with people on your Iberia flight who are returning home to Madrid. Hint at your great desire to taste the authentic food of the country you're visiting. Have the same discussion with shopkeepers, or the nice people at the next table in a restaurant with whom you've started talking. One way or another, I almost never fail to get a home-cooked meal at somebody's home—one of the most useful info-gathering experiences on earth.

9. Another way to experience a country's food from the inside is to buy some and cook it yourself. If it's feasible, take an apartment rather than stay in a hotel; lots of large cities have apartments for rent, for tourists just like us, at weekly rates. Then you'll have a kitchen, into which you can bring and sample all the goodies you've picked up at local markets. Even if you don't have a kitchen, don't fail to cruise the local markets—both open-air farmer-type markets and supermarkets. You will learn plenty. If you don't have a kitchen available to you, and if you're dying to taste what you're seeing at the markets, you can always buy ready-to-eat items—like cheese, cold cuts, salads, fruit—and have a picnic (outside in warm weather, in your hotel room in cold weather).

10. Take cooking classes. Look for ads in American food magazines that announce classes in foreign countries; there are many that are run by Americans for American travelers. This can be fine, as long as they bring in local teachers who are dedicated to the real food of the country. Try to get some names of Americans who took classes at any given school, and contact these people to see what they thought. There are some schools in Europe—often connected with wineries—that provide "cooking school vacations": a whole week or two weeks, centered on daily cooking classes. These can be a great way to advance your knowledge.

People on the Road Don't Take You Seriously in Your Quest for Authentic Food. There's a whole world out there just itching to ignore you when you say, "I want to taste authentic local cooking." That's why you have to repeat it over and over again, like a mantra. If the person you're talking to speaks reasonable English, explain your quest in detail, supplying the emotional history behind your need. Make an impression. Lie if you have to; tell him or her that you're a journalist, on assignment to taste the real food of the country. Do whatever it takes—but make it clear to restaurateurs, or to people from whom you're seeking restaurant advice, that *you want the real thing!*

Initially, you may have trouble getting anything at all. A few years back, I led a group of Americans on a gastronomic tour of Thailand. We arrived late Saturday night and went to bed champing at the bit to taste Thai food in Bangkok. When we boarded our tour bus the next morning, we asked our Thailand guide, who knew full well we were a gastronomic group, where lunch was going to be. "Well, during lunchtime we're going to a jewelry workshop," she said. "If you want lunch after that, back at the hotel you can get anything you want." Sensing trouble, I said, "Most of us would rather skip the jewelry and go to an authentic Thai restaurant for lunch." She looked perplexed, then said, "Thai restaurants aren't open for Sunday lunch." This contradicted what I'd read in my books, but I couldn't budge her. Finally, amidst the beautiful temples and pagodas we were visiting in the morning, I managed to get a consensus from the group: everyone in it was willing to boycott the tourist-trap jewel shop and to set off with me looking for lunch. When I told her, she caved. "Okay," she said, "I'll take you to a place I know." She did, it was fabulous, and our trip was off to a great start. Had I not persisted, however, my first meal in Thailand might well have been southern fried chicken.

Something else frustrated us in Thailand, as it does in all countries with spicy-hot cuisine: they never trust that Americans like it hot. Once again, you have to say over and over: "Please serve us the food exactly the way you like to eat it. We like really spicy food." I was a dinner guest once in Goa, one of India's spiciest regions, at a private home; despite my letters to my hosts, the letters of the travel agency that set the dinner up, and the exhortations of our local tour guide (whom I lectured in advance of the dinner about my desire for authentically spicy food)—well, you guessed it. The food had not a lick of spice in it, and many of the dishes were Americanized versions of the local food. This was a meal to introduce me to Goan food—and there wasn't even any vindaloo on the menu. When I discreetly inquired about vindaloo, they said, "Vindaloo? Oh, you wouldn't like vindaloo." Aaaargh!

One reason this happens is that people in foreign countries want you to like them—and their food. It's not hostility that's messing up your quest—it's ill-placed niceness. Remember that all they know of American food may be McDonald's, and they can't begin to imagine that you really want something else. It's your job to convince them!

Once, I was on a wine writers' trip in northern Italy, and we were given a lunch at one of Italy's largest wineries. Food-wise, they did well; they prepared a wonderful meal featuring local cuisine, including a hand-rolled pasta called bigoli that I shall never forget. We couldn't wait to see what they drink with bigoli in the region—so our jaws (and spirits) dropped when they served us an American Chardonnay. "We just acquired this American winery," they told us, "and we thought you'd love to taste something from your own country." Don't they get it? No, they often don't. Remember that.

Another factor that mucks up your quest for authenticity is the internationalization of food and your host's well-intentioned desire to show you what he or she considers to be the most up-to-date cooking of his or her region. Unfortunately, today, the most "impressive" restaurants in some regions are fusion-confusion, one-world kind of deals. I'll never forget arriving in Vigo, a lovely town in Galicia, in northwest Spain, with the largest fish market in Europe and a great tradition of Gallego seafood cooking. My hosts promised me that dinner would be at the best restaurant in Vigo, and I couldn't wait to get myself around those local shellfish specialities. I couldn't believe it when I wound up at a place that was serving foie gras with a fruit sauce, fish fillets with potato scales, and beef tenderloin with a wine sauce. And, oh yes, crème brûlée. The locals didn't realize that you can get this kind of food in any city in the world today. For them, truly, this restaurant was a big deal—something new, something cutting edge. For me, unfortunately—despite the sweet people I was with—it was a big drag. Be careful! Be clear about what you're looking for! Remember the mantra: "I want to taste authentic local cooking! I want to taste authentic local cooking! I want to taste authentic local cooking!" Sometimes I feel like wearing a badge with those words on it, translated into local dialect. Oftentimes you need it.

INDEX

Page numbers in **boldface** refer to recipes.